Hidden deep in our genes is the truth.

life is in danger

bloodshed all over the worl

vault

awing its way to the surface.

Damian A. Wassel
Publisher
Adrian F. Wassel
Editor-In-Chief
Nathan C. Gooden
Senior Artist
Tim Daniel
EVP Design & Production
David Dissanayake
VP Sales & Marketing
Ian Baldessari
Production Manager
Rebecca Taylor
Managing Editor, Wonderbound
Syndee Barwick
Director, Sales & Marketing, Book Trade
Sonja Synak
Art Director
Alex Scola
Social Media Strategy
Dan Crary
Director, Events & Social Commerce
Der-shing Helmer
Managing Editor, Vault

acts of senseless violence

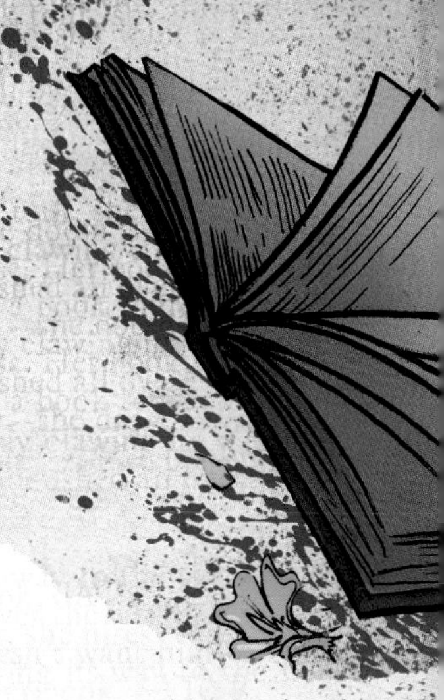

het of the coming collapse

For information about foreign or multimedia rights,
contact: rights@vaultcomics.com

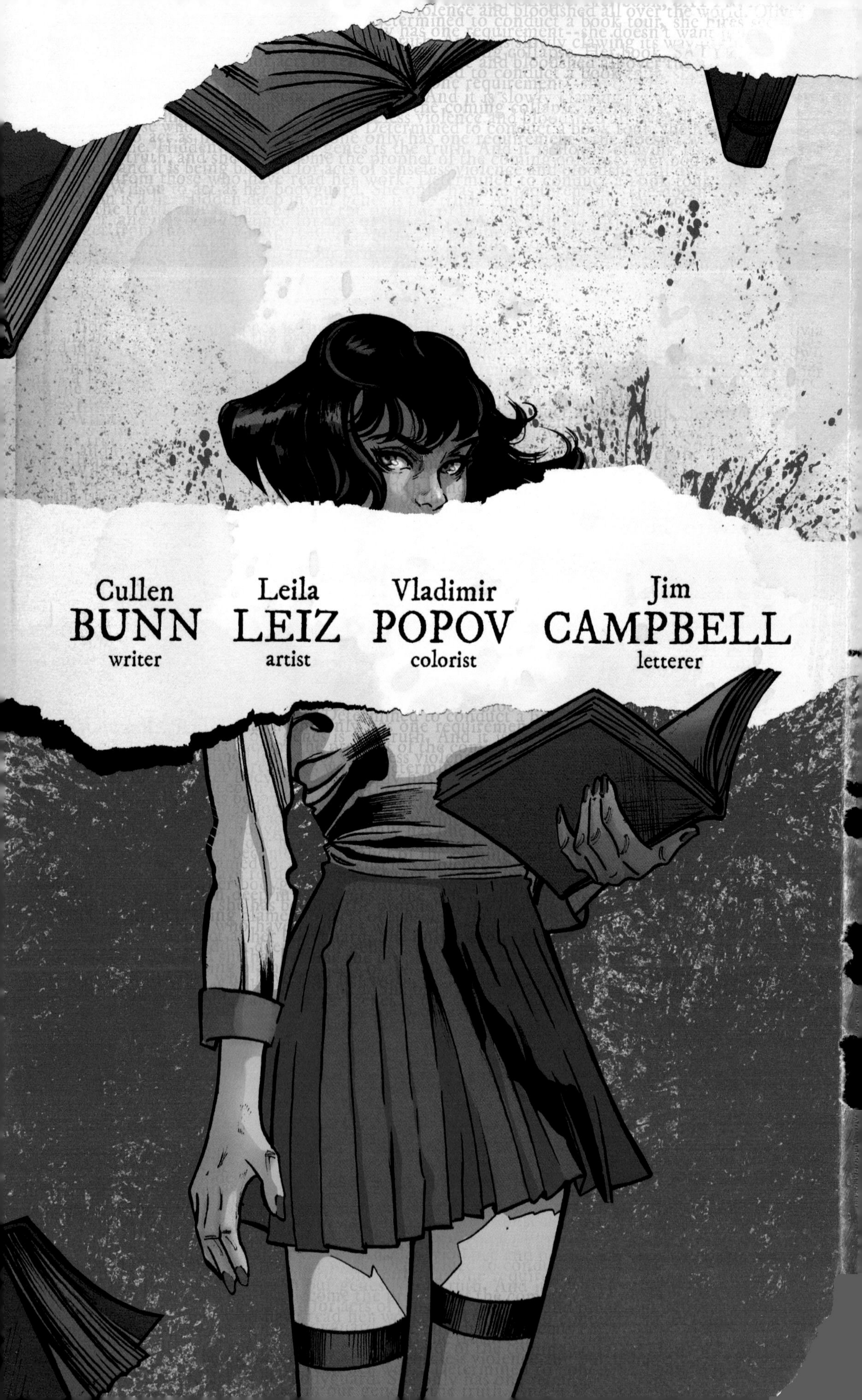
Cullen
BUNN
writer
Leila
LEIZ
artist
Vladimir
POPOV
colorist
Jim
CAMPBELL
letterer

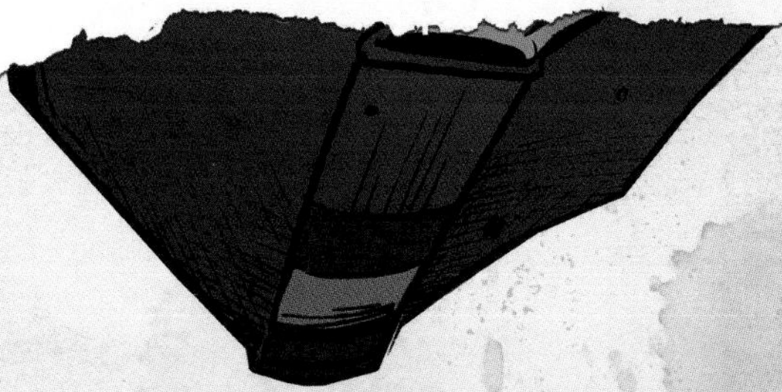

VAULT PRESENTS

THE LAST BOOK YOU'LL EVER READ

Civilization is a lie.

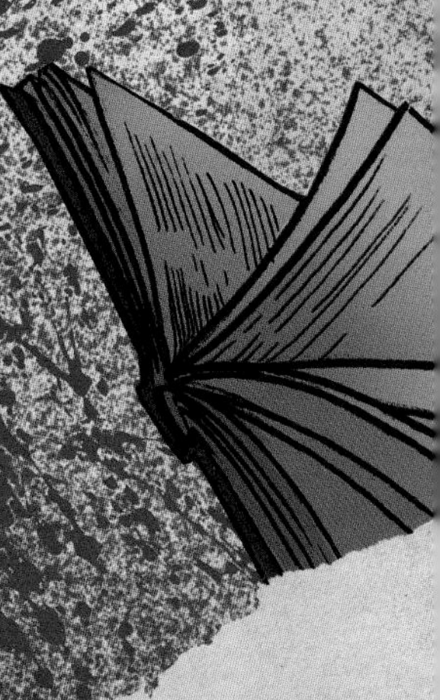

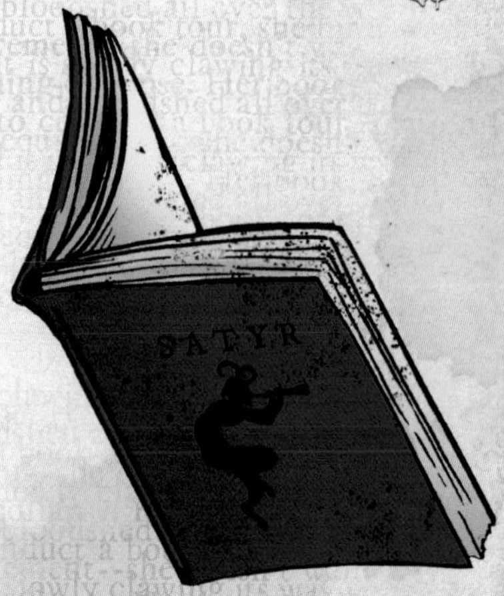
SATYR

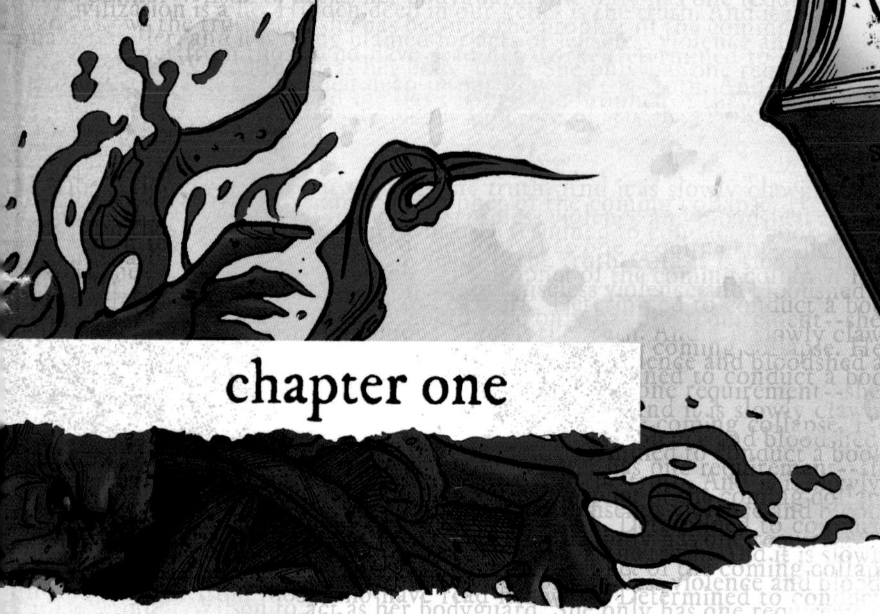

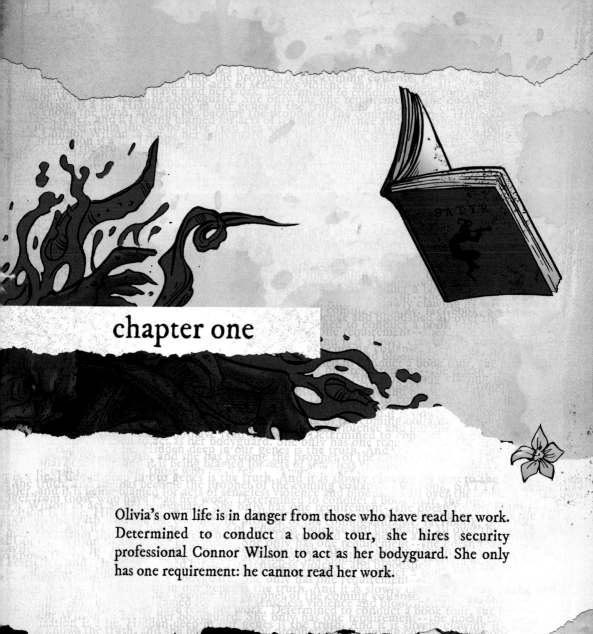

chapter one

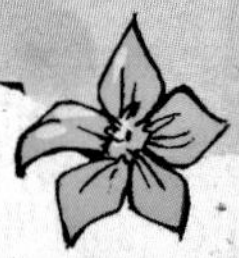

Olivia's own life is in danger from those who have read her work. Determined to conduct a book tour, she hires security professional Connor Wilson to act as her bodyguard. She only has one requirement: he cannot read her work.

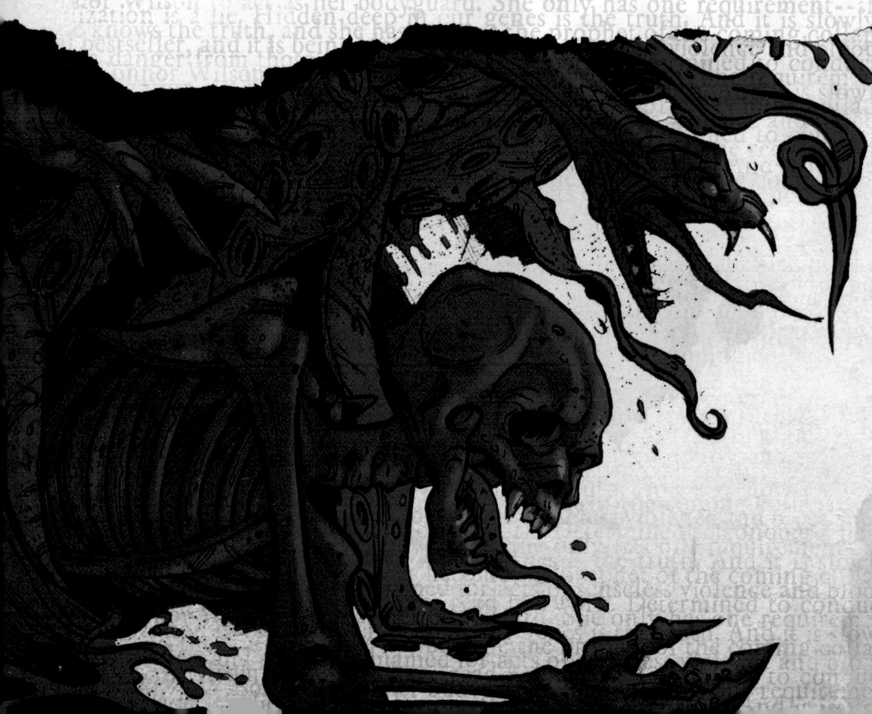

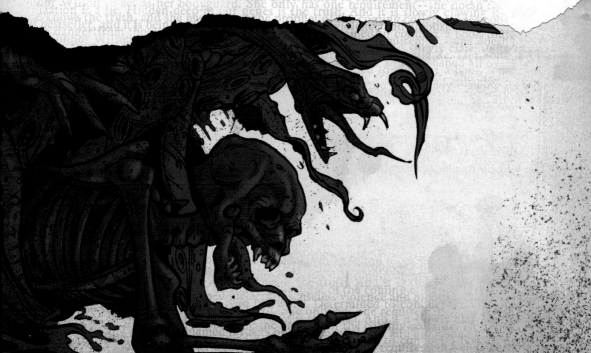

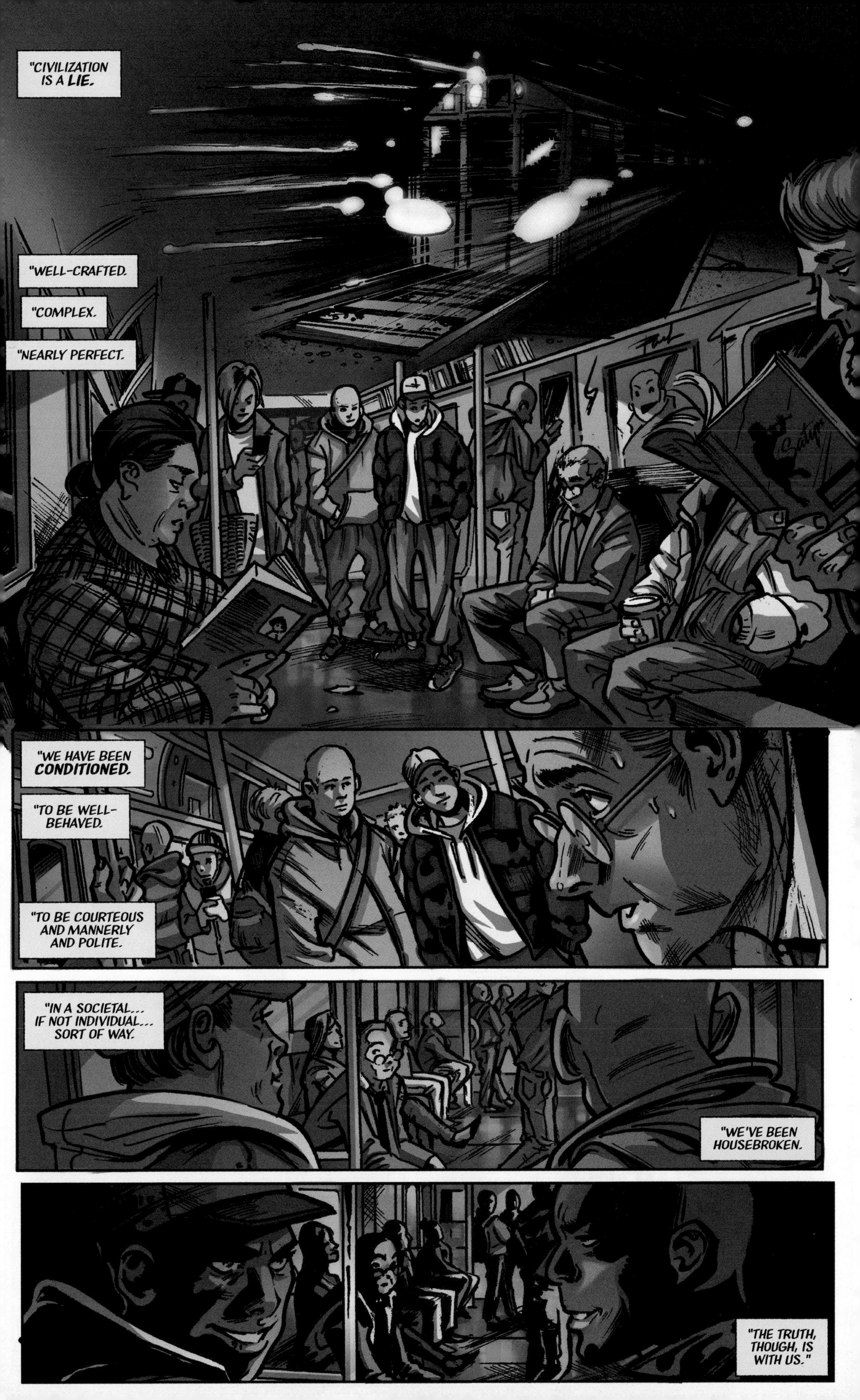
"CIVILIZATION IS A LIE.
"WELL-CRAFTED.
"COMPLEX.
"NEARLY PERFECT.
"WE HAVE BEEN CONDITIONED.
"TO BE WELL-BEHAVED.
"TO BE COURTEOUS AND MANNERLY AND POLITE.
"IN A SOCIETAL... IF NOT INDIVIDUAL... SORT OF WAY.
"WE'VE BEEN HOUSEBROKEN.
"THE TRUTH, THOUGH, IS WITH US."

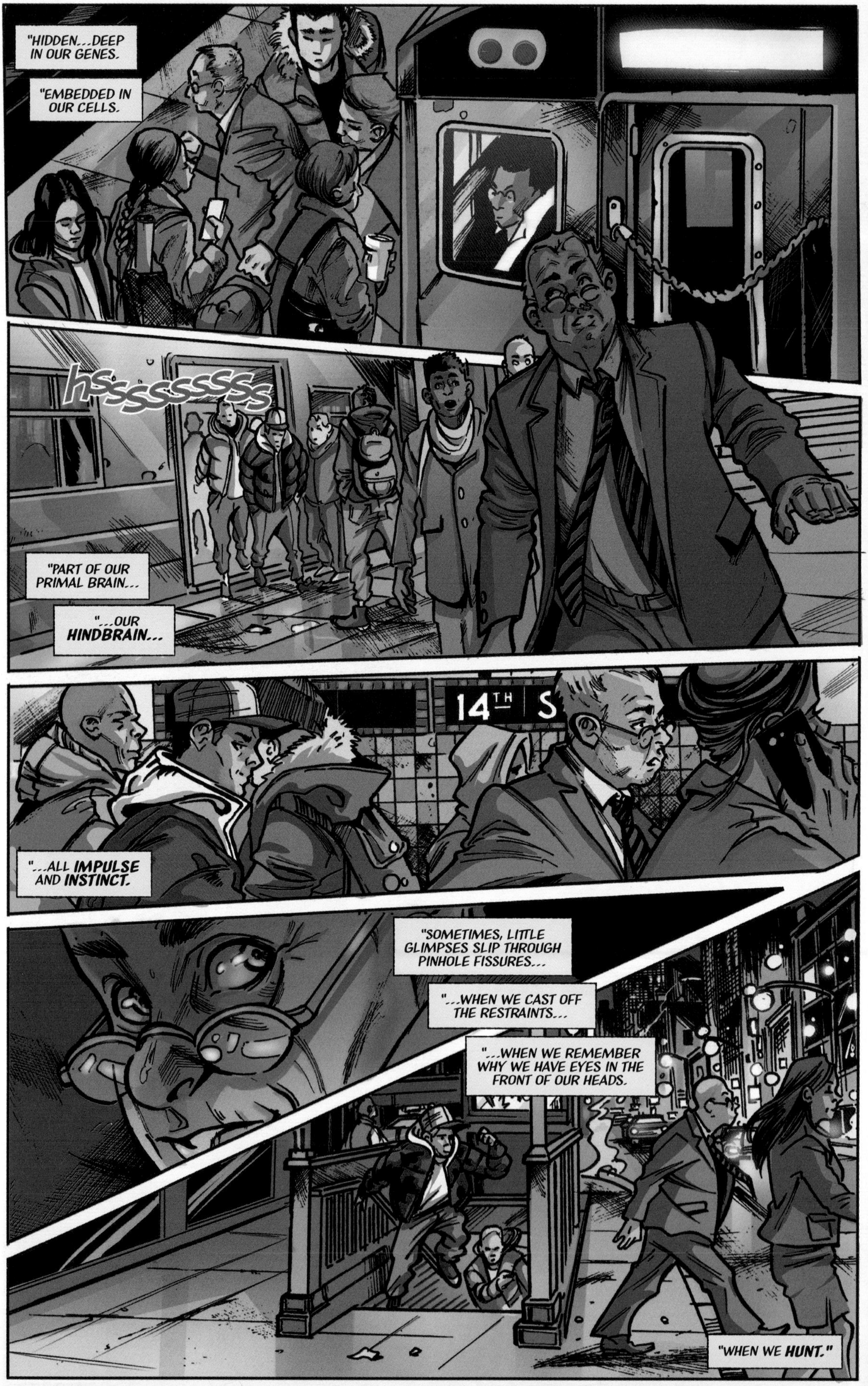
"HIDDEN...DEEP IN OUR GENES.
"EMBEDDED IN OUR CELLS.
hsssssssss
"PART OF OUR PRIMAL BRAIN...
"...OUR HINDBRAIN...
14TH S
"...ALL IMPULSE AND INSTINCT.
"SOMETIMES, LITTLE GLIMPSES SLIP THROUGH PINHOLE FISSURES...
"...WHEN WE CAST OFF THE RESTRAINTS...
"...WHEN WE REMEMBER WHY WE HAVE EYES IN THE FRONT OF OUR HEADS.
"WHEN WE HUNT."

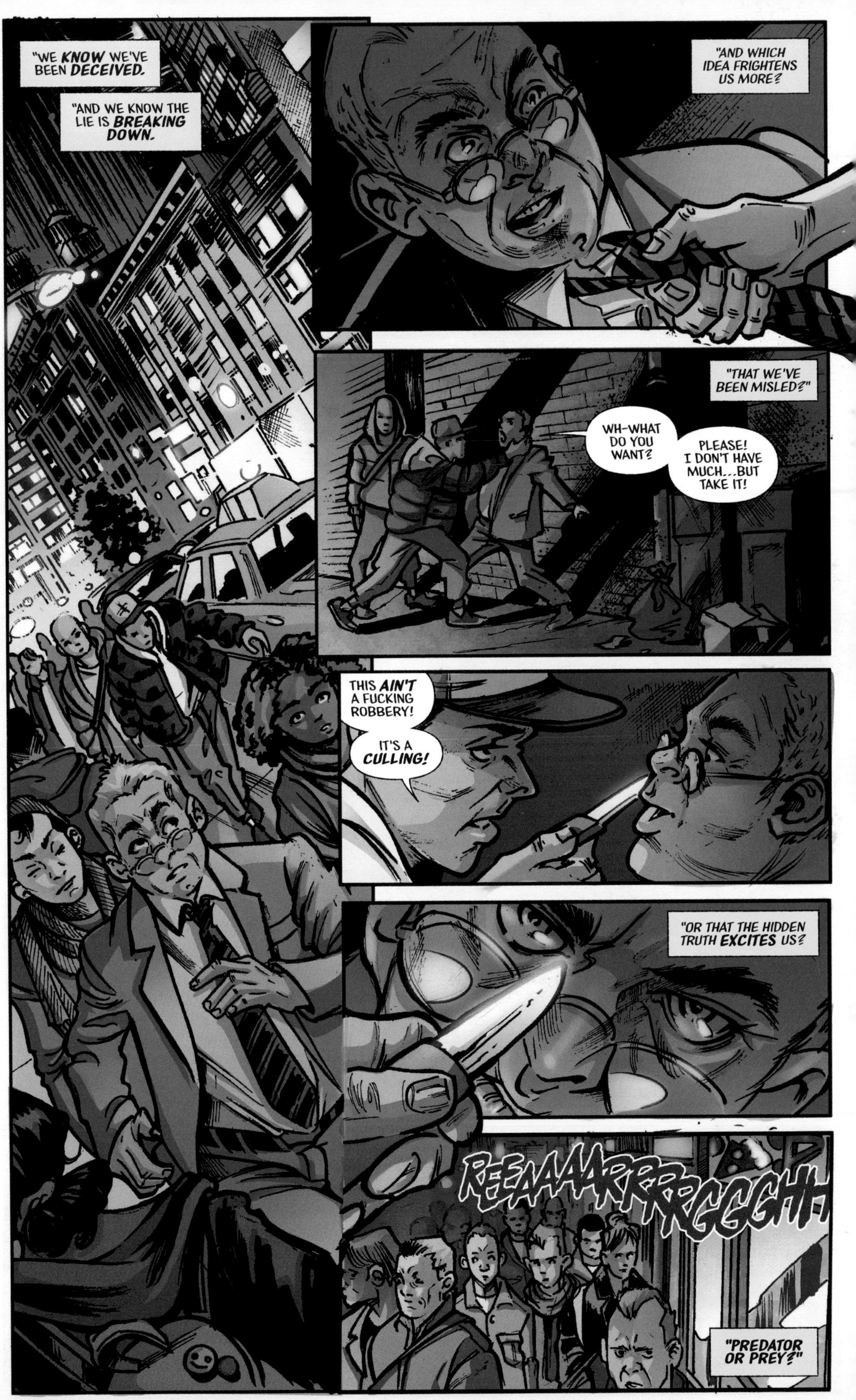
"WE **KNOW** WE'VE BEEN **DECEIVED.**
"AND WE KNOW THE LIE IS **BREAKING DOWN.**
"AND WHICH IDEA FRIGHTENS US MORE?
"THAT WE'VE BEEN MISLED?"
WH-WHAT DO YOU WANT?
PLEASE! I DON'T HAVE MUCH...BUT TAKE IT!
THIS **AIN'T** A FUCKING ROBBERY!
IT'S A **CULLING!**
"OR THAT THE HIDDEN TRUTH **EXCITES** US?
REEAAAARRRRGGGHH
"PREDATOR OR PREY?"

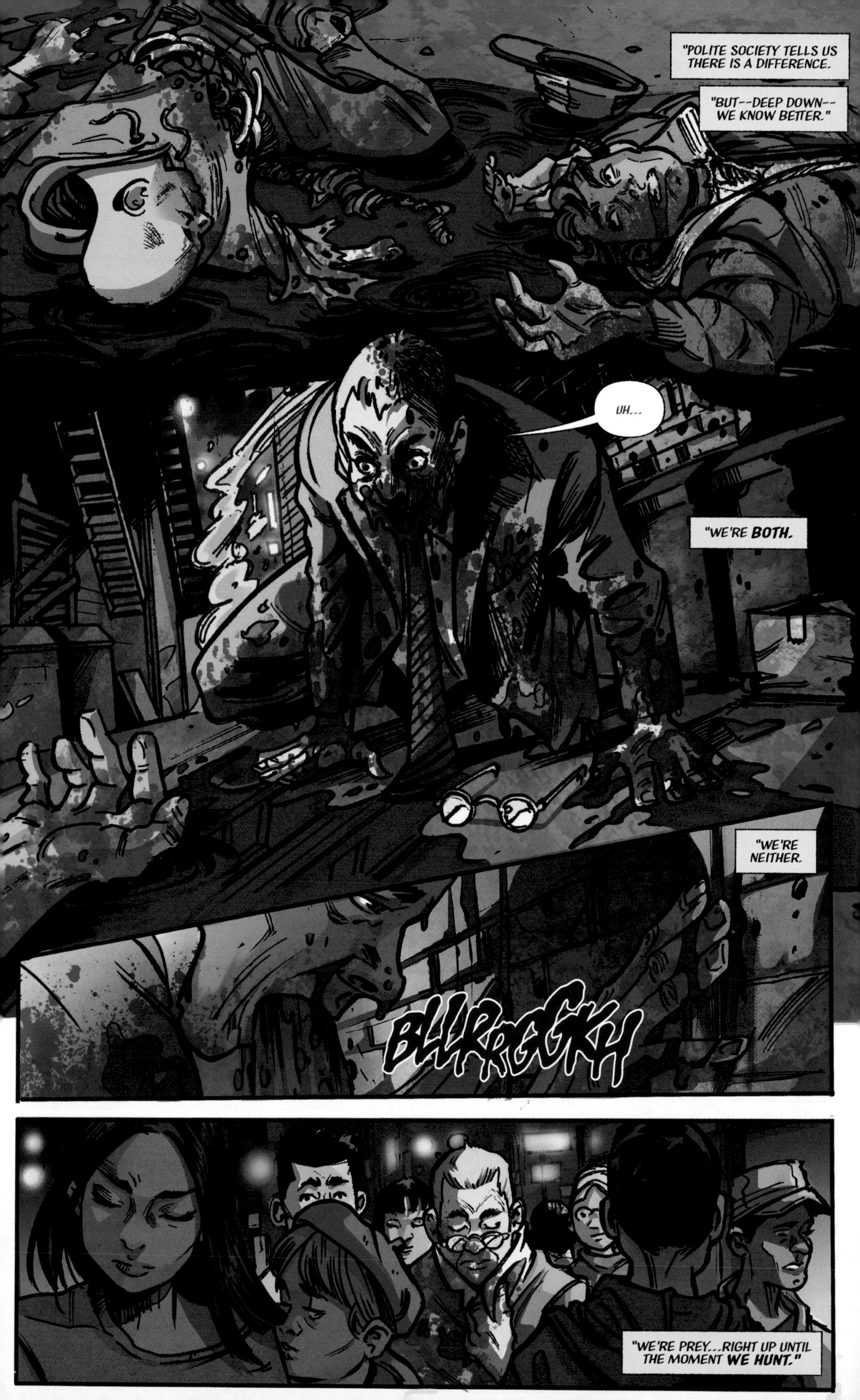
"POLITE SOCIETY TELLS US THERE IS A DIFFERENCE.
"BUT--DEEP DOWN--WE KNOW BETTER."
UH...
"WE'RE BOTH.
"WE'RE NEITHER.
BLURGGKH
"WE'RE PREY...RIGHT UP UNTIL THE MOMENT WE HUNT."

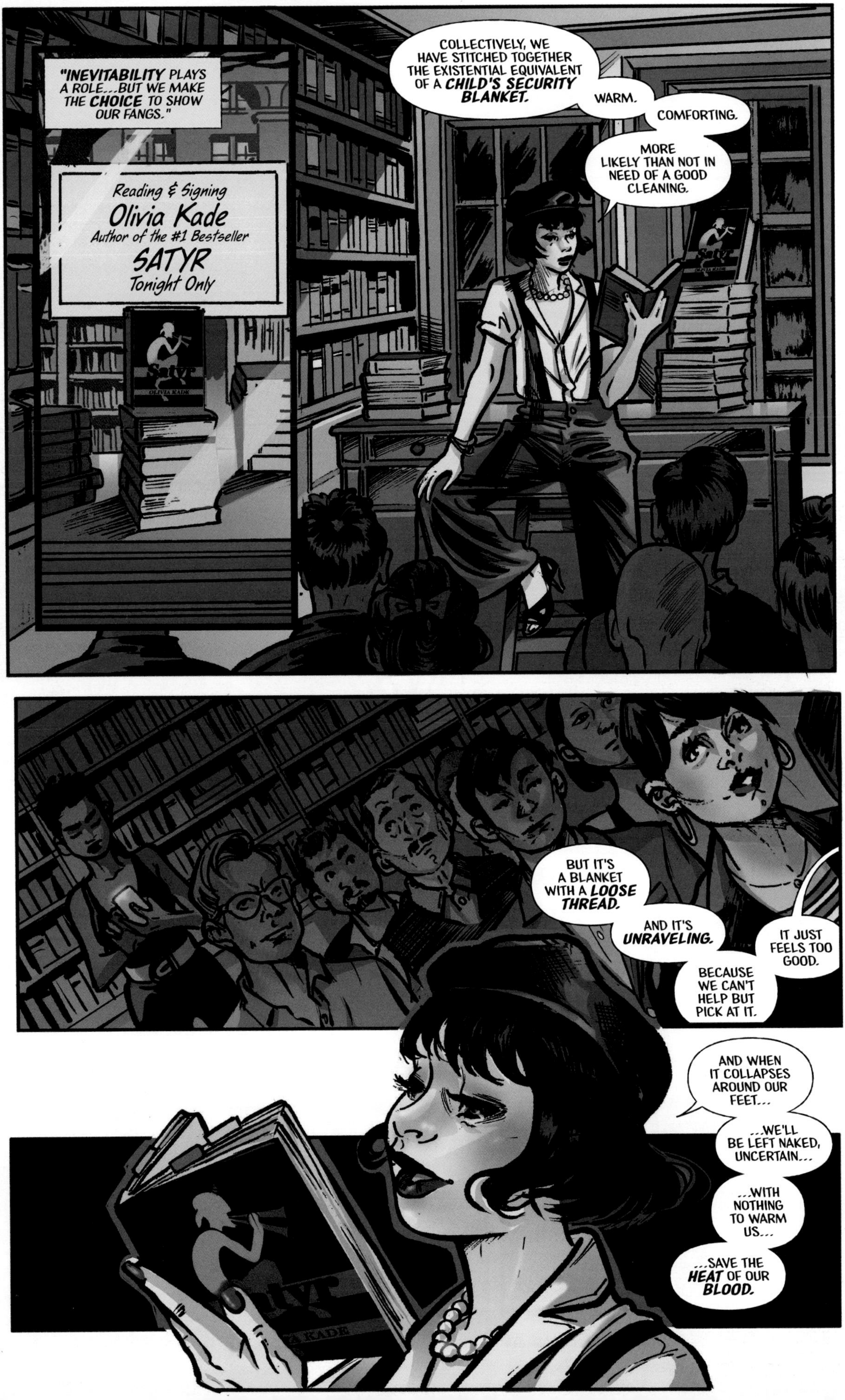
"INEVITABILITY PLAYS A ROLE... BUT WE MAKE THE CHOICE TO SHOW OUR FANGS."
Reading & Signing
Olivia Kade
Author of the #1 Bestseller
SATYR
Tonight Only
Satyr
OLIVIA KADE
COLLECTIVELY, WE HAVE STITCHED TOGETHER THE EXISTENTIAL EQUIVALENT OF A CHILD'S SECURITY BLANKET.
WARM.
COMFORTING.
MORE LIKELY THAN NOT IN NEED OF A GOOD CLEANING.
BUT IT'S A BLANKET WITH A LOOSE THREAD.
AND IT'S UNRAVELING.
BECAUSE WE CAN'T HELP BUT PICK AT IT.
IT JUST FEELS TOO GOOD.
AND WHEN IT COLLAPSES AROUND OUR FEET...
...WE'LL BE LEFT NAKED, UNCERTAIN...
...WITH NOTHING TO WARM US...
...SAVE THE HEAT OF OUR BLOOD.

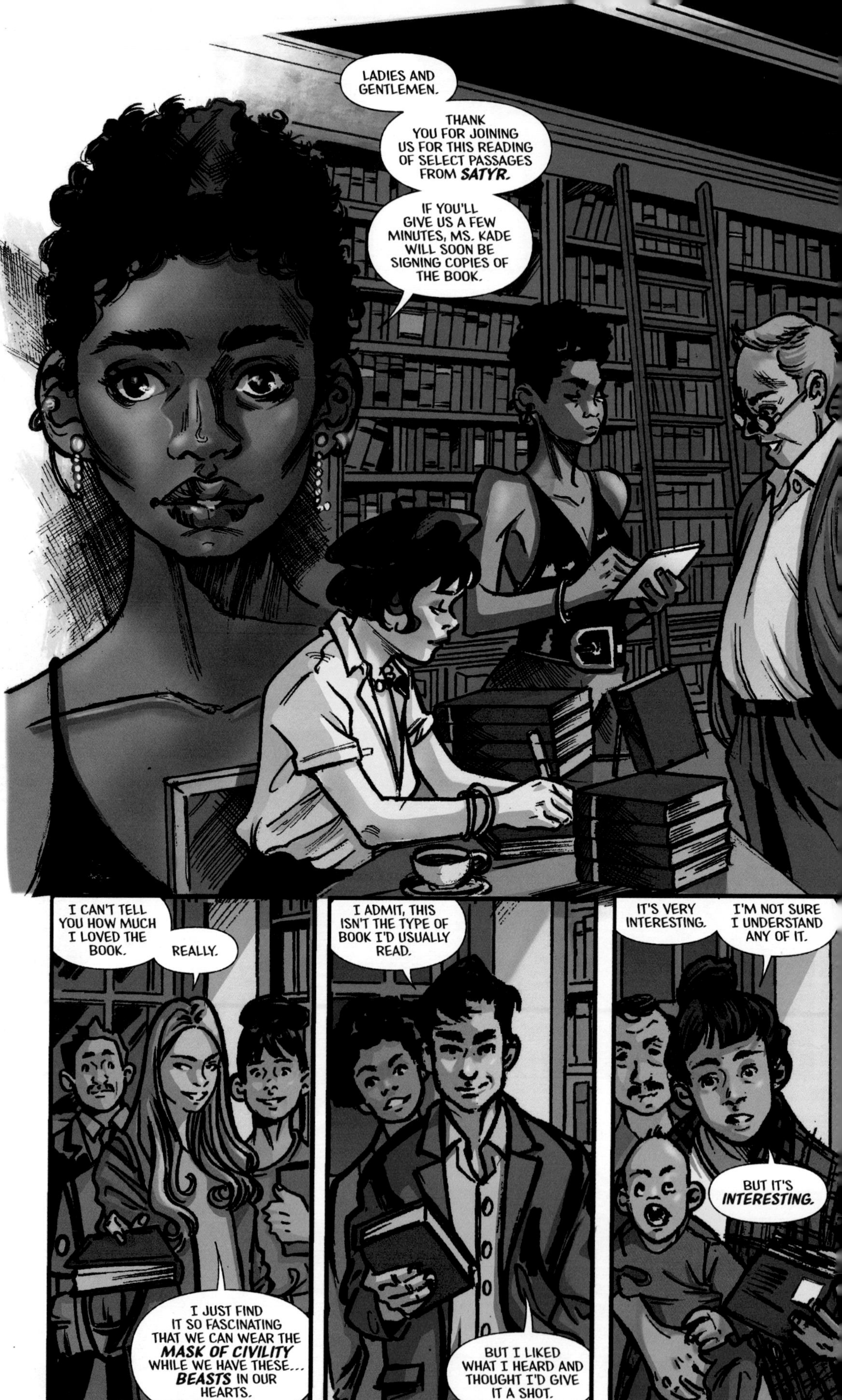
LADIES AND GENTLEMEN.
THANK YOU FOR JOINING US FOR THIS READING OF SELECT PASSAGES FROM *SATYR.*
IF YOU'LL GIVE US A FEW MINUTES, MS. KADE WILL SOON BE SIGNING COPIES OF THE BOOK.
I CAN'T TELL YOU HOW MUCH I LOVED THE BOOK.
REALLY.
I JUST FIND IT SO FASCINATING THAT WE CAN WEAR THE *MASK OF CIVILITY* WHILE WE HAVE THESE... *BEASTS* IN OUR HEARTS.
I ADMIT, THIS ISN'T THE TYPE OF BOOK I'D USUALLY READ.
BUT I LIKED WHAT I HEARD AND THOUGHT I'D GIVE IT A SHOT.
IT'S VERY INTERESTING.
I'M NOT SURE I UNDERSTAND ANY OF IT.
BUT IT'S *INTERESTING.*

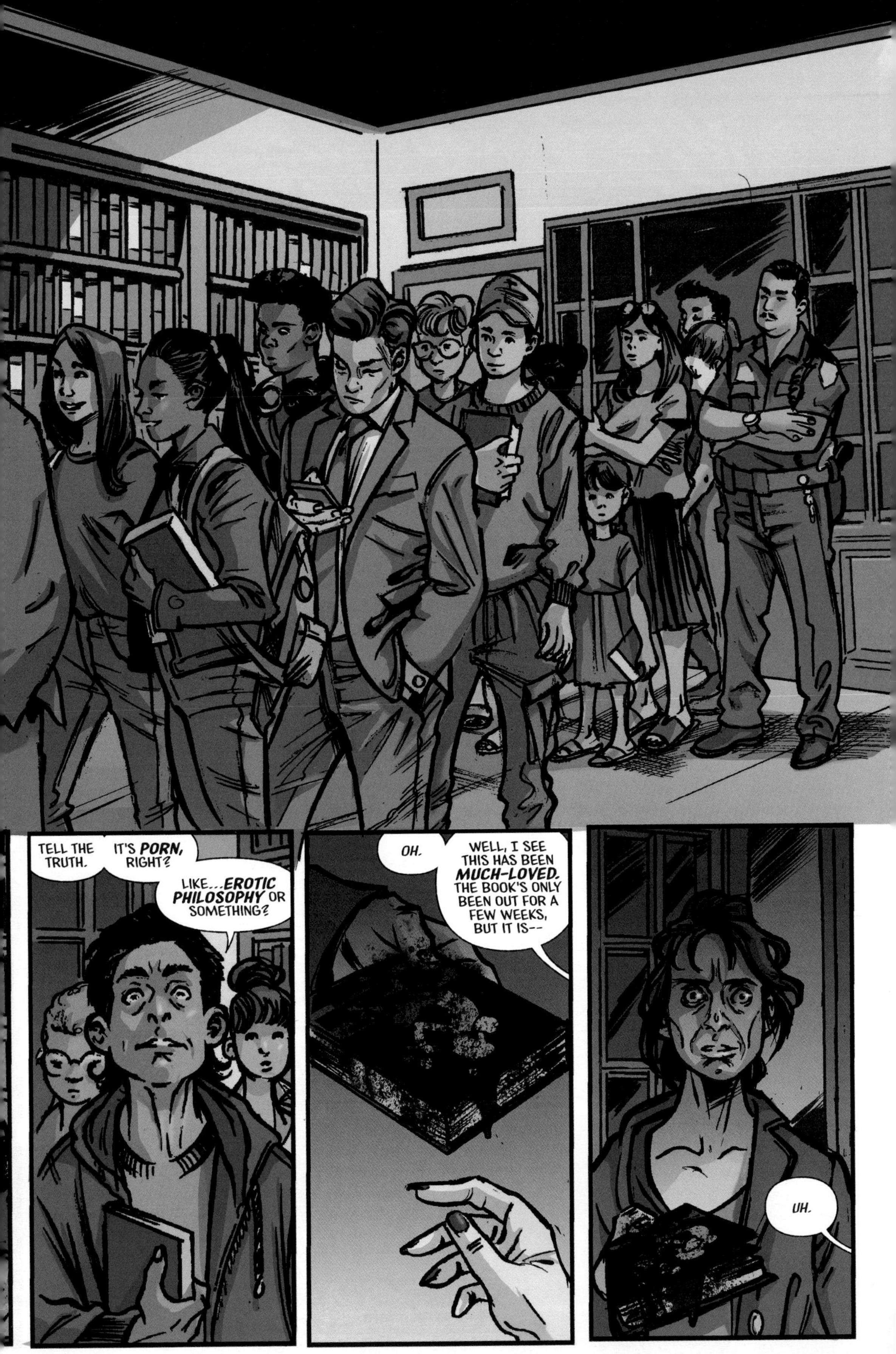
TELL THE TRUTH.
IT'S PORN, RIGHT?
LIKE...EROTIC PHILOSOPHY OR SOMETHING?
OH.
WELL, I SEE THIS HAS BEEN MUCH-LOVED. THE BOOK'S ONLY BEEN OUT FOR A FEW WEEKS, BUT IT IS--
UH.

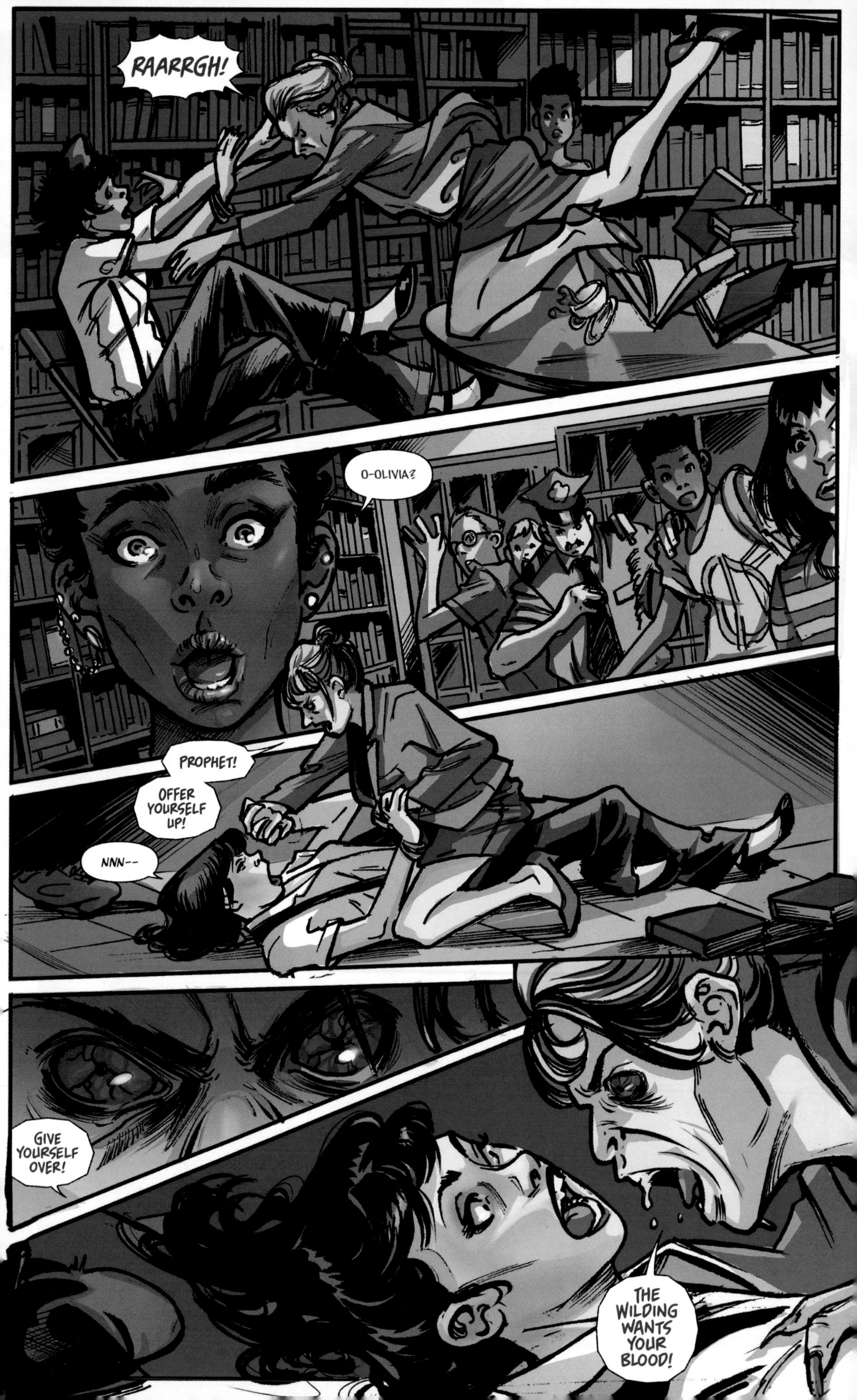
RAARRGH!
O-OLIVIA?
PROPHET!
OFFER YOURSELF UP!
NNN--
GIVE YOURSELF OVER!
THE WILDING WANTS YOUR BLOOD!

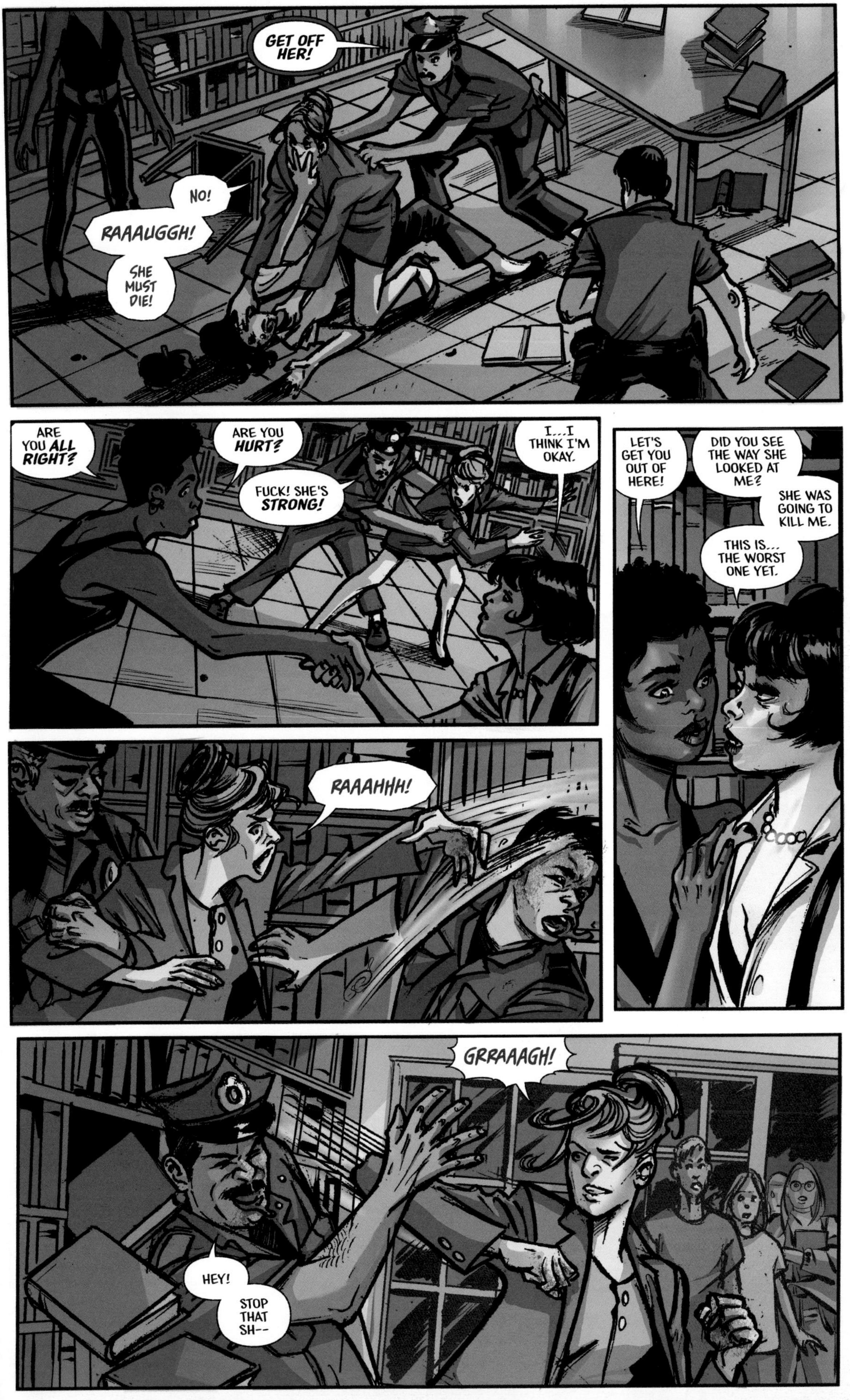
GET OFF HER!
NO!
RAAAUGGH!
SHE MUST DIE!
ARE YOU ALL RIGHT?
ARE YOU HURT?
FUCK! SHE'S STRONG!
I... I THINK I'M OKAY.
LET'S GET YOU OUT OF HERE!
DID YOU SEE THE WAY SHE LOOKED AT ME?
SHE WAS GOING TO KILL ME.
THIS IS... THE WORST ONE YET.
RAAAHHH!
GRRAAAGH!
HEY!
STOP THAT SH--

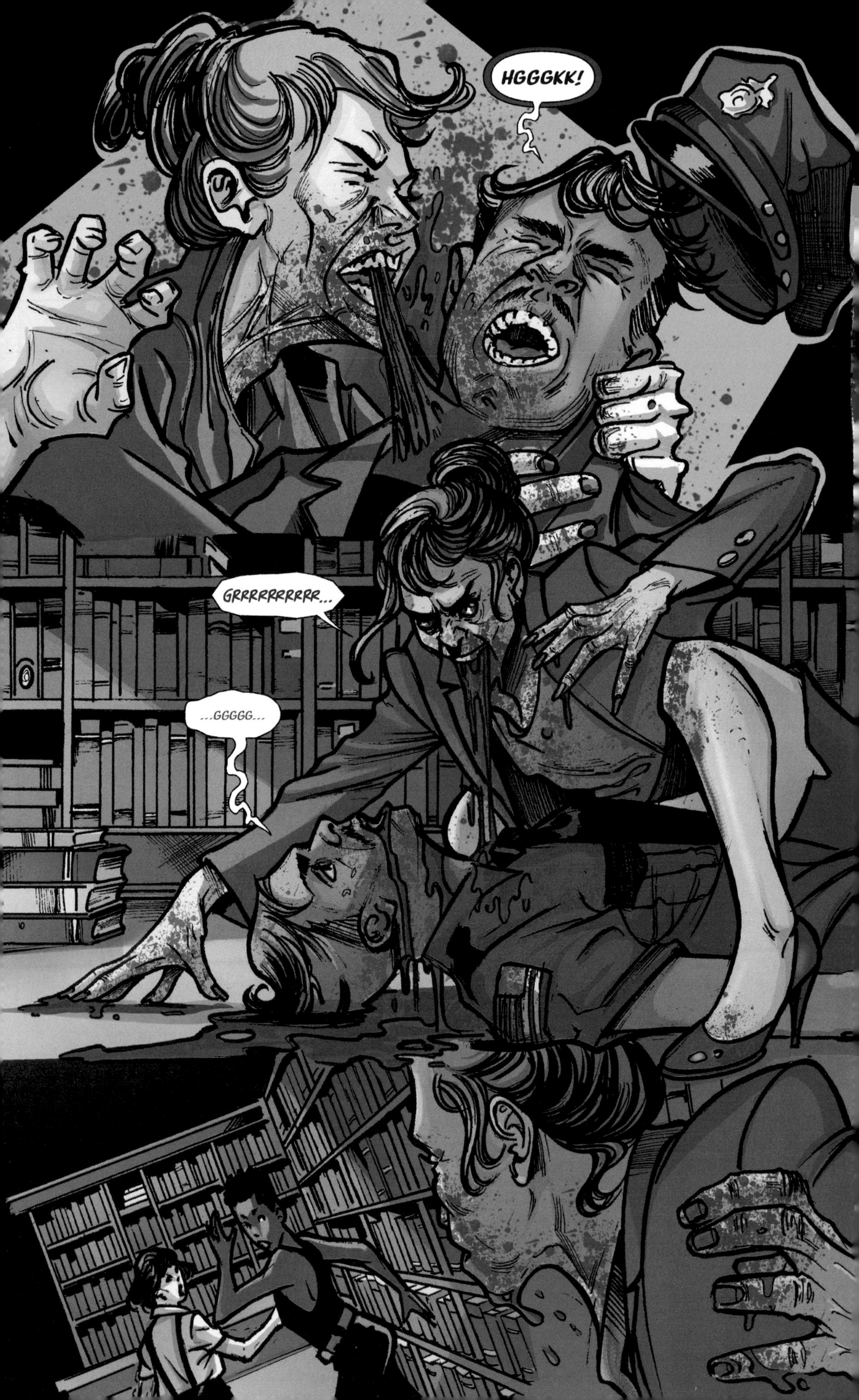
HGGGKK!
GRRRRRRRRRR...
...GGGGG...

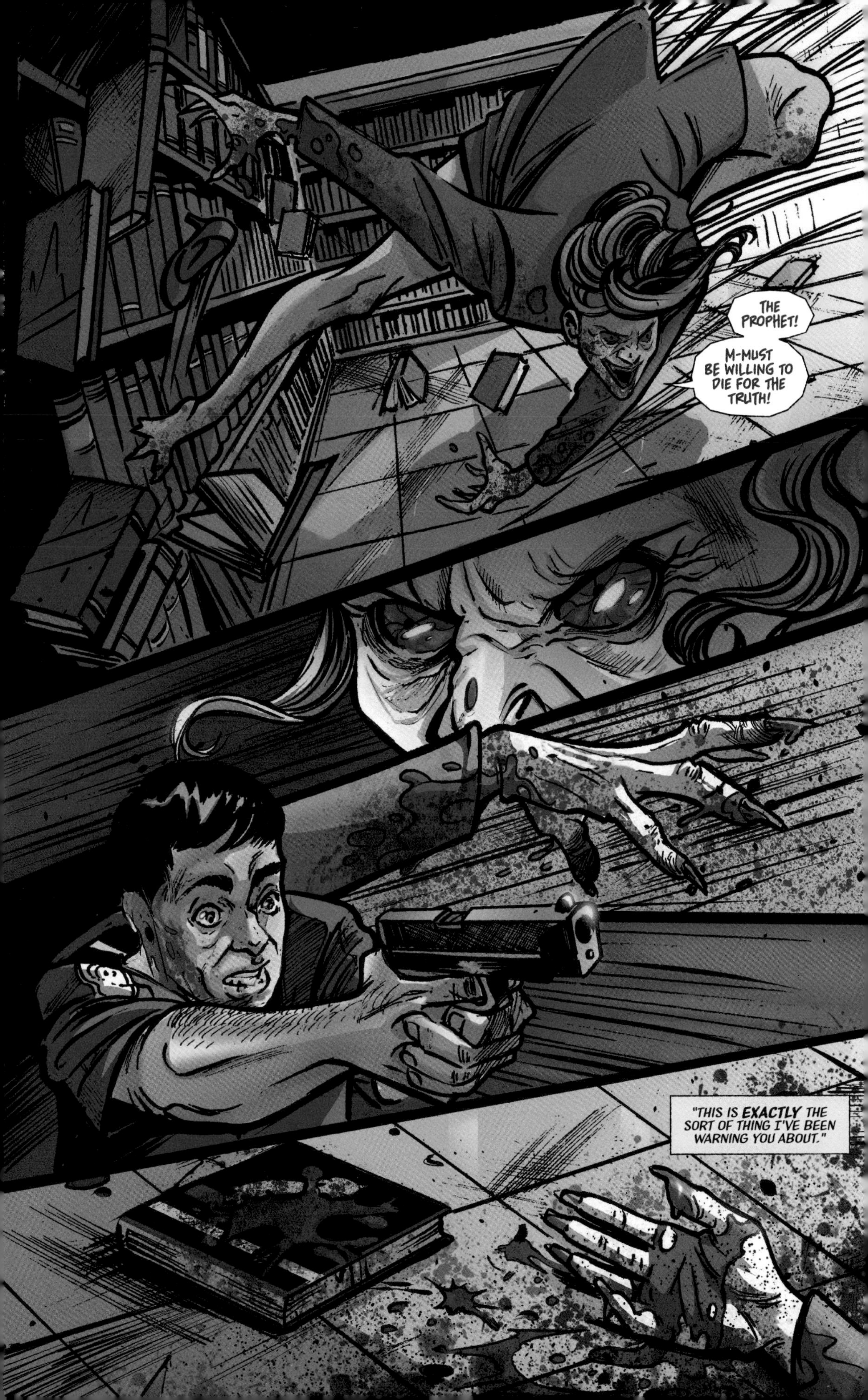
THE PROPHET!
M-MUST BE WILLING TO DIE FOR THE TRUTH!
"THIS IS **EXACTLY** THE SORT OF THING I'VE BEEN WARNING YOU ABOUT."

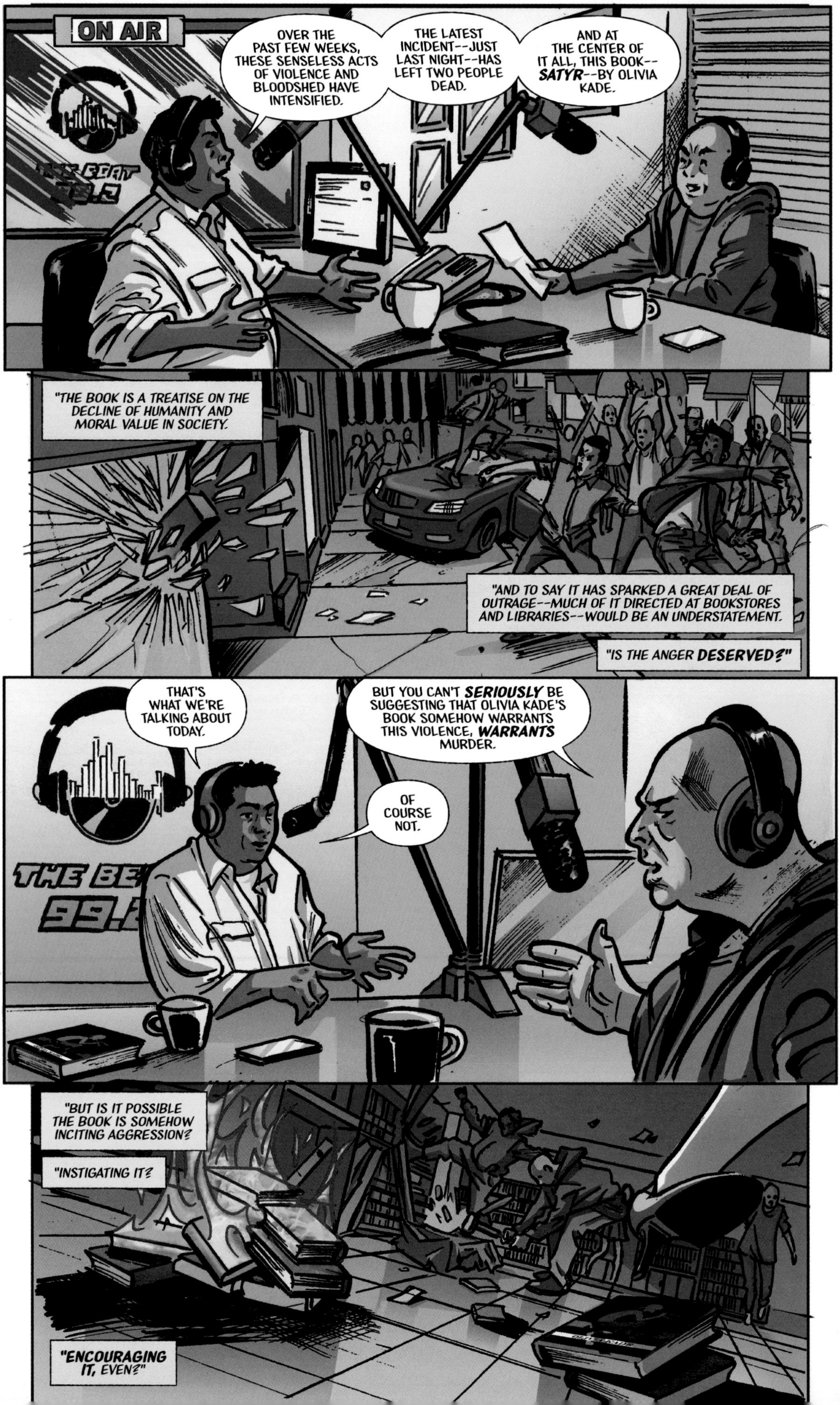
ON AIR
OVER THE PAST FEW WEEKS, THESE SENSELESS ACTS OF VIOLENCE AND BLOODSHED HAVE INTENSIFIED.
THE LATEST INCIDENT--JUST LAST NIGHT--HAS LEFT TWO PEOPLE DEAD.
AND AT THE CENTER OF IT ALL, THIS BOOK--*SATYR*--BY OLIVIA KADE.
"THE BOOK IS A TREATISE ON THE DECLINE OF HUMANITY AND MORAL VALUE IN SOCIETY.
"AND TO SAY IT HAS SPARKED A GREAT DEAL OF OUTRAGE--MUCH OF IT DIRECTED AT BOOKSTORES AND LIBRARIES--WOULD BE AN UNDERSTATEMENT.
"IS THE ANGER **DESERVED?**"
THAT'S WHAT WE'RE TALKING ABOUT TODAY.
BUT YOU CAN'T ***SERIOUSLY*** BE SUGGESTING THAT OLIVIA KADE'S BOOK SOMEHOW WARRANTS THIS VIOLENCE, ***WARRANTS*** MURDER.
OF COURSE NOT.
"BUT IS IT POSSIBLE THE BOOK IS SOMEHOW INCITING AGGRESSION?
"INSTIGATING IT?
"**ENCOURAGING IT,** EVEN?"

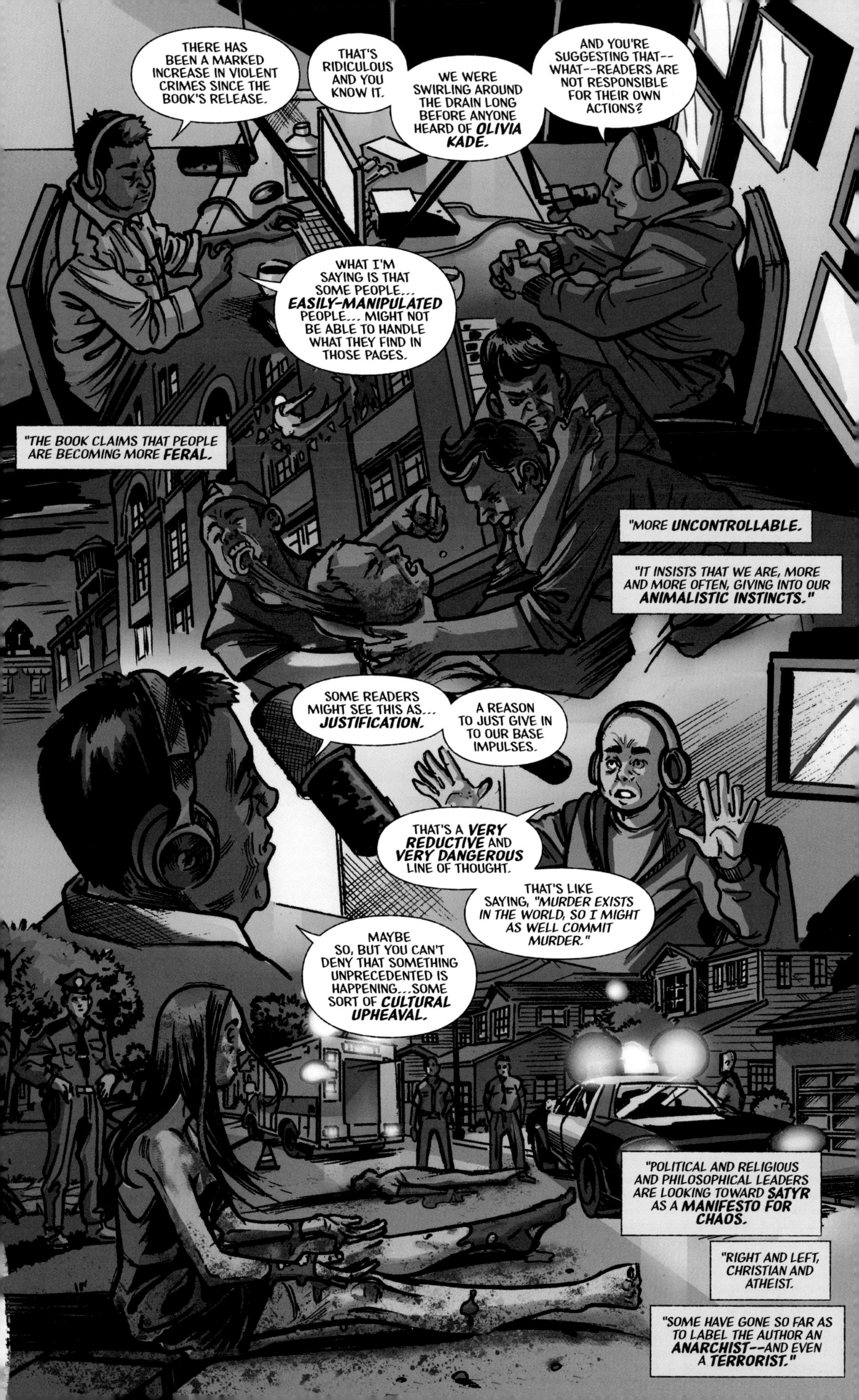
THERE HAS BEEN A MARKED INCREASE IN VIOLENT CRIMES SINCE THE BOOK'S RELEASE.
THAT'S RIDICULOUS AND YOU KNOW IT.
WE WERE SWIRLING AROUND THE DRAIN LONG BEFORE ANYONE HEARD OF OLIVIA KADE.
AND YOU'RE SUGGESTING THAT-- WHAT--READERS ARE NOT RESPONSIBLE FOR THEIR OWN ACTIONS?
WHAT I'M SAYING IS THAT SOME PEOPLE... EASILY-MANIPULATED PEOPLE... MIGHT NOT BE ABLE TO HANDLE WHAT THEY FIND IN THOSE PAGES.
"THE BOOK CLAIMS THAT PEOPLE ARE BECOMING MORE FERAL.
"MORE UNCONTROLLABLE.
"IT INSISTS THAT WE ARE, MORE AND MORE OFTEN, GIVING INTO OUR ANIMALISTIC INSTINCTS."
SOME READERS MIGHT SEE THIS AS... JUSTIFICATION.
A REASON TO JUST GIVE IN TO OUR BASE IMPULSES.
THAT'S A VERY REDUCTIVE AND VERY DANGEROUS LINE OF THOUGHT.
THAT'S LIKE SAYING, "MURDER EXISTS IN THE WORLD, SO I MIGHT AS WELL COMMIT MURDER."
MAYBE SO, BUT YOU CAN'T DENY THAT SOMETHING UNPRECEDENTED IS HAPPENING...SOME SORT OF CULTURAL UPHEAVAL.
"POLITICAL AND RELIGIOUS AND PHILOSOPHICAL LEADERS ARE LOOKING TOWARD SATYR AS A MANIFESTO FOR CHAOS.
"RIGHT AND LEFT, CHRISTIAN AND ATHEIST.
"SOME HAVE GONE SO FAR AS TO LABEL THE AUTHOR AN ANARCHIST--AND EVEN A TERRORIST."

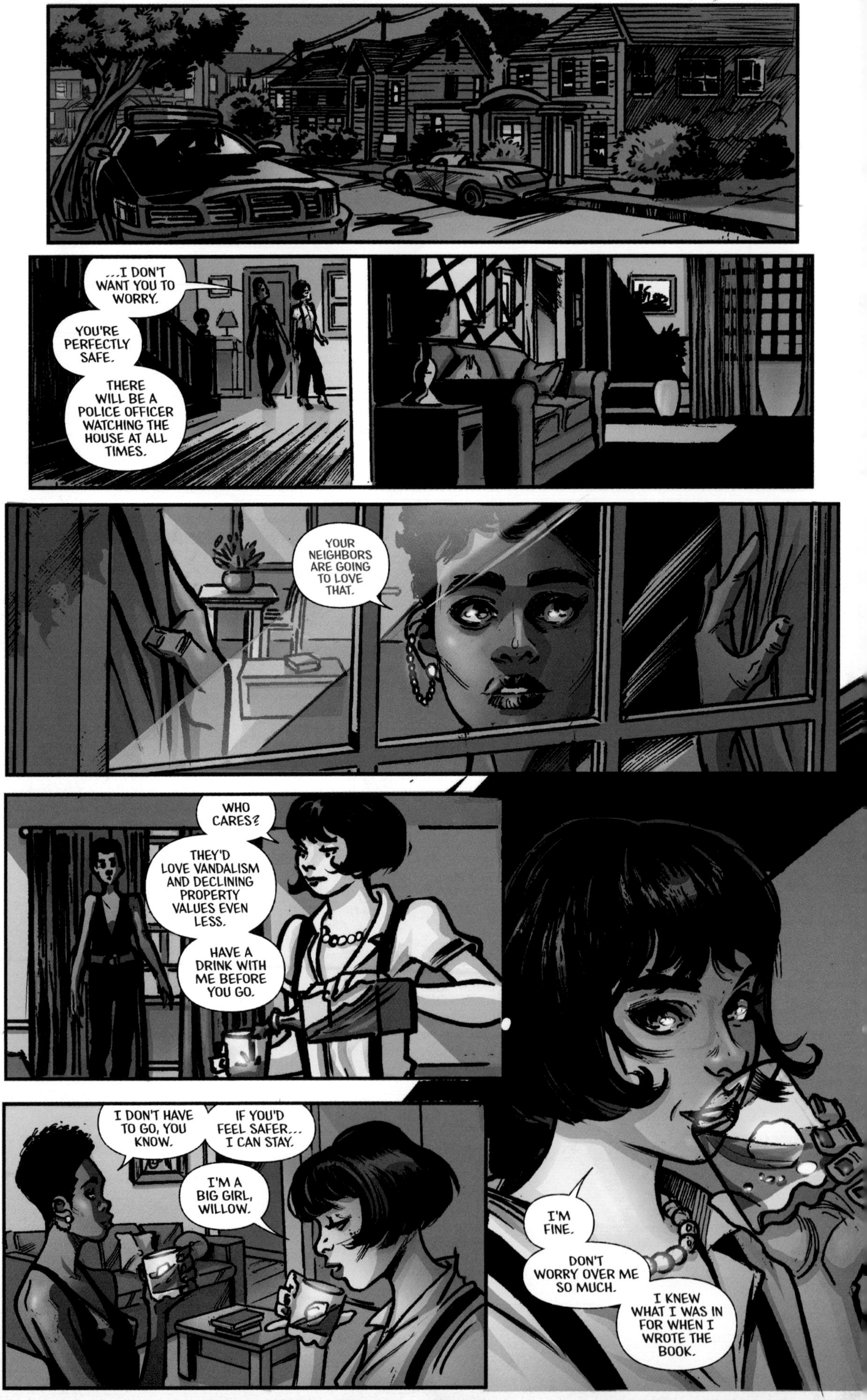
...I DON'T WANT YOU TO WORRY.
YOU'RE PERFECTLY SAFE.
THERE WILL BE A POLICE OFFICER WATCHING THE HOUSE AT ALL TIMES.
YOUR NEIGHBORS ARE GOING TO LOVE THAT.
WHO CARES?
THEY'D LOVE VANDALISM AND DECLINING PROPERTY VALUES EVEN LESS.
HAVE A DRINK WITH ME BEFORE YOU GO.
I DON'T HAVE TO GO, YOU KNOW.
IF YOU'D FEEL SAFER... I CAN STAY.
I'M A BIG GIRL, WILLOW.
I'M FINE.
DON'T WORRY OVER ME SO MUCH.
I KNEW WHAT I WAS IN FOR WHEN I WROTE THE BOOK.

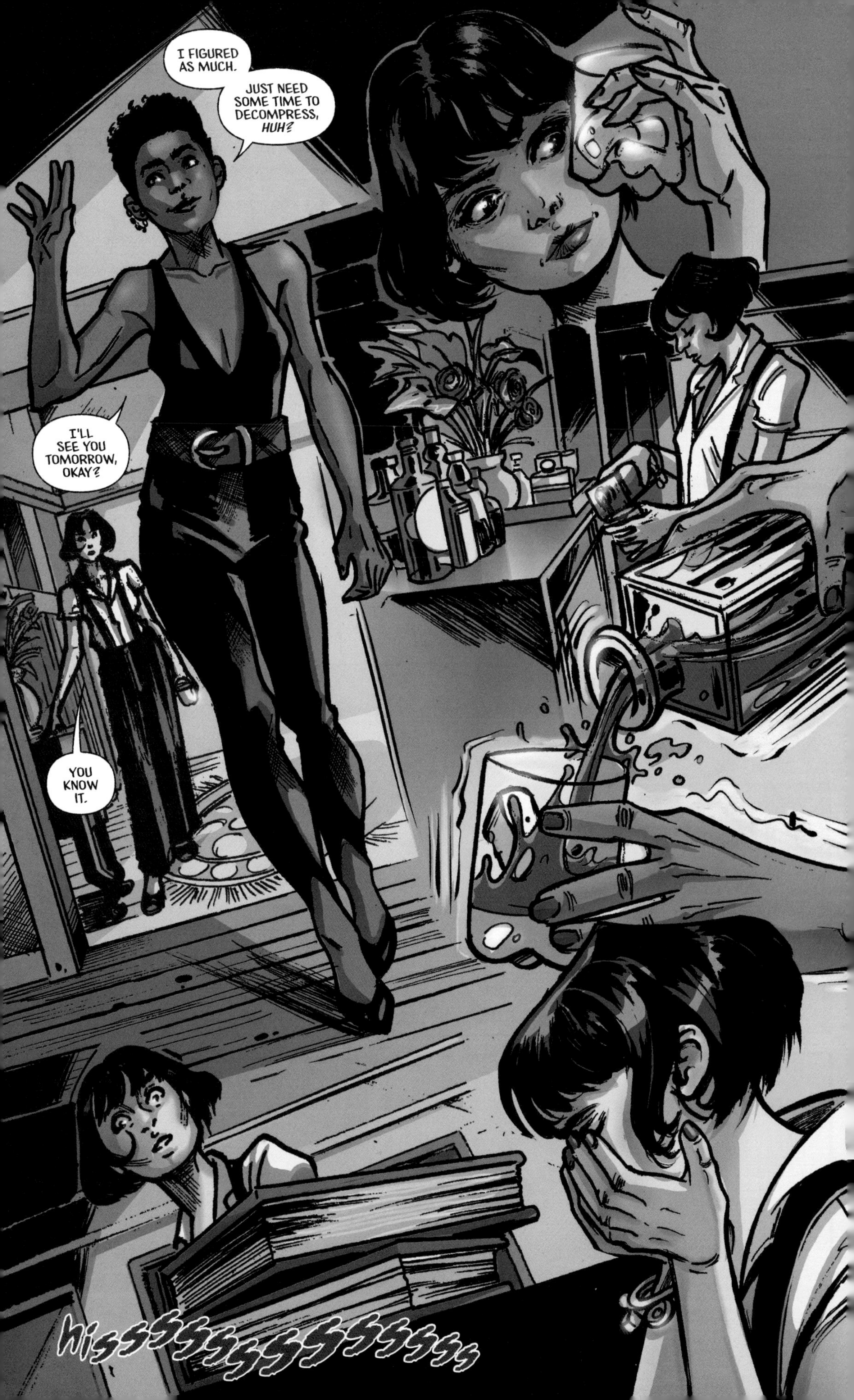
I FIGURED AS MUCH.
JUST NEED SOME TIME TO DECOMPRESS, *HUH?*
I'LL SEE YOU TOMORROW, OKAY?
YOU KNOW IT.
hisssssssssssssss

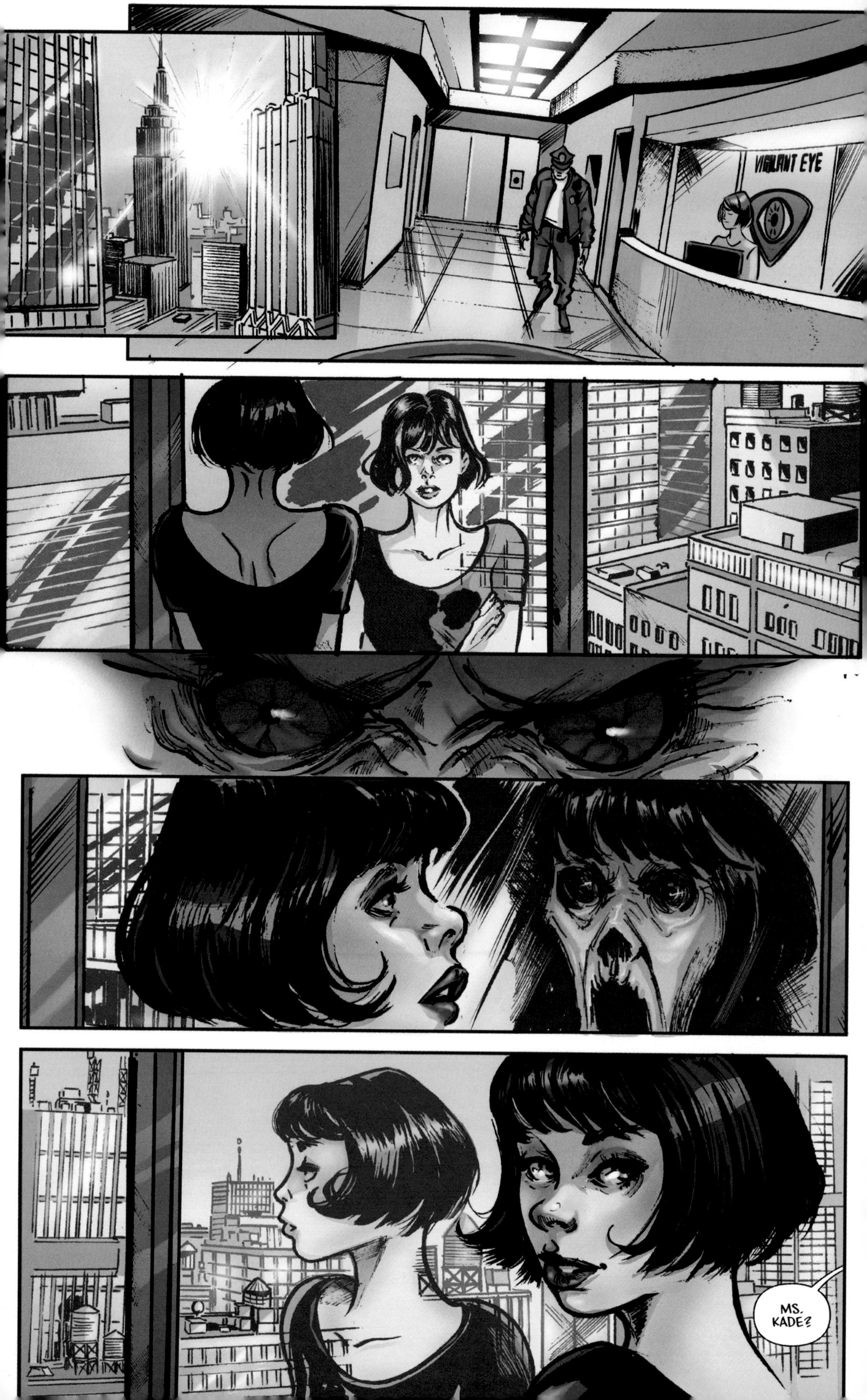
VIGILANT EYE
MS. KADE?

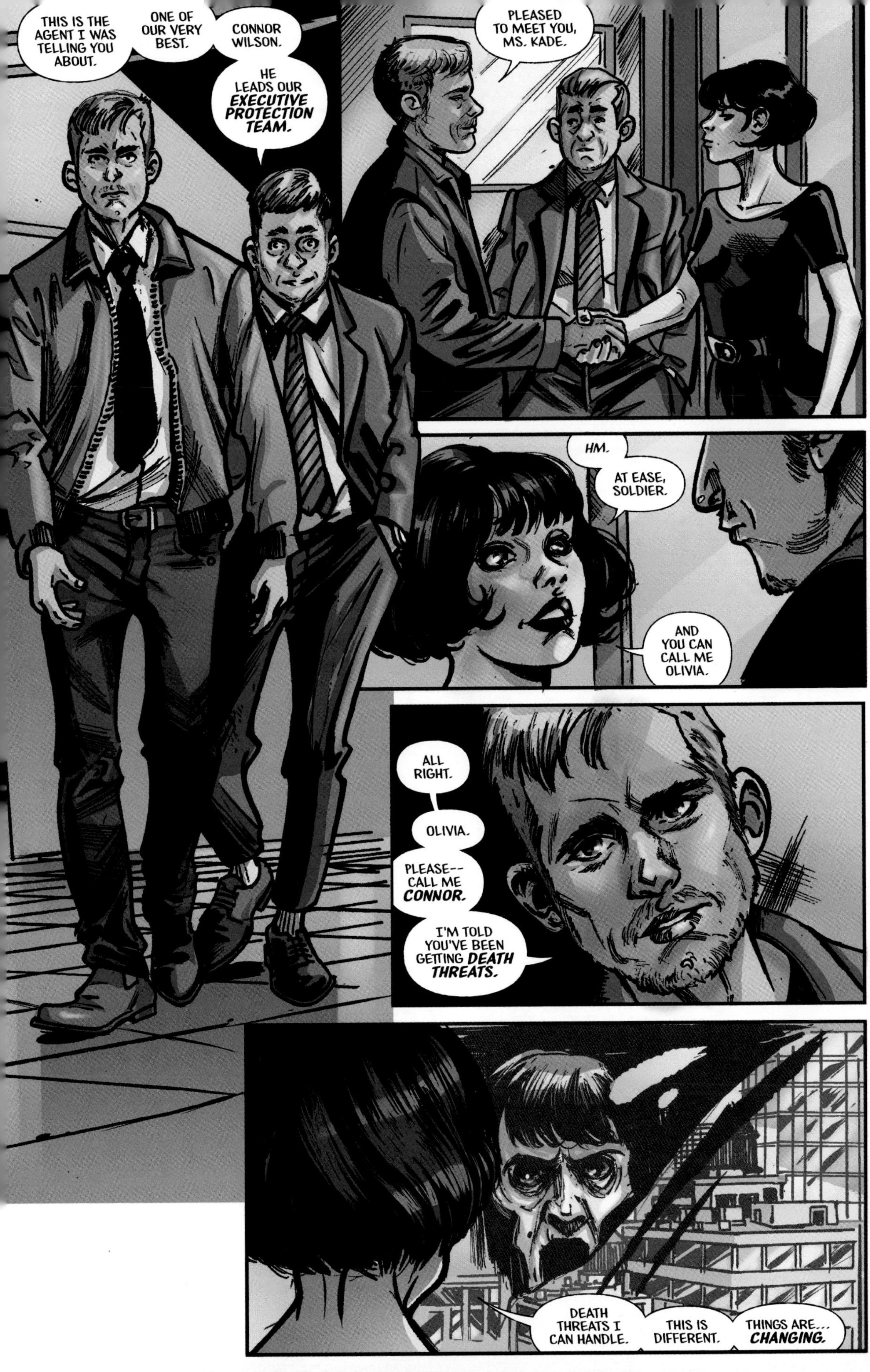
THIS IS THE AGENT I WAS TELLING YOU ABOUT.
ONE OF OUR VERY BEST.
CONNOR WILSON.
HE LEADS OUR EXECUTIVE PROTECTION TEAM.
PLEASED TO MEET YOU, MS. KADE.
HM.
AT EASE, SOLDIER.
AND YOU CAN CALL ME OLIVIA.
ALL RIGHT.
OLIVIA.
PLEASE-- CALL ME CONNOR.
I'M TOLD YOU'VE BEEN GETTING DEATH THREATS.
DEATH THREATS I CAN HANDLE.
THIS IS DIFFERENT.
THINGS ARE... CHANGING.

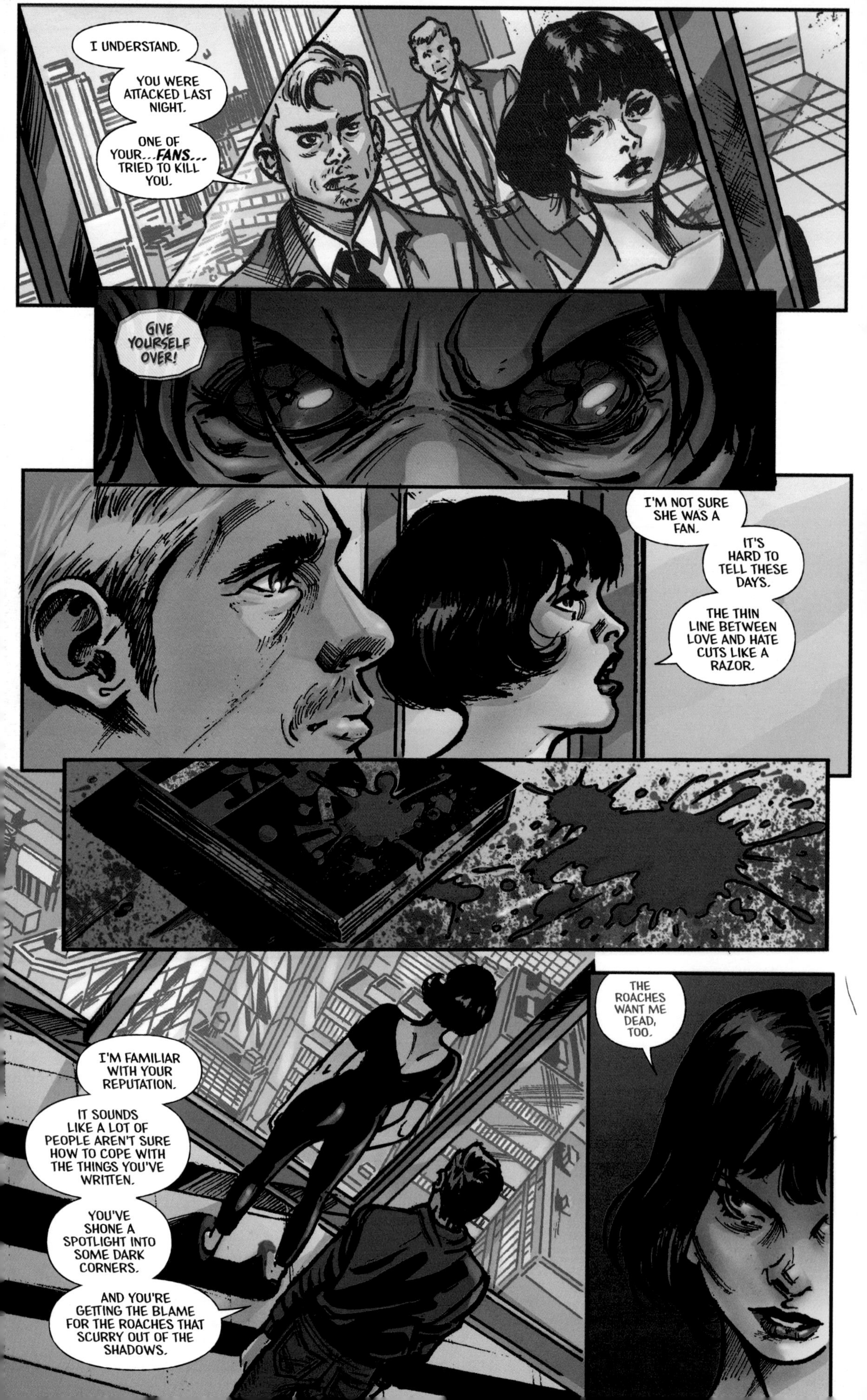
I UNDERSTAND.
YOU WERE ATTACKED LAST NIGHT.
ONE OF YOUR... FANS... TRIED TO KILL YOU.
GIVE YOURSELF OVER!
I'M NOT SURE SHE WAS A FAN.
IT'S HARD TO TELL THESE DAYS.
THE THIN LINE BETWEEN LOVE AND HATE CUTS LIKE A RAZOR.
I'M FAMILIAR WITH YOUR REPUTATION.
IT SOUNDS LIKE A LOT OF PEOPLE AREN'T SURE HOW TO COPE WITH THE THINGS YOU'VE WRITTEN.
YOU'VE SHONE A SPOTLIGHT INTO SOME DARK CORNERS.
AND YOU'RE GETTING THE BLAME FOR THE ROACHES THAT SCURRY OUT OF THE SHADOWS.
THE ROACHES WANT ME DEAD, TOO.

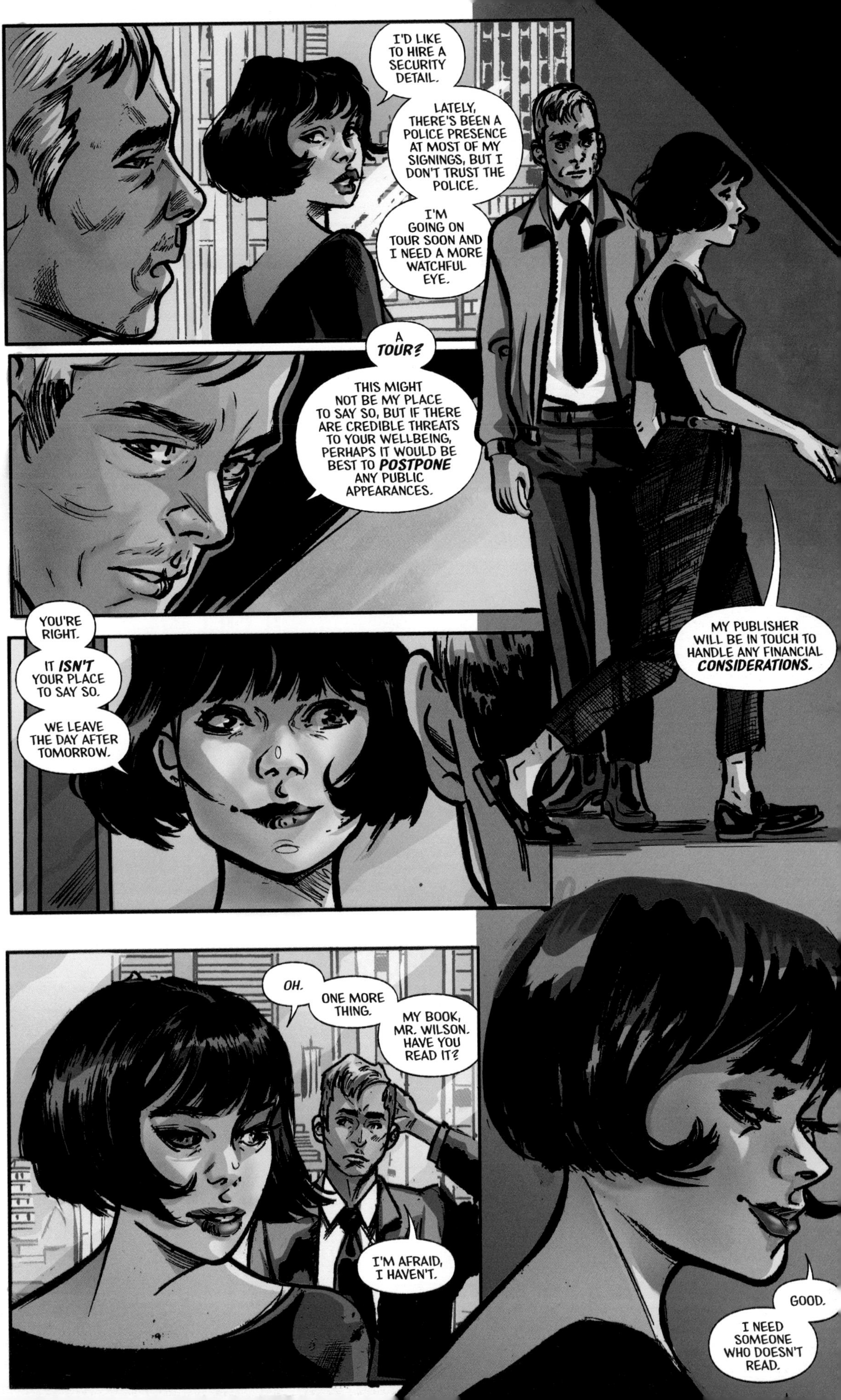
I'D LIKE TO HIRE A SECURITY DETAIL.
LATELY, THERE'S BEEN A POLICE PRESENCE AT MOST OF MY SIGNINGS, BUT I DON'T TRUST THE POLICE.
I'M GOING ON TOUR SOON AND I NEED A MORE WATCHFUL EYE.
A *TOUR?*
THIS MIGHT NOT BE MY PLACE TO SAY SO, BUT IF THERE ARE CREDIBLE THREATS TO YOUR WELLBEING, PERHAPS IT WOULD BE BEST TO *POSTPONE* ANY PUBLIC APPEARANCES.
YOU'RE RIGHT.
IT *ISN'T* YOUR PLACE TO SAY SO.
WE LEAVE THE DAY AFTER TOMORROW.
MY PUBLISHER WILL BE IN TOUCH TO HANDLE ANY FINANCIAL *CONSIDERATIONS.*
OH.
ONE MORE THING.
MY BOOK, MR. WILSON. HAVE YOU READ IT?
I'M AFRAID, I HAVEN'T.
GOOD.
I NEED SOMEONE WHO DOESN'T READ.

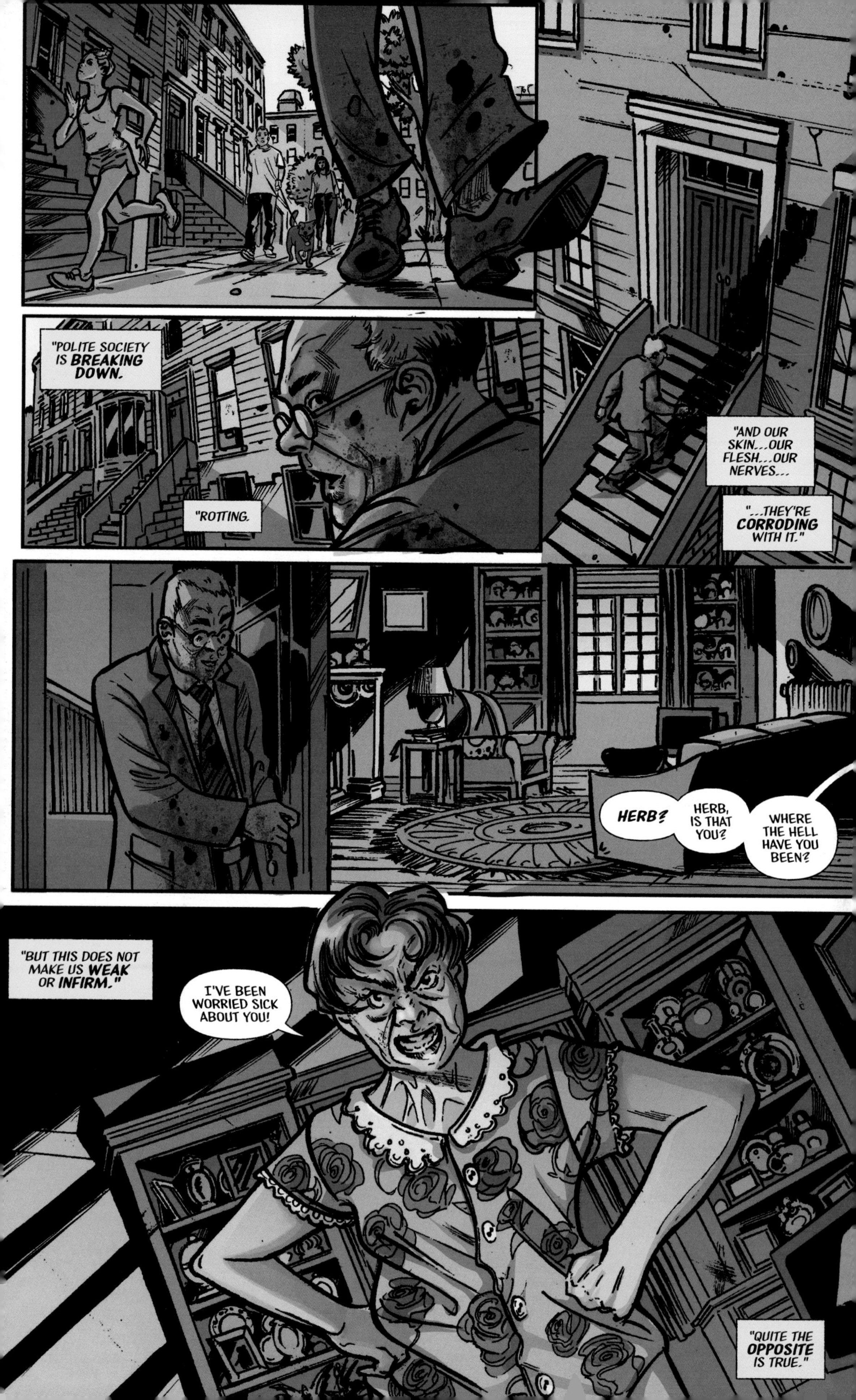
"POLITE SOCIETY IS BREAKING DOWN.
"ROTTING.
"AND OUR SKIN...OUR FLESH...OUR NERVES...
"...THEY'RE CORRODING WITH IT."
HERB?
HERB, IS THAT YOU?
WHERE THE HELL HAVE YOU BEEN?
"BUT THIS DOES NOT MAKE US WEAK OR INFIRM."
I'VE BEEN WORRIED SICK ABOUT YOU!
"QUITE THE OPPOSITE IS TRUE."

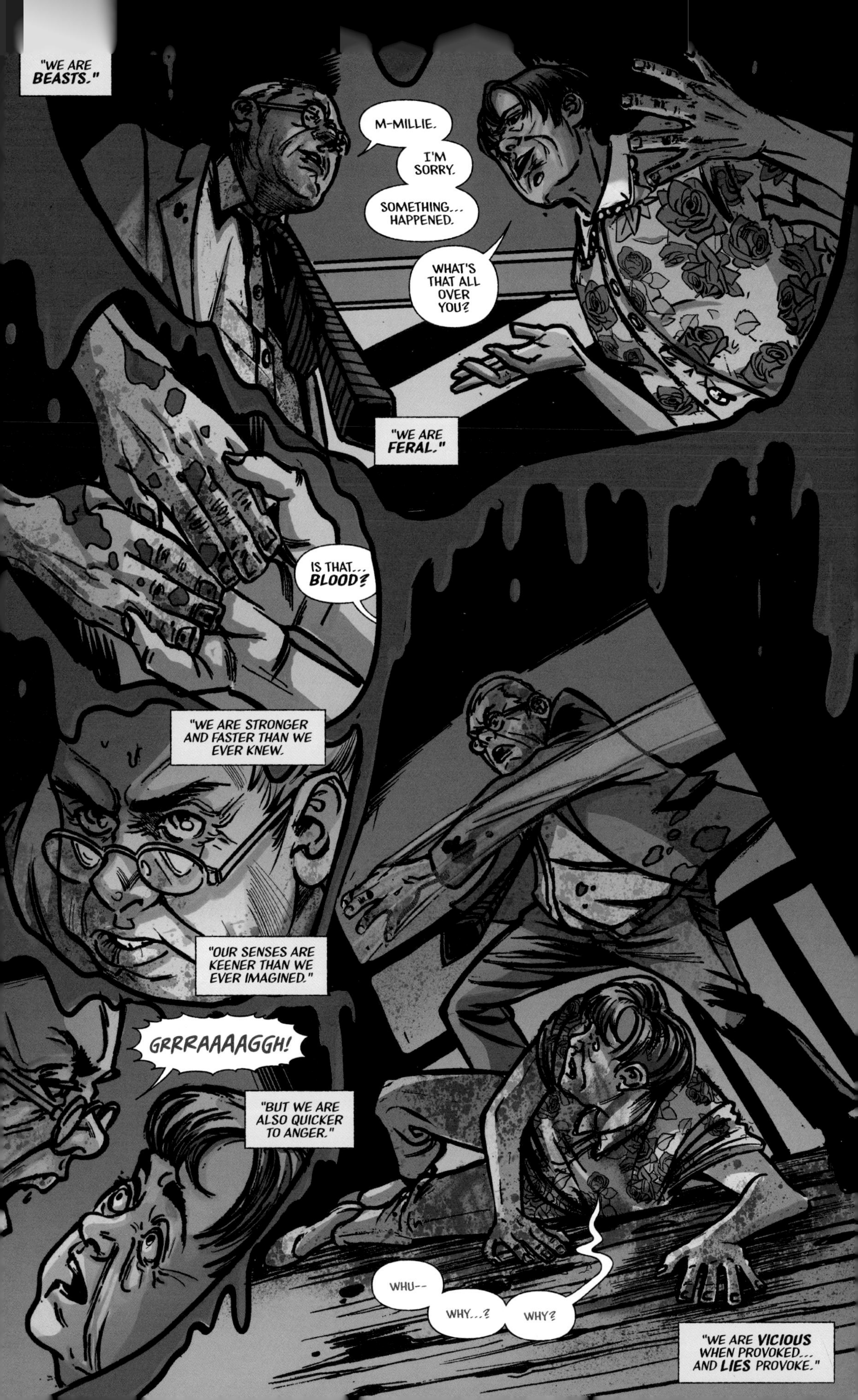
"WE ARE BEASTS."
M-MILLIE.
I'M SORRY.
SOMETHING... HAPPENED.
WHAT'S THAT ALL OVER YOU?
"WE ARE FERAL."
IS THAT... BLOOD?
"WE ARE STRONGER AND FASTER THAN WE EVER KNEW.
"OUR SENSES ARE KEENER THAN WE EVER IMAGINED."
GRRRAAAAGGH!
"BUT WE ARE ALSO QUICKER TO ANGER."
WHU--
WHY...?
WHY?
"WE ARE VICIOUS WHEN PROVOKED... AND LIES PROVOKE."

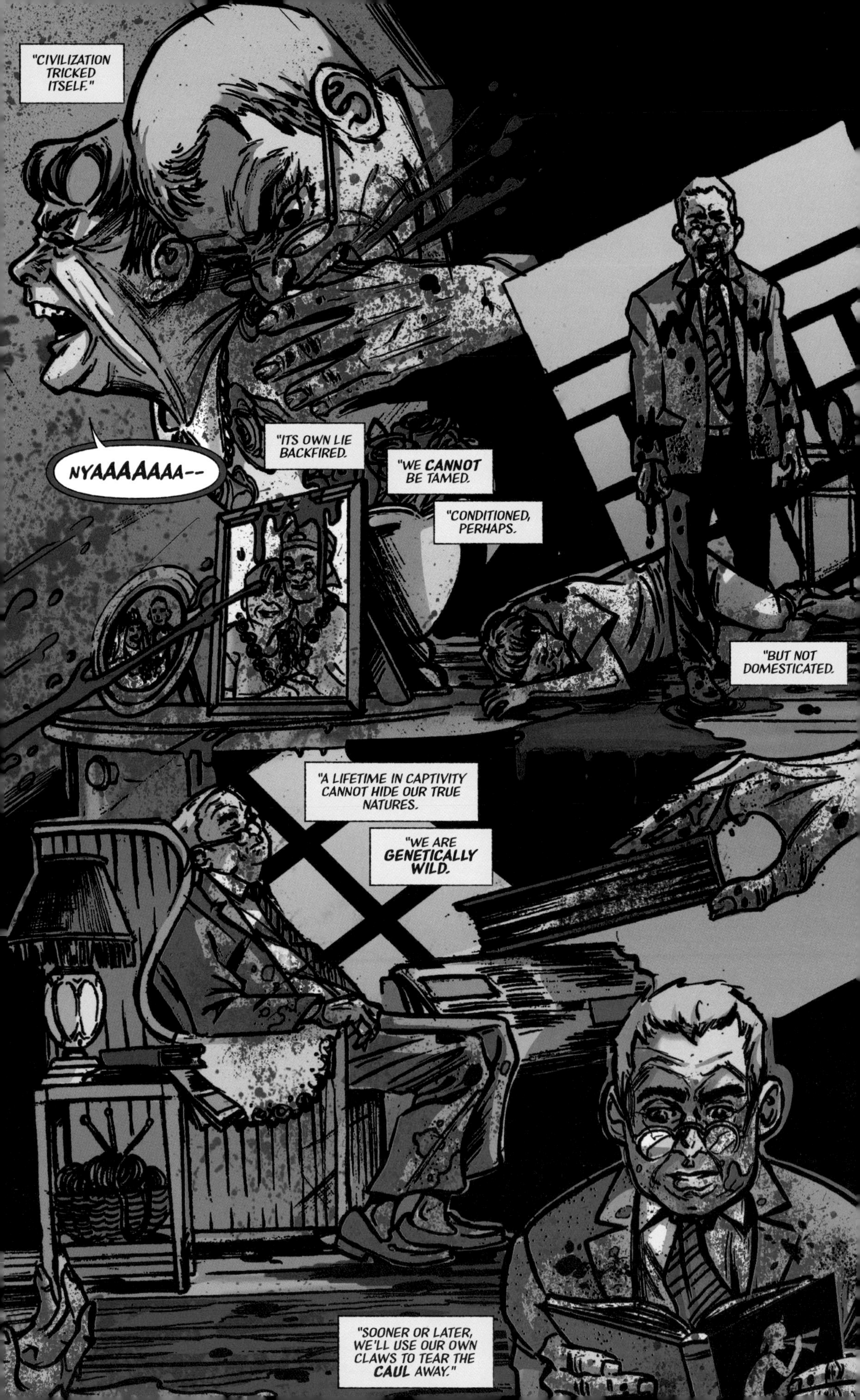
"CIVILIZATION TRICKED ITSELF."
NYAAAAAAA--
"ITS OWN LIE BACKFIRED.
"WE CANNOT BE TAMED.
"CONDITIONED, PERHAPS.
"BUT NOT DOMESTICATED.
"A LIFETIME IN CAPTIVITY CANNOT HIDE OUR TRUE NATURES.
"WE ARE GENETICALLY WILD.
"SOONER OR LATER, WE'LL USE OUR OWN CLAWS TO TEAR THE CAUL AWAY."

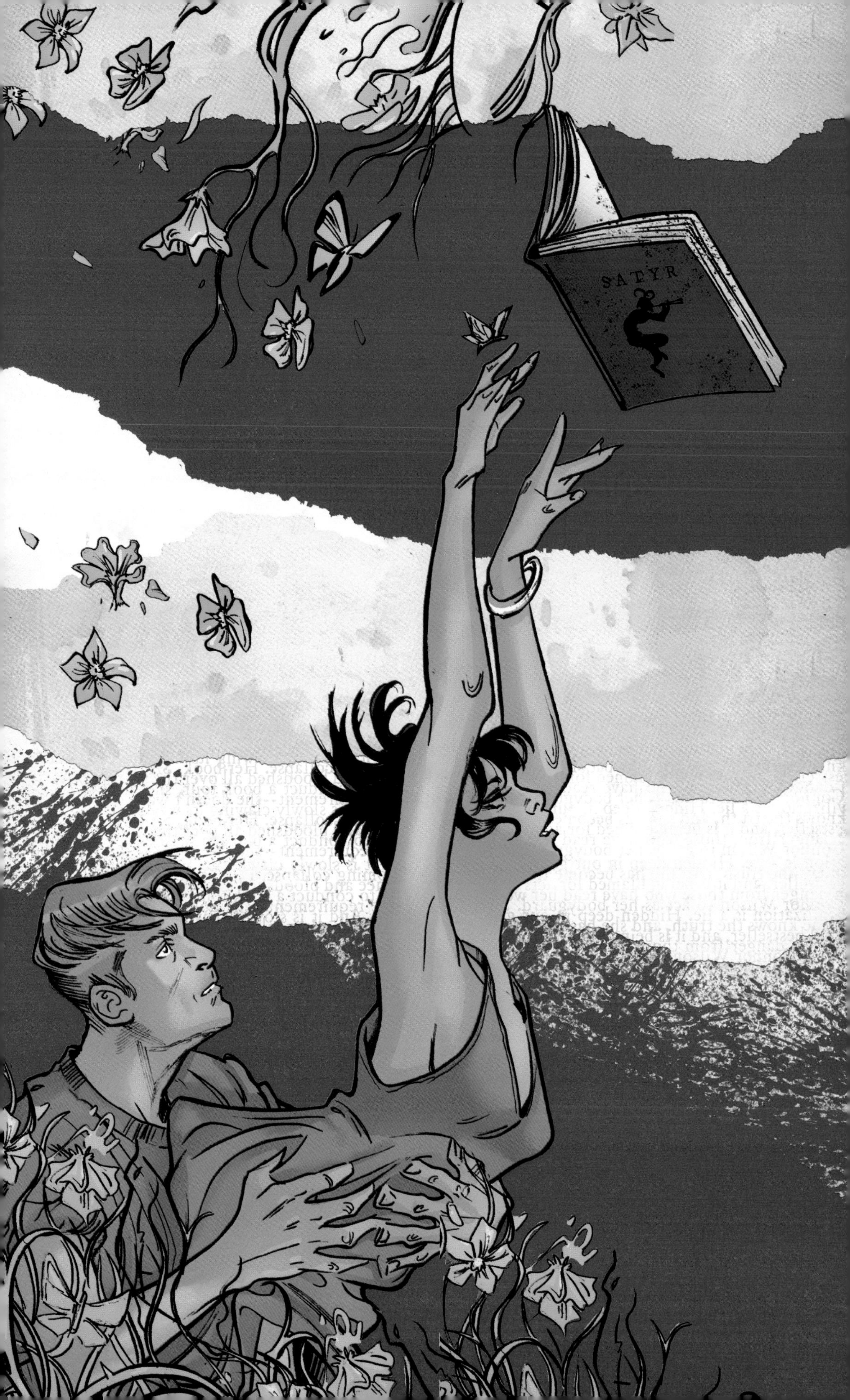
SATYR

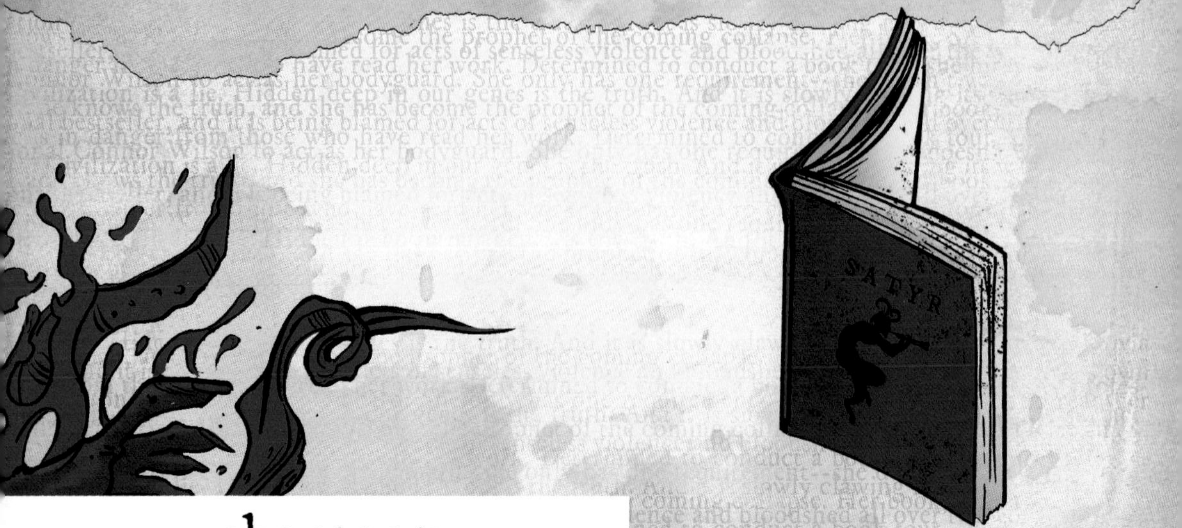
SATYR

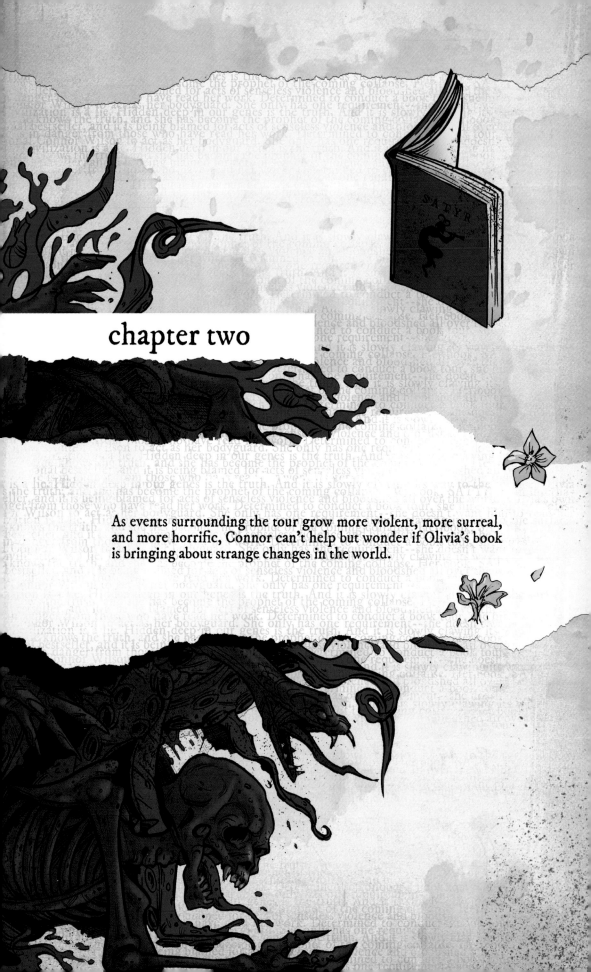

chapter two

As events surrounding the tour grow more violent, more surreal, and more horrific, Connor can't help but wonder if Olivia's book is bringing about strange changes in the world.

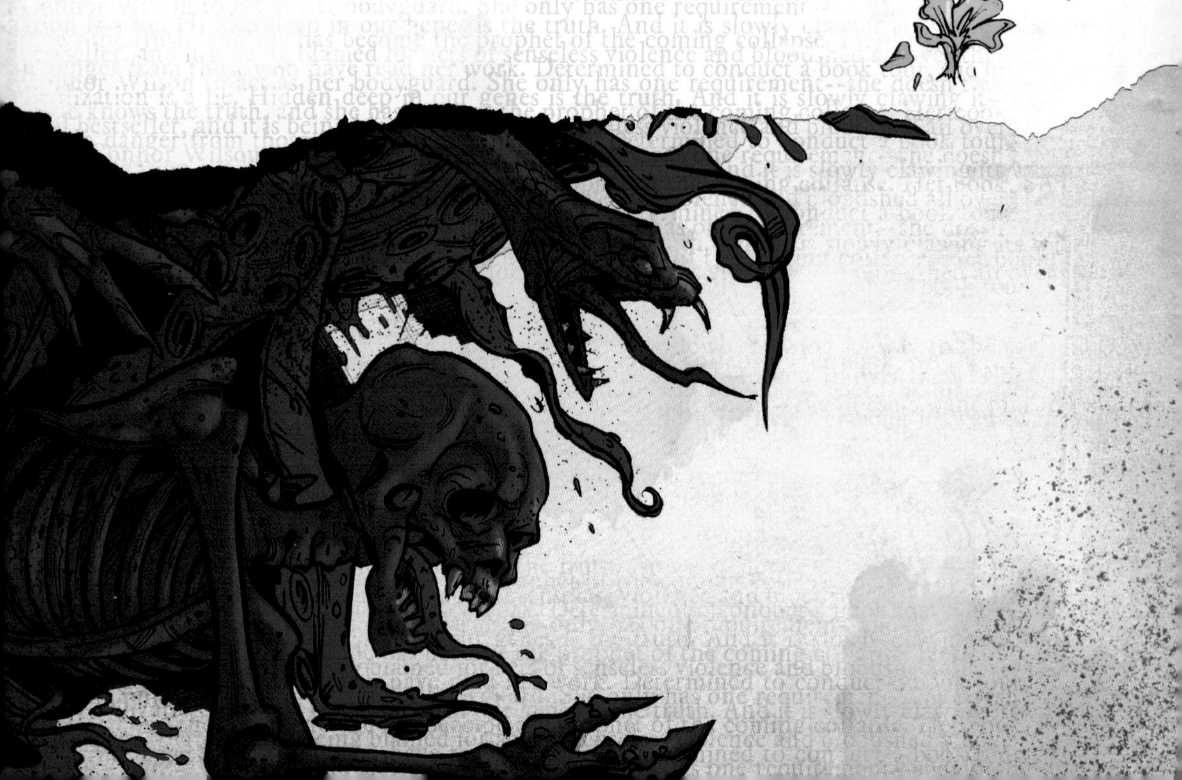

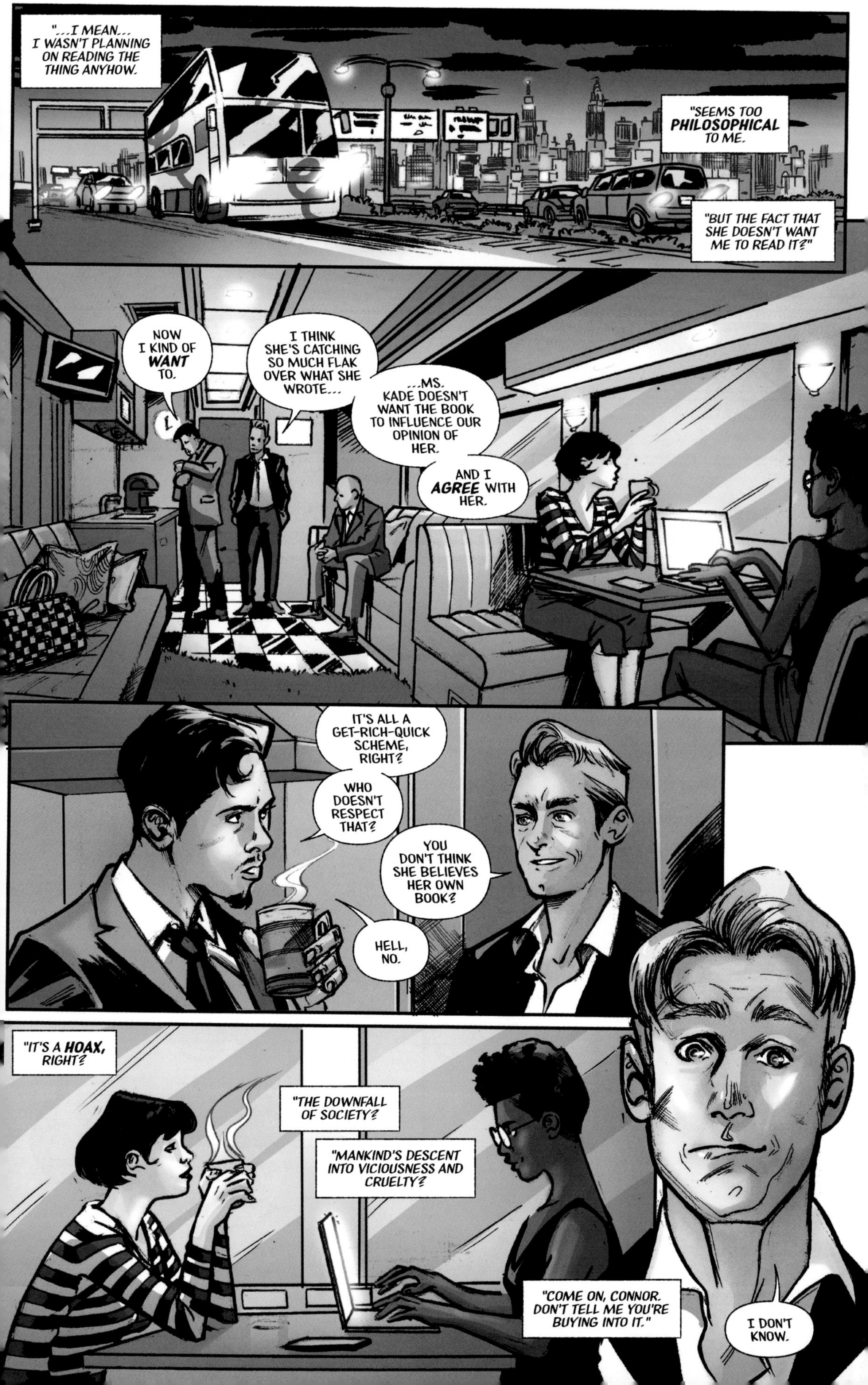
"...I MEAN... I WASN'T PLANNING ON READING THE THING ANYHOW.
"SEEMS TOO PHILOSOPHICAL TO ME.
"BUT THE FACT THAT SHE DOESN'T WANT ME TO READ IT?"
NOW I KIND OF WANT TO.
I THINK SHE'S CATCHING SO MUCH FLAK OVER WHAT SHE WROTE...
...MS. KADE DOESN'T WANT THE BOOK TO INFLUENCE OUR OPINION OF HER.
AND I AGREE WITH HER.
IT'S ALL A GET-RICH-QUICK SCHEME, RIGHT?
WHO DOESN'T RESPECT THAT?
YOU DON'T THINK SHE BELIEVES HER OWN BOOK?
HELL, NO.
"IT'S A HOAX, RIGHT?
"THE DOWNFALL OF SOCIETY?
"MANKIND'S DESCENT INTO VICIOUSNESS AND CRUELTY?
"COME ON, CONNOR. DON'T TELL ME YOU'RE BUYING INTO IT."
I DON'T KNOW.

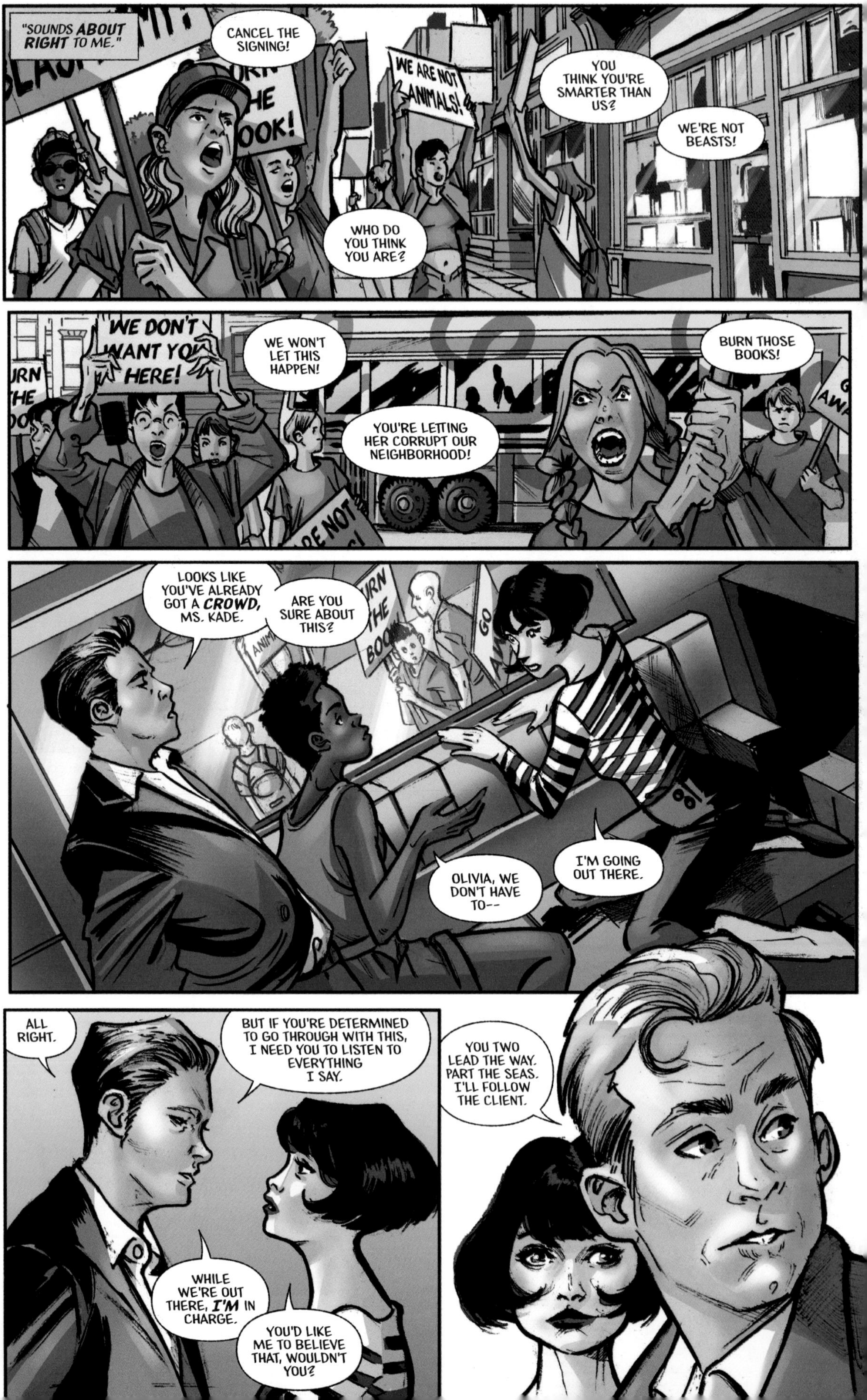
"SOUNDS ABOUT RIGHT TO ME."
CANCEL THE SIGNING!
WE ARE NOT ANIMALS!
YOU THINK YOU'RE SMARTER THAN US?
WE'RE NOT BEASTS!
WHO DO YOU THINK YOU ARE?
WE DON'T
HERE!
WE WON'T LET THIS HAPPEN!
YOU'RE LETTING HER CORRUPT OUR NEIGHBORHOOD!
BURN THOSE BOOKS!
LOOKS LIKE YOU'VE ALREADY GOT A CROWD, MS. KADE.
ARE YOU SURE ABOUT THIS?
OLIVIA, WE DON'T HAVE TO--
I'M GOING OUT THERE.
ALL RIGHT.
BUT IF YOU'RE DETERMINED TO GO THROUGH WITH THIS, I NEED YOU TO LISTEN TO EVERYTHING I SAY.
WHILE WE'RE OUT THERE, I'M IN CHARGE.
YOU'D LIKE ME TO BELIEVE THAT, WOULDN'T YOU?
YOU TWO LEAD THE WAY. PART THE SEAS. I'LL FOLLOW THE CLIENT.

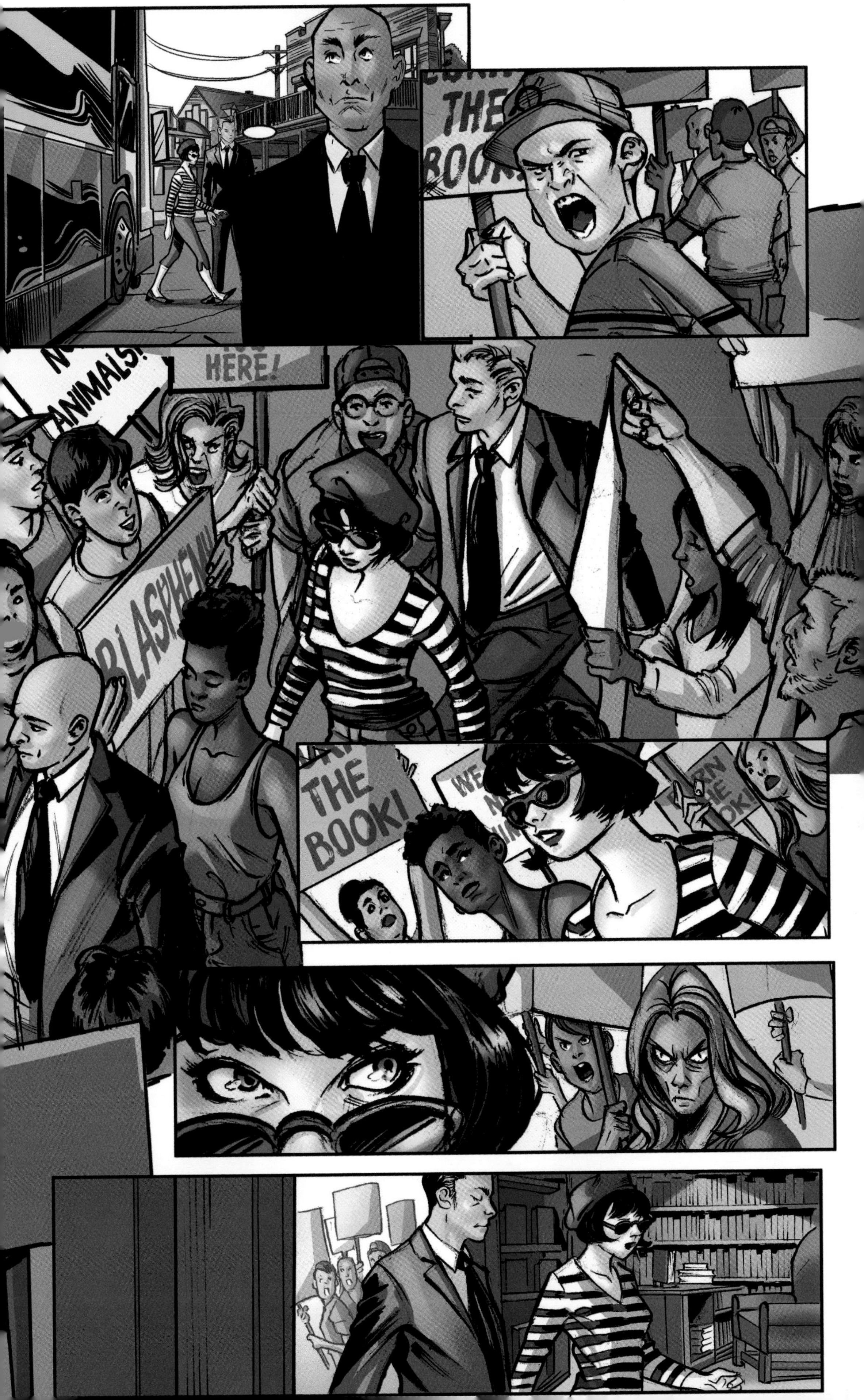
ANIMALS!
HERE!
THE BOOK!

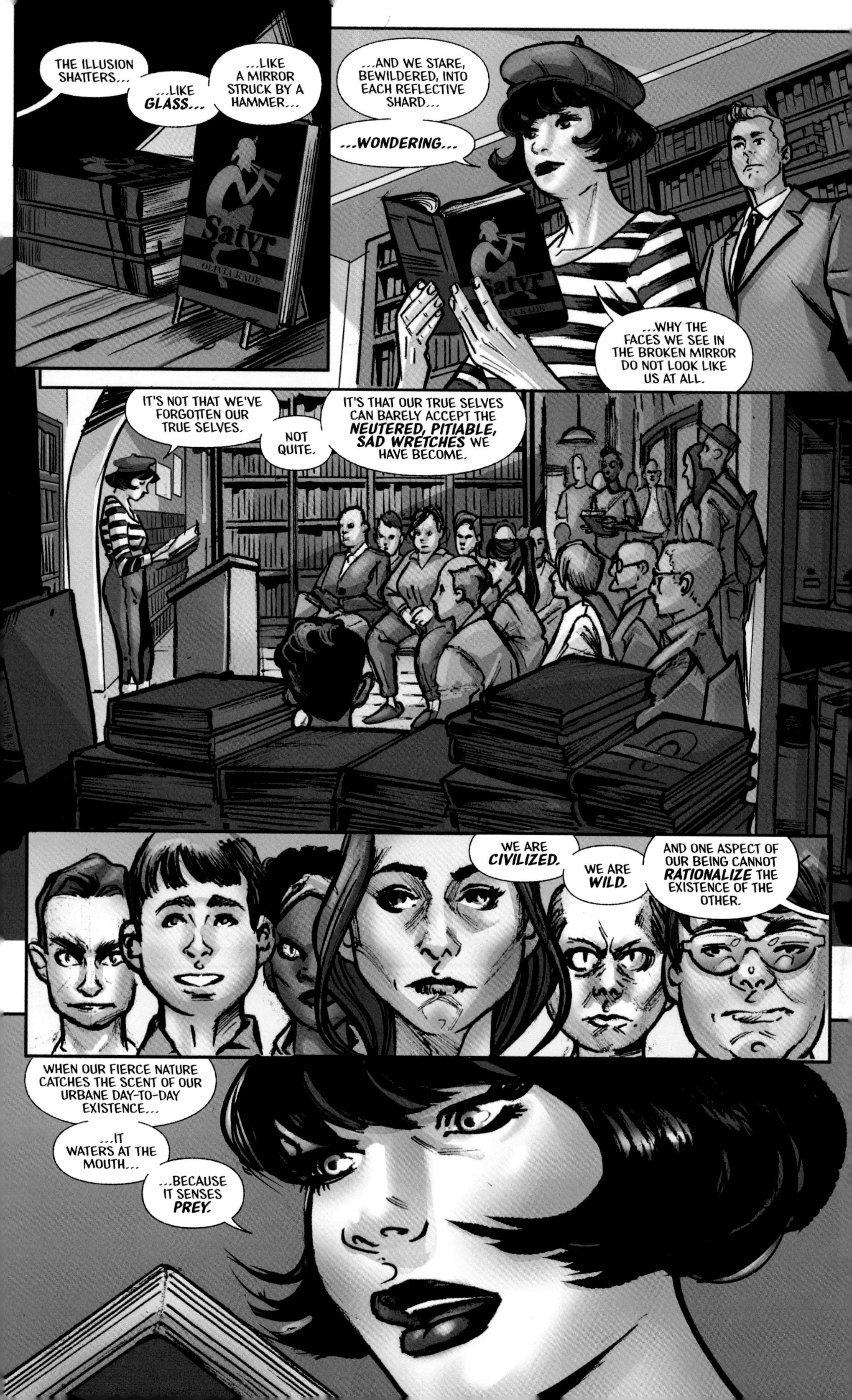
THE ILLUSION SHATTERS...
...LIKE GLASS...
...LIKE A MIRROR STRUCK BY A HAMMER...
Satyr
OLIVIA KADE
...AND WE STARE, BEWILDERED, INTO EACH REFLECTIVE SHARD...
...WONDERING...
...WHY THE FACES WE SEE IN THE BROKEN MIRROR DO NOT LOOK LIKE US AT ALL.
IT'S NOT THAT WE'VE FORGOTTEN OUR TRUE SELVES.
NOT QUITE.
IT'S THAT OUR TRUE SELVES CAN BARELY ACCEPT THE NEUTERED, PITIABLE, SAD WRETCHES WE HAVE BECOME.
WE ARE CIVILIZED.
WE ARE WILD.
AND ONE ASPECT OF OUR BEING CANNOT RATIONALIZE THE EXISTENCE OF THE OTHER.
WHEN OUR FIERCE NATURE CATCHES THE SCENT OF OUR URBANE DAY-TO-DAY EXISTENCE...
...IT WATERS AT THE MOUTH...
...BECAUSE IT SENSES PREY.

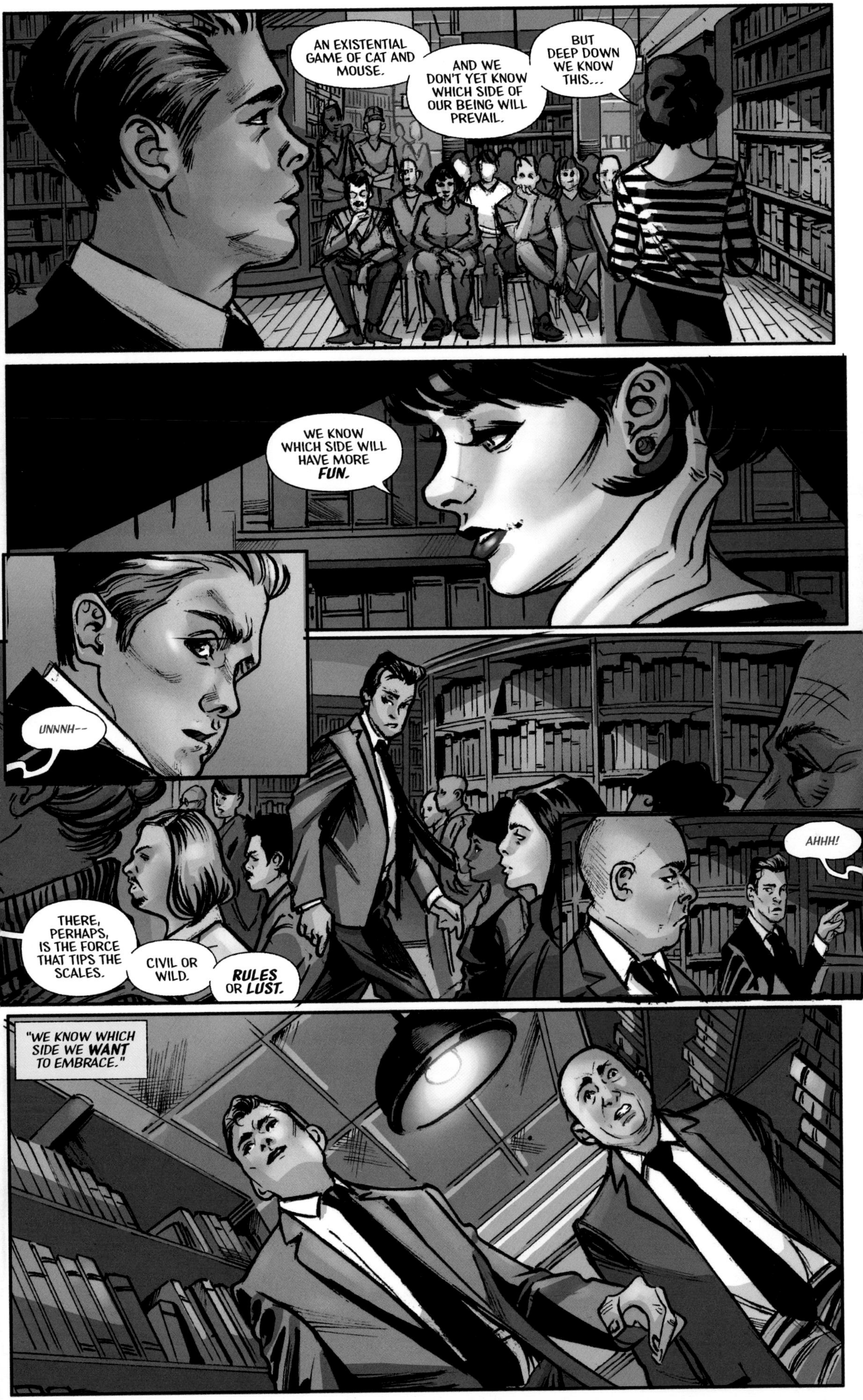
AN EXISTENTIAL GAME OF CAT AND MOUSE.
AND WE DON'T YET KNOW WHICH SIDE OF OUR BEING WILL PREVAIL.
BUT DEEP DOWN WE KNOW THIS...
WE KNOW WHICH SIDE WILL HAVE MORE FUN.
UNNNH--
AHHH!
THERE, PERHAPS, IS THE FORCE THAT TIPS THE SCALES.
CIVIL OR WILD.
RULES OR LUST.
"WE KNOW WHICH SIDE WE WANT TO EMBRACE."

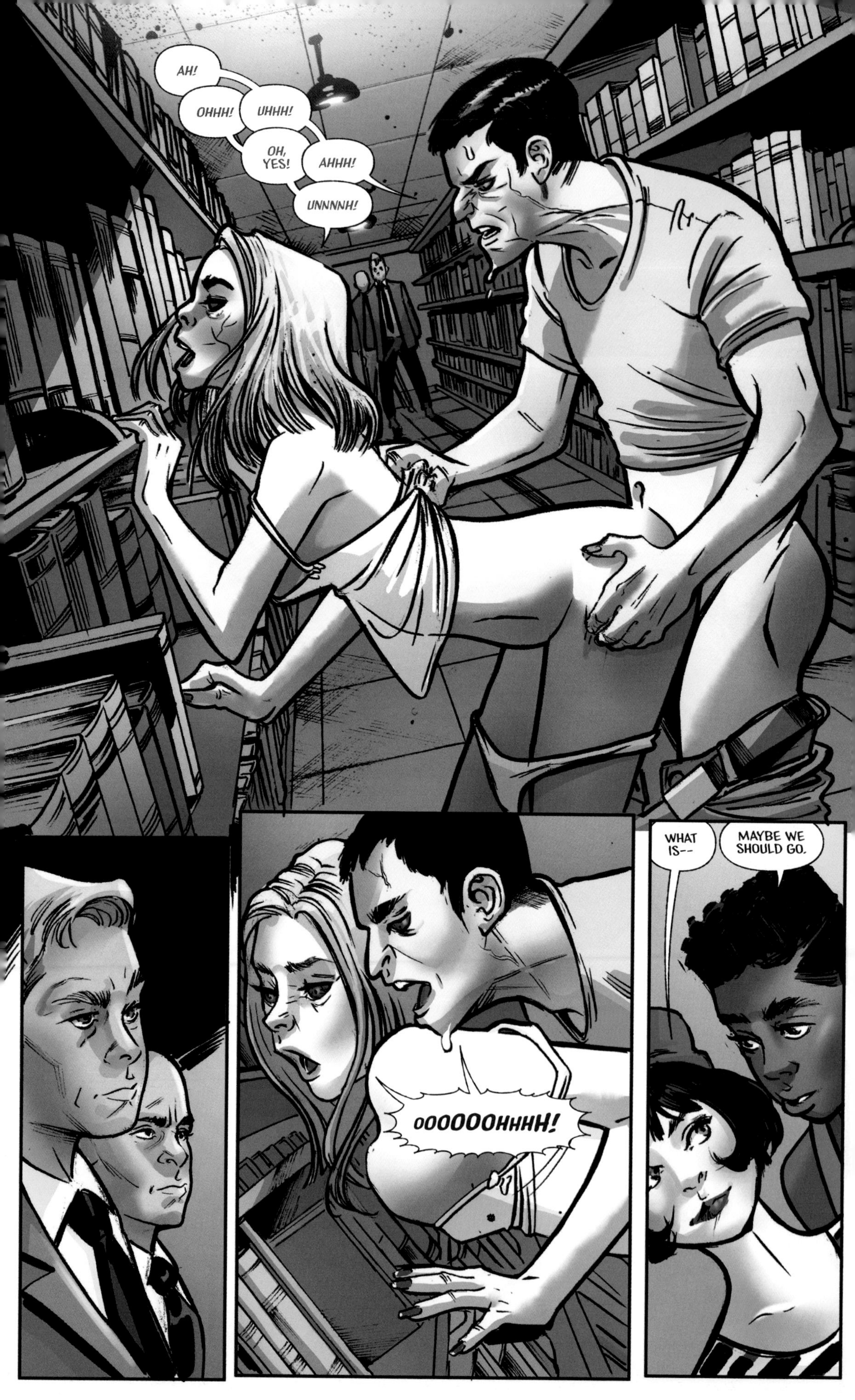
AH!
OHHH!
UHHH!
OH, YES!
AHHH!
UNNNNH!
OOOOOOHHHH!
WHAT IS--
MAYBE WE SHOULD GO.

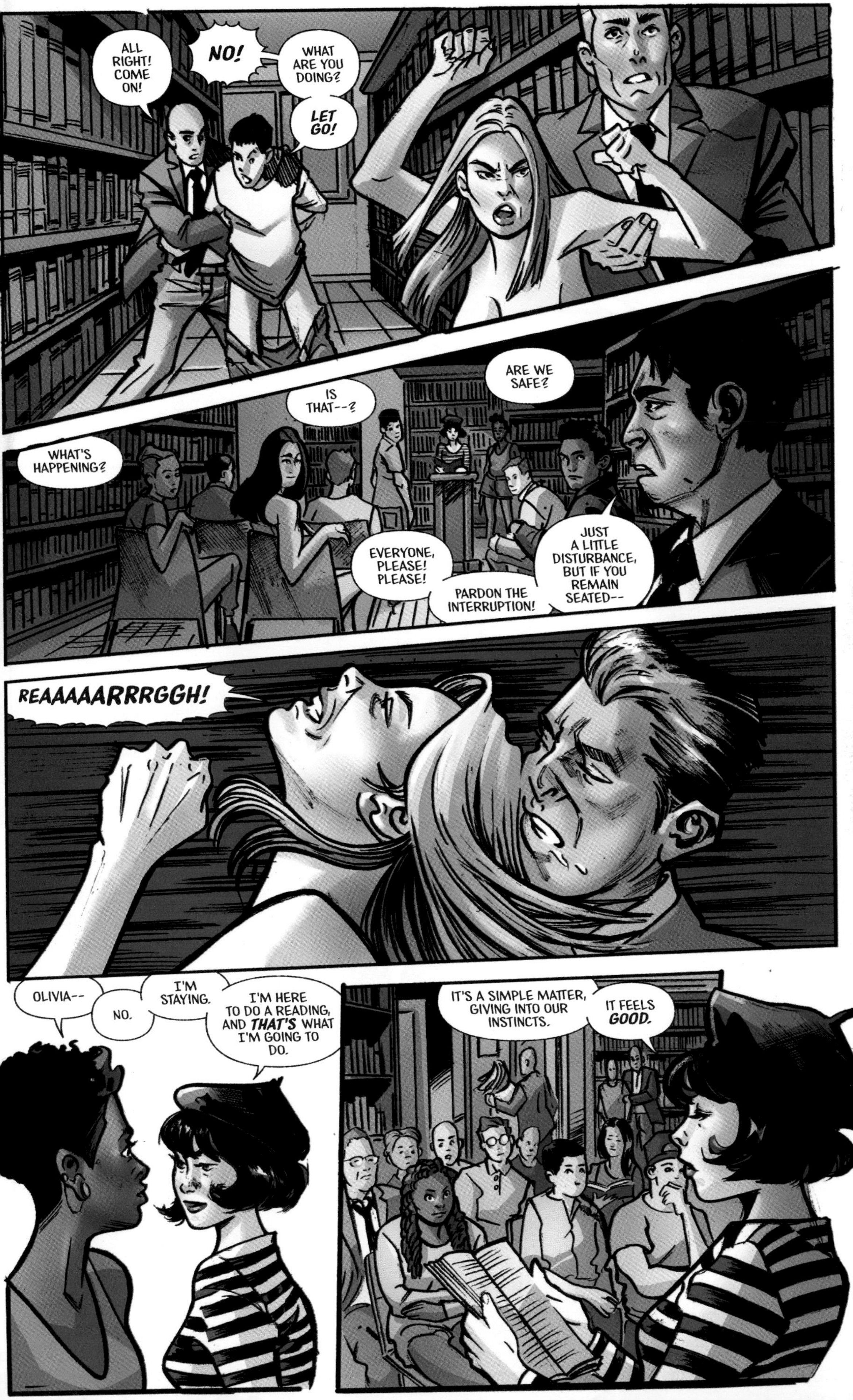
ALL RIGHT! COME ON!
NO!
WHAT ARE YOU DOING?
LET GO!
WHAT'S HAPPENING?
IS THAT--?
ARE WE SAFE?
EVERYONE, PLEASE! PLEASE!
PARDON THE INTERRUPTION!
JUST A LITTLE DISTURBANCE, BUT IF YOU REMAIN SEATED--
REAAAAARRRGGH!
OLIVIA--
NO.
I'M STAYING.
I'M HERE TO DO A READING, AND THAT'S WHAT I'M GOING TO DO.
IT'S A SIMPLE MATTER, GIVING INTO OUR INSTINCTS.
IT FEELS GOOD.

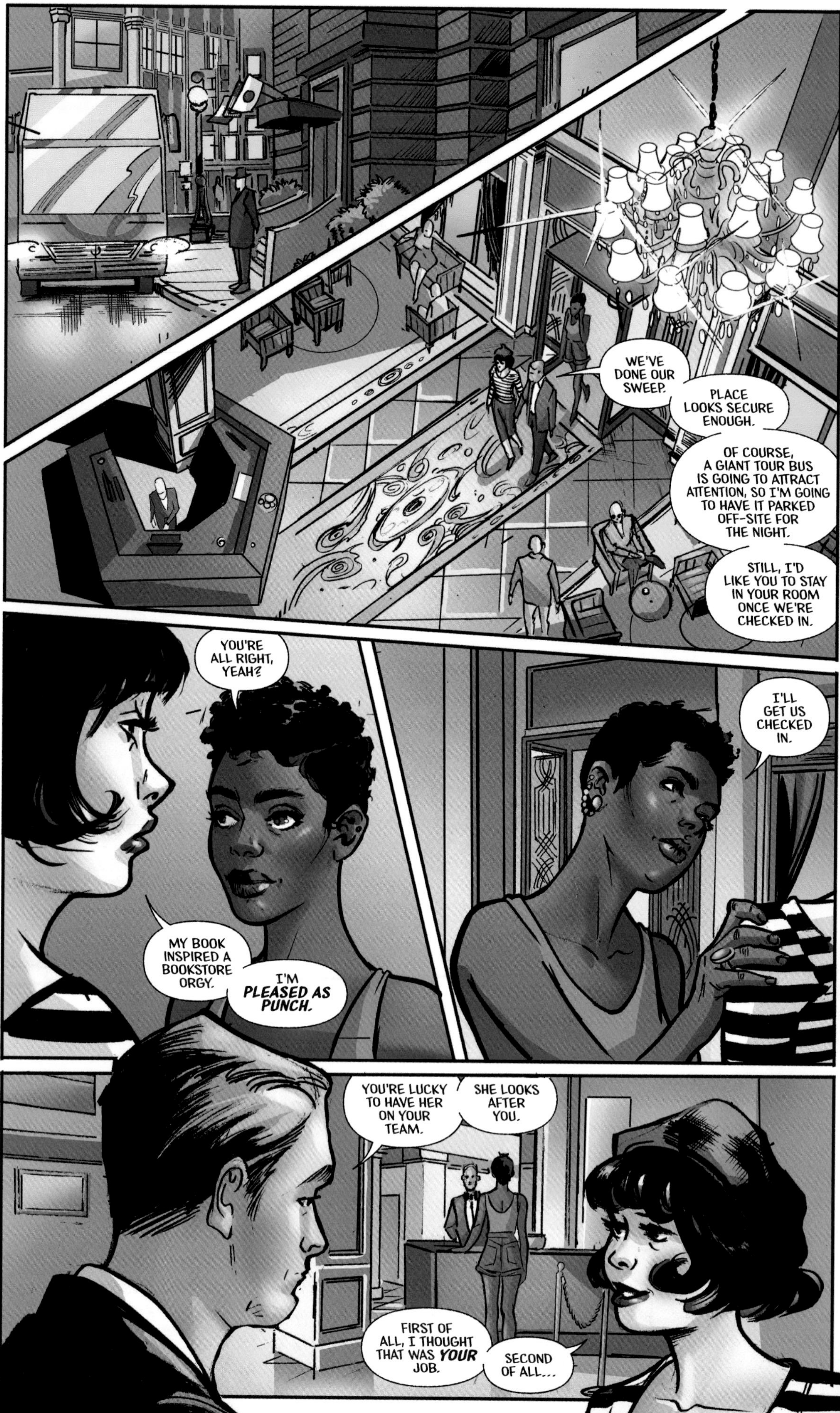

WE'VE DONE OUR SWEEP.
PLACE LOOKS SECURE ENOUGH.
OF COURSE, A GIANT TOUR BUS IS GOING TO ATTRACT ATTENTION, SO I'M GOING TO HAVE IT PARKED OFF-SITE FOR THE NIGHT.
STILL, I'D LIKE YOU TO STAY IN YOUR ROOM ONCE WE'RE CHECKED IN.
YOU'RE ALL RIGHT, YEAH?
MY BOOK INSPIRED A BOOKSTORE ORGY.
I'M PLEASED AS PUNCH.
I'LL GET US CHECKED IN.
YOU'RE LUCKY TO HAVE HER ON YOUR TEAM.
SHE LOOKS AFTER YOU.
FIRST OF ALL, I THOUGHT THAT WAS YOUR JOB.
SECOND OF ALL...

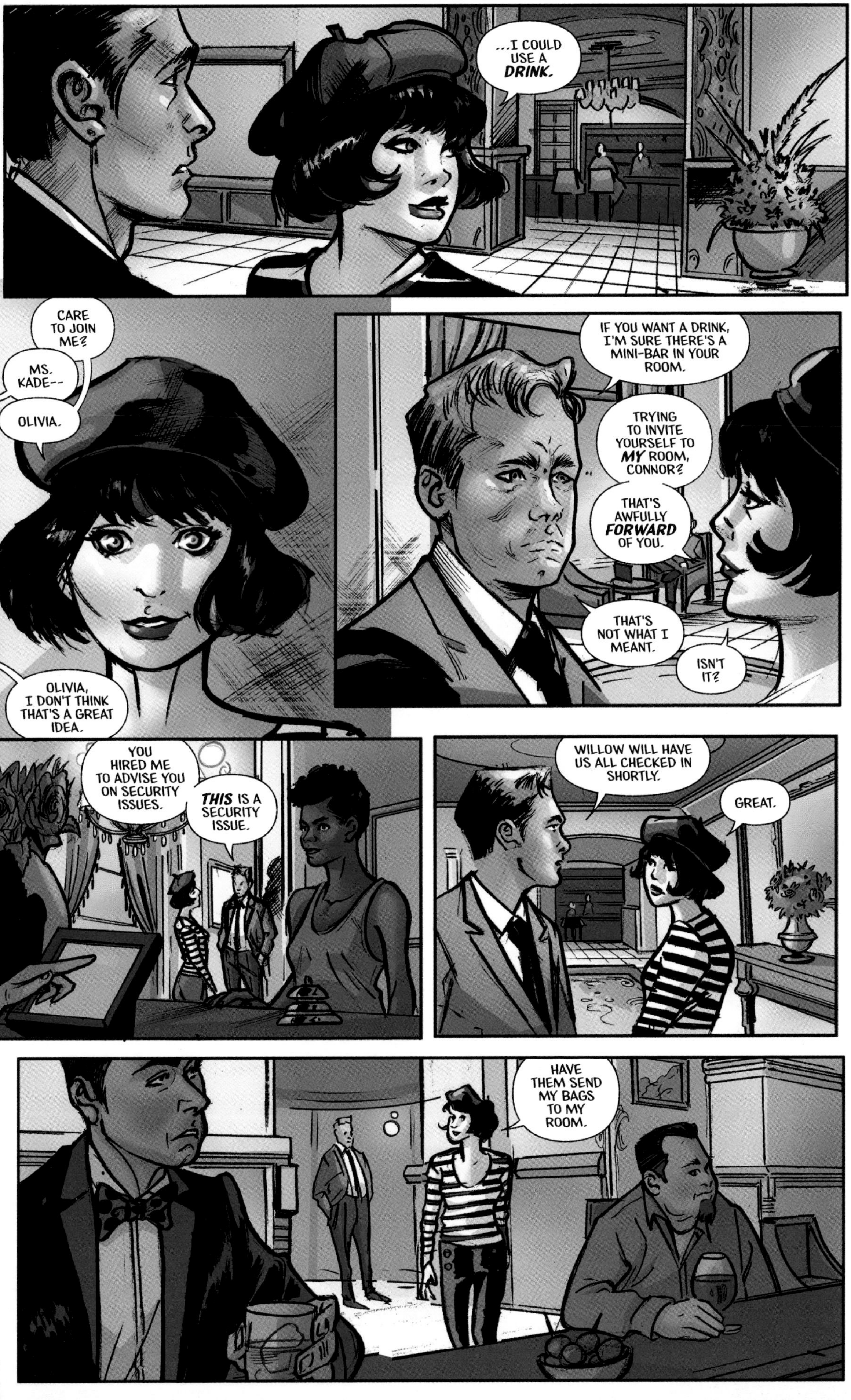
...I COULD USE A DRINK.
CARE TO JOIN ME?
MS. KADE--
OLIVIA.
OLIVIA, I DON'T THINK THAT'S A GREAT IDEA.
IF YOU WANT A DRINK, I'M SURE THERE'S A MINI-BAR IN YOUR ROOM.
TRYING TO INVITE YOURSELF TO MY ROOM, CONNOR?
THAT'S AWFULLY FORWARD OF YOU.
THAT'S NOT WHAT I MEANT.
ISN'T IT?
YOU HIRED ME TO ADVISE YOU ON SECURITY ISSUES.
THIS IS A SECURITY ISSUE.
WILLOW WILL HAVE US ALL CHECKED IN SHORTLY.
GREAT.
HAVE THEM SEND MY BAGS TO MY ROOM.

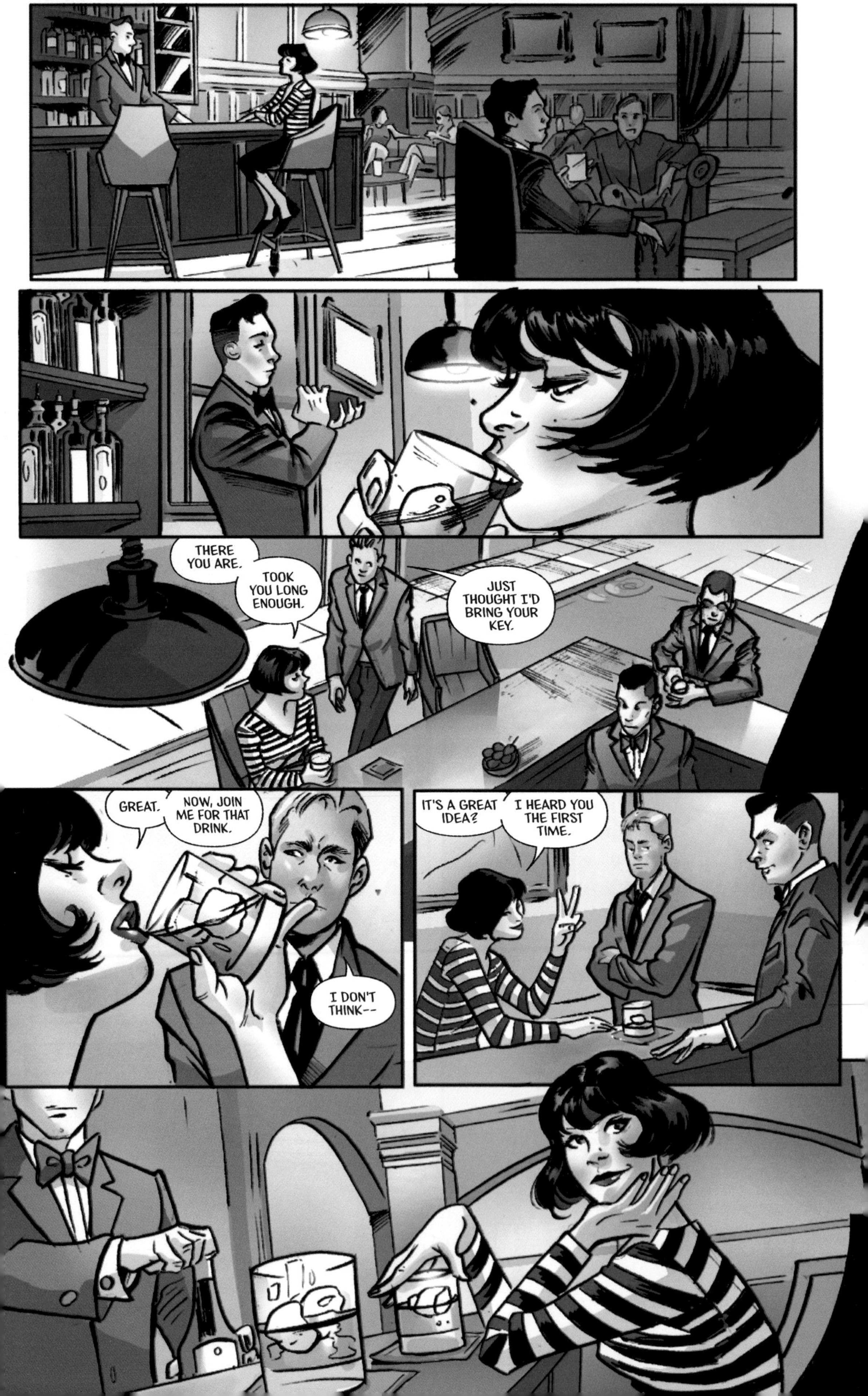
THERE YOU ARE.
TOOK YOU LONG ENOUGH.
JUST THOUGHT I'D BRING YOUR KEY.
GREAT.
NOW, JOIN ME FOR THAT DRINK.
I DON'T THINK--
IT'S A GREAT IDEA?
I HEARD YOU THE FIRST TIME.

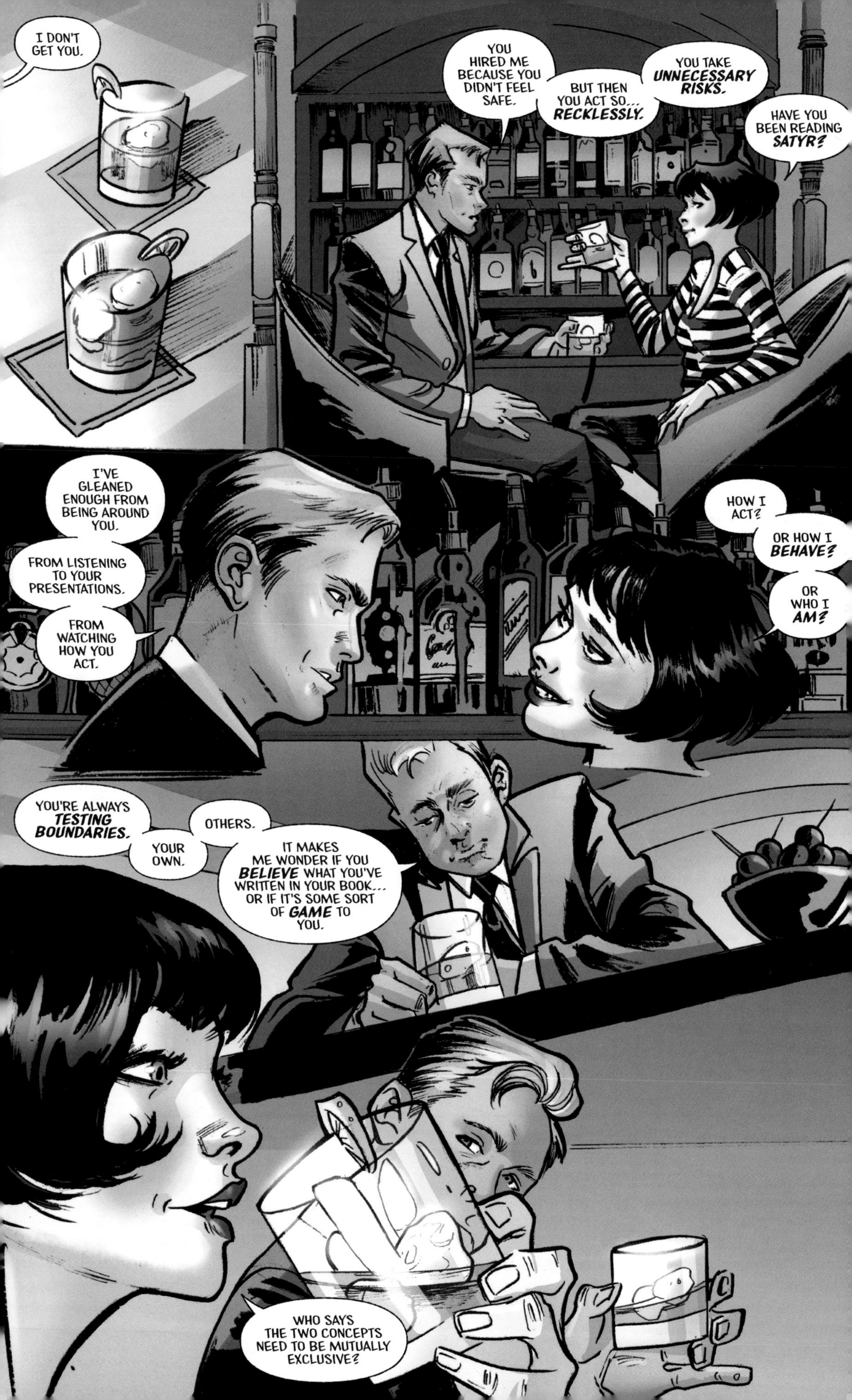
I DON'T GET YOU.
YOU HIRED ME BECAUSE YOU DIDN'T FEEL SAFE.
BUT THEN YOU ACT SO... RECKLESSLY.
YOU TAKE UNNECESSARY RISKS.
HAVE YOU BEEN READING SATYR?
I'VE GLEANED ENOUGH FROM BEING AROUND YOU.
FROM LISTENING TO YOUR PRESENTATIONS.
FROM WATCHING HOW YOU ACT.
HOW I ACT?
OR HOW I BEHAVE?
OR WHO I AM?
YOU'RE ALWAYS TESTING BOUNDARIES.
YOUR OWN.
OTHERS.
IT MAKES ME WONDER IF YOU BELIEVE WHAT YOU'VE WRITTEN IN YOUR BOOK... OR IF IT'S SOME SORT OF GAME TO YOU.
WHO SAYS THE TWO CONCEPTS NEED TO BE MUTUALLY EXCLUSIVE?

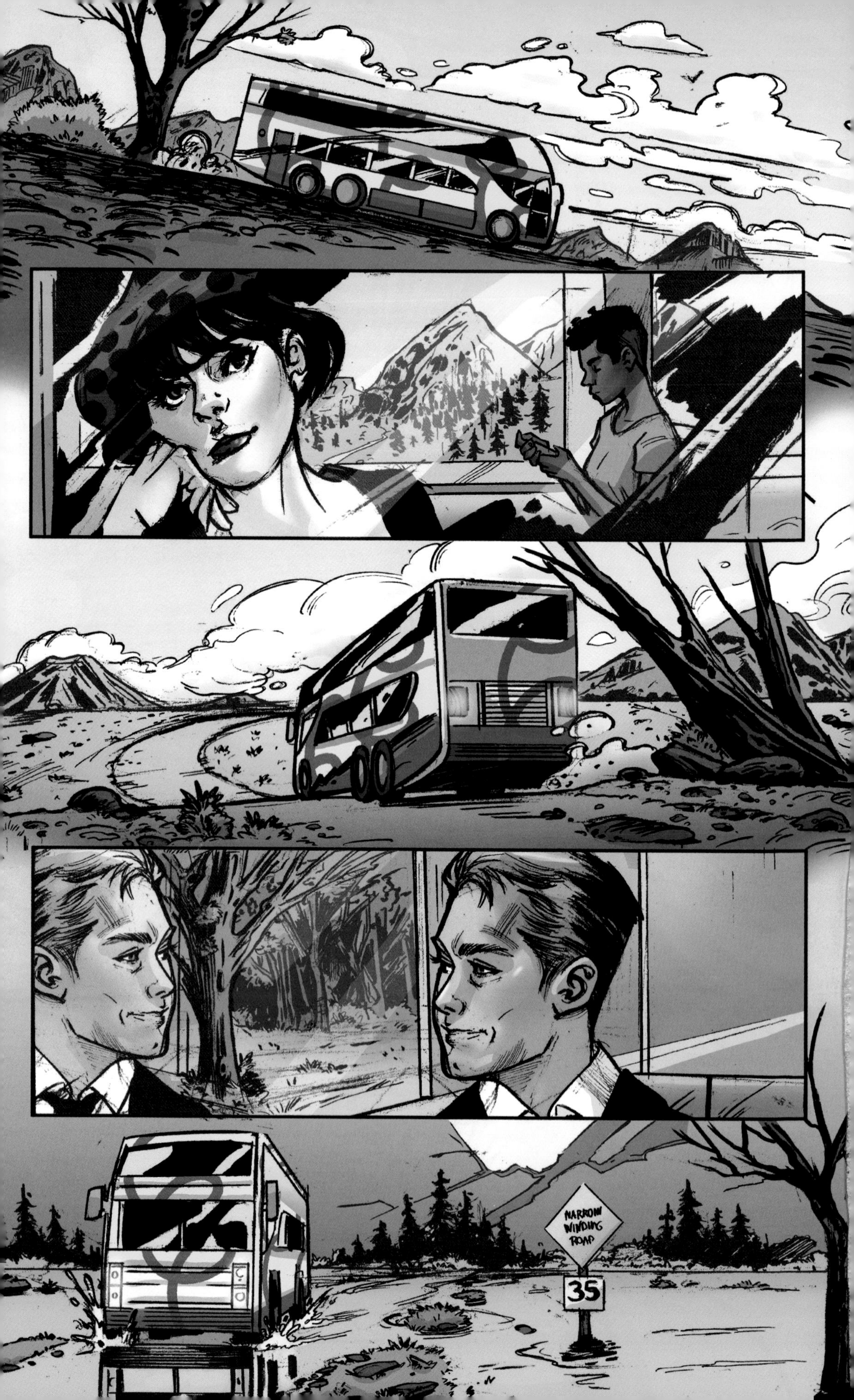
NARROW WINDING ROAD
35

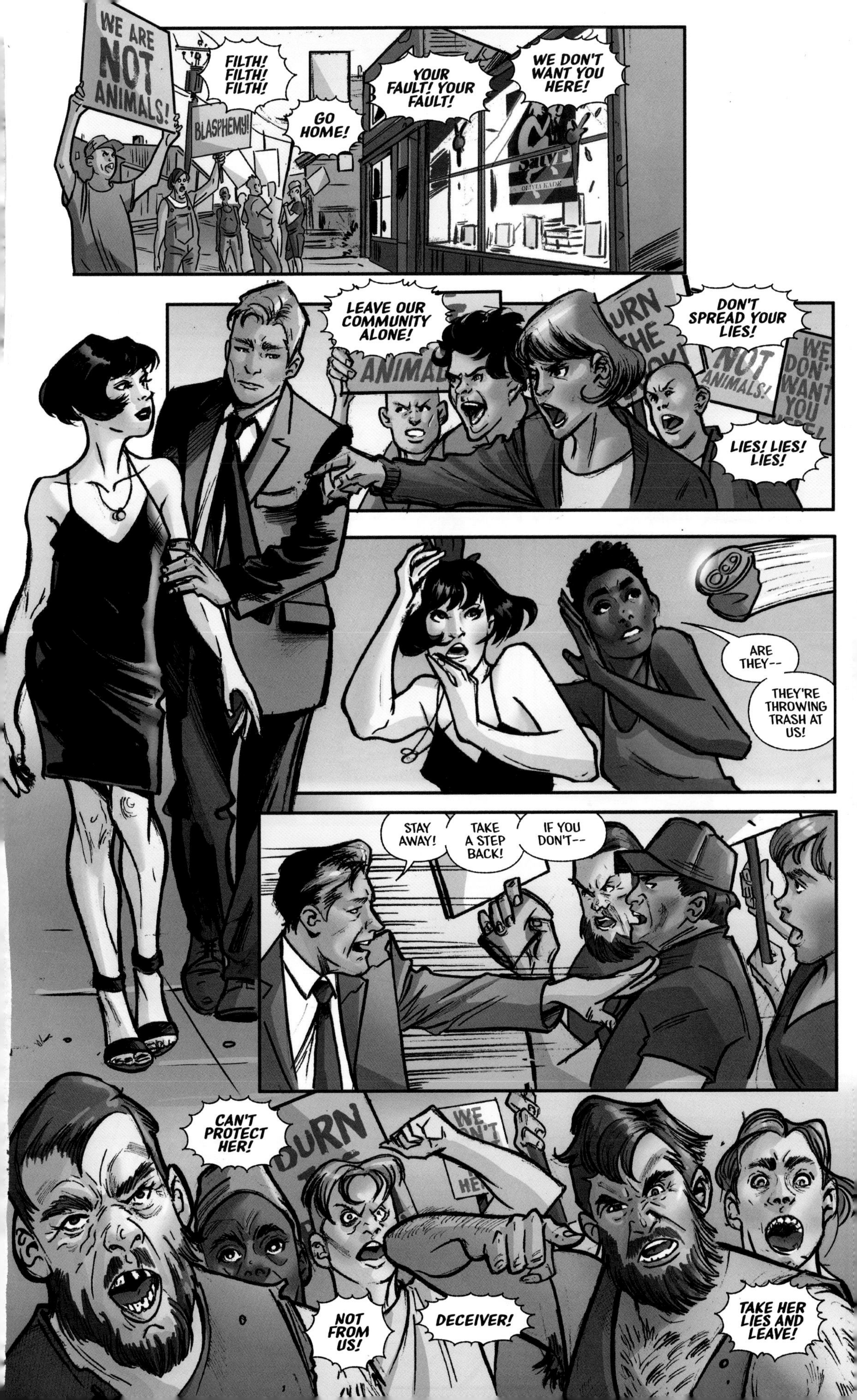
WE ARE NOT ANIMALS!
BLASPHEMY!
FILTH! FILTH! FILTH!
GO HOME!
YOUR FAULT! YOUR FAULT!
WE DON'T WANT YOU HERE!
LEAVE OUR COMMUNITY ALONE!
NOT ANIMALS!
DON'T SPREAD YOUR LIES!
LIES! LIES! LIES!
ARE THEY--
THEY'RE THROWING TRASH AT US!
STAY AWAY!
TAKE A STEP BACK!
IF YOU DON'T--
CAN'T PROTECT HER!
NOT FROM US!
DECEIVER!
TAKE HER LIES AND LEAVE!

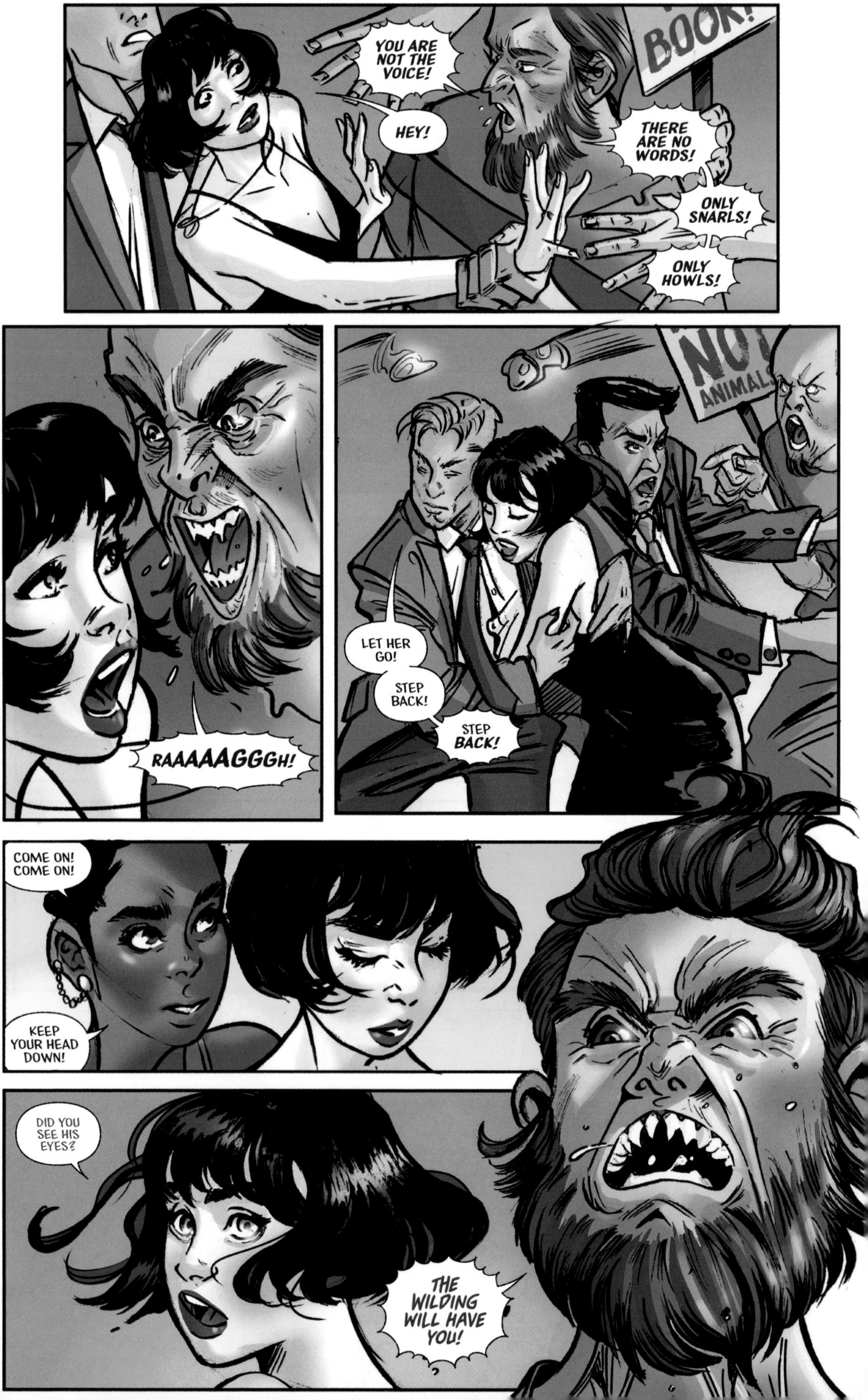
BOOK!
YOU ARE NOT THE VOICE!
HEY!
THERE ARE NO WORDS!
ONLY SNARLS!
ONLY HOWLS!
RAAAAAGGGH!
LET HER GO!
STEP BACK!
STEP BACK!
COME ON! COME ON!
KEEP YOUR HEAD DOWN!
DID YOU SEE HIS EYES?
THE WILDING WILL HAVE YOU!

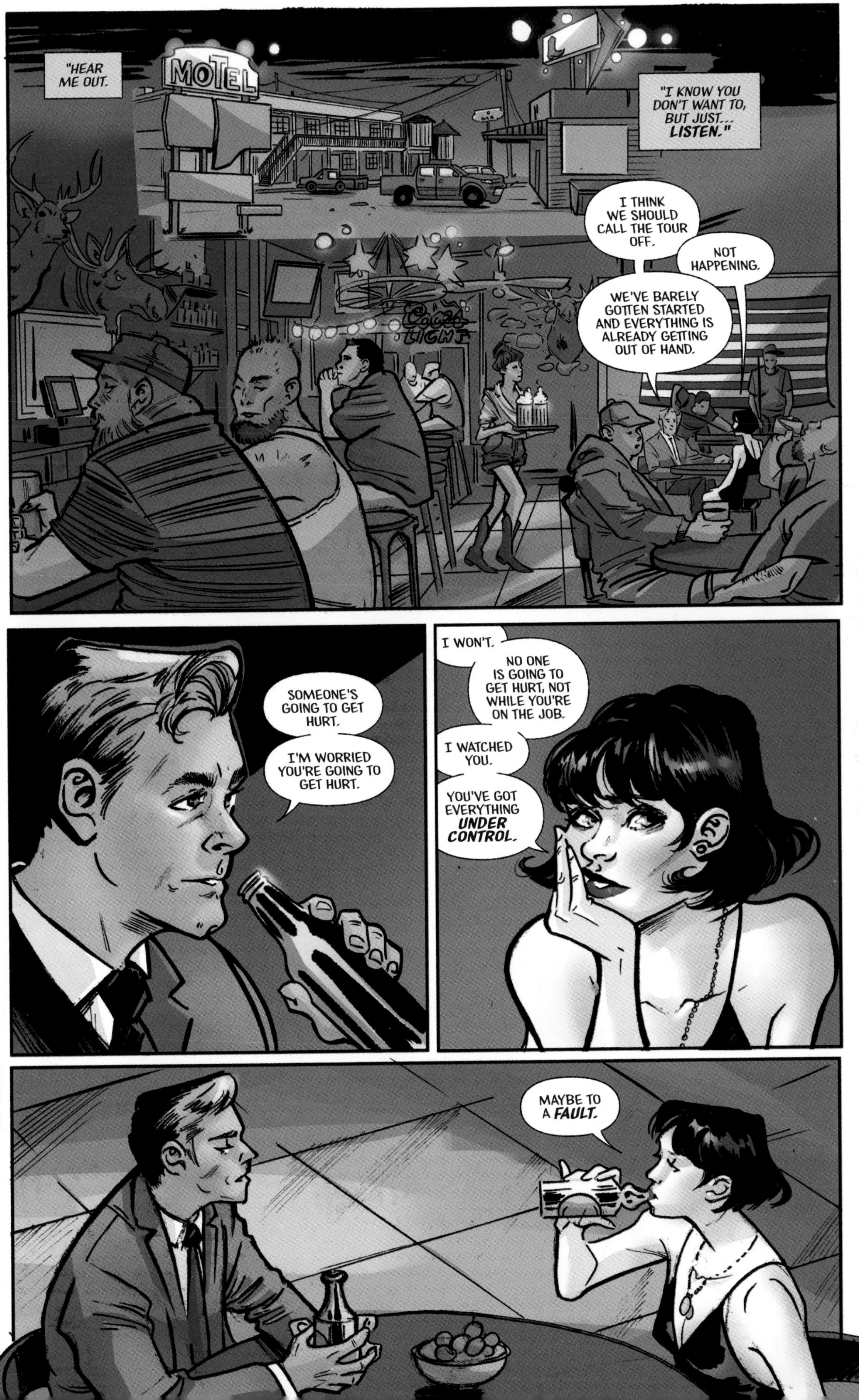
"HEAR ME OUT.
MOTEL
"I KNOW YOU DON'T WANT TO, BUT JUST... LISTEN."
I THINK WE SHOULD CALL THE TOUR OFF.
NOT HAPPENING.
WE'VE BARELY GOTTEN STARTED AND EVERYTHING IS ALREADY GETTING OUT OF HAND.
SOMEONE'S GOING TO GET HURT.
I'M WORRIED YOU'RE GOING TO GET HURT.
I WON'T.
NO ONE IS GOING TO GET HURT, NOT WHILE YOU'RE ON THE JOB.
I WATCHED YOU.
YOU'VE GOT EVERYTHING UNDER CONTROL.
MAYBE TO A FAULT.

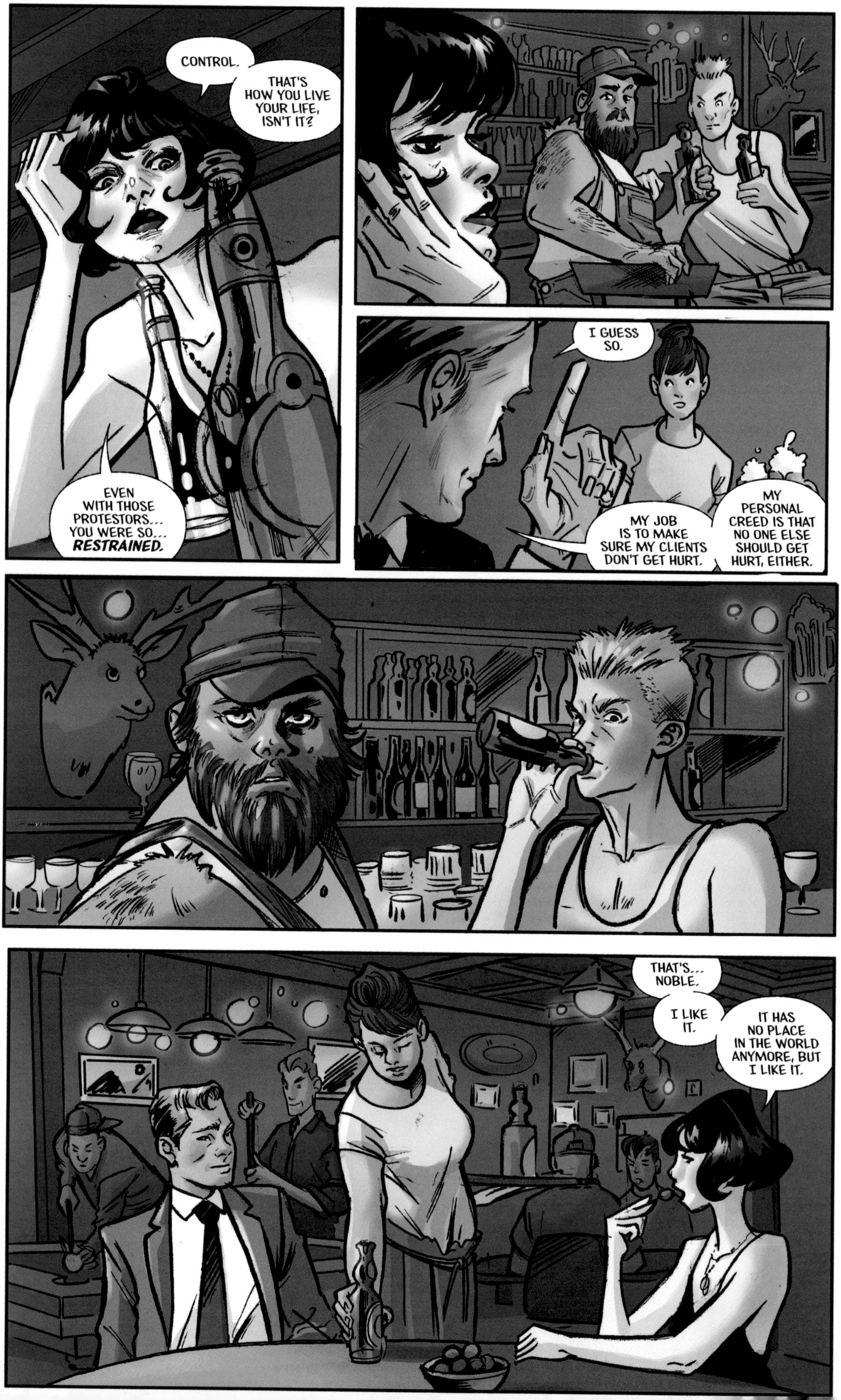
CONTROL.
THAT'S HOW YOU LIVE YOUR LIFE, ISN'T IT?
EVEN WITH THOSE PROTESTORS... YOU WERE SO... ***RESTRAINED.***
I GUESS SO.
MY JOB IS TO MAKE SURE MY CLIENTS DON'T GET HURT.
MY PERSONAL CREED IS THAT NO ONE ELSE SHOULD GET HURT, EITHER.
THAT'S... NOBLE.
I LIKE IT.
IT HAS NO PLACE IN THE WORLD ANYMORE, BUT I LIKE IT.

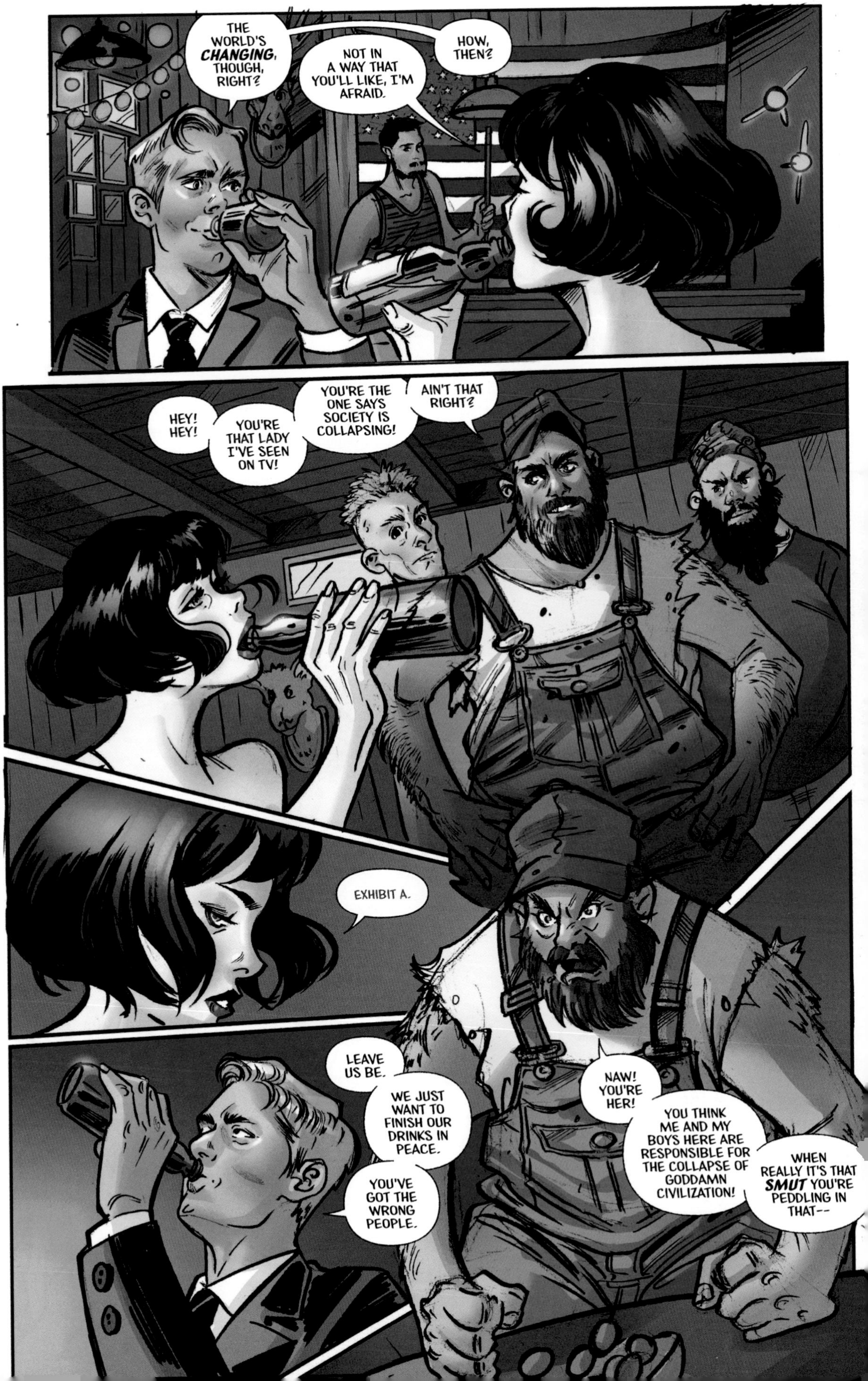
THE WORLD'S CHANGING, THOUGH, RIGHT?
NOT IN A WAY THAT YOU'LL LIKE, I'M AFRAID.
HOW, THEN?
HEY! HEY!
YOU'RE THAT LADY I'VE SEEN ON TV!
YOU'RE THE ONE SAYS SOCIETY IS COLLAPSING!
AIN'T THAT RIGHT?
EXHIBIT A.
LEAVE US BE.
WE JUST WANT TO FINISH OUR DRINKS IN PEACE.
YOU'VE GOT THE WRONG PEOPLE.
NAW! YOU'RE HER!
YOU THINK ME AND MY BOYS HERE ARE RESPONSIBLE FOR THE COLLAPSE OF GODDAMN CIVILIZATION!
WHEN REALLY IT'S THAT SMUT YOU'RE PEDDLING IN THAT--

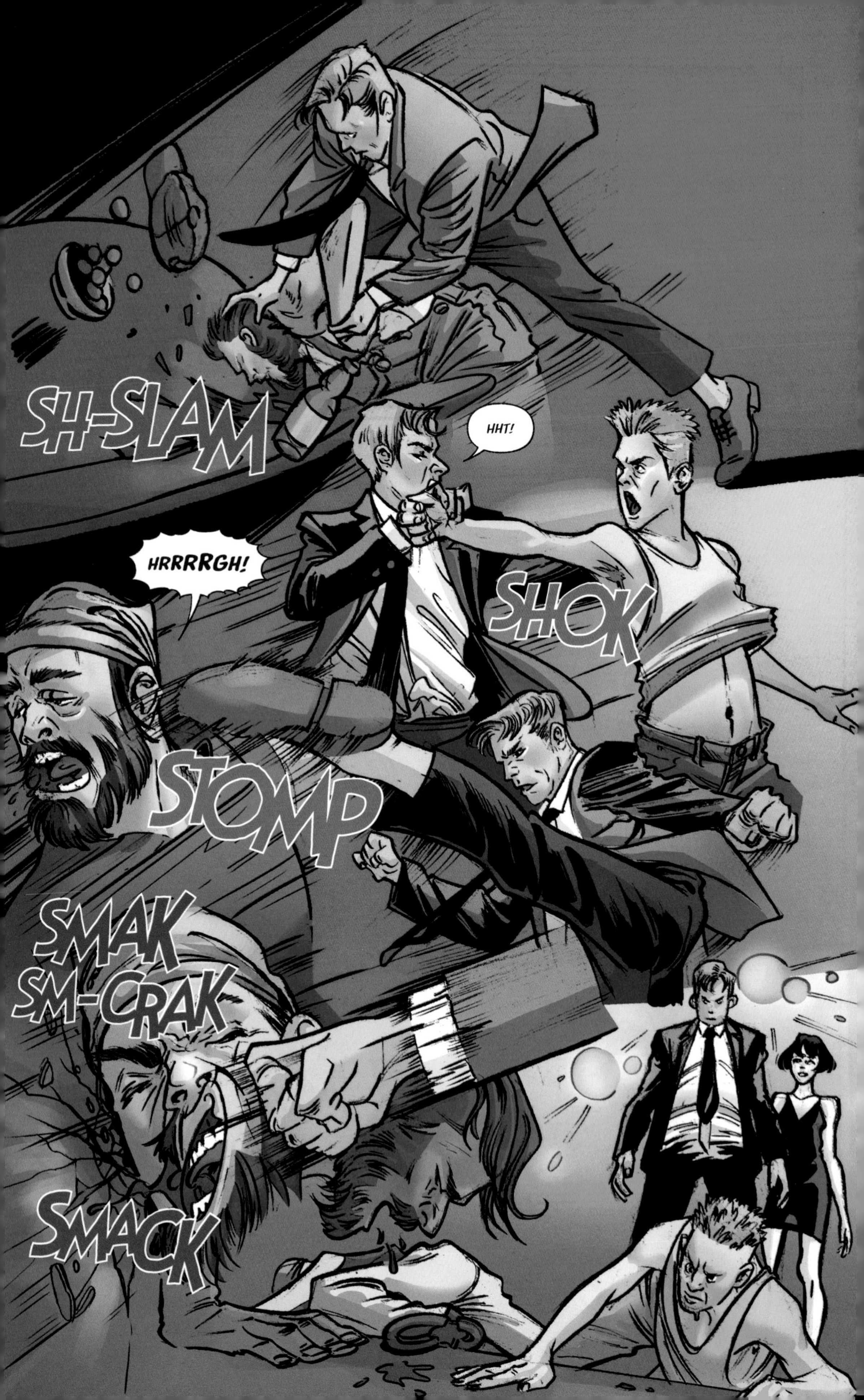
SH-SLAM
HHT!
HRRRRGH!
SHOK
STOMP
SMAK
SM-CRAK
SMACK

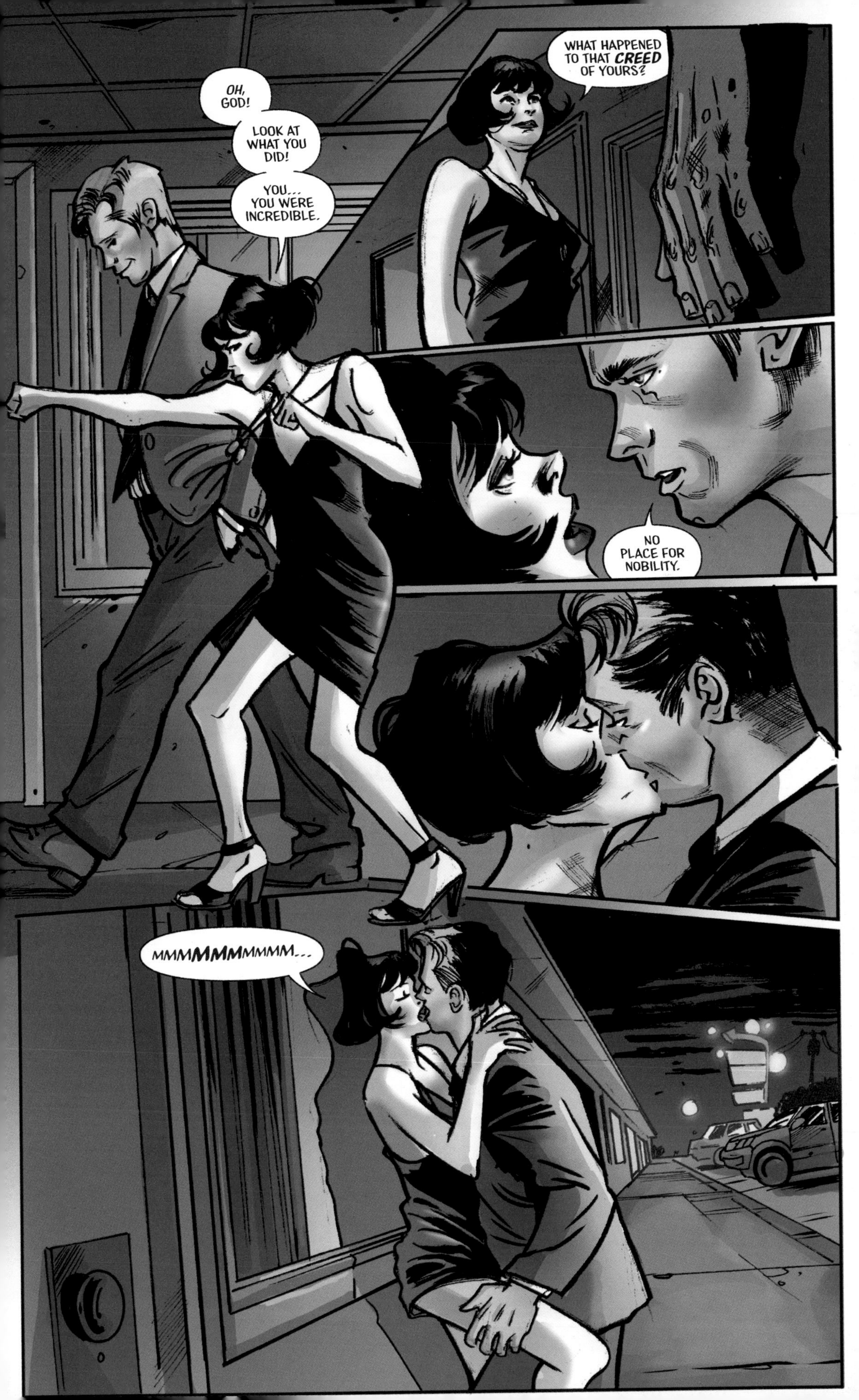
OH, GOD!
LOOK AT WHAT YOU DID!
YOU... YOU WERE INCREDIBLE.
WHAT HAPPENED TO THAT CREED OF YOURS?
NO PLACE FOR NOBILITY.
MMMMMMMMMMM...

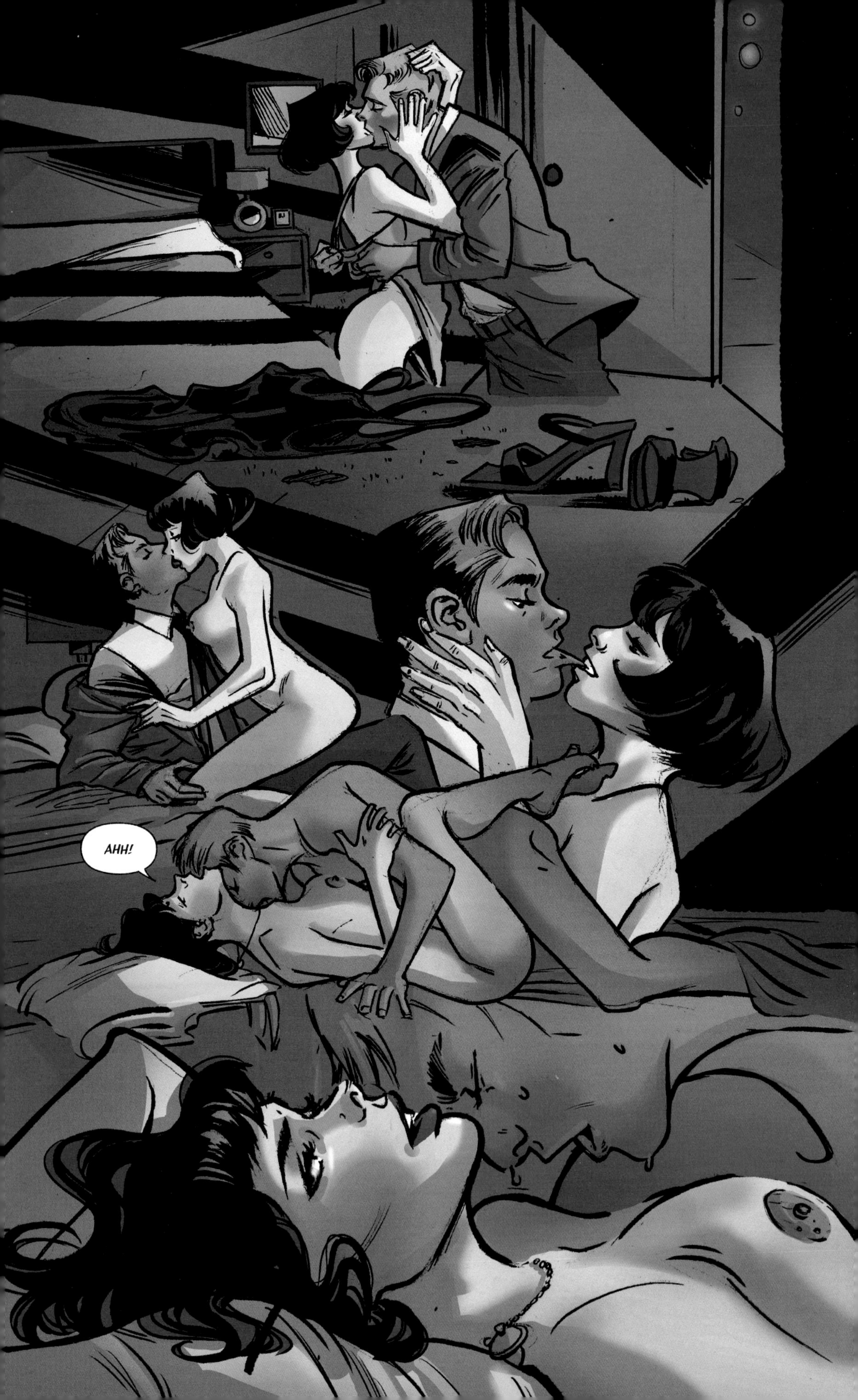
AHH!

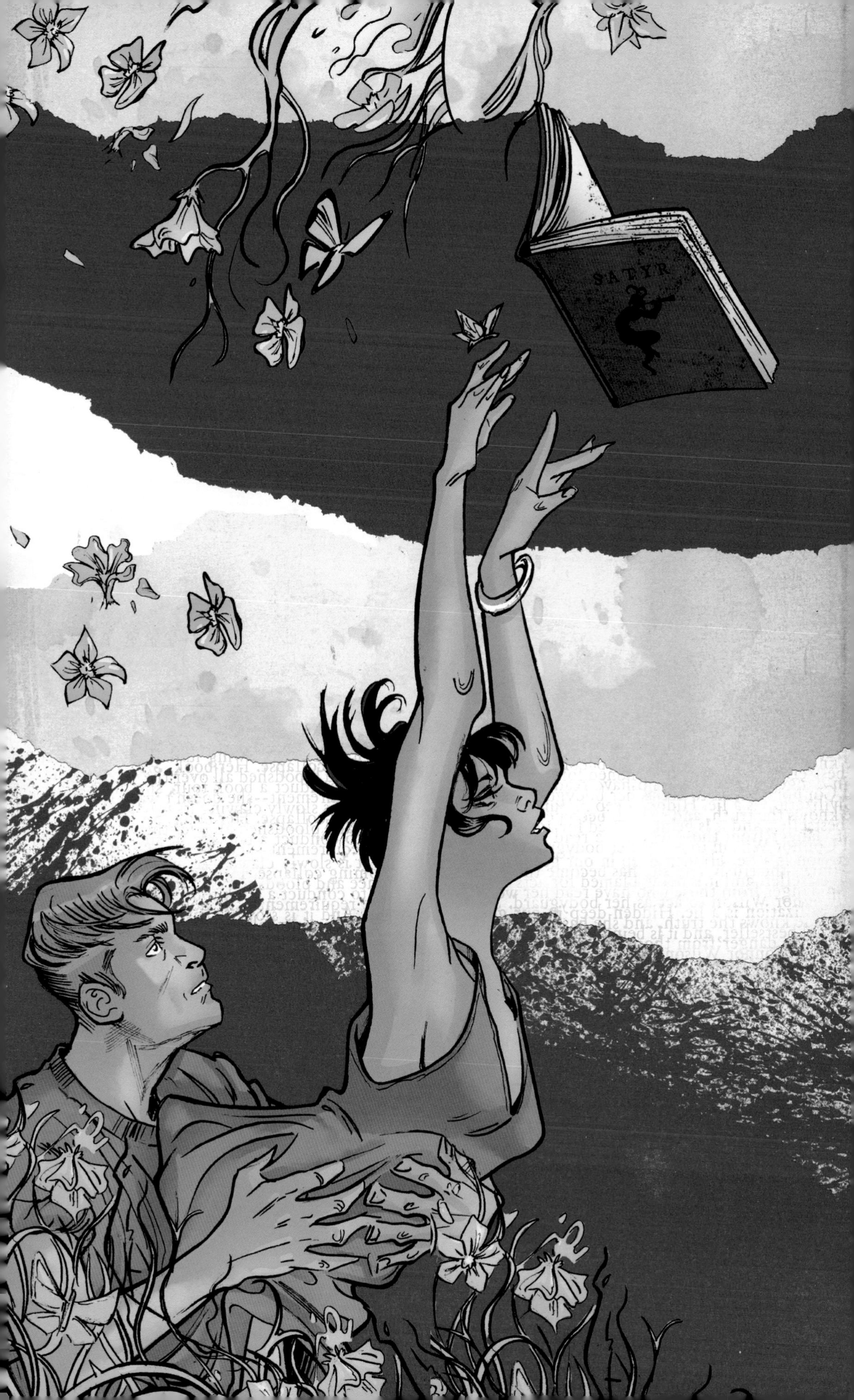
SATYR

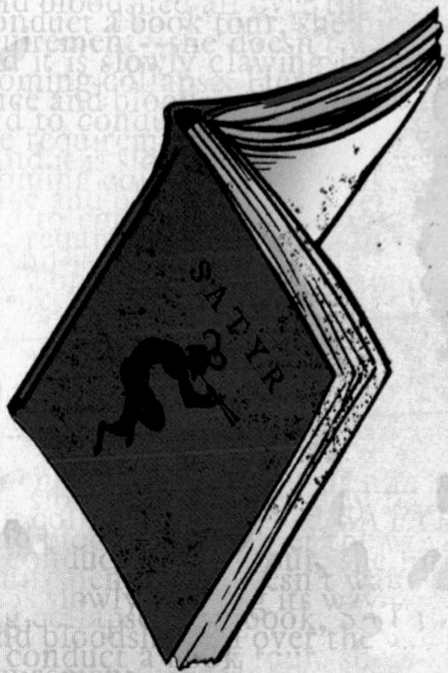
SATYR

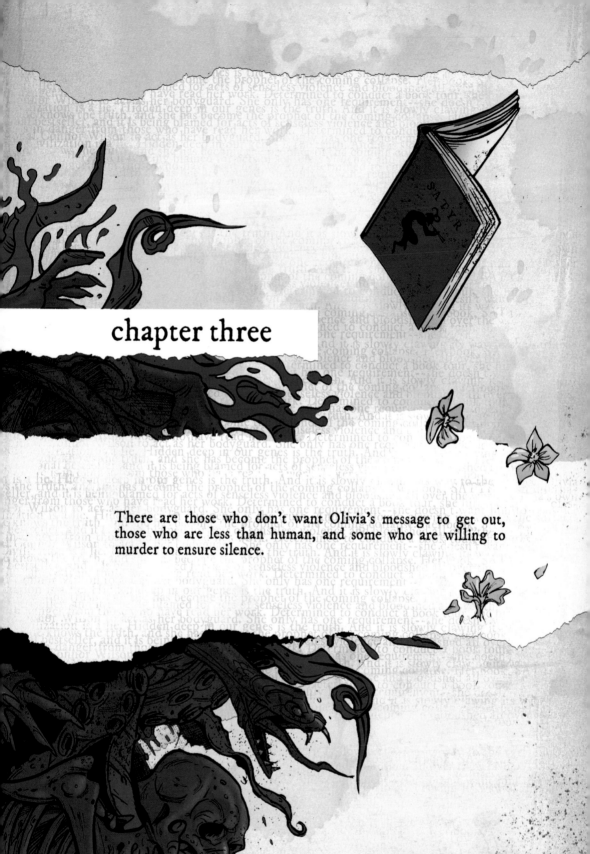

chapter three

There are those who don't want Olivia's message to get out, those who are less than human, and some who are willing to murder to ensure silence.

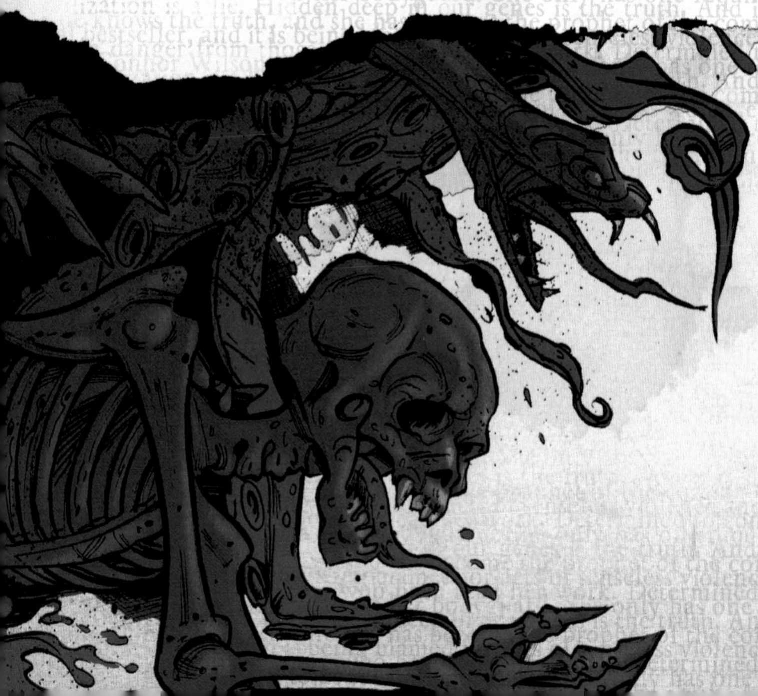

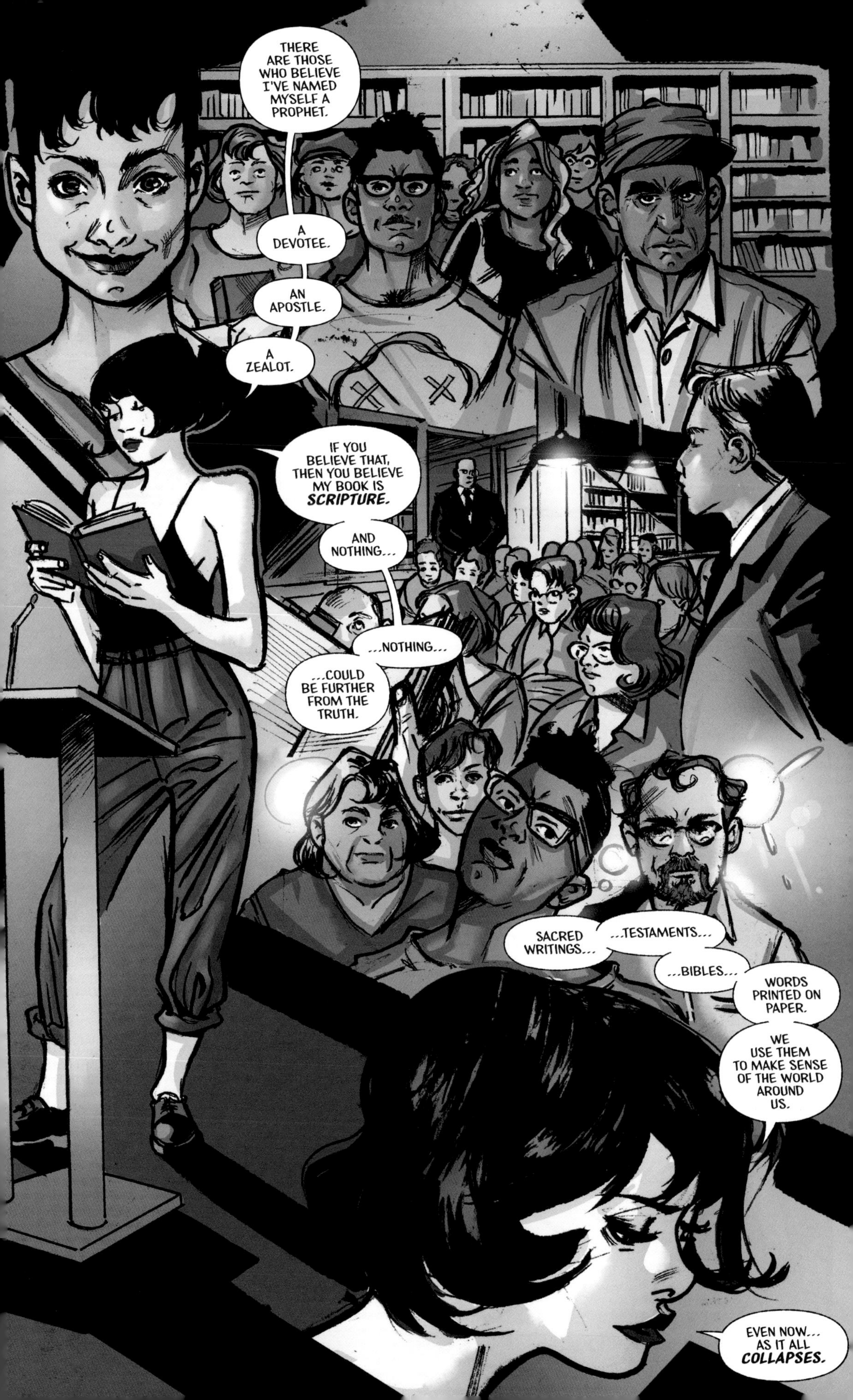
THERE ARE THOSE WHO BELIEVE I'VE NAMED MYSELF A PROPHET.
A DEVOTEE.
AN APOSTLE.
A ZEALOT.
IF YOU BELIEVE THAT, THEN YOU BELIEVE MY BOOK IS *SCRIPTURE.*
AND NOTHING...
...NOTHING...
...COULD BE FURTHER FROM THE TRUTH.
SACRED WRITINGS...
...TESTAMENTS...
...BIBLES...
WORDS PRINTED ON PAPER.
WE USE THEM TO MAKE SENSE OF THE WORLD AROUND US.
EVEN NOW... AS IT ALL *COLLAPSES.*

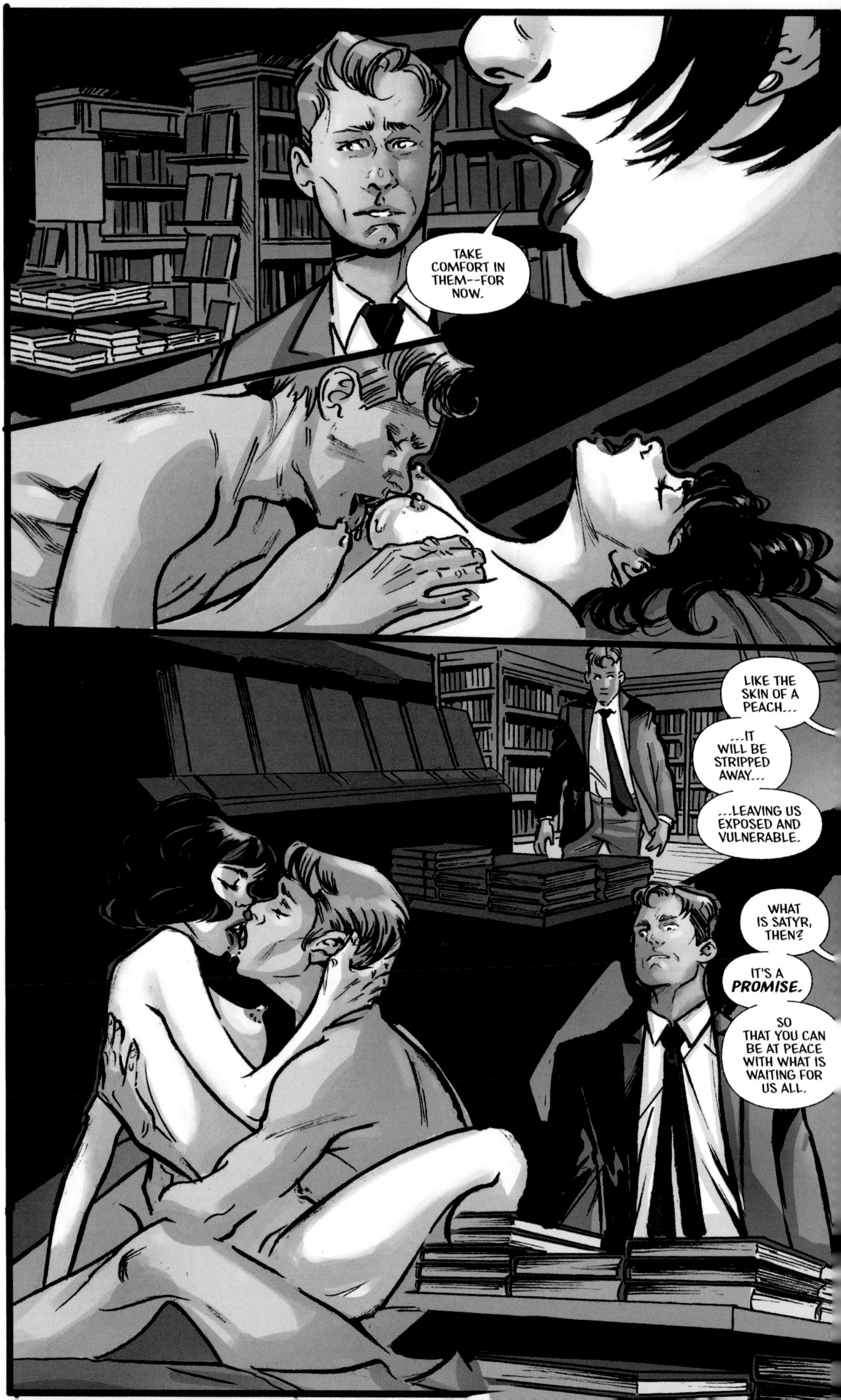
TAKE COMFORT IN THEM--FOR NOW.
LIKE THE SKIN OF A PEACH...
...IT WILL BE STRIPPED AWAY...
...LEAVING US EXPOSED AND VULNERABLE.
WHAT IS SATYR, THEN?
IT'S A PROMISE.
SO THAT YOU CAN BE AT PEACE WITH WHAT IS WAITING FOR US ALL.

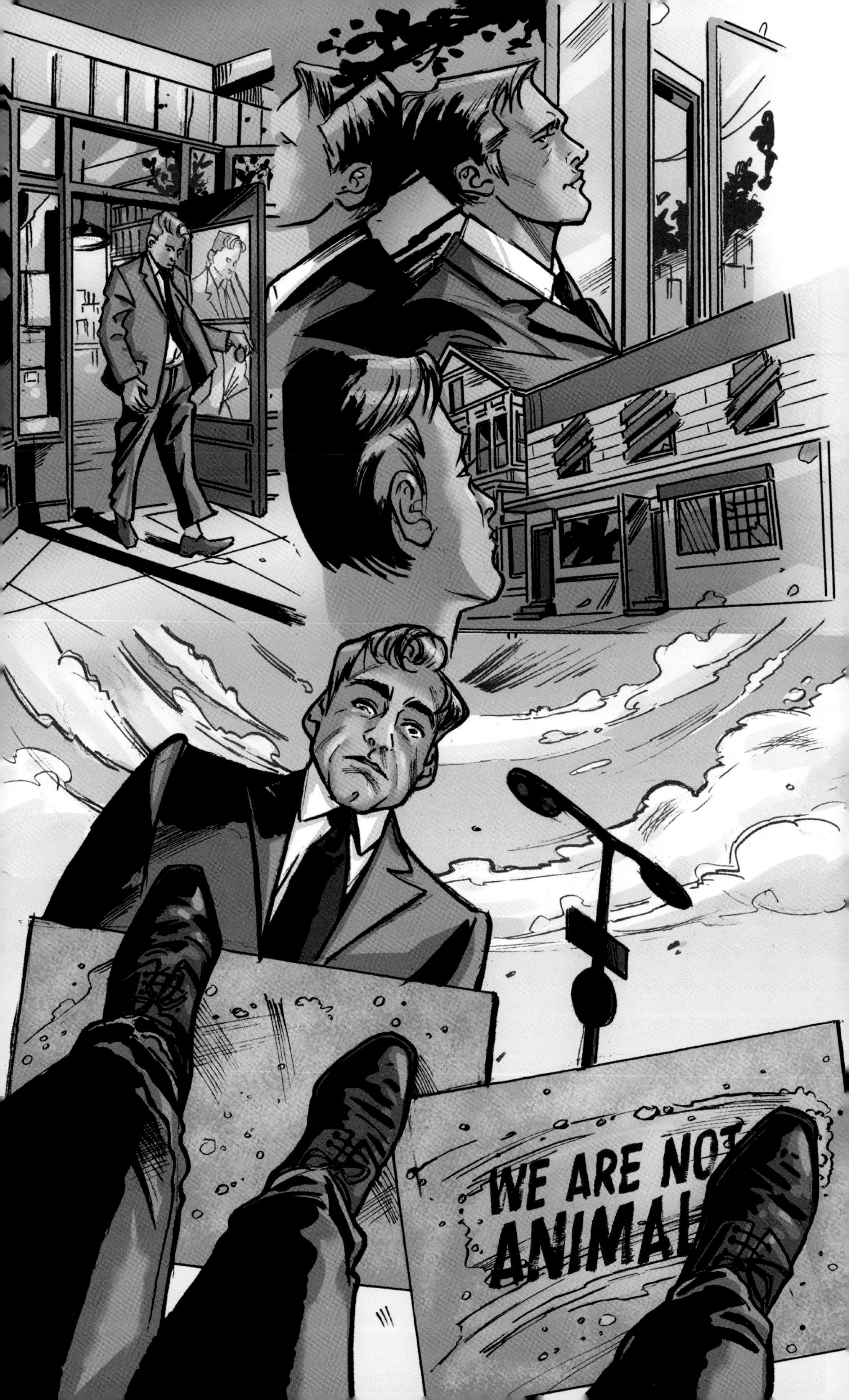
WE ARE NOT
ANIMAL

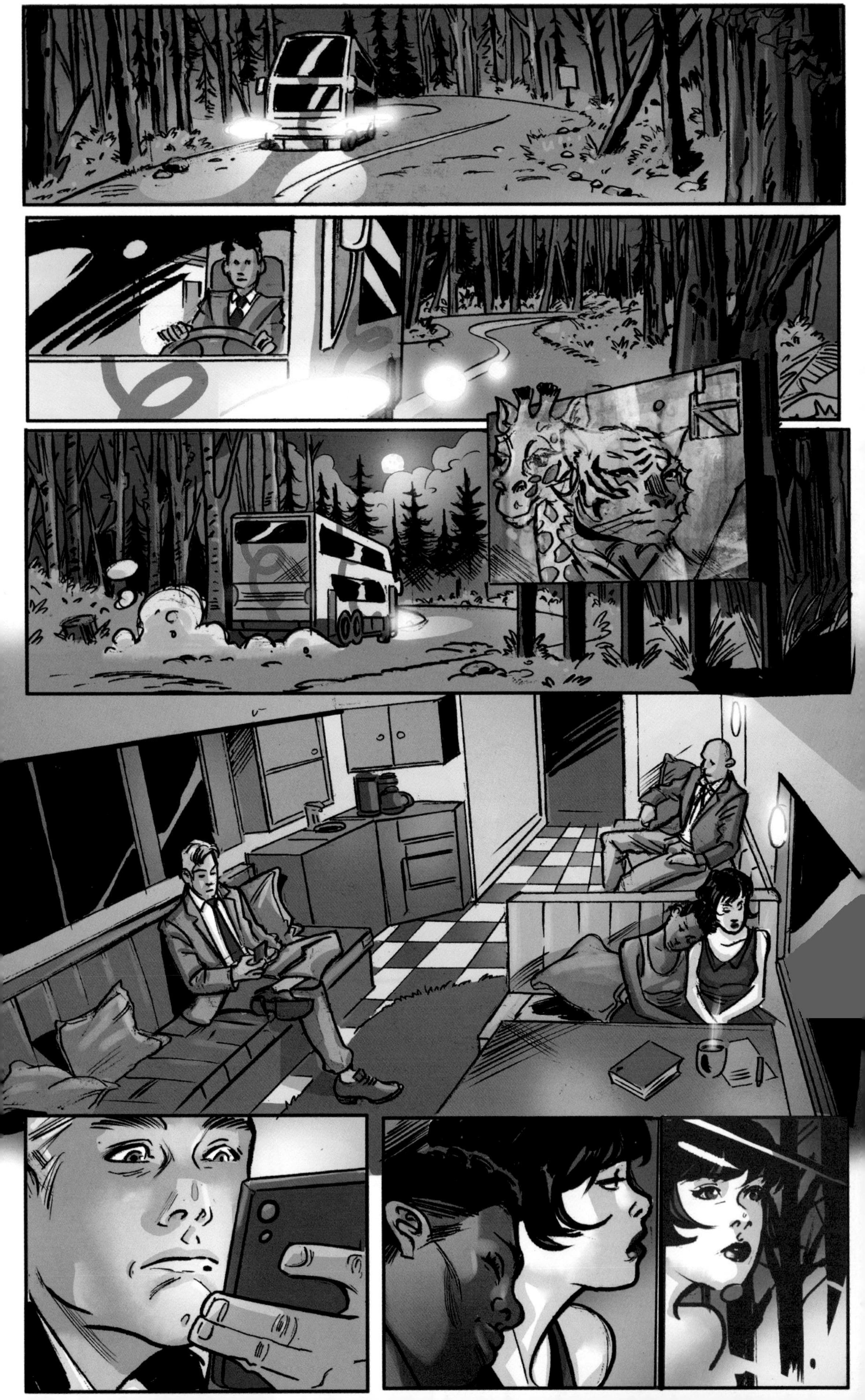

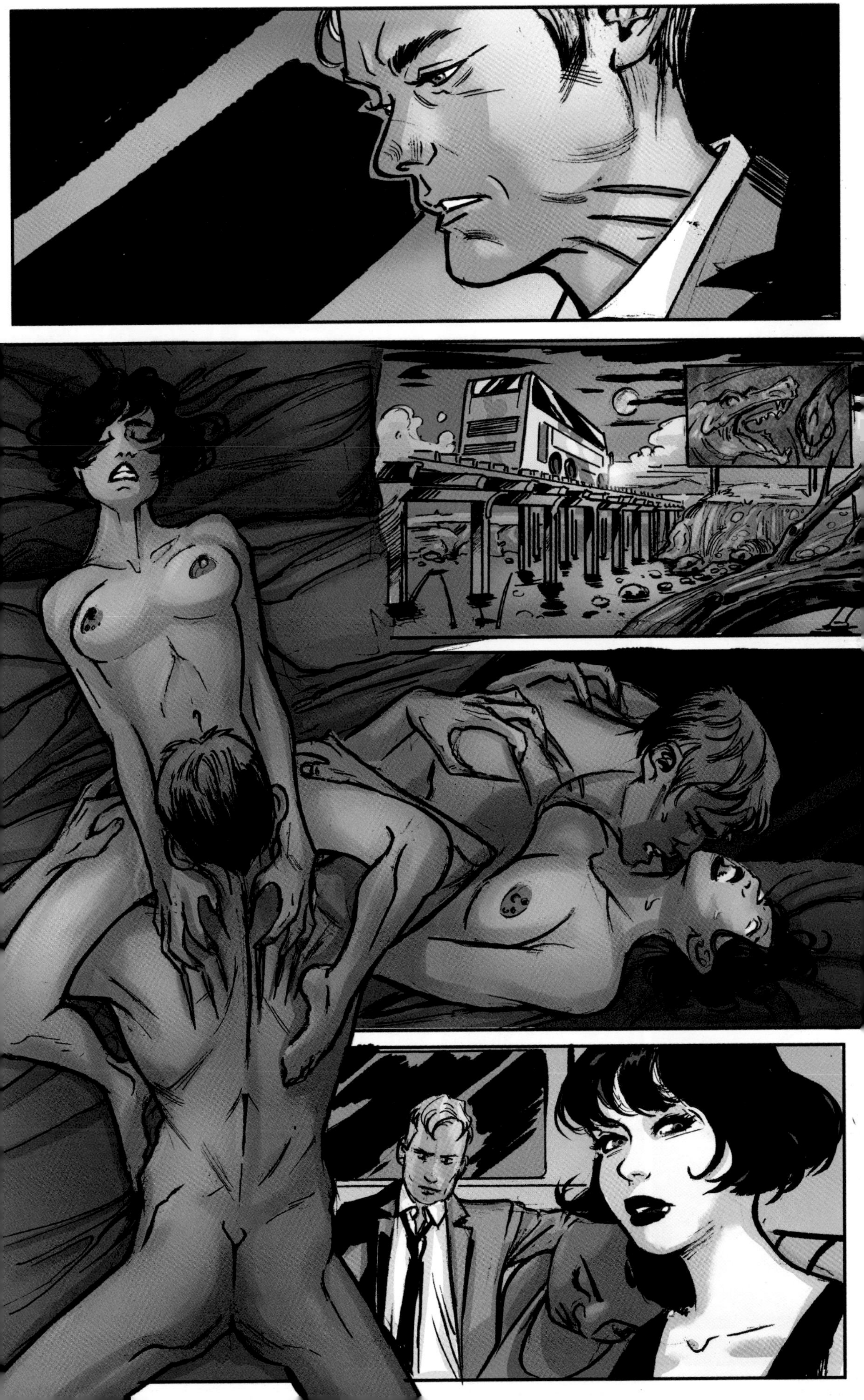

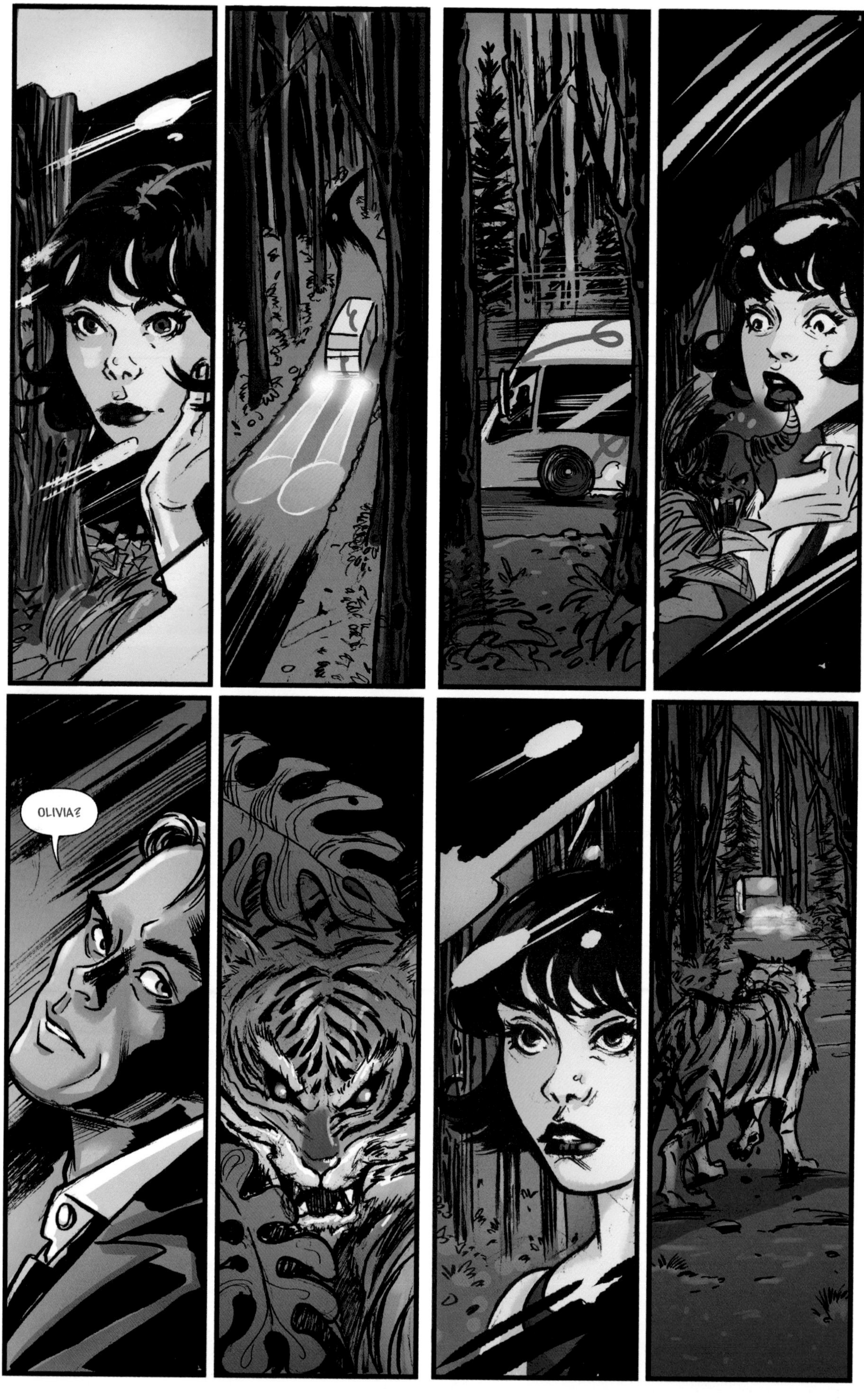
OLIVIA?

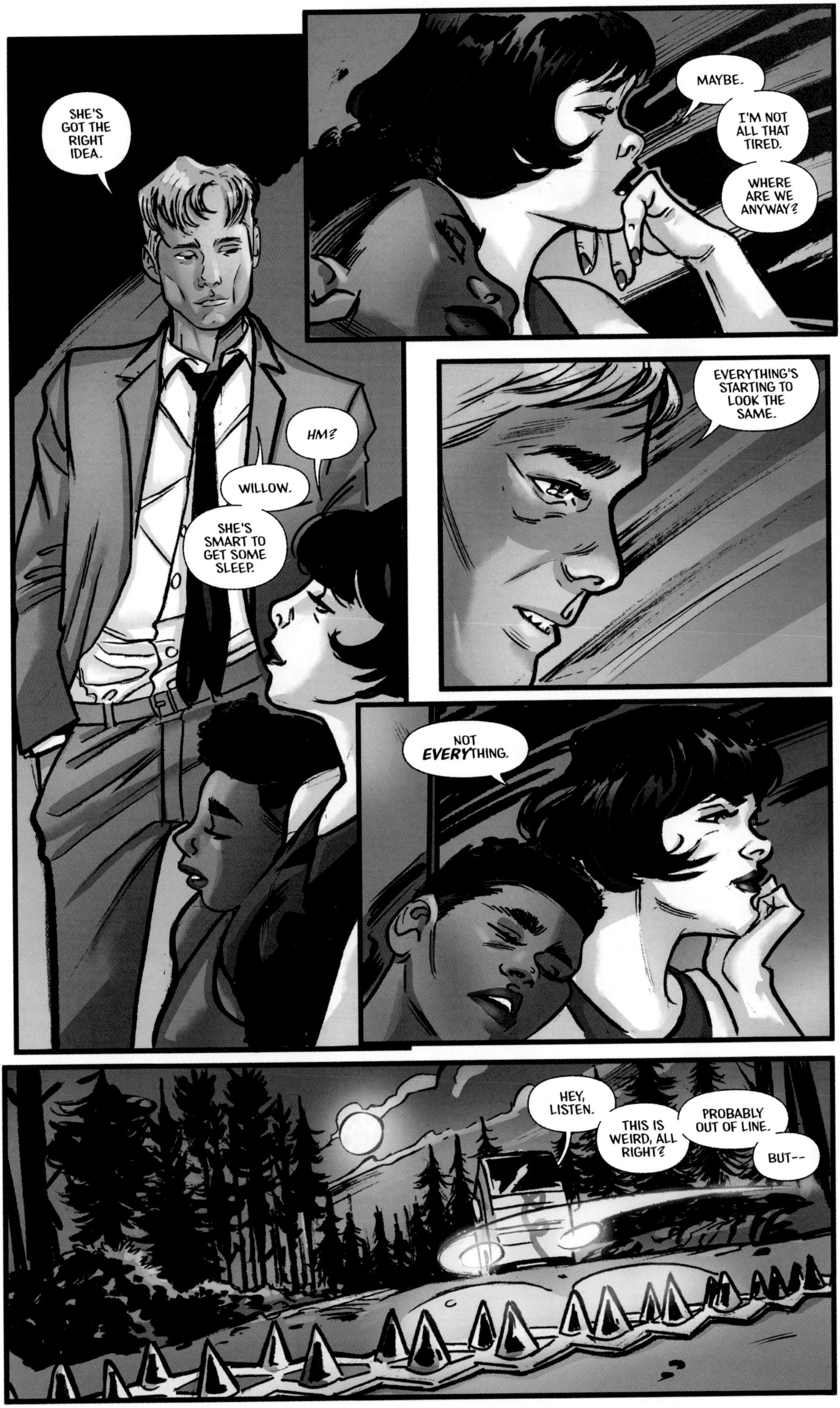
SHE'S GOT THE RIGHT IDEA.
MAYBE.
I'M NOT ALL THAT TIRED.
WHERE ARE WE ANYWAY?
HM?
WILLOW.
SHE'S SMART TO GET SOME SLEEP.
EVERYTHING'S STARTING TO LOOK THE SAME.
NOT EVERYTHING.
HEY, LISTEN.
THIS IS WEIRD, ALL RIGHT?
PROBABLY OUT OF LINE.
BUT--

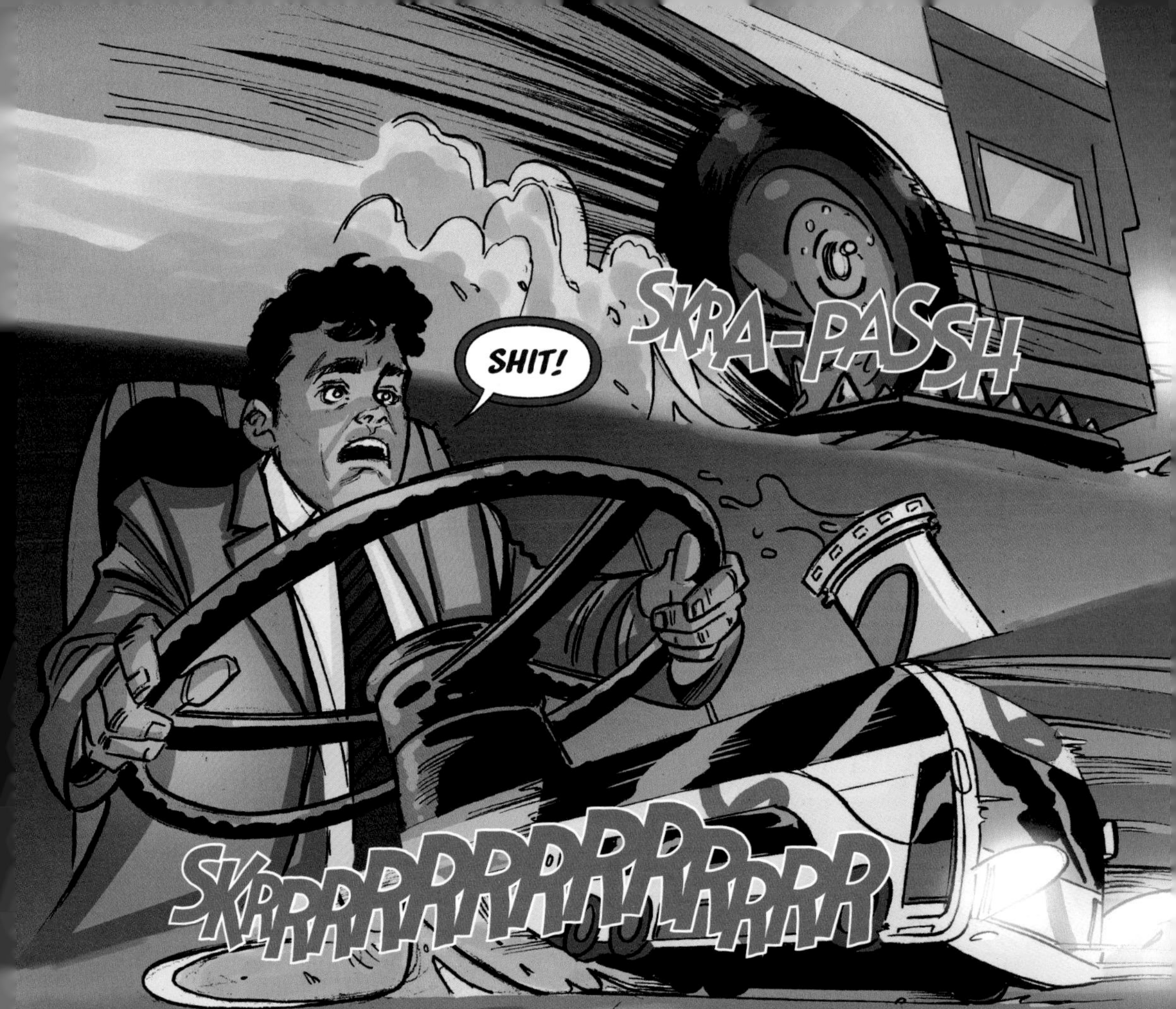
SHIT!
SKRA-PASSH
SKRRRRRRRRRRRRRR

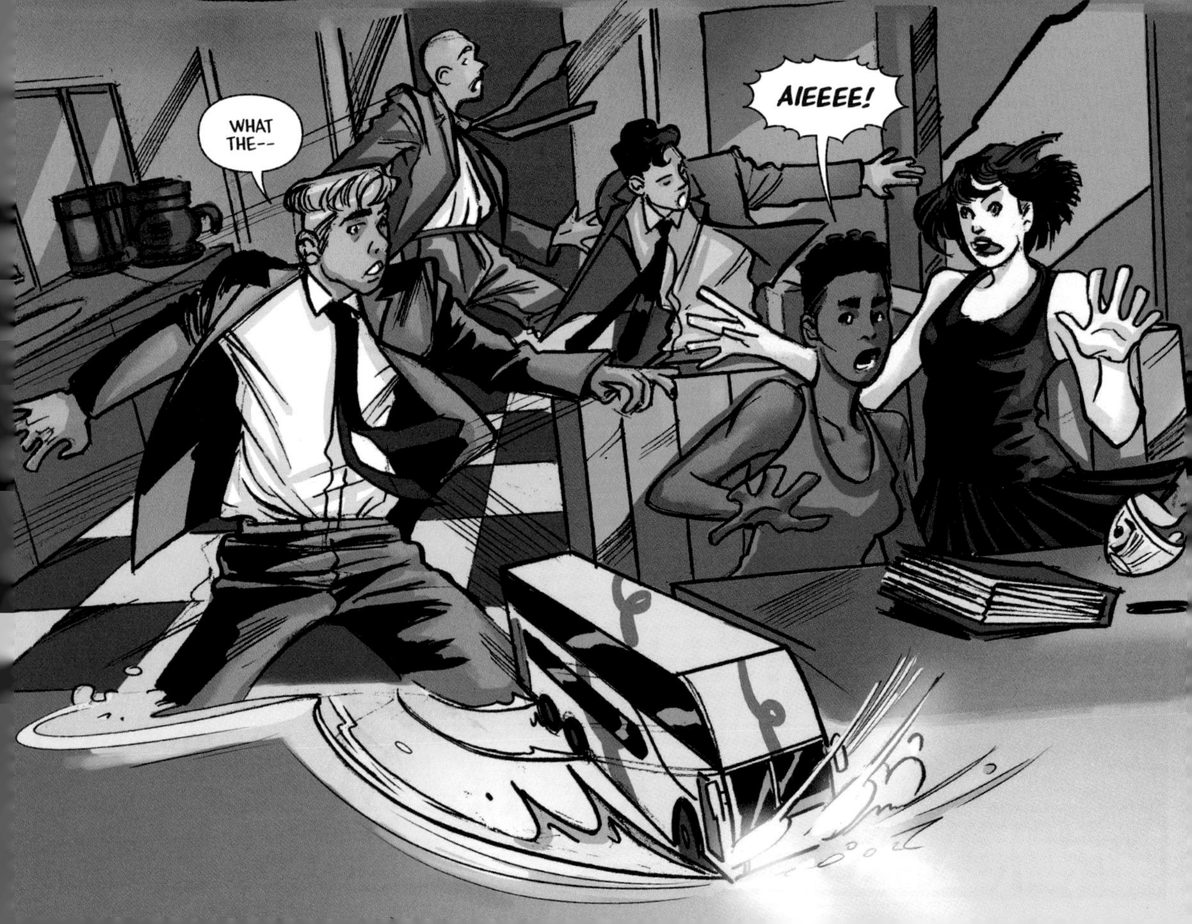
WHAT THE--
AIEEEE!

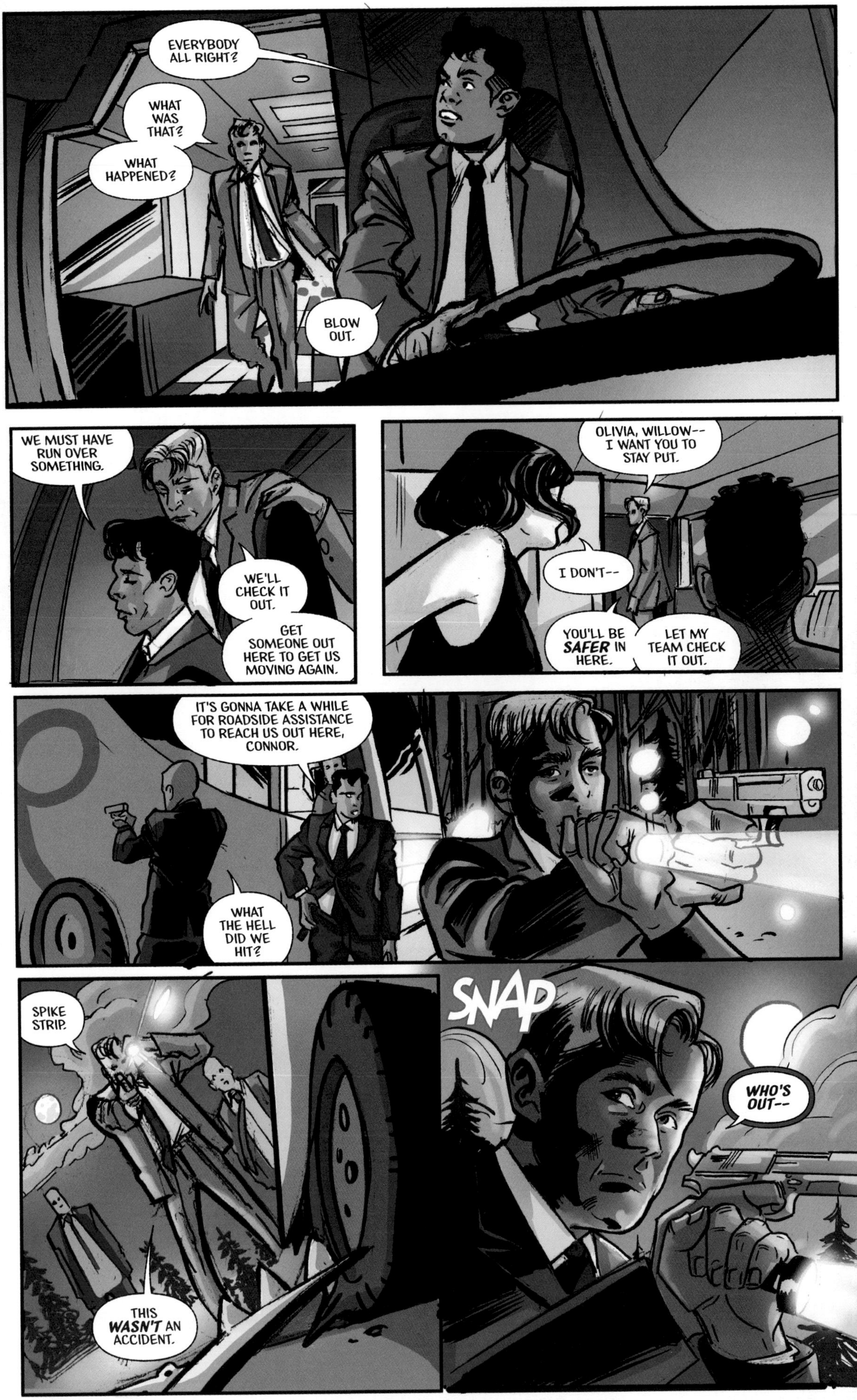
EVERYBODY ALL RIGHT?
WHAT WAS THAT?
WHAT HAPPENED?
BLOW OUT.
WE MUST HAVE RUN OVER SOMETHING.
WE'LL CHECK IT OUT.
GET SOMEONE OUT HERE TO GET US MOVING AGAIN.
OLIVIA, WILLOW-- I WANT YOU TO STAY PUT.
I DON'T--
YOU'LL BE *SAFER* IN HERE.
LET MY TEAM CHECK IT OUT.
IT'S GONNA TAKE A WHILE FOR ROADSIDE ASSISTANCE TO REACH US OUT HERE, CONNOR.
WHAT THE HELL DID WE HIT?
SPIKE STRIP.
THIS *WASN'T* AN ACCIDENT.
SNAP
WHO'S OUT--

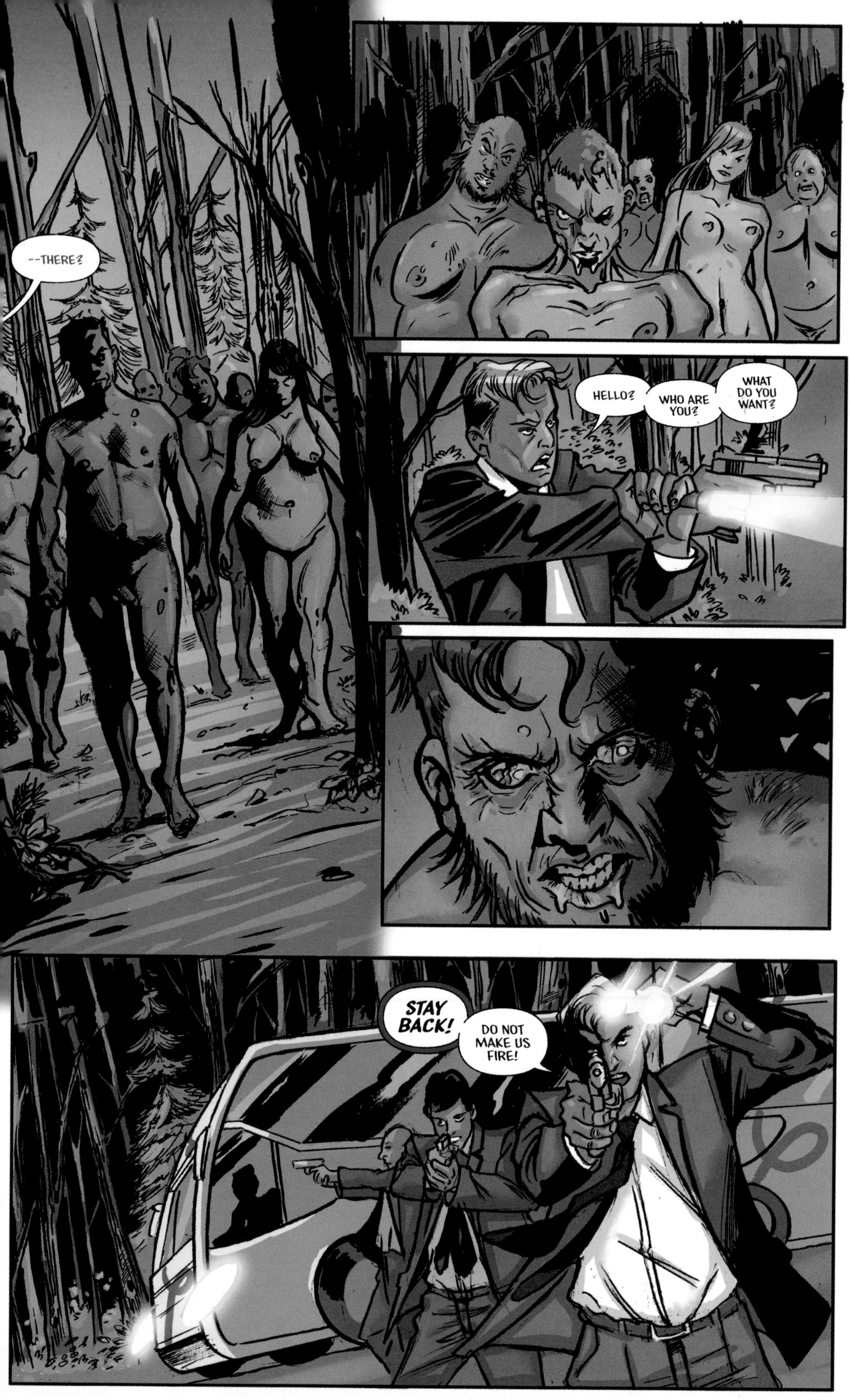
--THERE?
HELLO?
WHO ARE YOU?
WHAT DO YOU WANT?
STAY BACK!
DO NOT MAKE US FIRE!

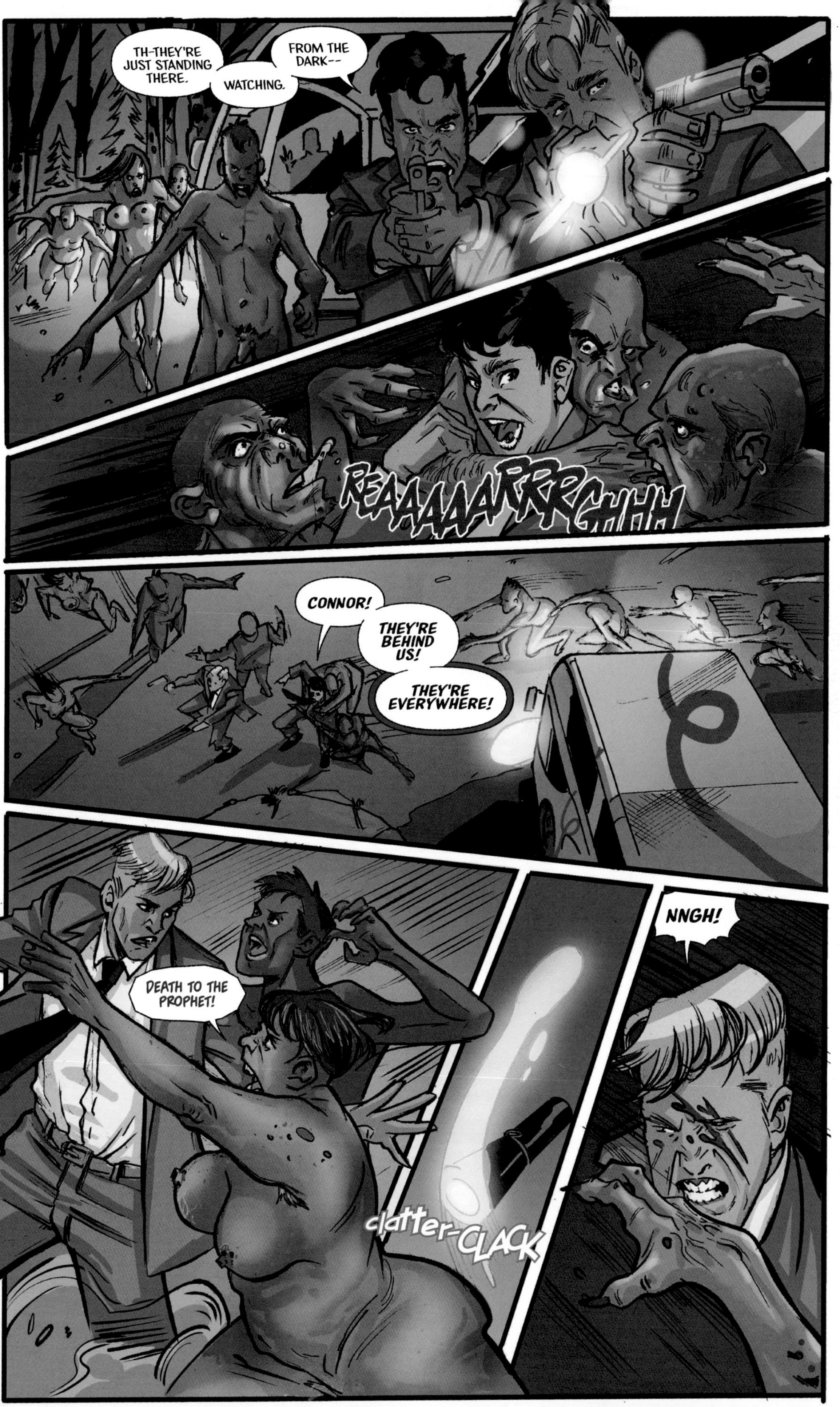
TH-THEY'RE JUST STANDING THERE.
WATCHING.
FROM THE DARK--
REAAAAARRRGHHH
CONNOR!
THEY'RE BEHIND US!
THEY'RE EVERYWHERE!
DEATH TO THE PROPHET!
clatter-CLACK
NNGH!

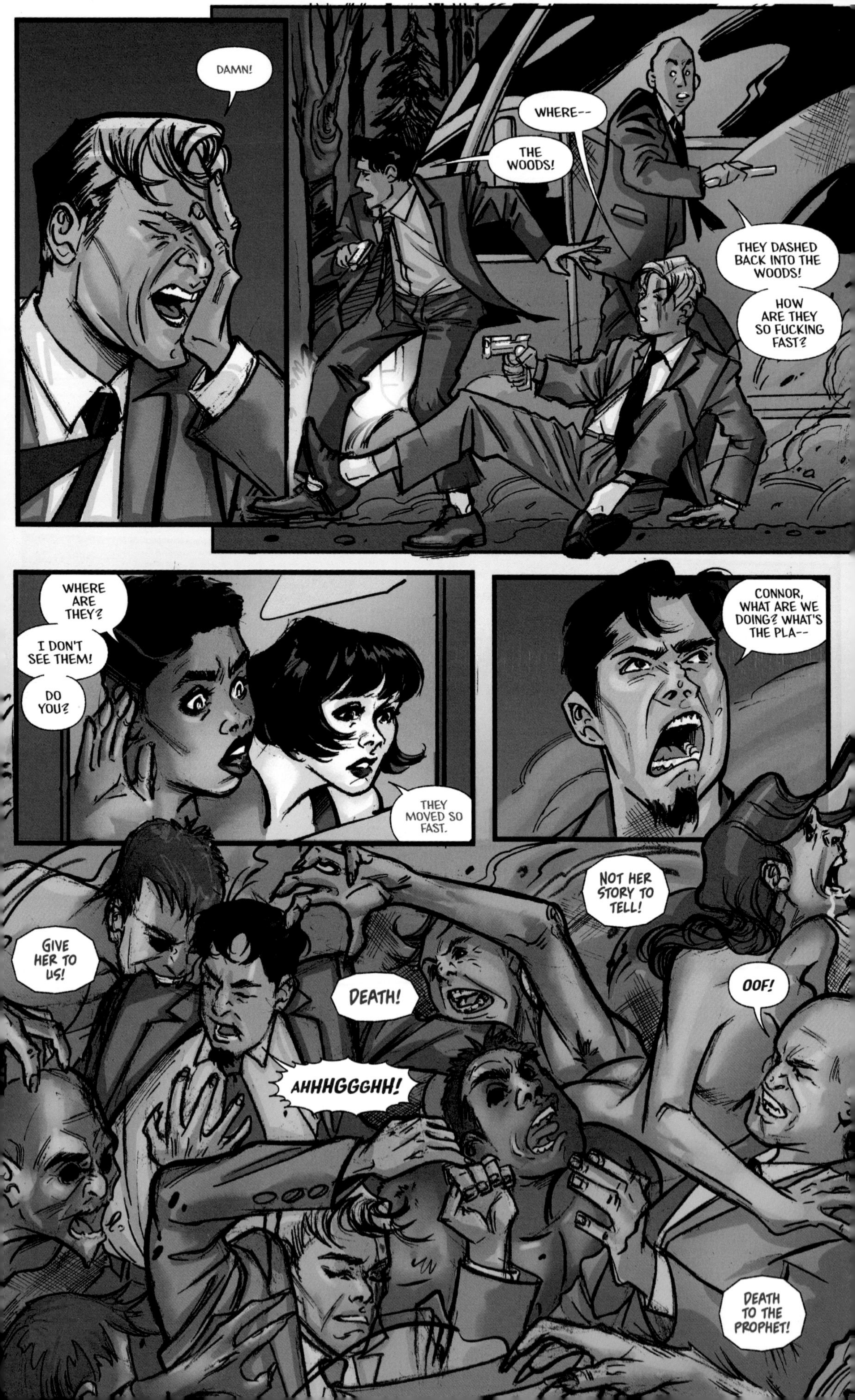
DAMN!
WHERE--
THE WOODS!
THEY DASHED BACK INTO THE WOODS!
HOW ARE THEY SO FUCKING FAST?
WHERE ARE THEY?
I DON'T SEE THEM!
DO YOU?
THEY MOVED SO FAST.
CONNOR, WHAT ARE WE DOING? WHAT'S THE PLA--
GIVE HER TO US!
DEATH!
NOT HER STORY TO TELL!
OOF!
AHHHGGGHH!
DEATH TO THE PROPHET!

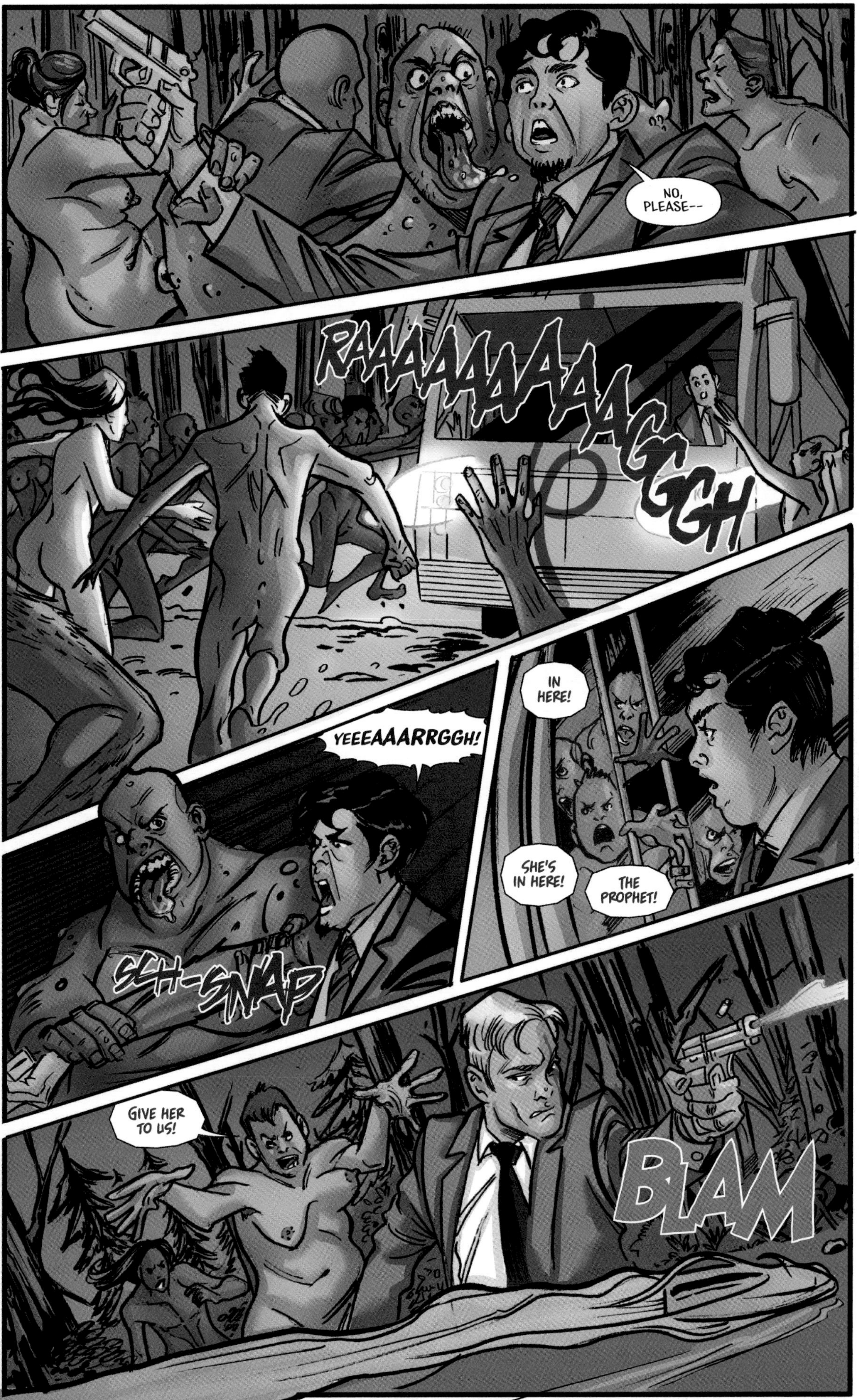
NO, PLEASE--
RAAAAAAAAAAGGGH
YEEEAAARRGGH!
SCH-SNAP
IN HERE!
SHE'S IN HERE!
THE PROPHET!
GIVE HER TO US!
BLAM

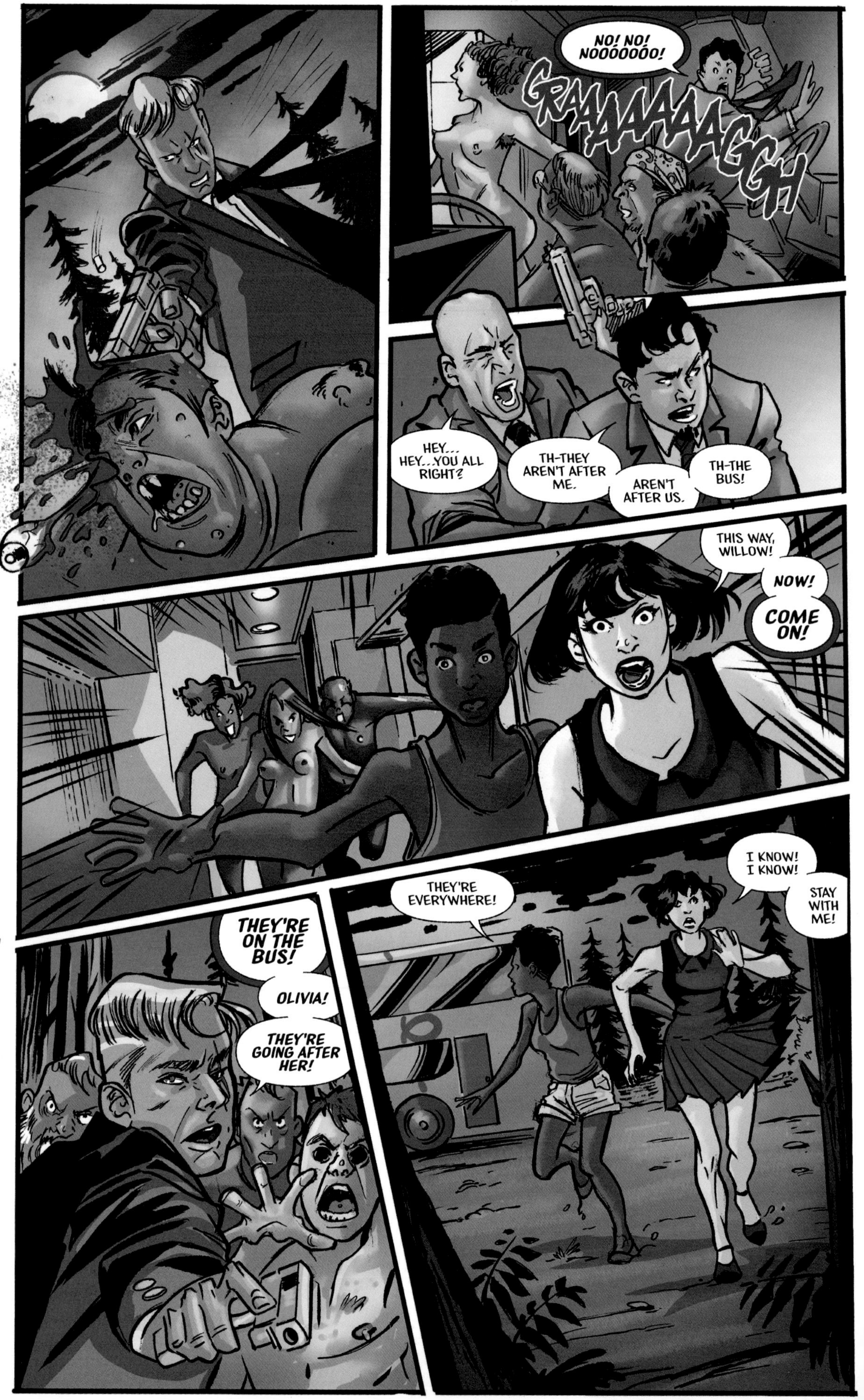
NO! NO! NOOOOOOO!
GRAAAAAAAGGH
HEY... HEY...YOU ALL RIGHT?
TH-THEY AREN'T AFTER ME.
AREN'T AFTER US.
TH-THE BUS!
THIS WAY, WILLOW!
NOW!
COME ON!
THEY'RE ON THE BUS!
OLIVIA!
THEY'RE GOING AFTER HER!
THEY'RE EVERYWHERE!
I KNOW! I KNOW!
STAY WITH ME!

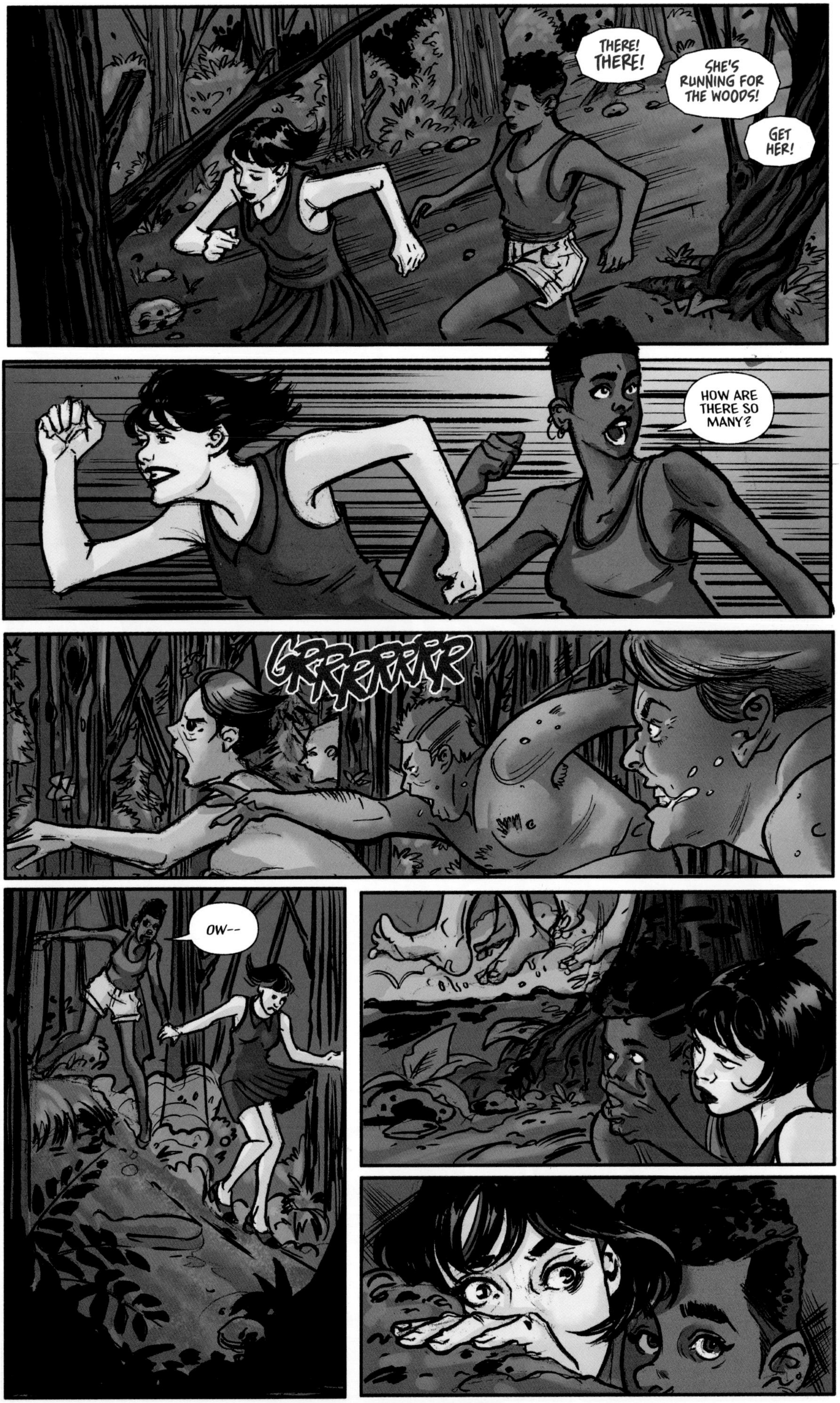
THERE! THERE!
SHE'S RUNNING FOR THE WOODS!
GET HER!
HOW ARE THERE SO MANY?
GRRRRRR
OW--

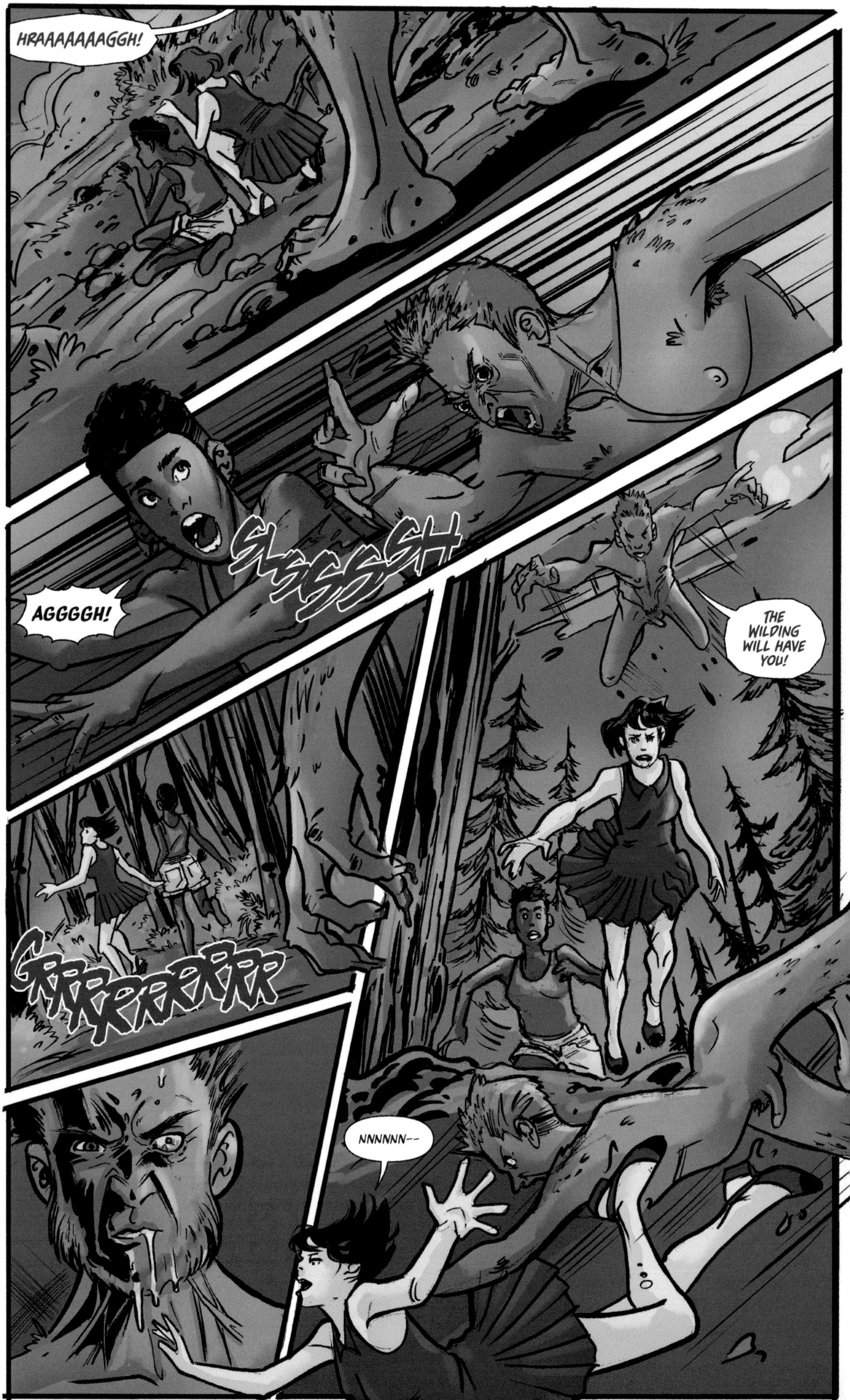
HRAAAAAAAGGH!
SLSSSSH
AGGGGH!
THE WILDING WILL HAVE YOU!
GRRRRRRRRR
NNNNNN--

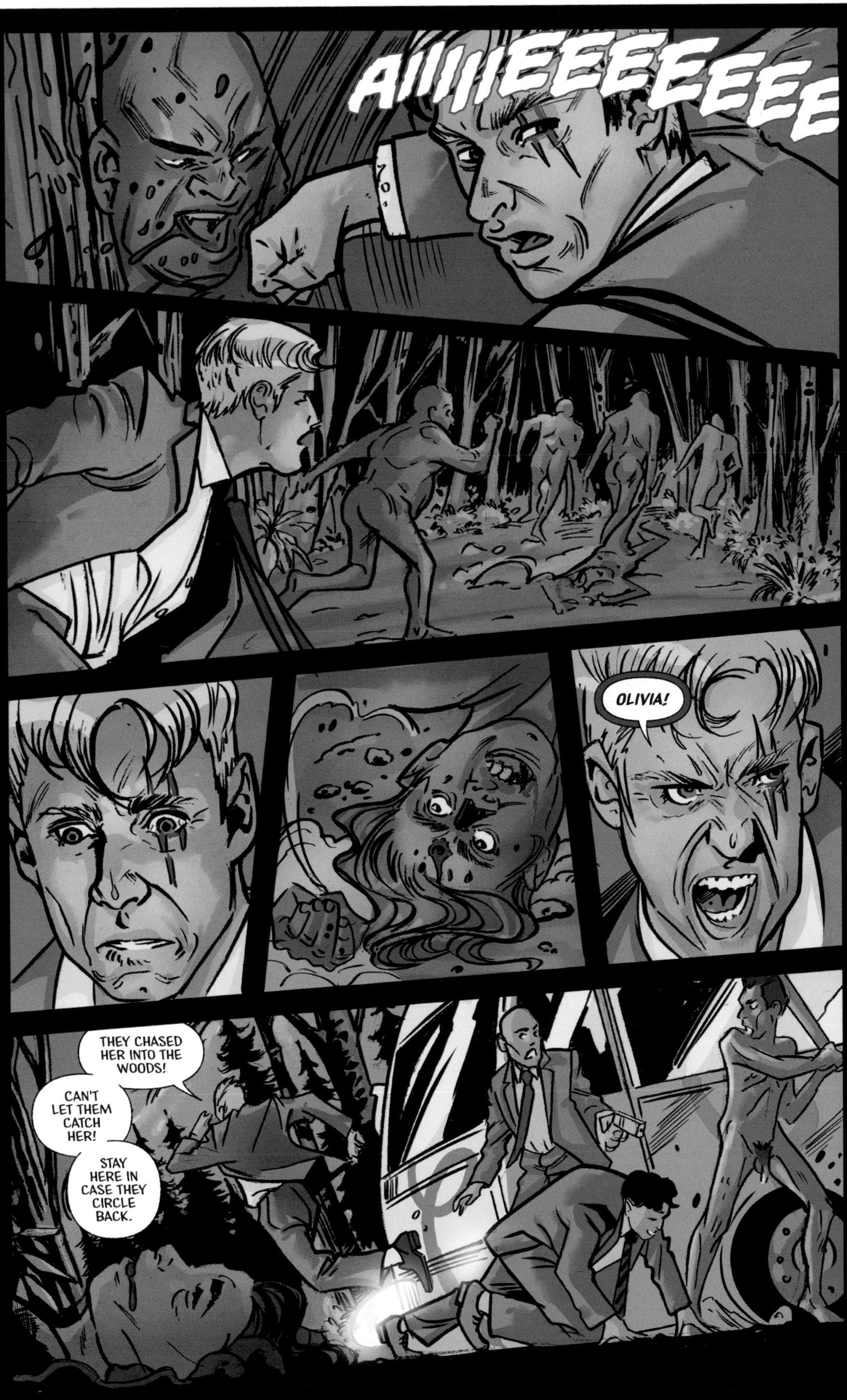
AIIIIEEEEEEEEE
OLIVIA!
THEY CHASED HER INTO THE WOODS!
CAN'T LET THEM CATCH HER!
STAY HERE IN CASE THEY CIRCLE BACK.

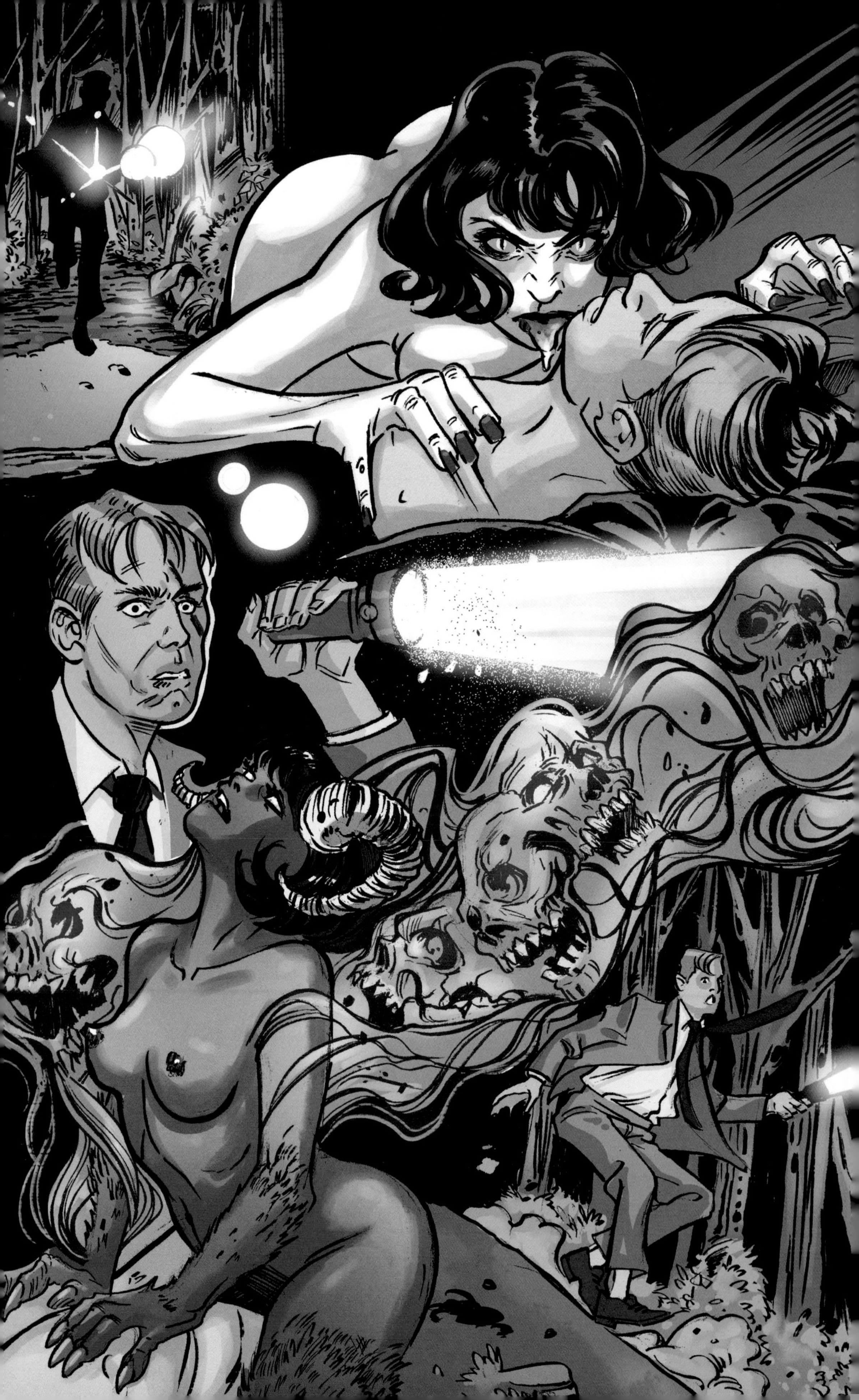

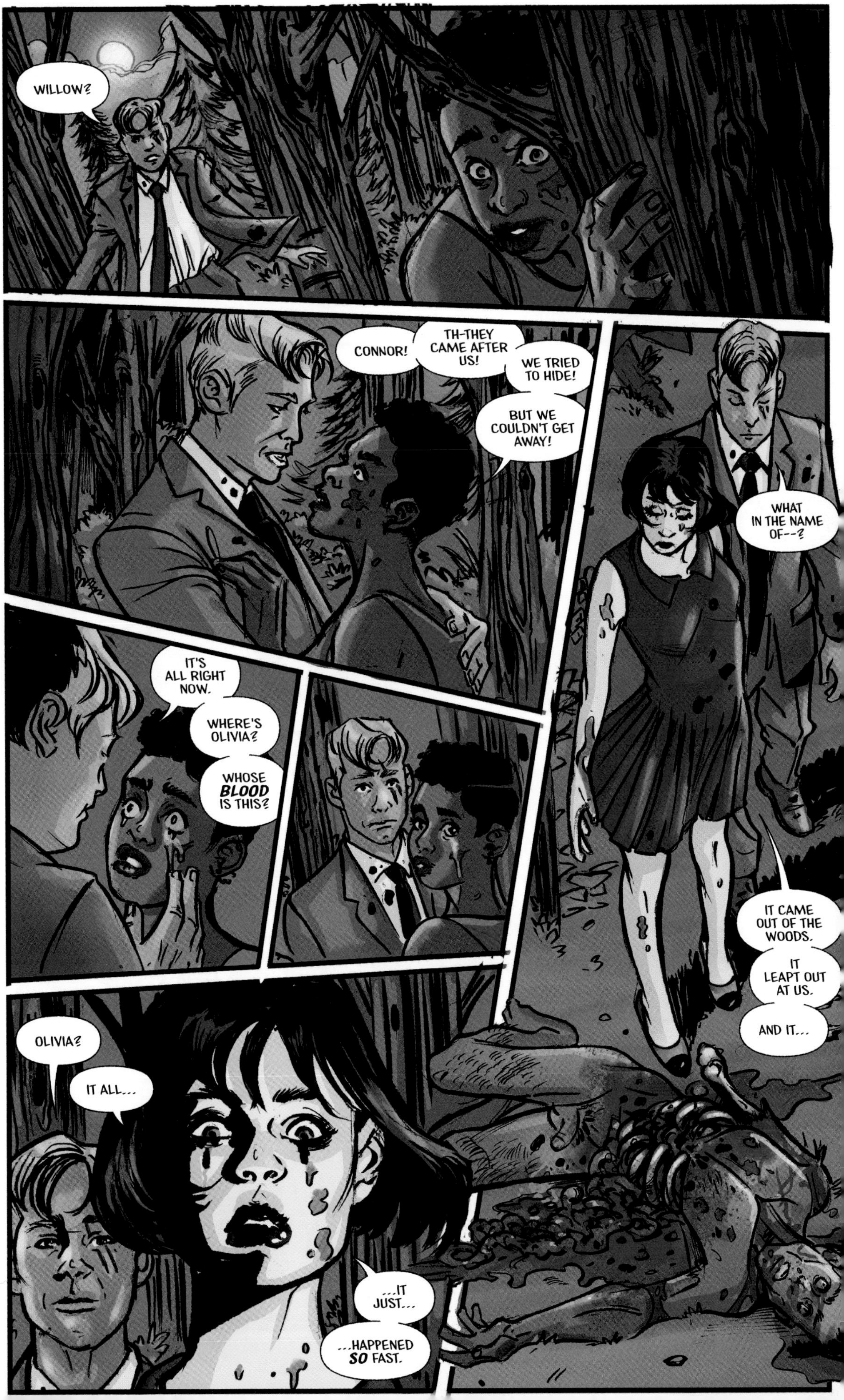
WILLOW?
CONNOR!
TH-THEY CAME AFTER US!
WE TRIED TO HIDE!
BUT WE COULDN'T GET AWAY!
WHAT IN THE NAME OF--?
IT'S ALL RIGHT NOW.
WHERE'S OLIVIA?
WHOSE BLOOD IS THIS?
IT CAME OUT OF THE WOODS.
IT LEAPT OUT AT US.
AND IT...
OLIVIA?
IT ALL...
...IT JUST...
...HAPPENED SO FAST.

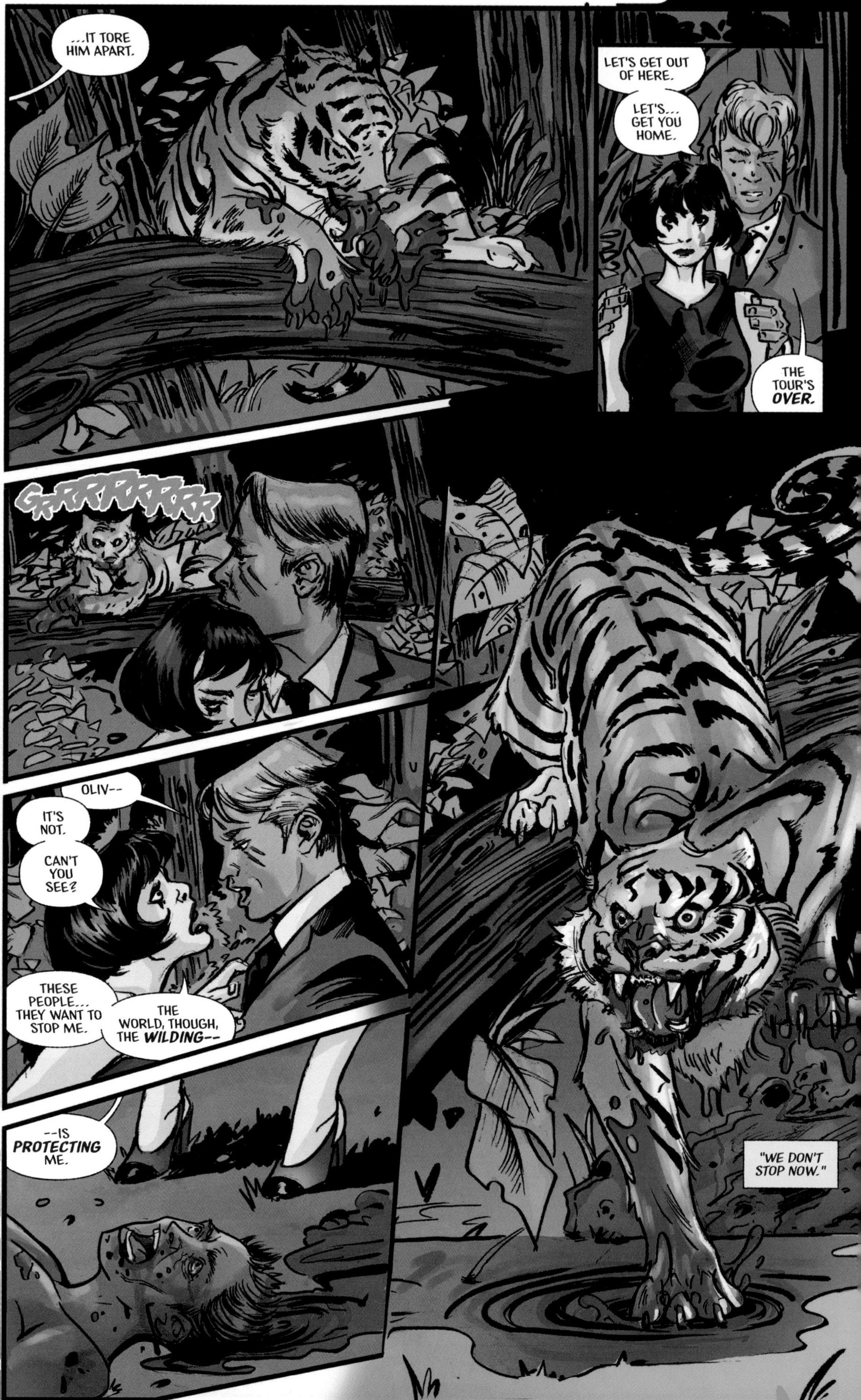
...IT TORE HIM APART.
LET'S GET OUT OF HERE.
LET'S... GET YOU HOME.
THE TOUR'S **OVER.**
GRRRRRRRRRR
OLIV--
IT'S NOT.
CAN'T YOU SEE?
THESE PEOPLE... THEY WANT TO STOP ME.
THE WORLD, THOUGH, THE **WILDING--**
--IS **PROTECTING** ME.
"WE DON'T STOP NOW."

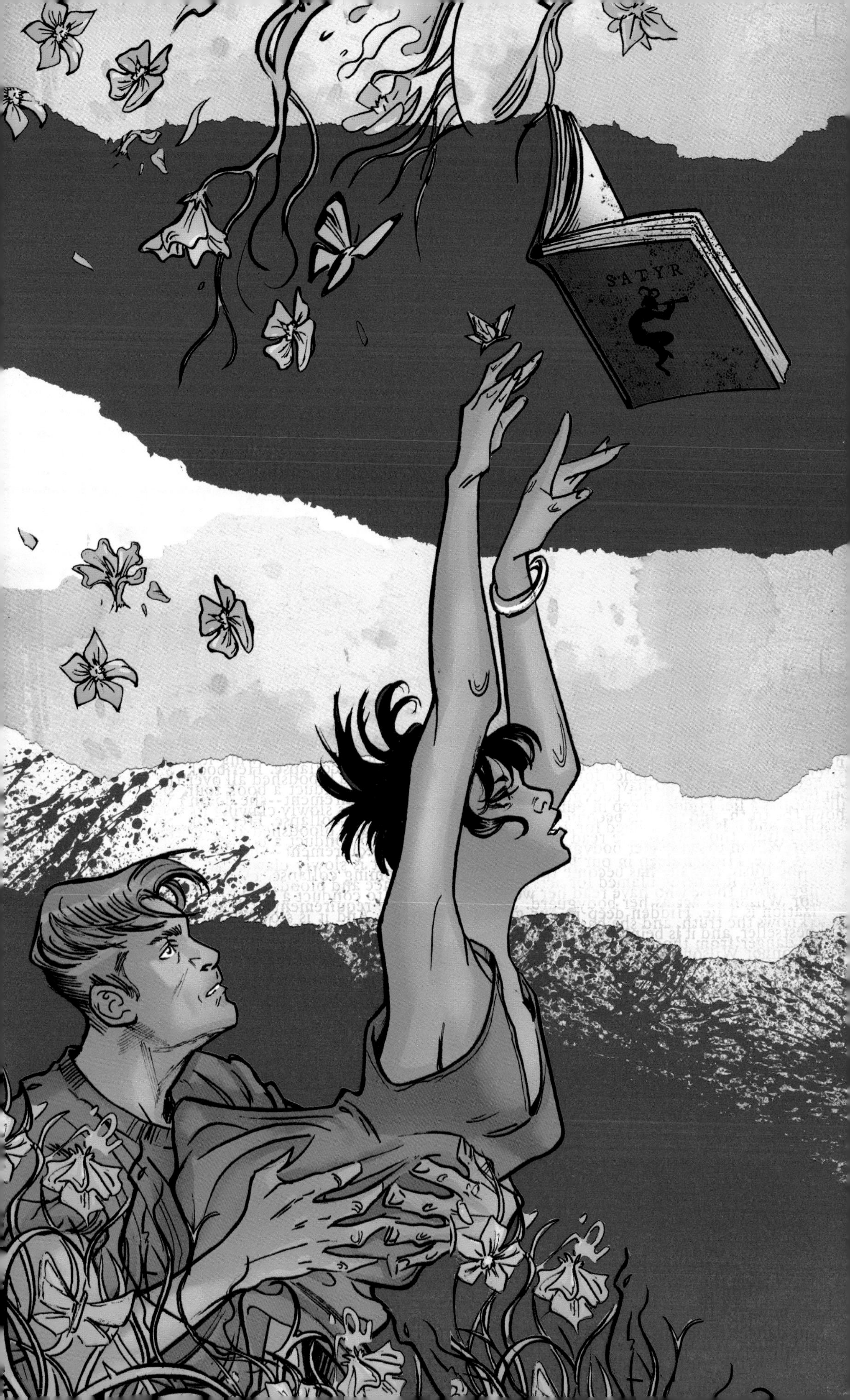
SATYR

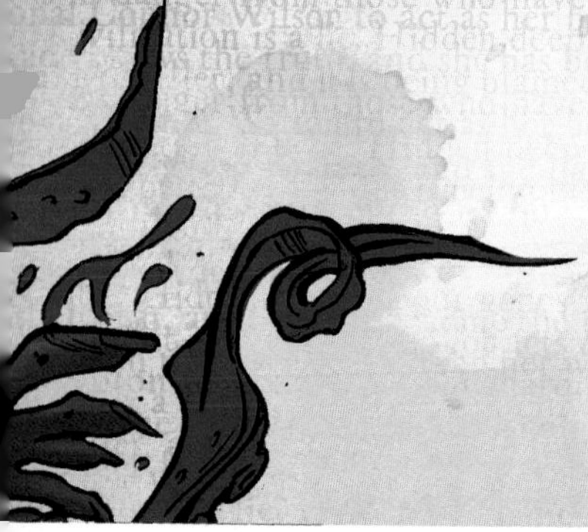

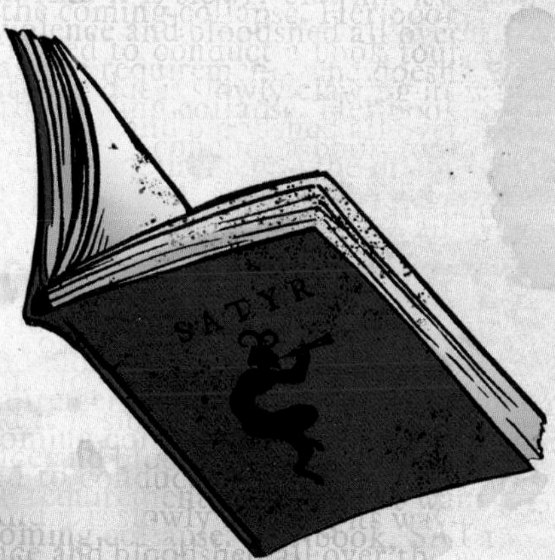

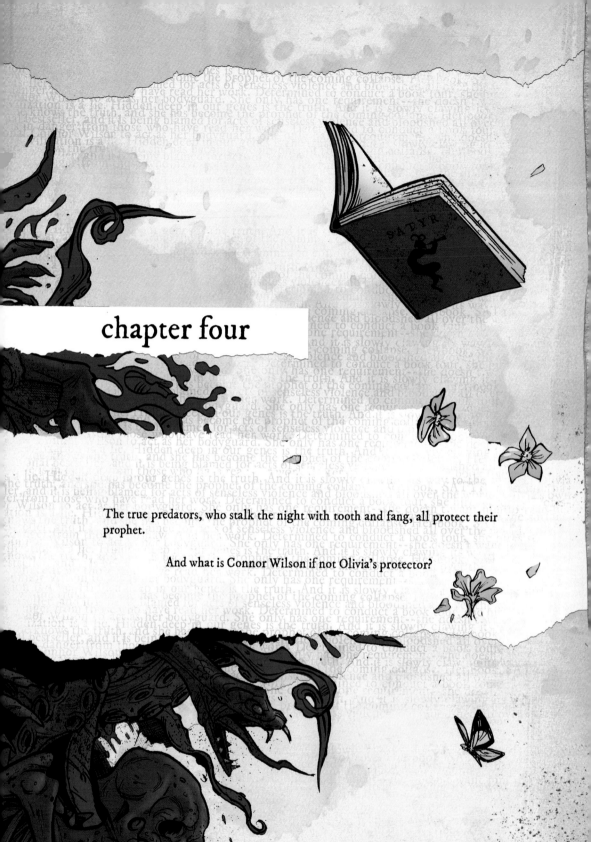

chapter four

The true predators, who stalk the night with tooth and fang, all protect their prophet.

And what is Connor Wilson if not Olivia's protector?

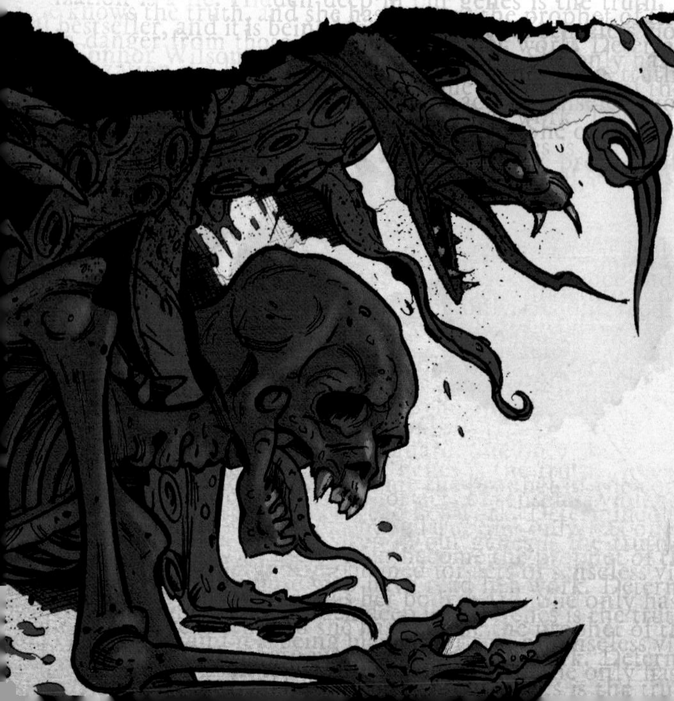

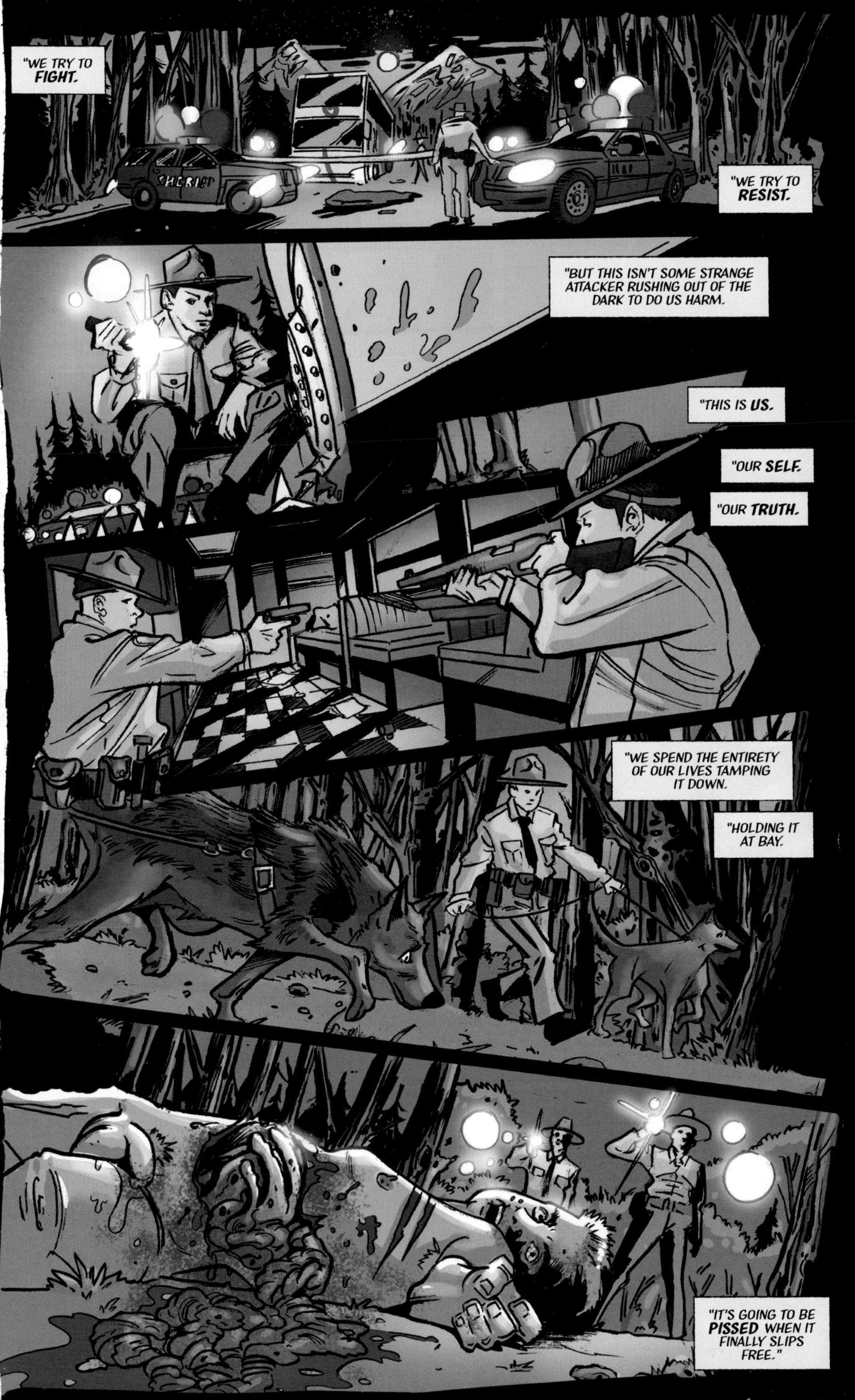
"WE TRY TO FIGHT.
"WE TRY TO RESIST.
"BUT THIS ISN'T SOME STRANGE ATTACKER RUSHING OUT OF THE DARK TO DO US HARM.
"THIS IS US.
"OUR SELF.
"OUR TRUTH.
"WE SPEND THE ENTIRETY OF OUR LIVES TAMPING IT DOWN.
"HOLDING IT AT BAY.
"IT'S GOING TO BE PISSED WHEN IT FINALLY SLIPS FREE."

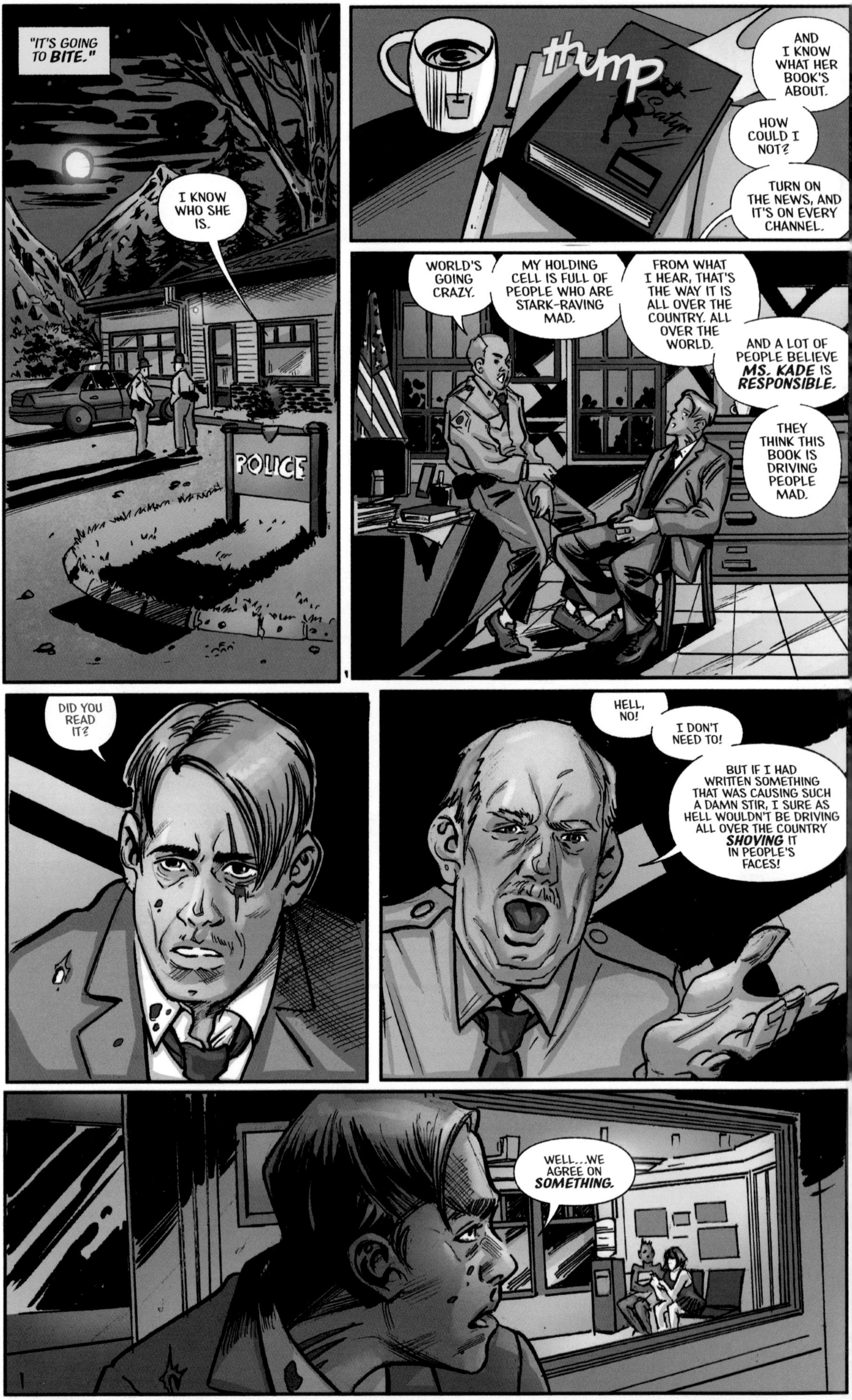
"IT'S GOING TO BITE."
I KNOW WHO SHE IS.
POLICE
thump
Satyr
AND I KNOW WHAT HER BOOK'S ABOUT.
HOW COULD I NOT?
TURN ON THE NEWS, AND IT'S ON EVERY CHANNEL.
WORLD'S GOING CRAZY.
MY HOLDING CELL IS FULL OF PEOPLE WHO ARE STARK-RAVING MAD.
FROM WHAT I HEAR, THAT'S THE WAY IT IS ALL OVER THE COUNTRY. ALL OVER THE WORLD.
AND A LOT OF PEOPLE BELIEVE MS. KADE IS RESPONSIBLE.
THEY THINK THIS BOOK IS DRIVING PEOPLE MAD.
DID YOU READ IT?
HELL, NO!
I DON'T NEED TO!
BUT IF I HAD WRITTEN SOMETHING THAT WAS CAUSING SUCH A DAMN STIR, I SURE AS HELL WOULDN'T BE DRIVING ALL OVER THE COUNTRY SHOVING IT IN PEOPLE'S FACES!
WELL...WE AGREE ON SOMETHING.

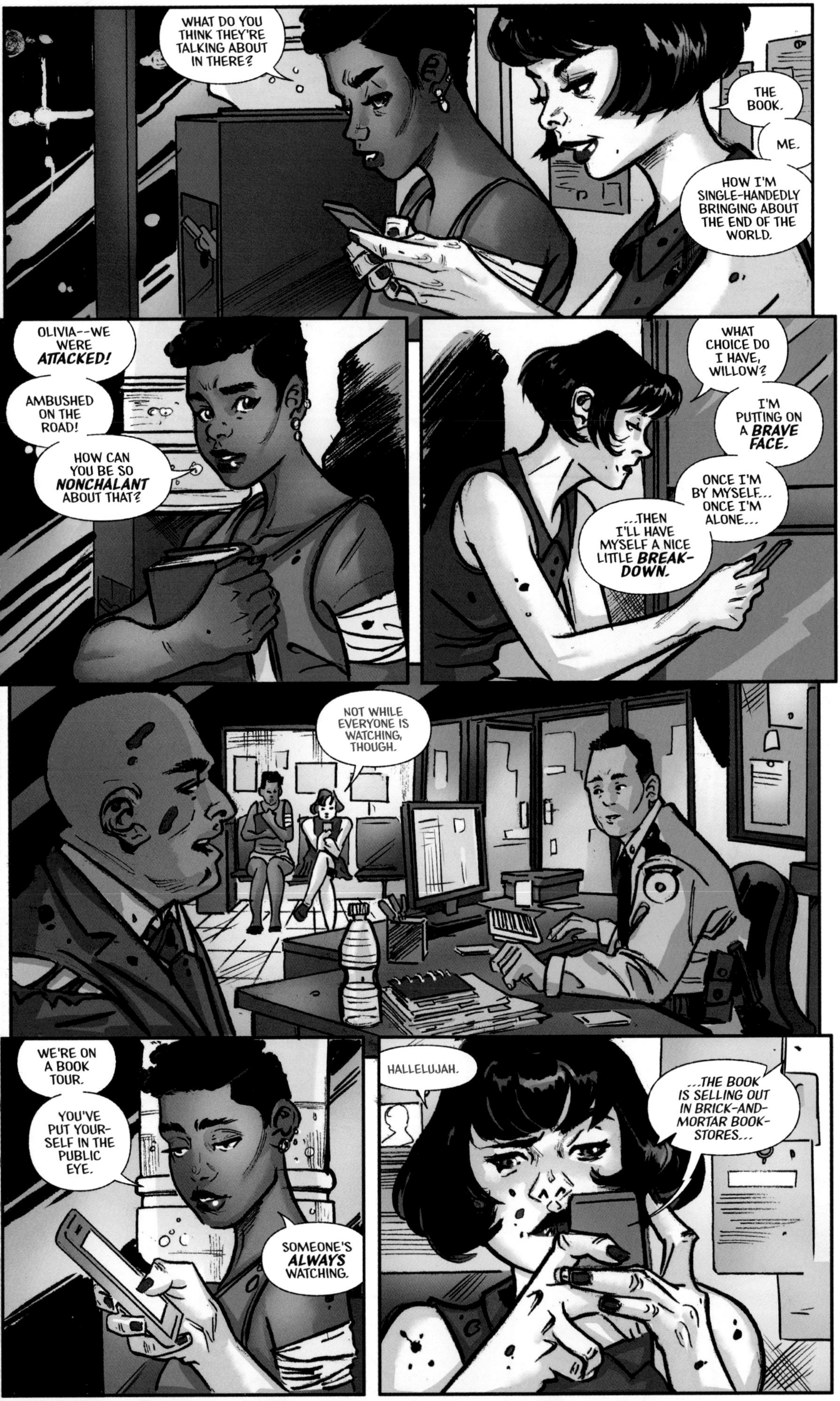
WHAT DO YOU THINK THEY'RE TALKING ABOUT IN THERE?
THE BOOK.
ME.
HOW I'M SINGLE-HANDEDLY BRINGING ABOUT THE END OF THE WORLD.
OLIVIA--WE WERE ATTACKED!
AMBUSHED ON THE ROAD!
HOW CAN YOU BE SO NONCHALANT ABOUT THAT?
WHAT CHOICE DO I HAVE, WILLOW?
I'M PUTTING ON A BRAVE FACE.
ONCE I'M BY MYSELF... ONCE I'M ALONE...
...THEN I'LL HAVE MYSELF A NICE LITTLE BREAK-DOWN.
NOT WHILE EVERYONE IS WATCHING, THOUGH.
WE'RE ON A BOOK TOUR.
YOU'VE PUT YOUR-SELF IN THE PUBLIC EYE.
SOMEONE'S ALWAYS WATCHING.
HALLELUJAH.
...THE BOOK IS SELLING OUT IN BRICK-AND-MORTAR BOOK-STORES...

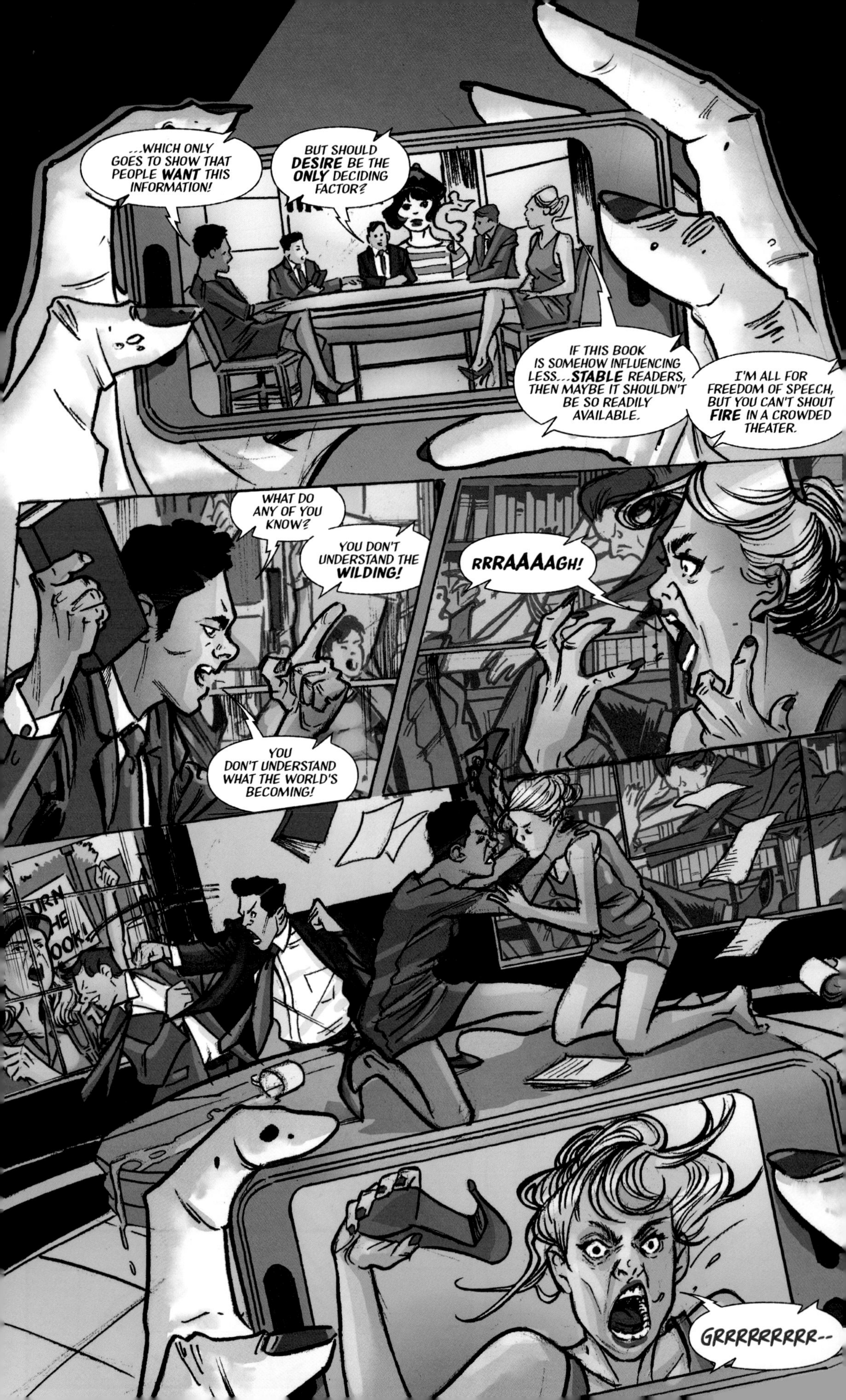
...WHICH ONLY GOES TO SHOW THAT PEOPLE WANT THIS INFORMATION!
BUT SHOULD DESIRE BE THE ONLY DECIDING FACTOR?
IF THIS BOOK IS SOMEHOW INFLUENCING LESS...STABLE READERS, THEN MAYBE IT SHOULDN'T BE SO READILY AVAILABLE.
I'M ALL FOR FREEDOM OF SPEECH, BUT YOU CAN'T SHOUT FIRE IN A CROWDED THEATER.
WHAT DO ANY OF YOU KNOW?
YOU DON'T UNDERSTAND THE WILDING!
YOU DON'T UNDERSTAND WHAT THE WORLD'S BECOMING!
RRRAAAAGH!
GRRRRRRRRR--

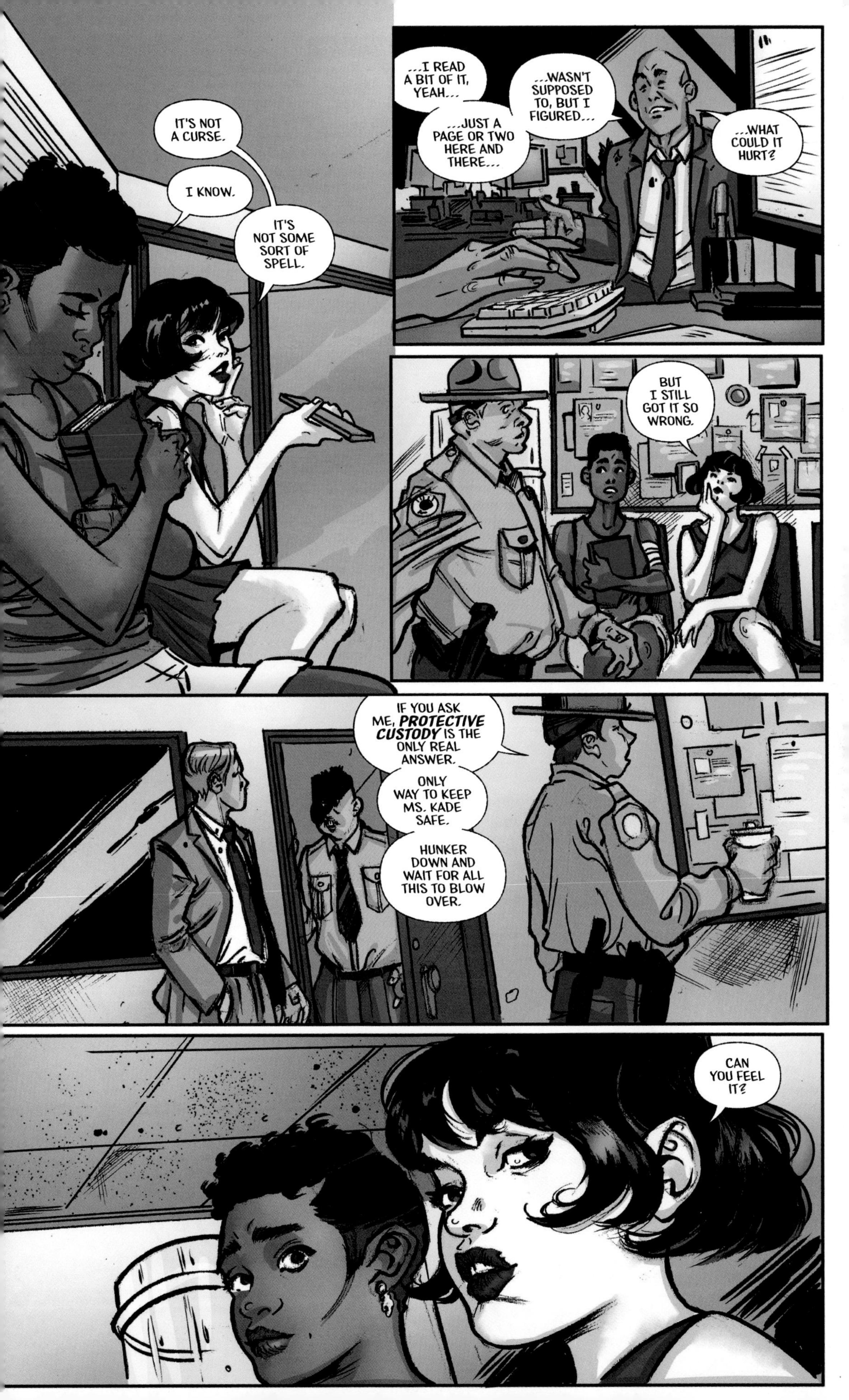
IT'S NOT A CURSE.
I KNOW.
IT'S NOT SOME SORT OF SPELL.
...I READ A BIT OF IT, YEAH...
...JUST A PAGE OR TWO HERE AND THERE...
...WASN'T SUPPOSED TO, BUT I FIGURED...
...WHAT COULD IT HURT?
BUT I STILL GOT IT SO WRONG.
IF YOU ASK ME, PROTECTIVE CUSTODY IS THE ONLY REAL ANSWER.
ONLY WAY TO KEEP MS. KADE SAFE.
HUNKER DOWN AND WAIT FOR ALL THIS TO BLOW OVER.
CAN YOU FEEL IT?

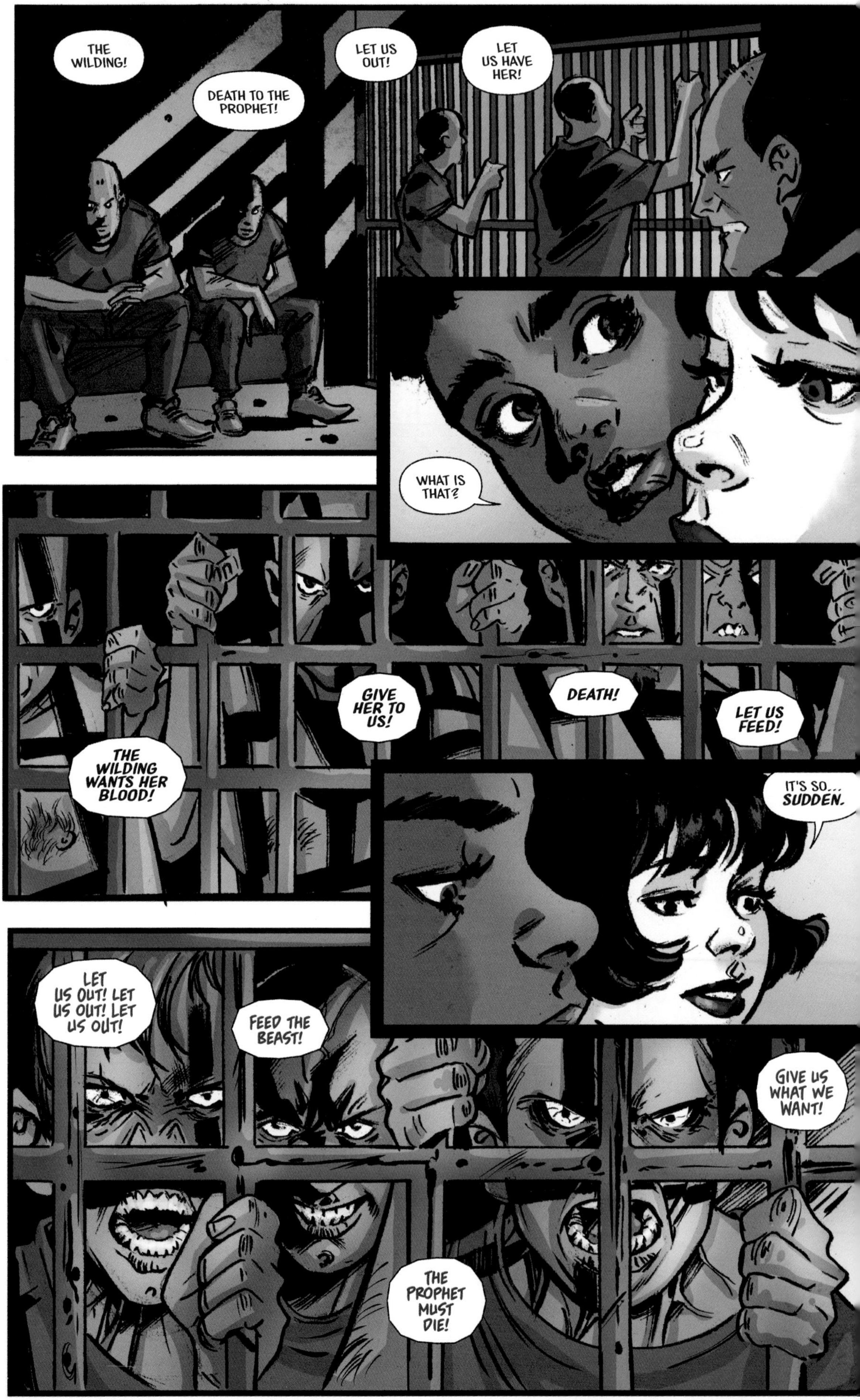
THE WILDING!
DEATH TO THE PROPHET!
LET US OUT!
LET US HAVE HER!
WHAT IS THAT?
GIVE HER TO US!
DEATH!
LET US FEED!
THE WILDING WANTS HER BLOOD!
IT'S SO... SUDDEN.
LET US OUT! LET US OUT! LET US OUT!
FEED THE BEAST!
GIVE US WHAT WE WANT!
THE PROPHET MUST DIE!

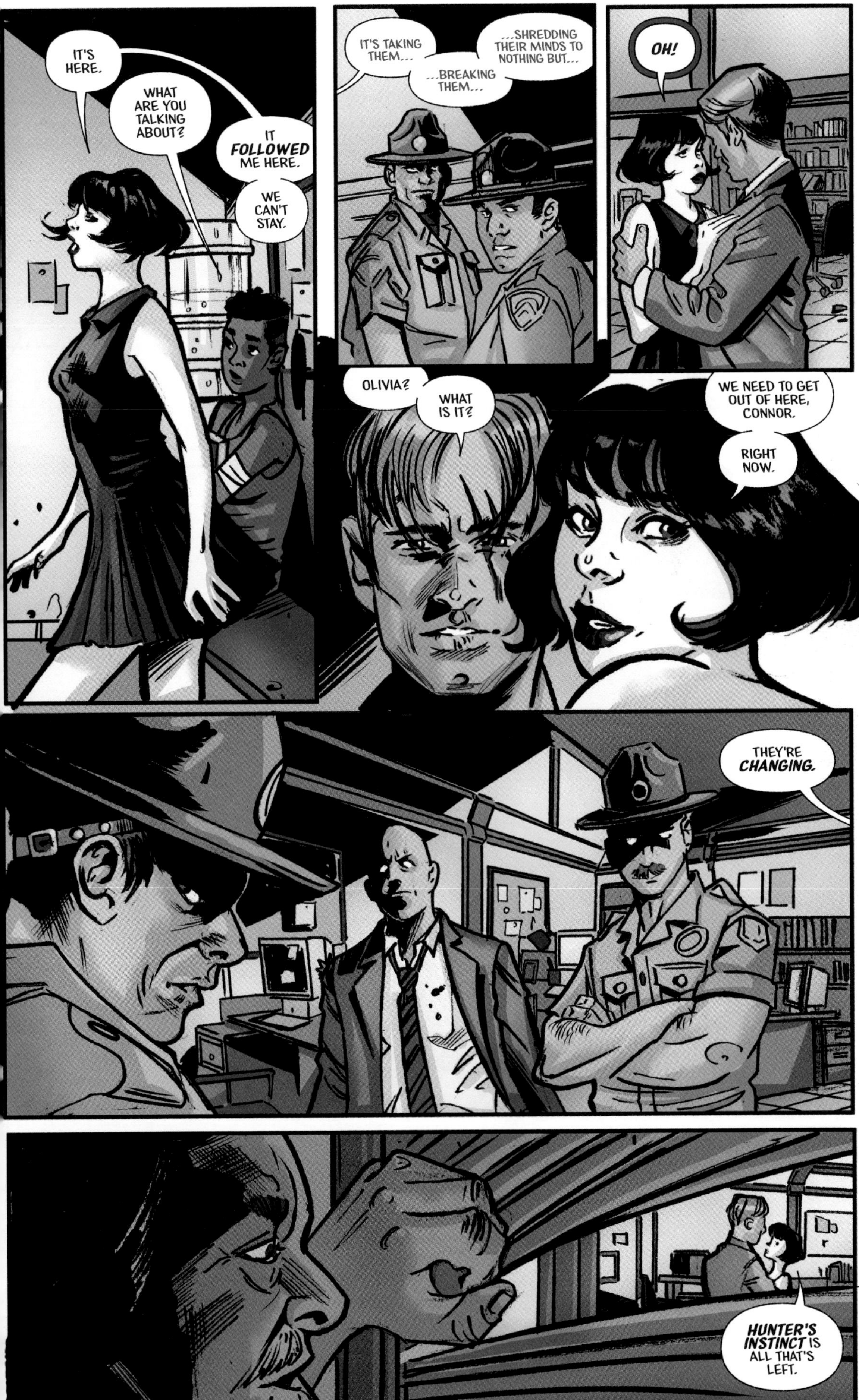
IT'S HERE.
WHAT ARE YOU TALKING ABOUT?
IT *FOLLOWED* ME HERE.
WE CAN'T STAY.
IT'S TAKING THEM...
...BREAKING THEM...
...SHREDDING THEIR MINDS TO NOTHING BUT...
OH!
OLIVIA?
WHAT IS IT?
WE NEED TO GET OUT OF HERE, CONNOR.
RIGHT NOW.
THEY'RE *CHANGING.*
HUNTER'S INSTINCT IS ALL THAT'S LEFT.

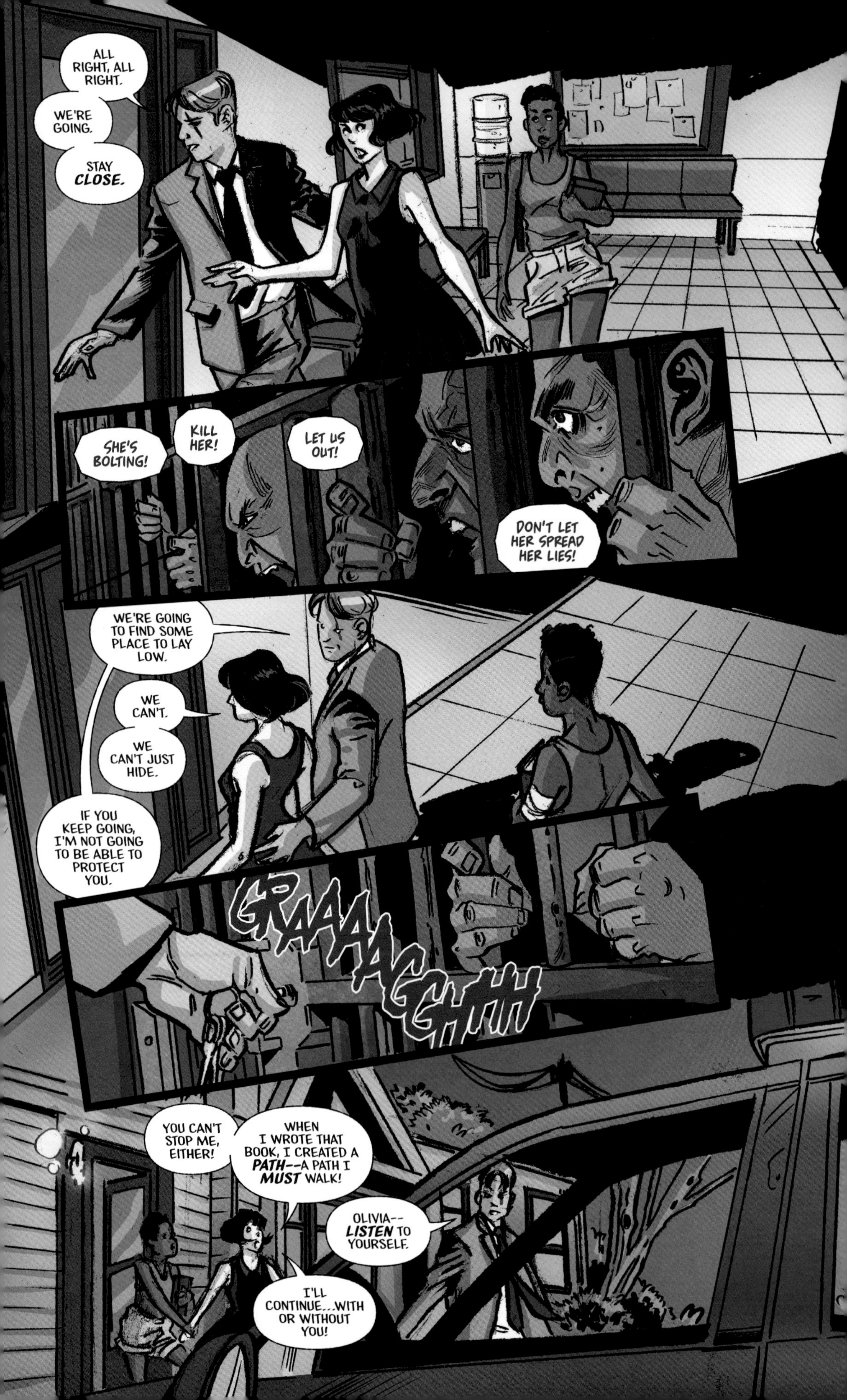
ALL RIGHT, ALL RIGHT.
WE'RE GOING.
STAY CLOSE.
SHE'S BOLTING!
KILL HER!
LET US OUT!
DON'T LET HER SPREAD HER LIES!
WE'RE GOING TO FIND SOME PLACE TO LAY LOW.
WE CAN'T.
WE CAN'T JUST HIDE.
IF YOU KEEP GOING, I'M NOT GOING TO BE ABLE TO PROTECT YOU.
GRAAAAAGGHHH
YOU CAN'T STOP ME, EITHER!
WHEN I WROTE THAT BOOK, I CREATED A PATH--A PATH I MUST WALK!
OLIVIA-- LISTEN TO YOURSELF.
I'LL CONTINUE...WITH OR WITHOUT YOU!

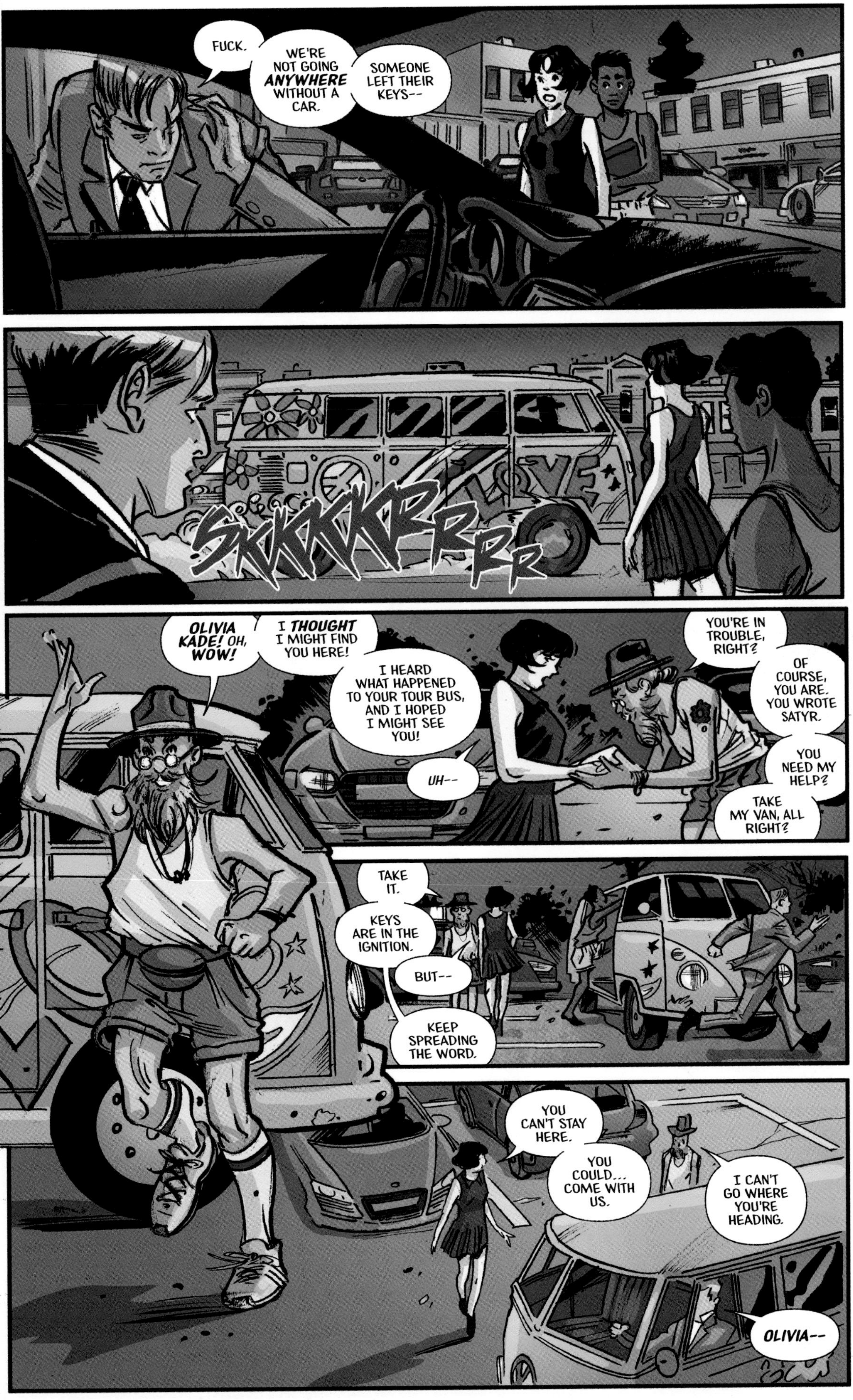
FUCK.
WE'RE NOT GOING ANYWHERE WITHOUT A CAR.
SOMEONE LEFT THEIR KEYS--
SKKKKRRRR
OLIVIA KADE! OH, WOW!
I THOUGHT I MIGHT FIND YOU HERE!
I HEARD WHAT HAPPENED TO YOUR TOUR BUS, AND I HOPED I MIGHT SEE YOU!
UH--
YOU'RE IN TROUBLE, RIGHT?
OF COURSE, YOU ARE. YOU WROTE SATYR.
YOU NEED MY HELP?
TAKE MY VAN, ALL RIGHT?
TAKE IT.
KEYS ARE IN THE IGNITION.
BUT--
KEEP SPREADING THE WORD.
YOU CAN'T STAY HERE.
YOU COULD... COME WITH US.
I CAN'T GO WHERE YOU'RE HEADING.
OLIVIA--

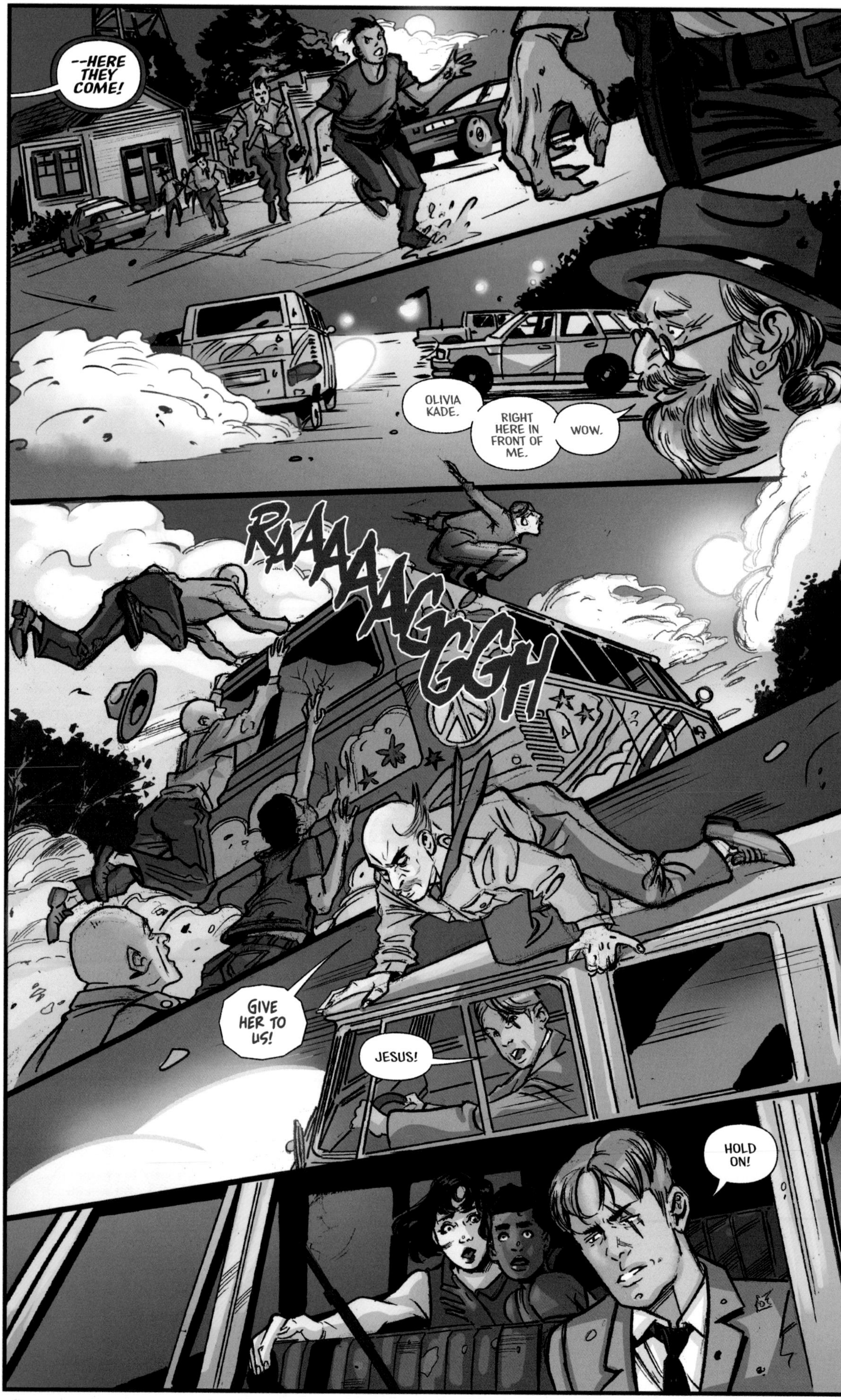
--HERE THEY COME!
OLIVIA KADE.
RIGHT HERE IN FRONT OF ME.
WOW.
RAAAAAGGGH
GIVE HER TO US!
JESUS!
HOLD ON!

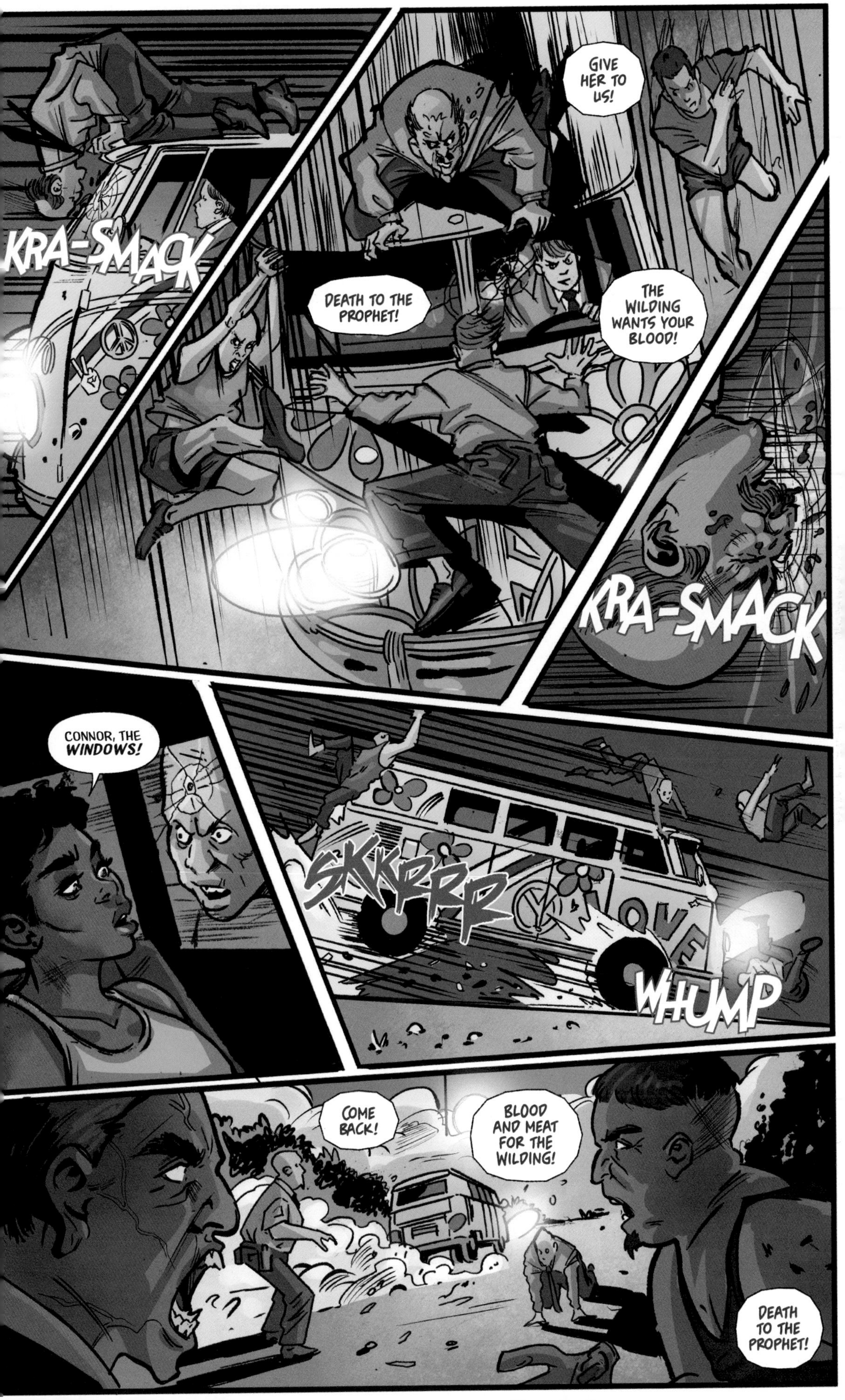
KRA-SMACK
GIVE HER TO US!
DEATH TO THE PROPHET!
THE WILDING WANTS YOUR BLOOD!
KRA-SMACK
CONNOR, THE WINDOWS!
SKKRRR
WHUMP
COME BACK!
BLOOD AND MEAT FOR THE WILDING!
DEATH TO THE PROPHET!

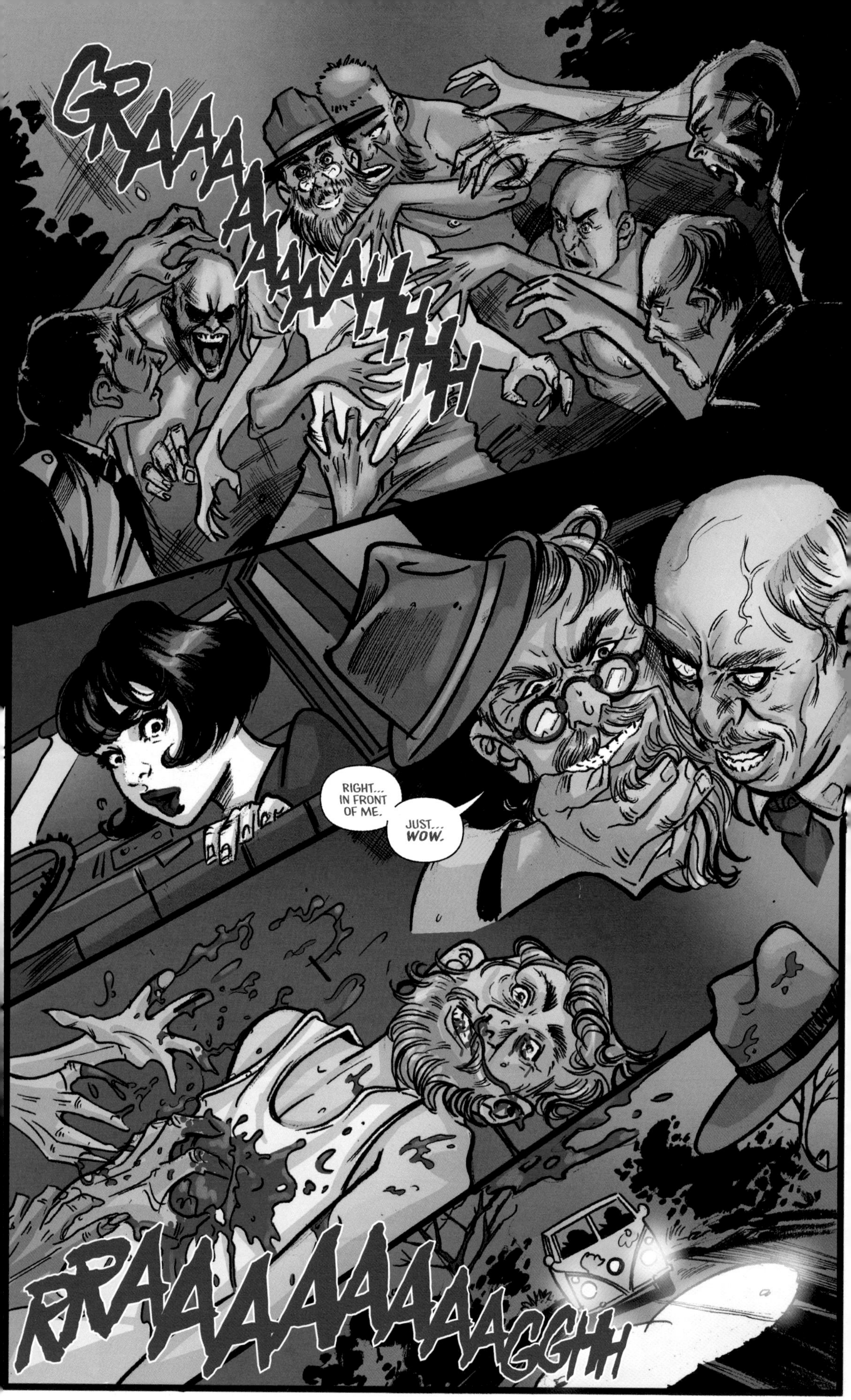
GRAAAAAAAAHHHH
RIGHT... IN FRONT OF ME.
JUST... WOW.
RRAAAAAAAAAGGHH

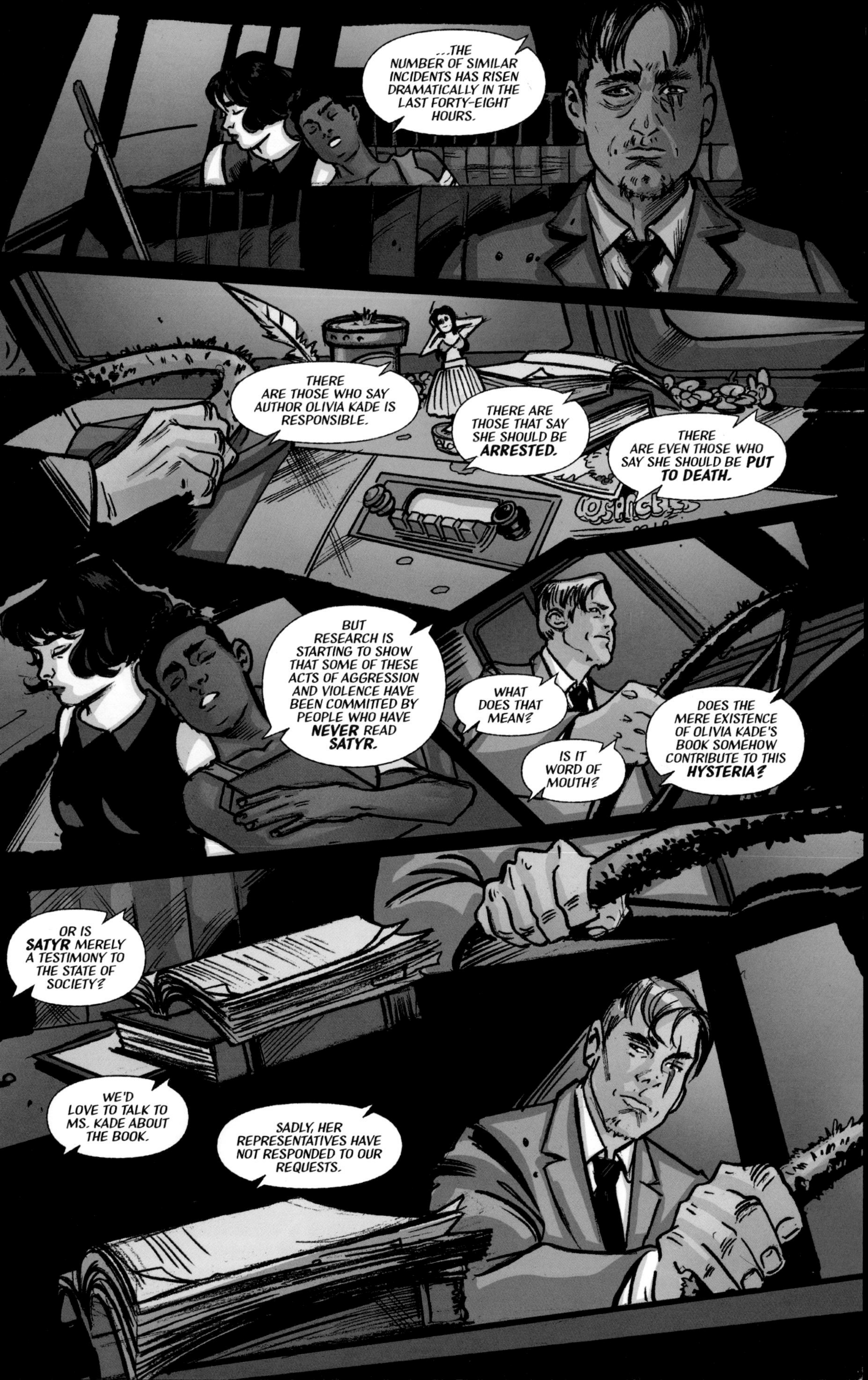
...THE NUMBER OF SIMILAR INCIDENTS HAS RISEN DRAMATICALLY IN THE LAST FORTY-EIGHT HOURS.
THERE ARE THOSE WHO SAY AUTHOR OLIVIA KADE IS RESPONSIBLE.
THERE ARE THOSE THAT SAY SHE SHOULD BE **ARRESTED.**
THERE ARE EVEN THOSE WHO SAY SHE SHOULD BE **PUT TO DEATH.**
BUT RESEARCH IS STARTING TO SHOW THAT SOME OF THESE ACTS OF AGGRESSION AND VIOLENCE HAVE BEEN COMMITTED BY PEOPLE WHO HAVE **NEVER** READ **SATYR.**
WHAT DOES THAT MEAN?
IS IT WORD OF MOUTH?
DOES THE MERE EXISTENCE OF OLIVIA KADE'S BOOK SOMEHOW CONTRIBUTE TO THIS **HYSTERIA?**
OR IS **SATYR** MERELY A TESTIMONY TO THE STATE OF SOCIETY?
WE'D LOVE TO TALK TO MS. KADE ABOUT THE BOOK.
SADLY, HER REPRESENTATIVES HAVE NOT RESPONDED TO OUR REQUESTS.

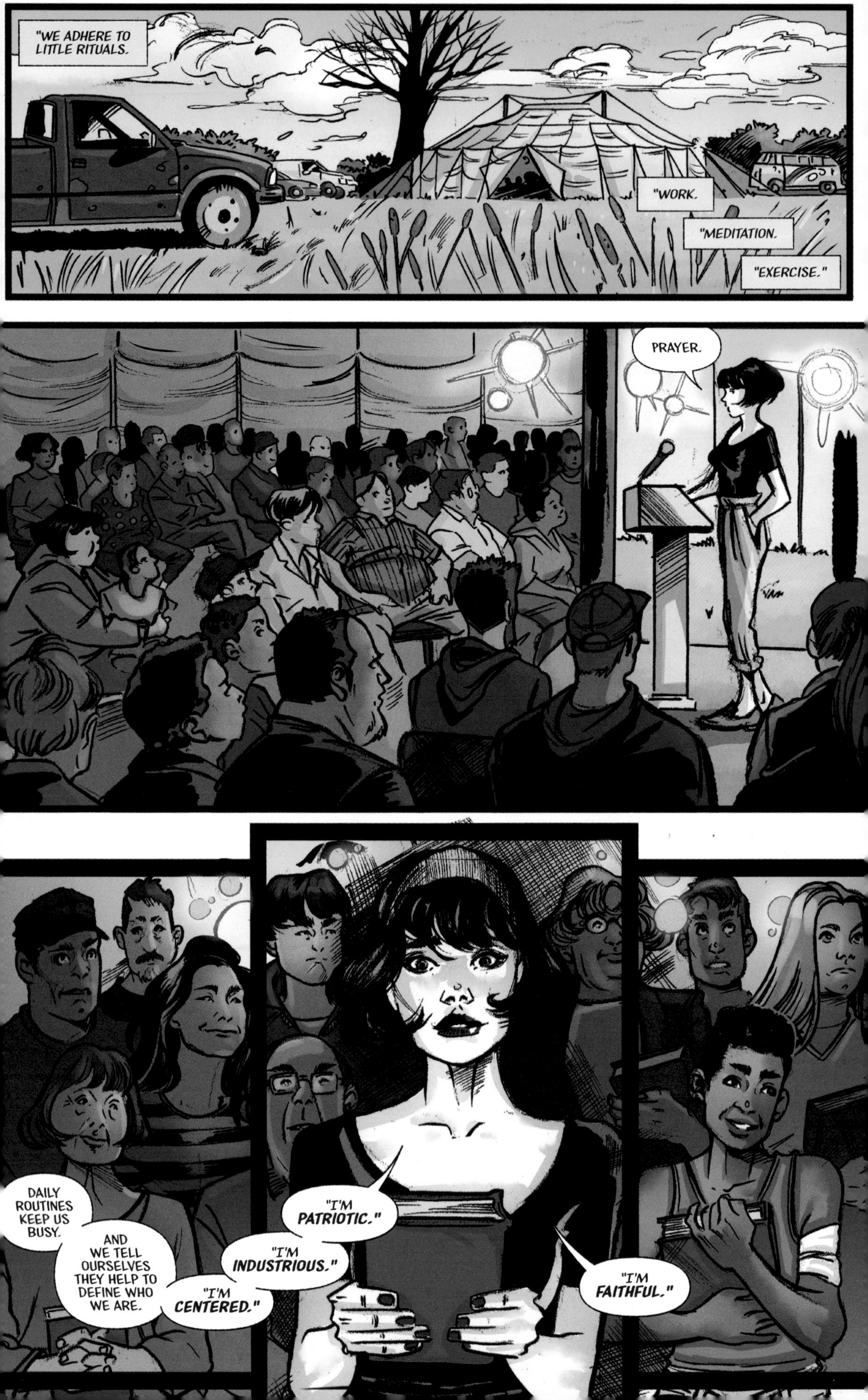
"WE ADHERE TO LITTLE RITUALS.
"WORK.
"MEDITATION.
"EXERCISE."
PRAYER.
DAILY ROUTINES KEEP US BUSY.
AND WE TELL OURSELVES THEY HELP TO DEFINE WHO WE ARE.
"I'M CENTERED."
"I'M INDUSTRIOUS."
"I'M PATRIOTIC."
"I'M FAITHFUL."

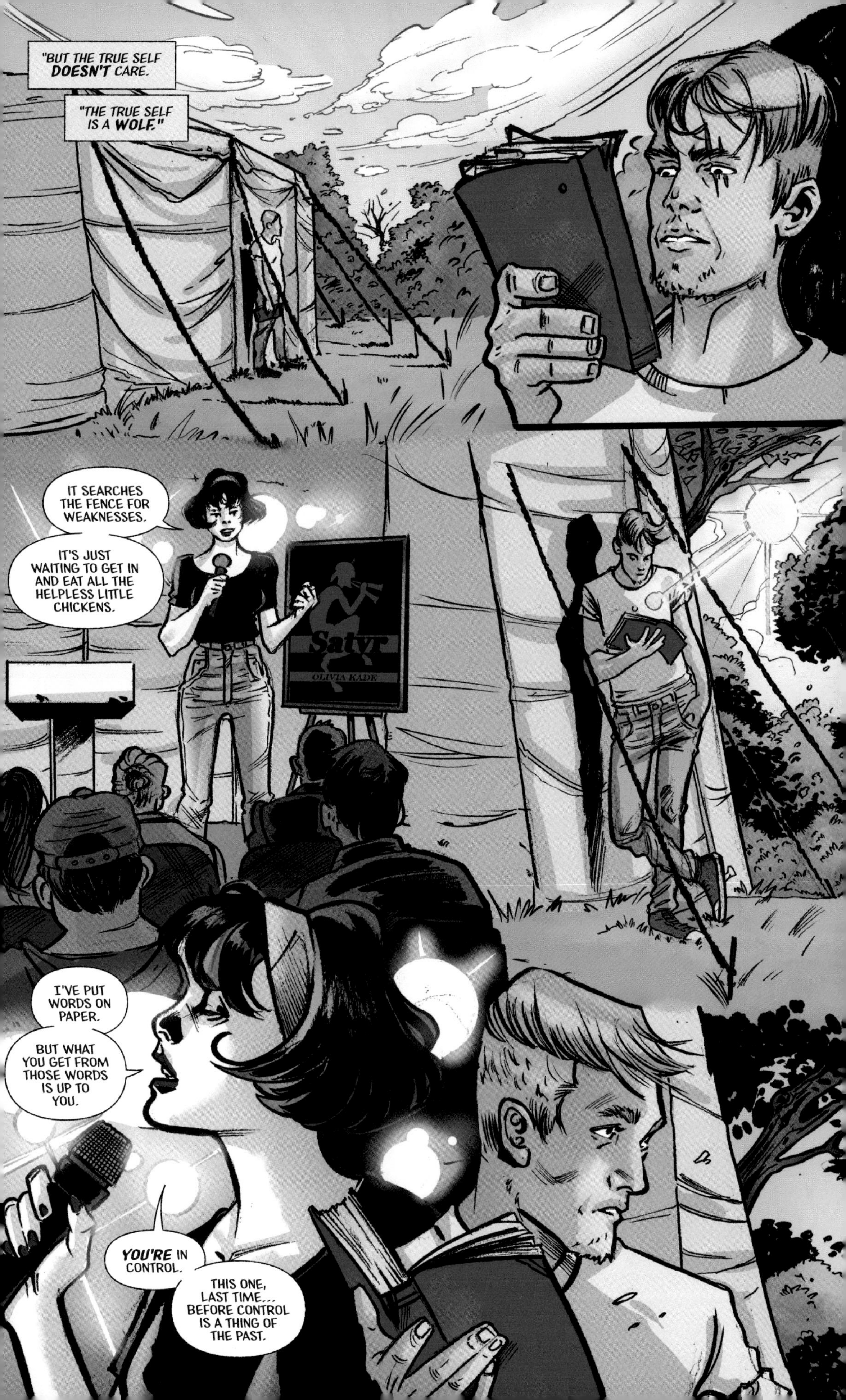
"BUT THE TRUE SELF DOESN'T CARE.
"THE TRUE SELF IS A WOLF."
IT SEARCHES THE FENCE FOR WEAKNESSES.
IT'S JUST WAITING TO GET IN AND EAT ALL THE HELPLESS LITTLE CHICKENS.
Satyr
OLIVIA KADE
I'VE PUT WORDS ON PAPER.
BUT WHAT YOU GET FROM THOSE WORDS IS UP TO YOU.
YOU'RE IN CONTROL.
THIS ONE, LAST TIME... BEFORE CONTROL IS A THING OF THE PAST.

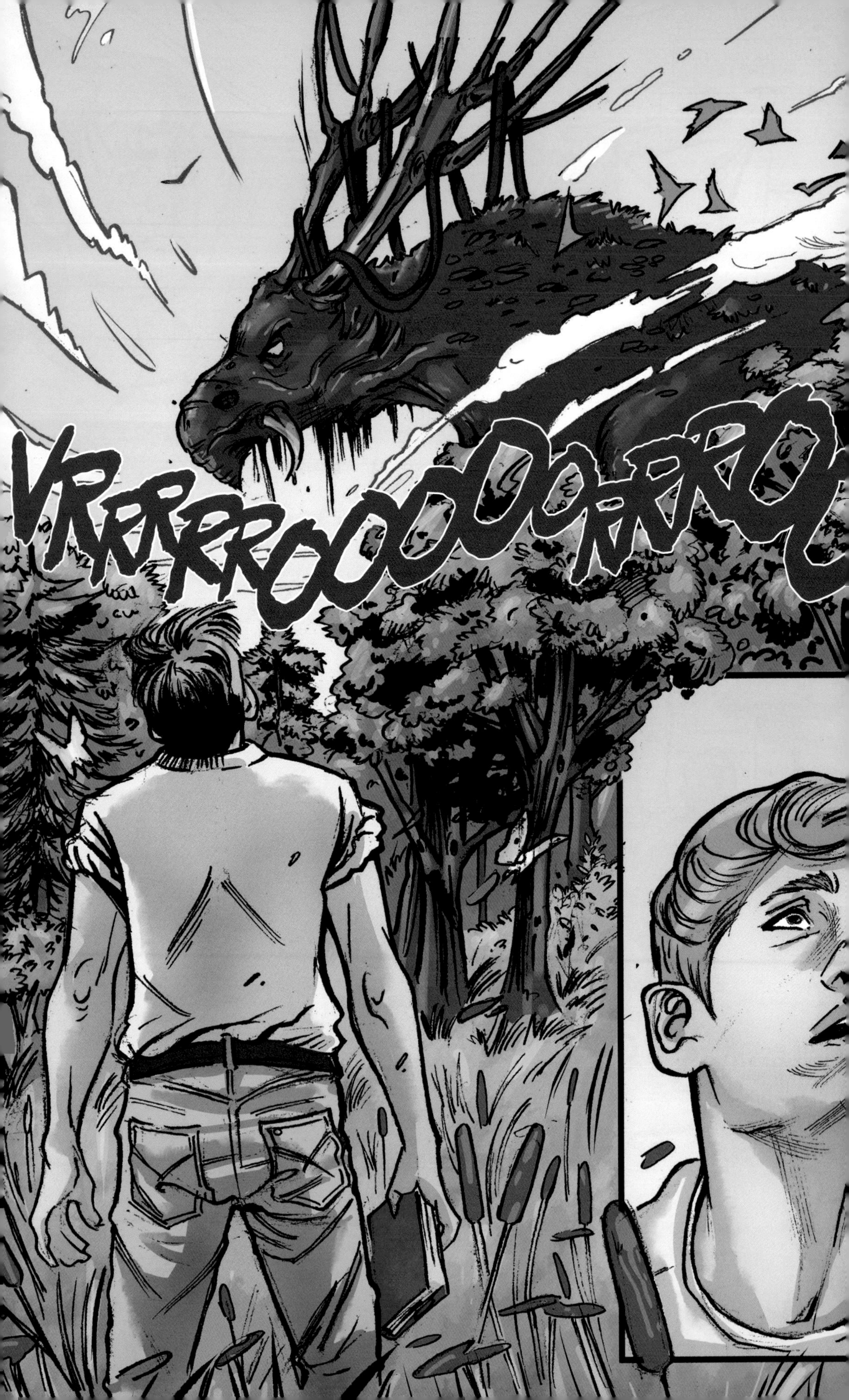
VRRRRROOOOOOORRRO

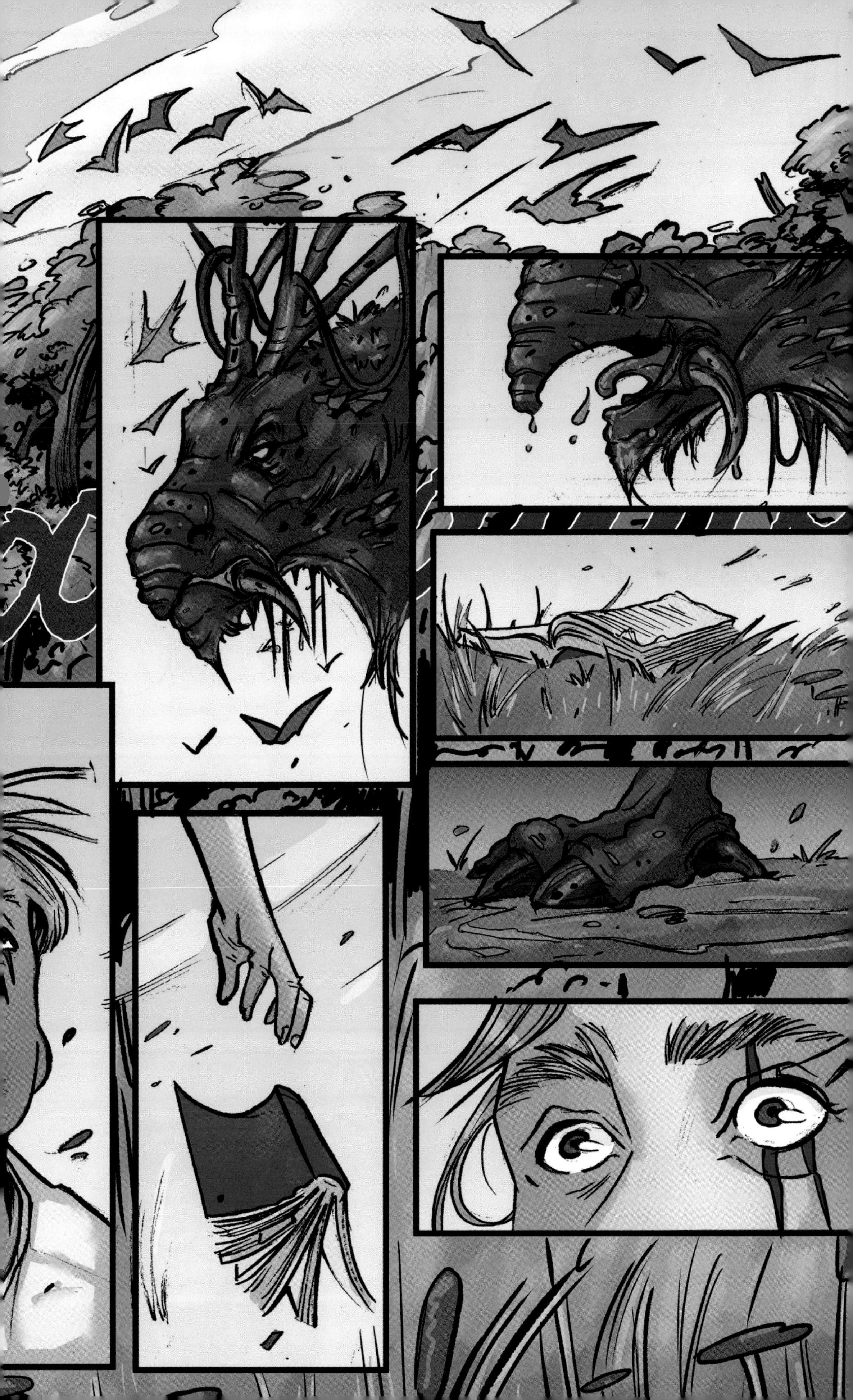

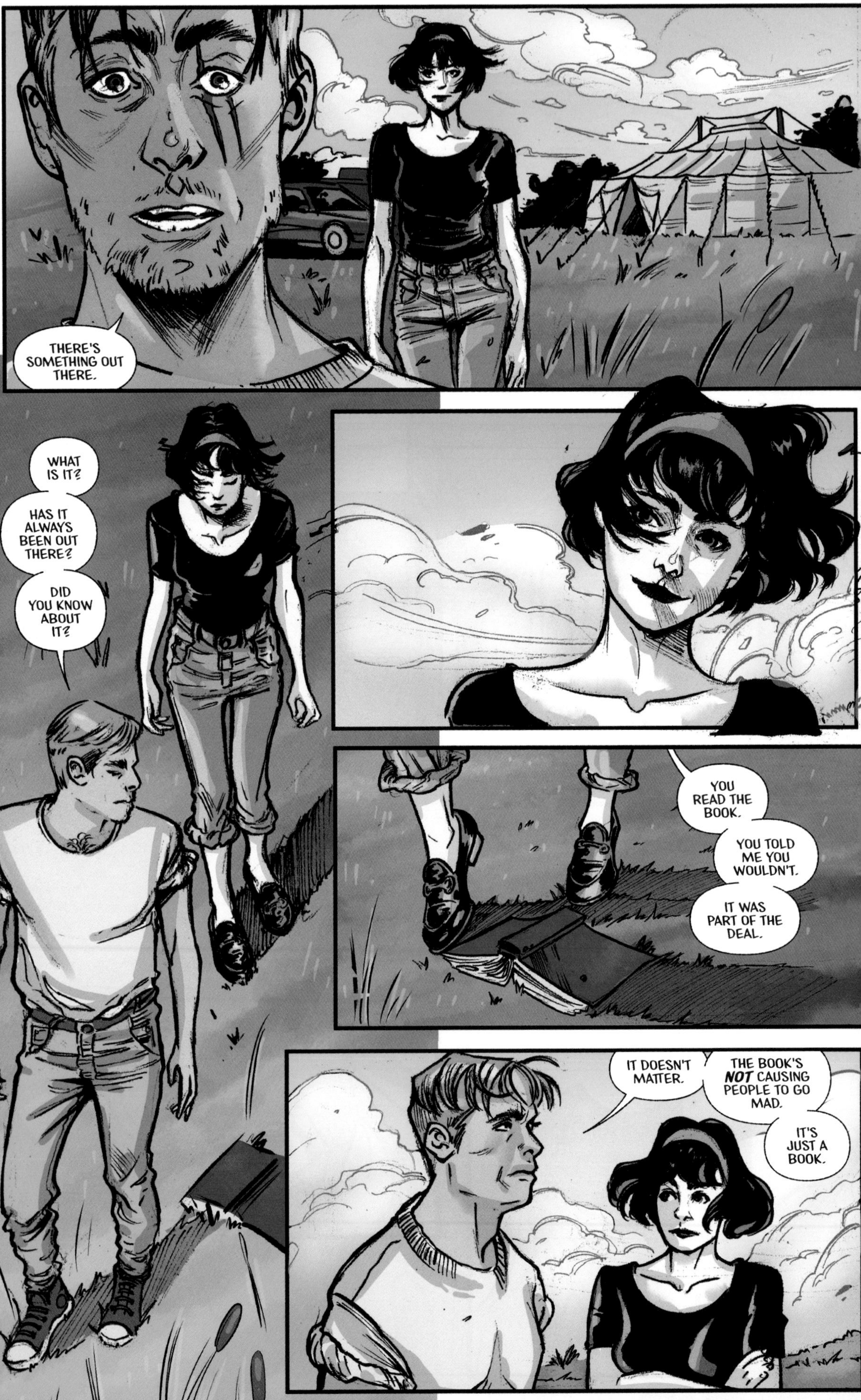
THERE'S SOMETHING OUT THERE.
WHAT IS IT?
HAS IT ALWAYS BEEN OUT THERE?
DID YOU KNOW ABOUT IT?
YOU READ THE BOOK.
YOU TOLD ME YOU WOULDN'T.
IT WAS PART OF THE DEAL.
IT DOESN'T MATTER.
THE BOOK'S ***NOT*** CAUSING PEOPLE TO GO MAD.
IT'S JUST A BOOK.

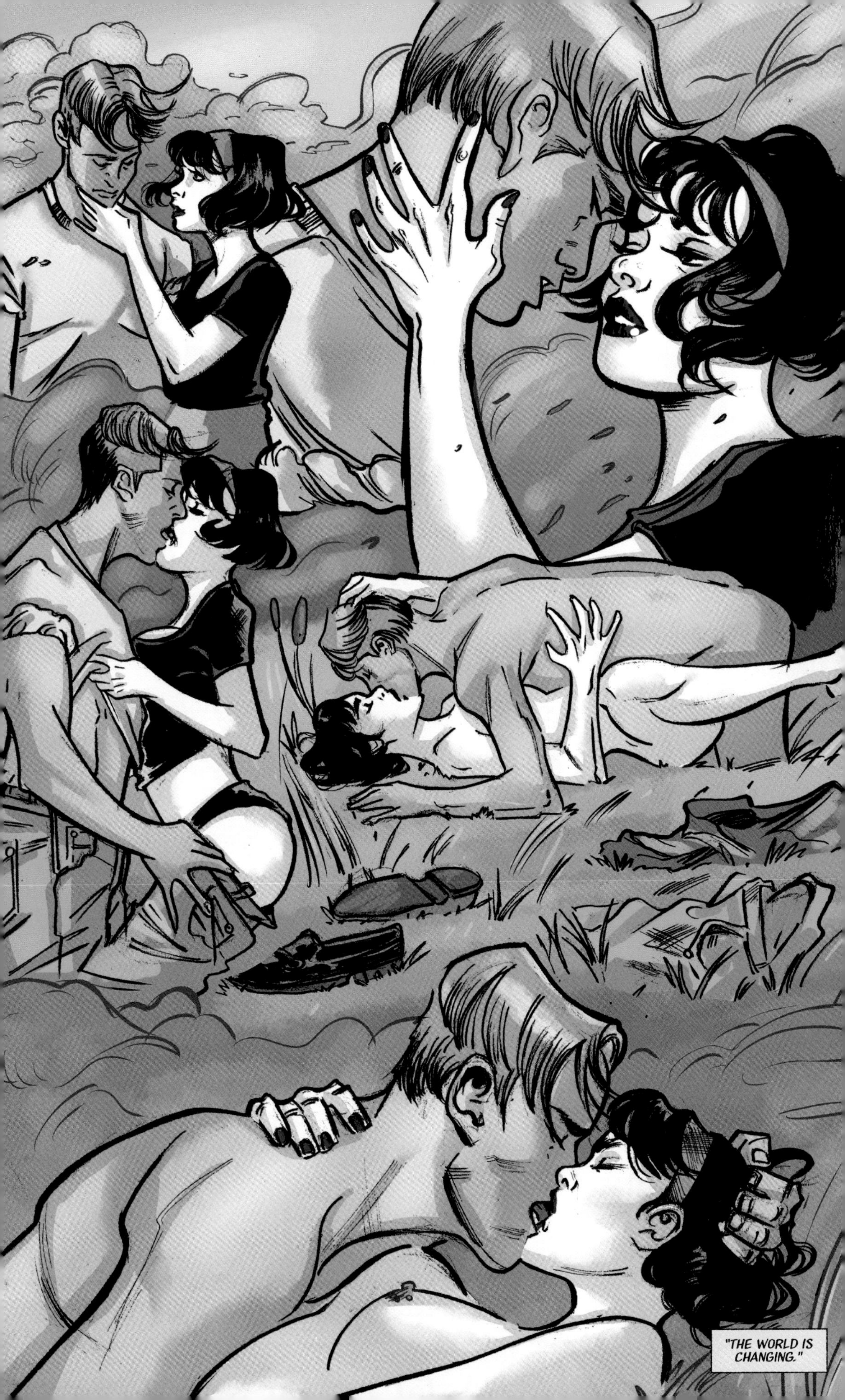
"THE WORLD IS CHANGING."

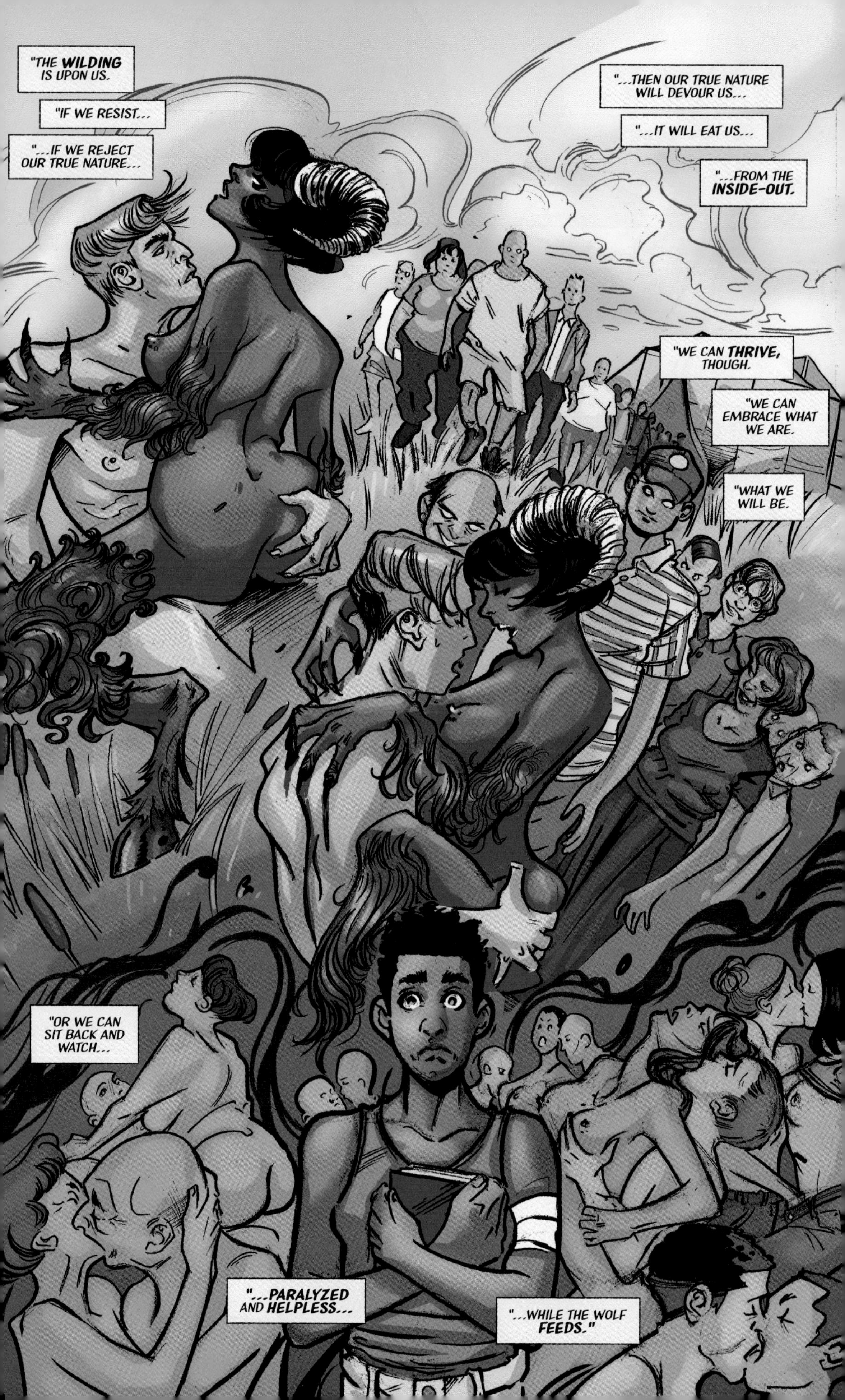
"THE WILDING IS UPON US.
"IF WE RESIST...
"...IF WE REJECT OUR TRUE NATURE...
"...THEN OUR TRUE NATURE WILL DEVOUR US...
"...IT WILL EAT US...
"...FROM THE INSIDE-OUT.
"WE CAN THRIVE, THOUGH.
"WE CAN EMBRACE WHAT WE ARE.
"WHAT WE WILL BE.
"OR WE CAN SIT BACK AND WATCH...
"...PARALYZED AND HELPLESS...
"...WHILE THE WOLF FEEDS."

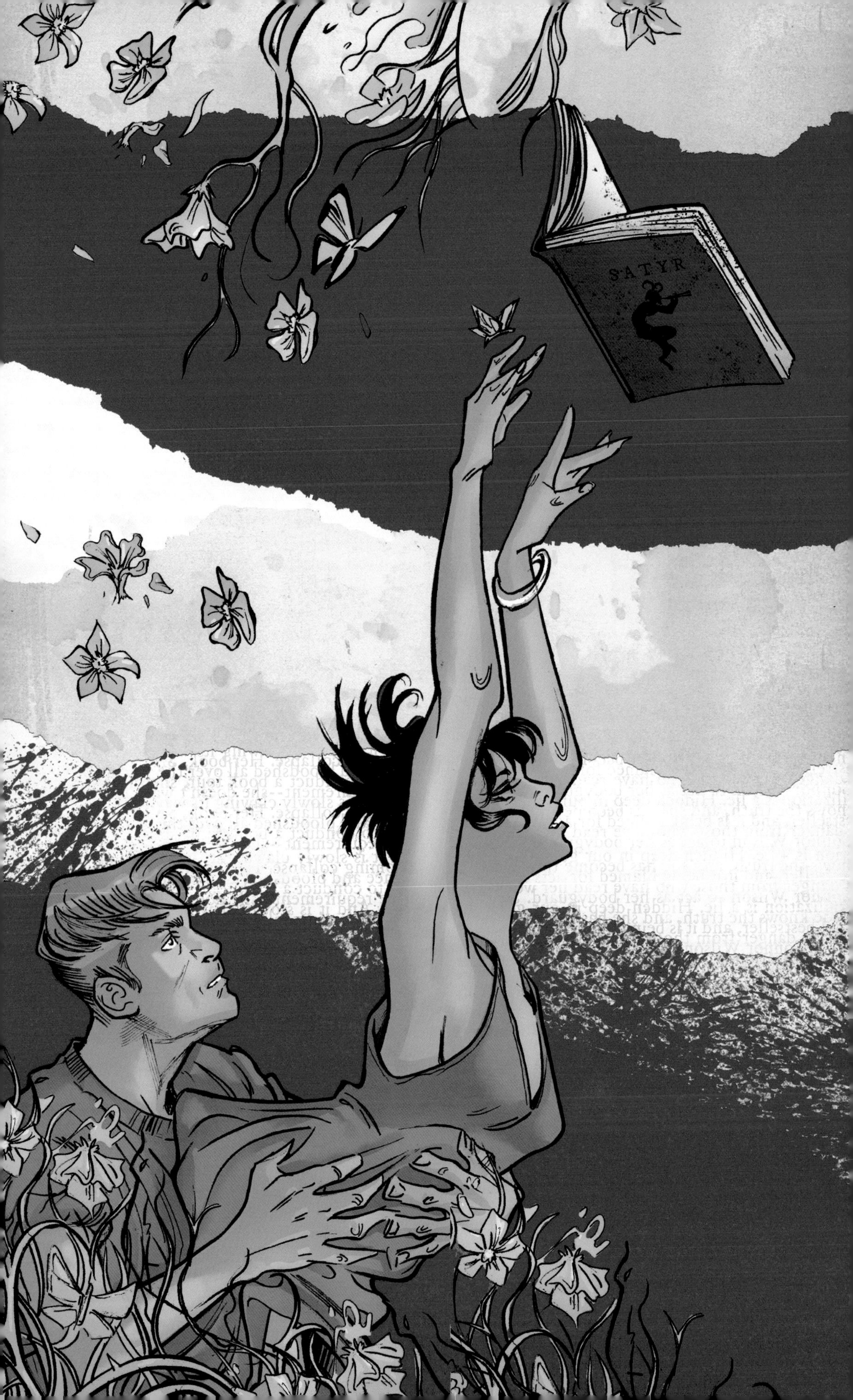
SATYR

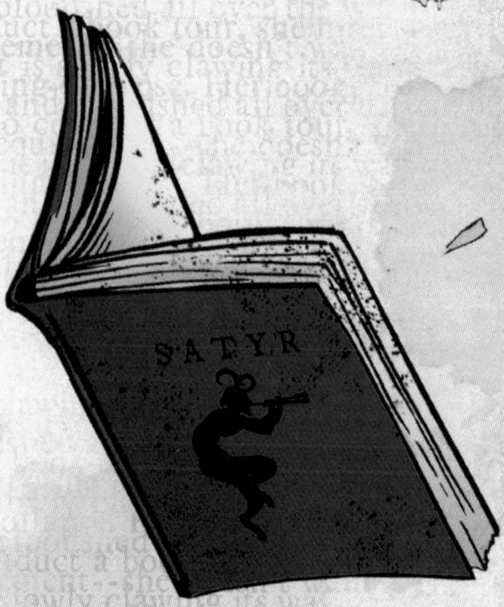
SATYR

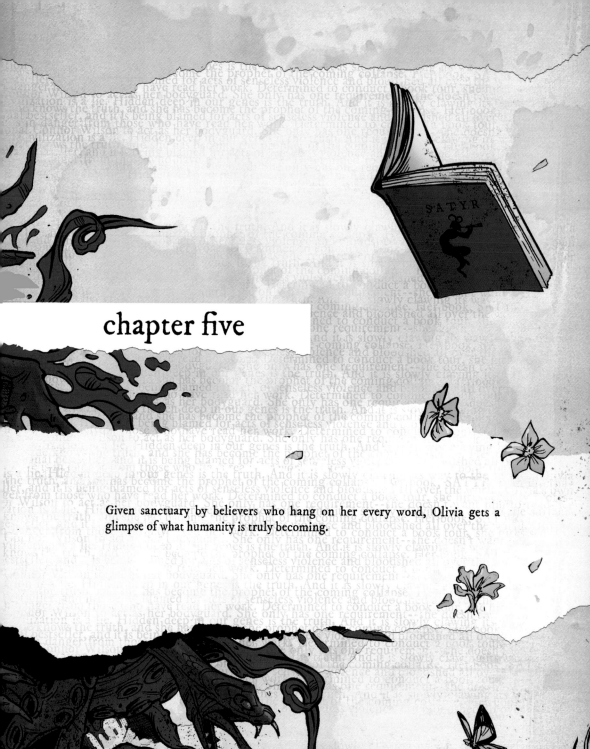

chapter five

Given sanctuary by believers who hang on her every word, Olivia gets a glimpse of what humanity is truly becoming.

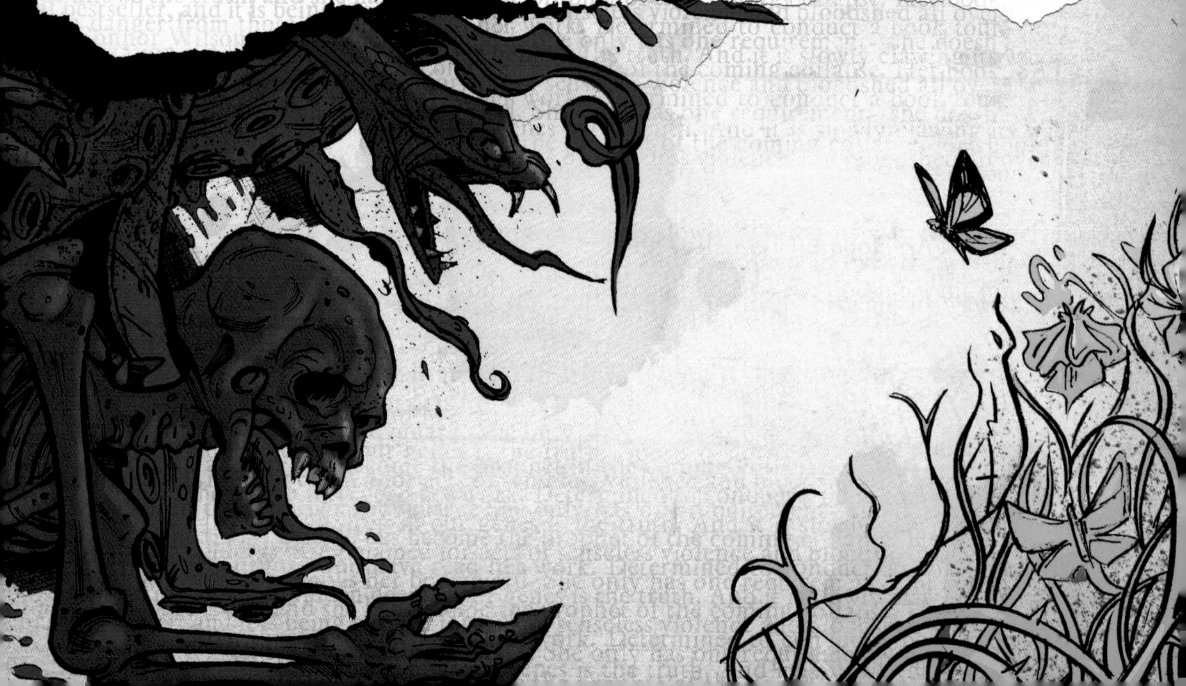

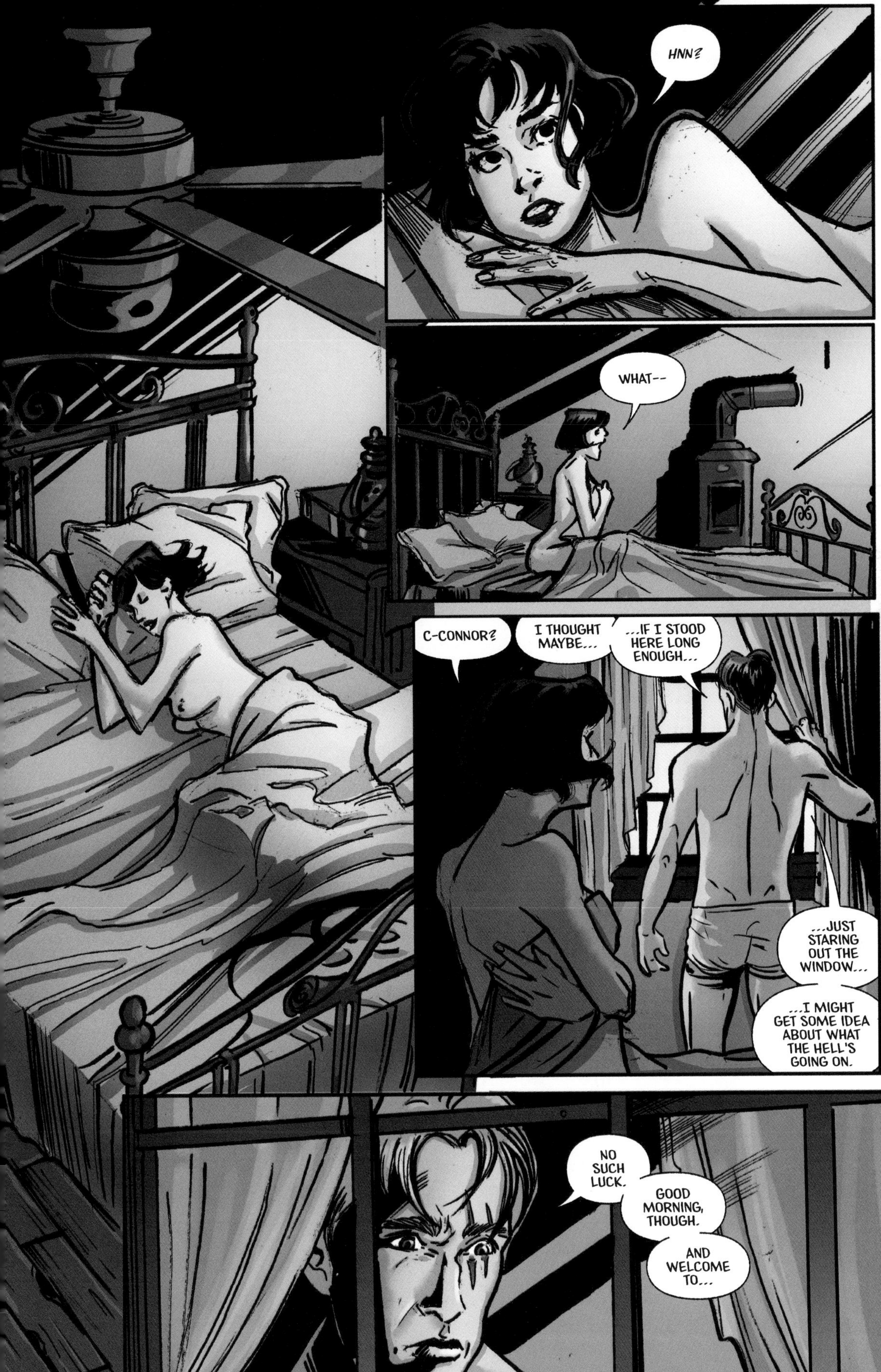
HNN?
WHAT--
C-CONNOR?
I THOUGHT MAYBE...
...IF I STOOD HERE LONG ENOUGH...
...JUST STARING OUT THE WINDOW...
...I MIGHT GET SOME IDEA ABOUT WHAT THE HELL'S GOING ON.
NO SUCH LUCK.
GOOD MORNING, THOUGH.
AND WELCOME TO...

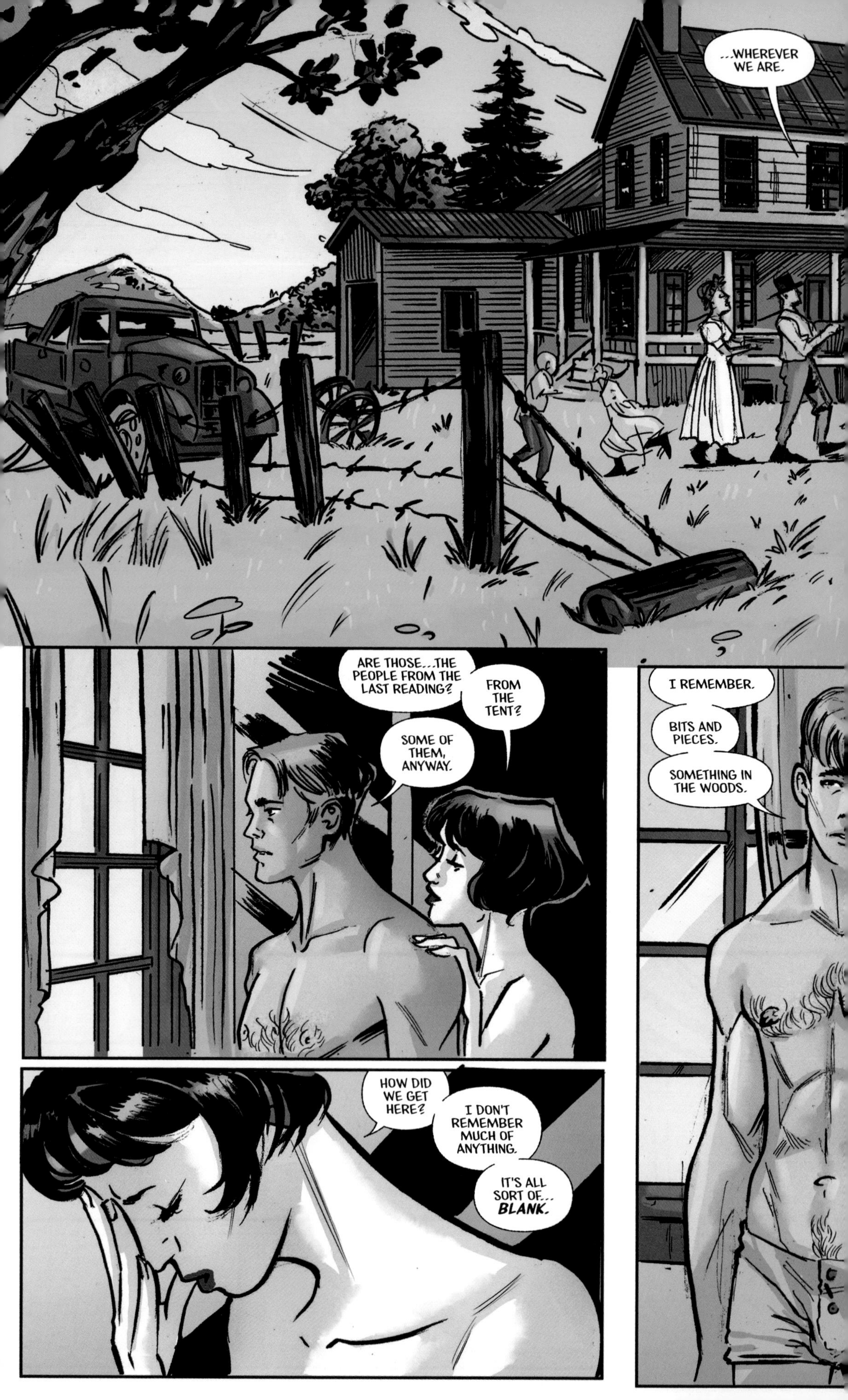
...WHEREVER WE ARE.
ARE THOSE...THE PEOPLE FROM THE LAST READING?
FROM THE TENT?
SOME OF THEM, ANYWAY.
I REMEMBER.
BITS AND PIECES.
SOMETHING IN THE WOODS.
HOW DID WE GET HERE?
I DON'T REMEMBER MUCH OF ANYTHING.
IT'S ALL SORT OF... *BLANK.*

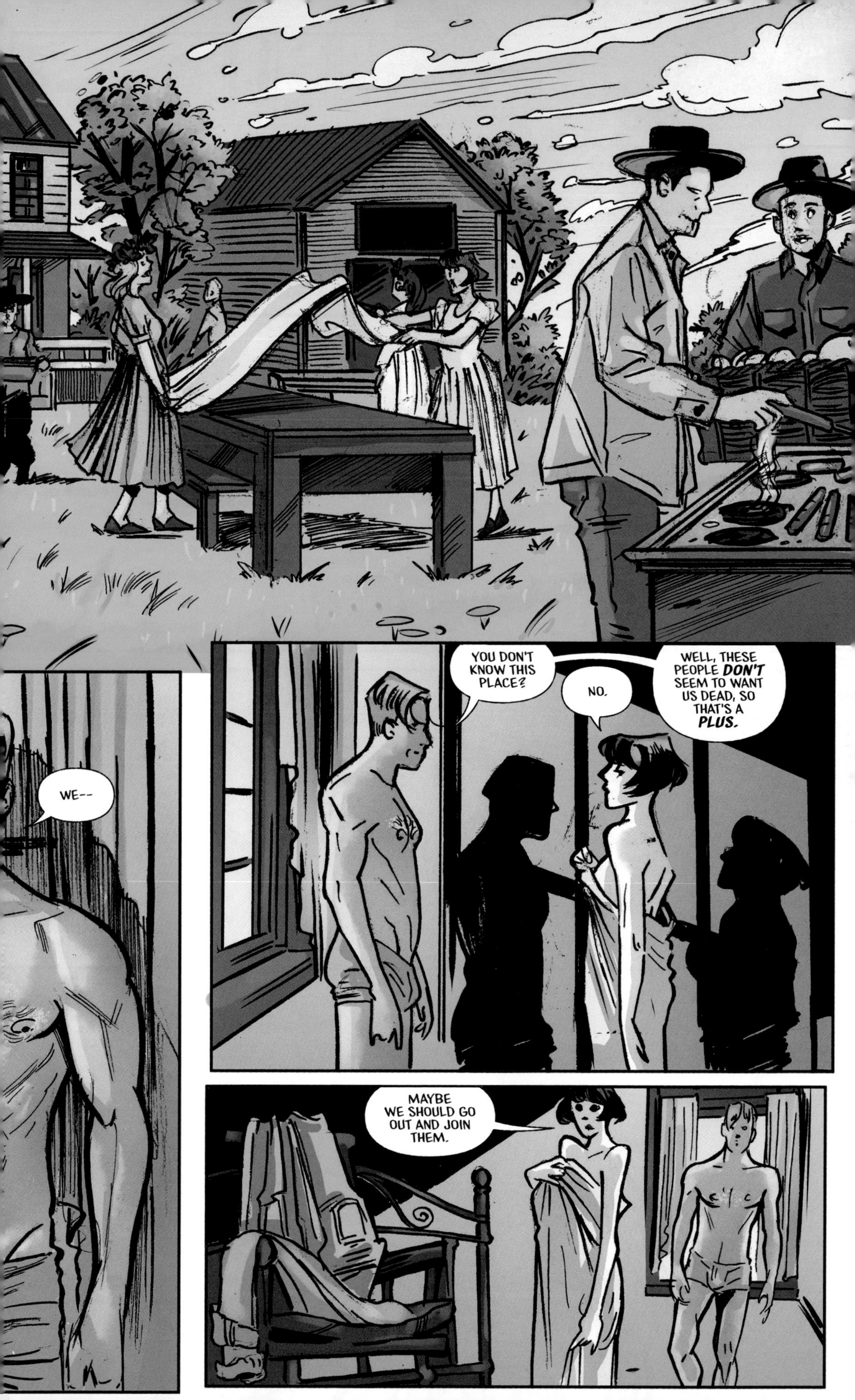
WE--
YOU DON'T KNOW THIS PLACE?
NO.
WELL, THESE PEOPLE DON'T SEEM TO WANT US DEAD, SO THAT'S A PLUS.
MAYBE WE SHOULD GO OUT AND JOIN THEM.

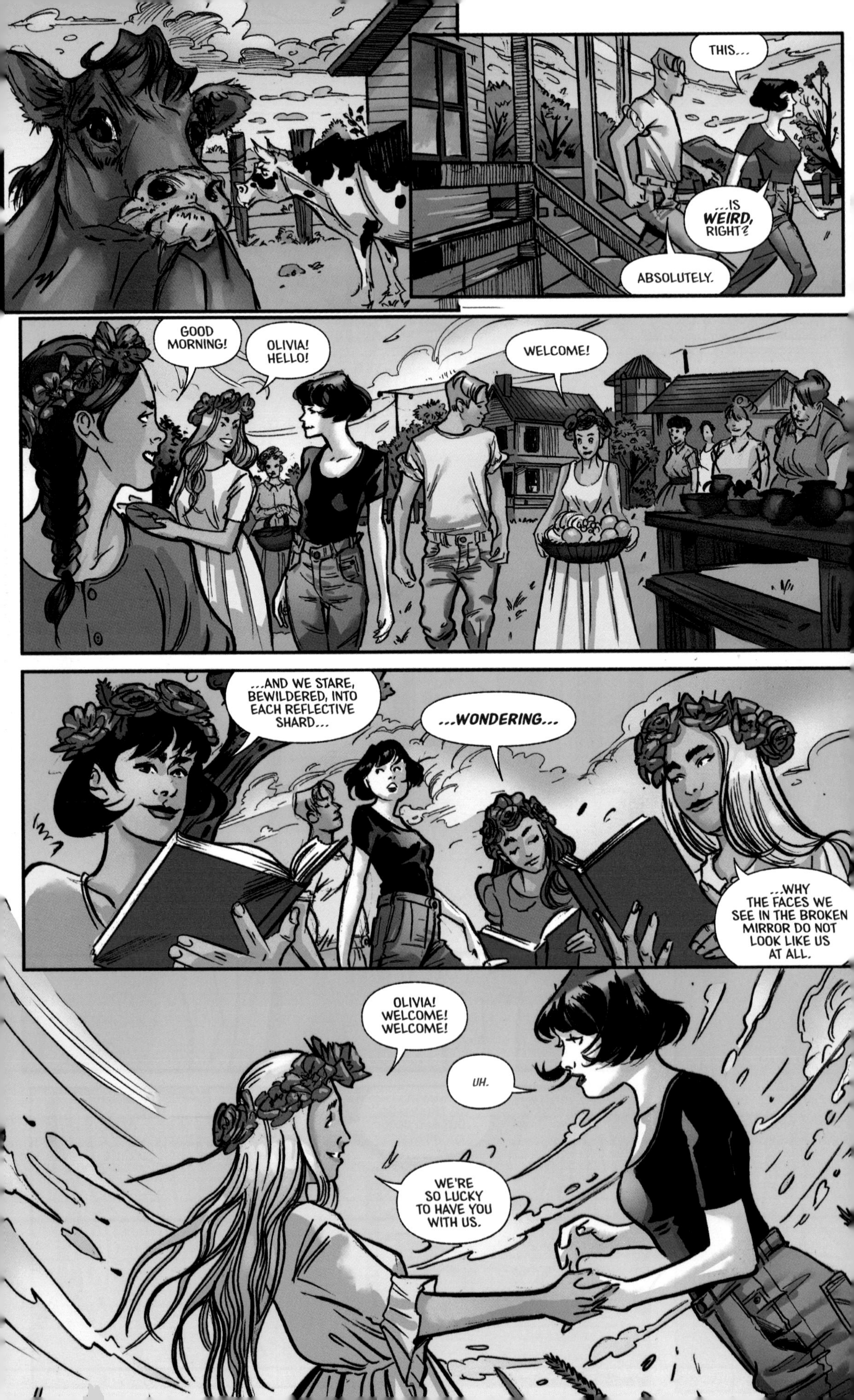
THIS...
...IS WEIRD, RIGHT?
ABSOLUTELY.
GOOD MORNING!
OLIVIA! HELLO!
WELCOME!
...AND WE STARE, BEWILDERED, INTO EACH REFLECTIVE SHARD...
...WONDERING...
...WHY THE FACES WE SEE IN THE BROKEN MIRROR DO NOT LOOK LIKE US AT ALL.
OLIVIA! WELCOME! WELCOME!
UH.
WE'RE SO LUCKY TO HAVE YOU WITH US.

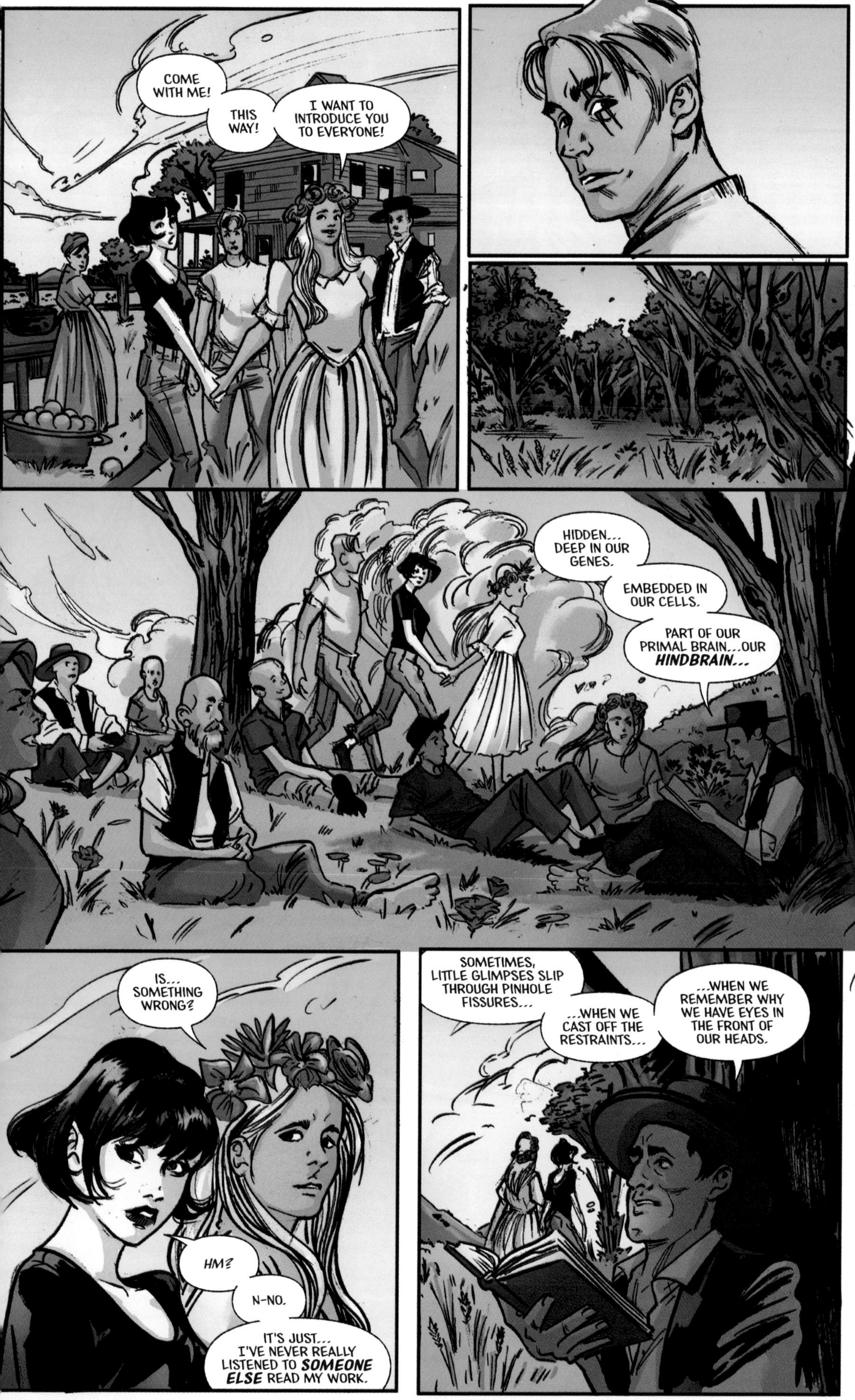
COME WITH ME!
THIS WAY!
I WANT TO INTRODUCE YOU TO EVERYONE!
HIDDEN... DEEP IN OUR GENES.
EMBEDDED IN OUR CELLS.
PART OF OUR PRIMAL BRAIN...OUR HINDBRAIN...
IS... SOMETHING WRONG?
HM?
N-NO.
IT'S JUST... I'VE NEVER REALLY LISTENED TO SOMEONE ELSE READ MY WORK.
SOMETIMES, LITTLE GLIMPSES SLIP THROUGH PINHOLE FISSURES...
...WHEN WE CAST OFF THE RESTRAINTS...
...WHEN WE REMEMBER WHY WE HAVE EYES IN THE FRONT OF OUR HEADS.

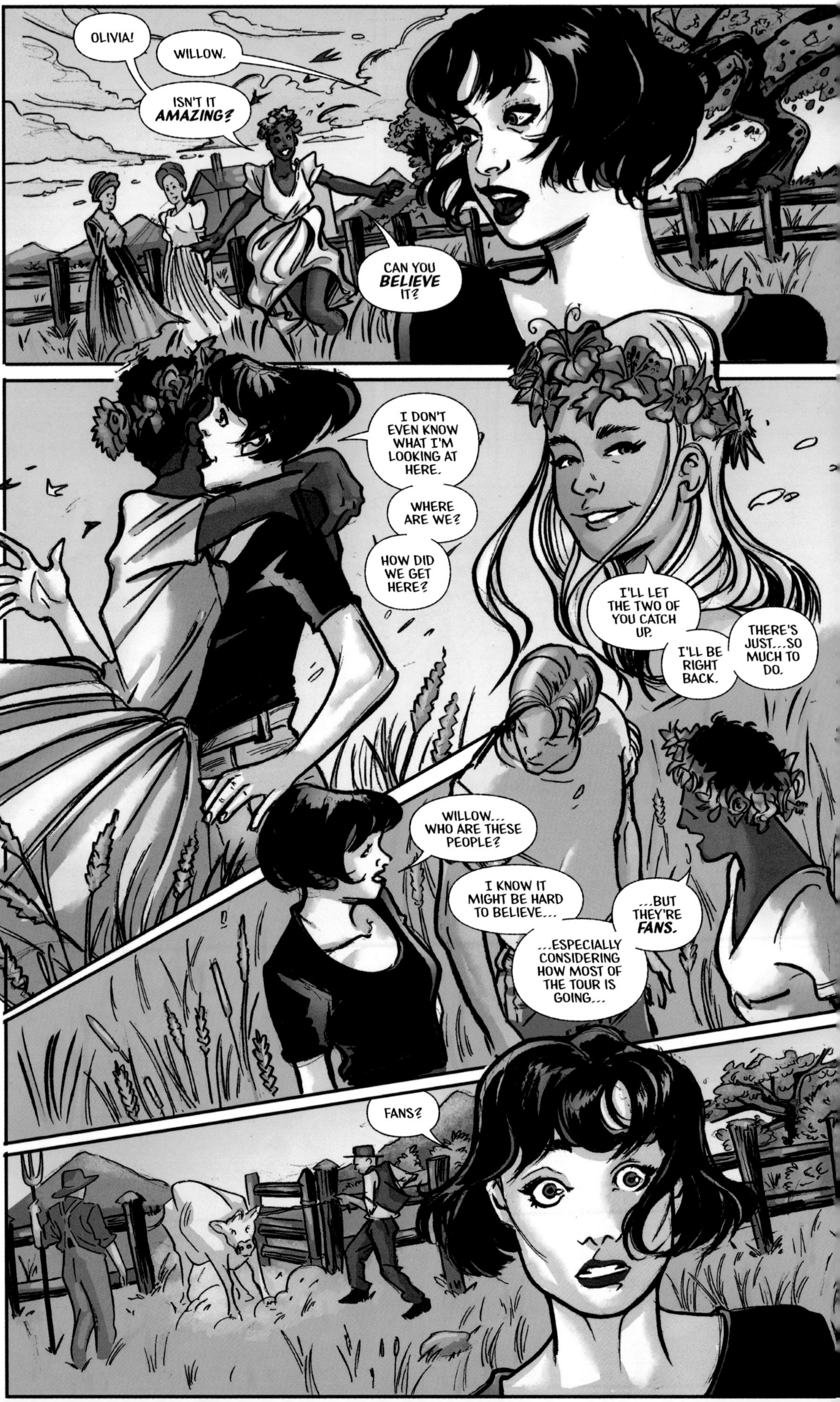
OLIVIA!
WILLOW.
ISN'T IT AMAZING?
CAN YOU BELIEVE IT?
I DON'T EVEN KNOW WHAT I'M LOOKING AT HERE.
WHERE ARE WE?
HOW DID WE GET HERE?
I'LL LET THE TWO OF YOU CATCH UP.
I'LL BE RIGHT BACK.
THERE'S JUST...SO MUCH TO DO.
WILLOW... WHO ARE THESE PEOPLE?
I KNOW IT MIGHT BE HARD TO BELIEVE...
...ESPECIALLY CONSIDERING HOW MOST OF THE TOUR IS GOING...
...BUT THEY'RE FANS.
FANS?

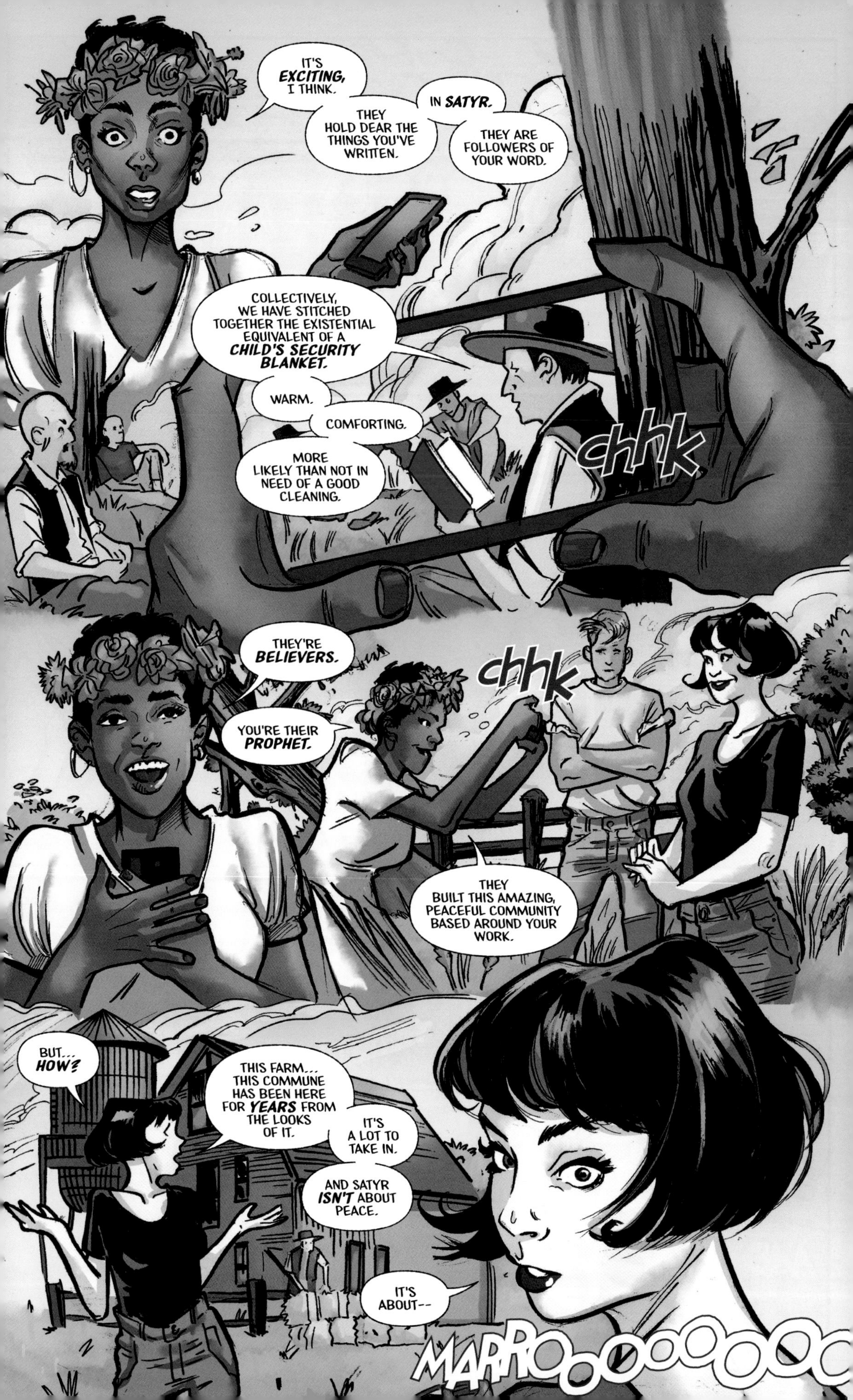
IT'S EXCITING, I THINK.
THEY HOLD DEAR THE THINGS YOU'VE WRITTEN.
IN SATYR.
THEY ARE FOLLOWERS OF YOUR WORD.
COLLECTIVELY, WE HAVE STITCHED TOGETHER THE EXISTENTIAL EQUIVALENT OF A CHILD'S SECURITY BLANKET.
WARM.
COMFORTING.
MORE LIKELY THAN NOT IN NEED OF A GOOD CLEANING.
chhk
THEY'RE BELIEVERS.
YOU'RE THEIR PROPHET.
chhk
THEY BUILT THIS AMAZING, PEACEFUL COMMUNITY BASED AROUND YOUR WORK.
BUT... HOW?
THIS FARM... THIS COMMUNE HAS BEEN HERE FOR YEARS FROM THE LOOKS OF IT.
IT'S A LOT TO TAKE IN.
AND SATYR ISN'T ABOUT PEACE.
IT'S ABOUT--
MARROOOOOOOO

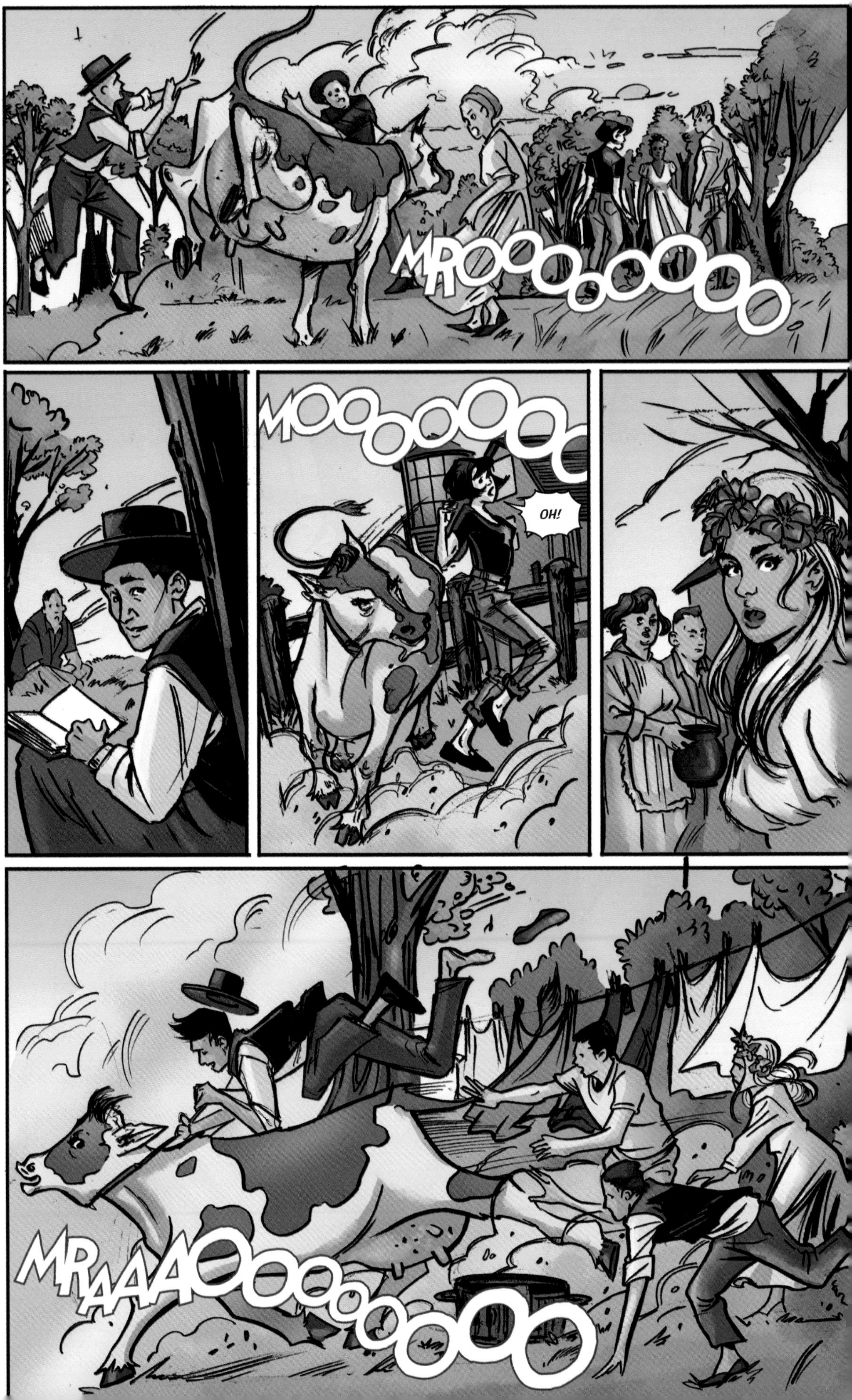
MROOOOOOOOO
MOOOOOOO
OH!
MRAAAOOOOOOOOO

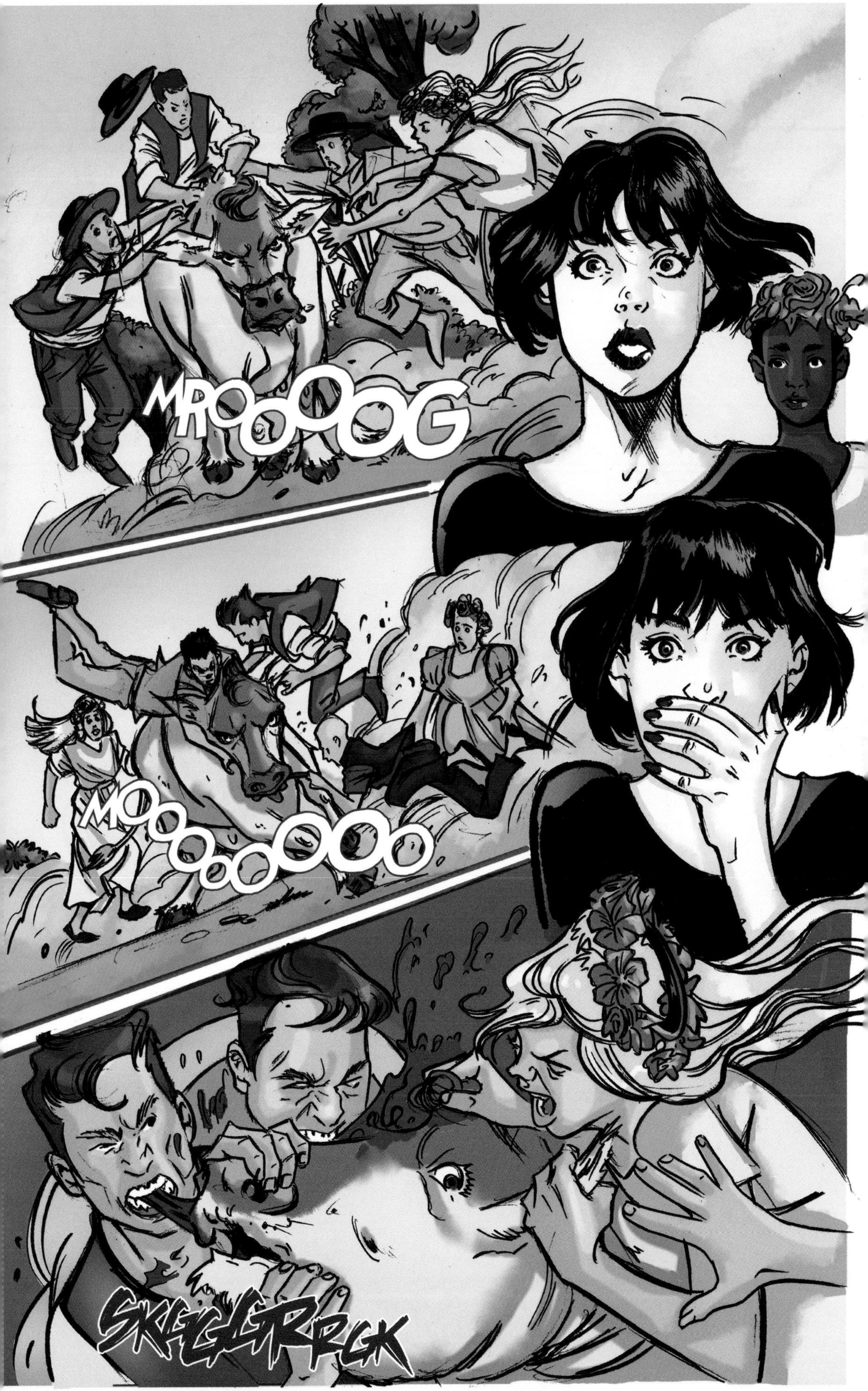
MROOOOOOG
MOOOOOOOOOO
SKLGLRRGK

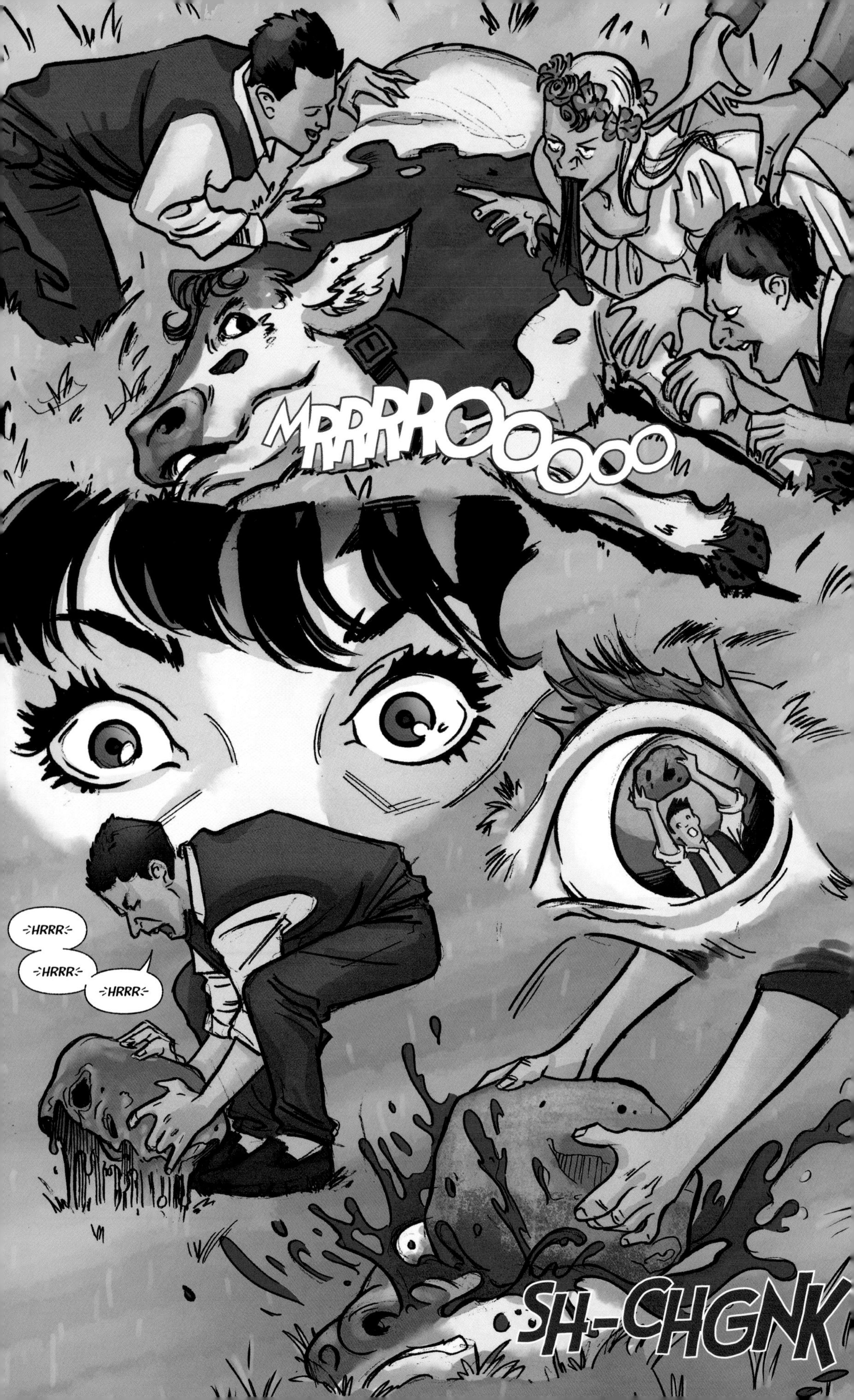
MRRRROOOOOO
HRRR
HRRR
HRRR
SH-CHGNK

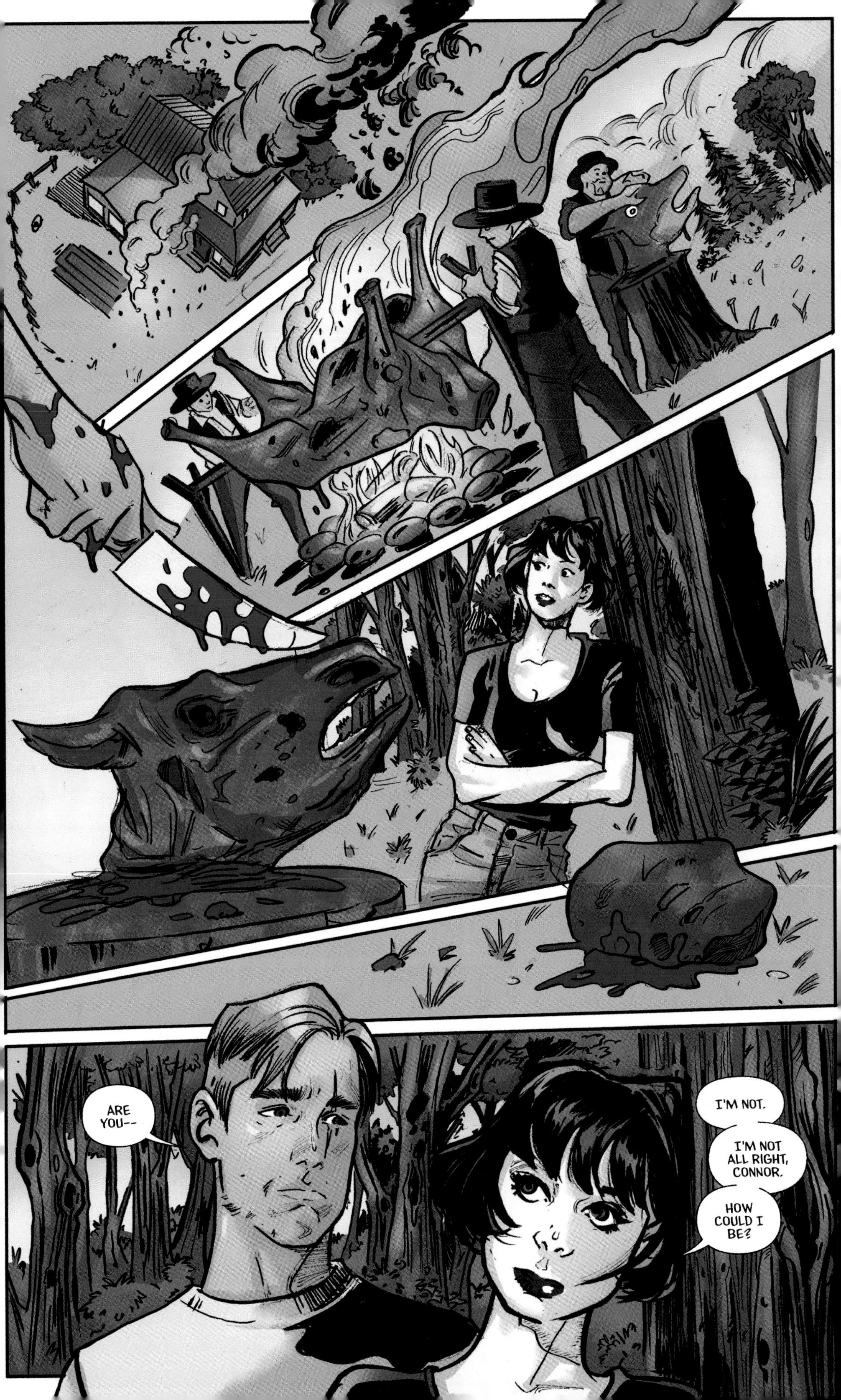
ARE YOU--
I'M NOT.
I'M NOT ALL RIGHT, CONNOR.
HOW COULD I BE?

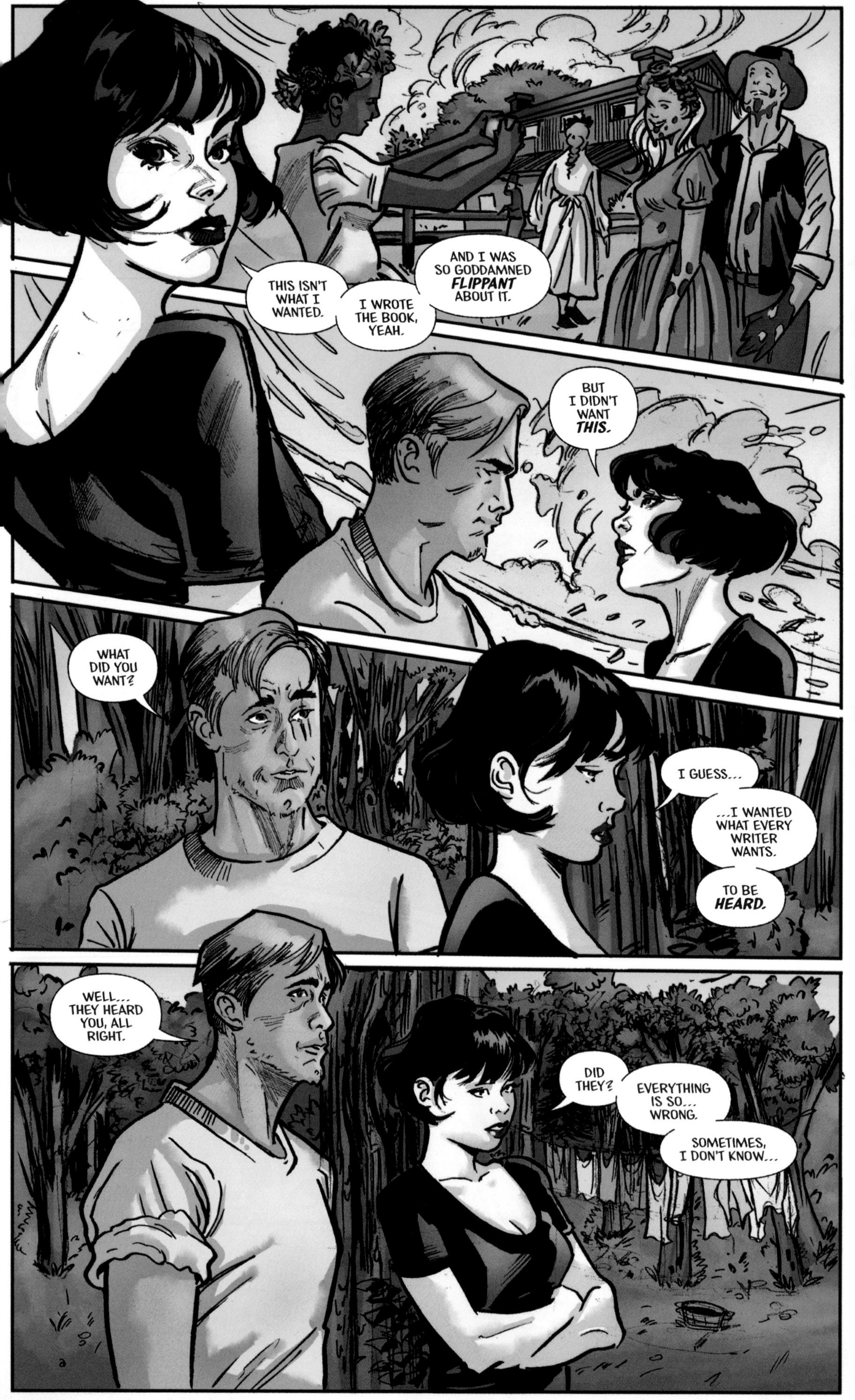

THIS ISN'T WHAT I WANTED.
I WROTE THE BOOK, YEAH.
AND I WAS SO GODDAMNED FLIPPANT ABOUT IT.
BUT I DIDN'T WANT THIS.
WHAT DID YOU WANT?
I GUESS...
...I WANTED WHAT EVERY WRITER WANTS.
TO BE HEARD.
WELL... THEY HEARD YOU, ALL RIGHT.
DID THEY?
EVERYTHING IS SO... WRONG.
SOMETIMES, I DON'T KNOW...

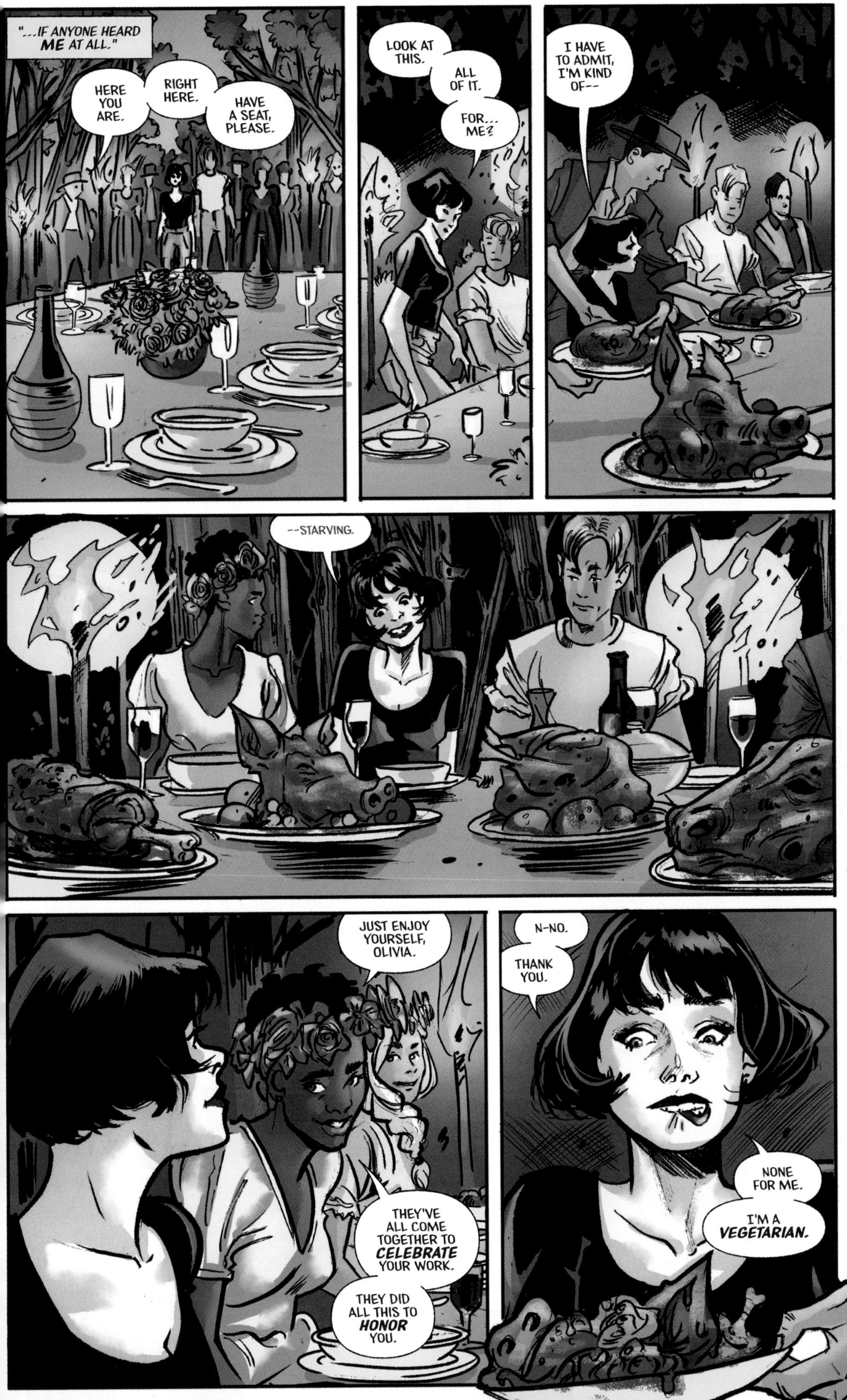
"...IF ANYONE HEARD ME AT ALL."
HERE YOU ARE.
RIGHT HERE.
HAVE A SEAT, PLEASE.
LOOK AT THIS.
ALL OF IT.
FOR... ME?
I HAVE TO ADMIT, I'M KIND OF--
--STARVING.
JUST ENJOY YOURSELF, OLIVIA.
THEY'VE ALL COME TOGETHER TO CELEBRATE YOUR WORK.
THEY DID ALL THIS TO HONOR YOU.
N-NO.
THANK YOU.
NONE FOR ME.
I'M A VEGETARIAN.

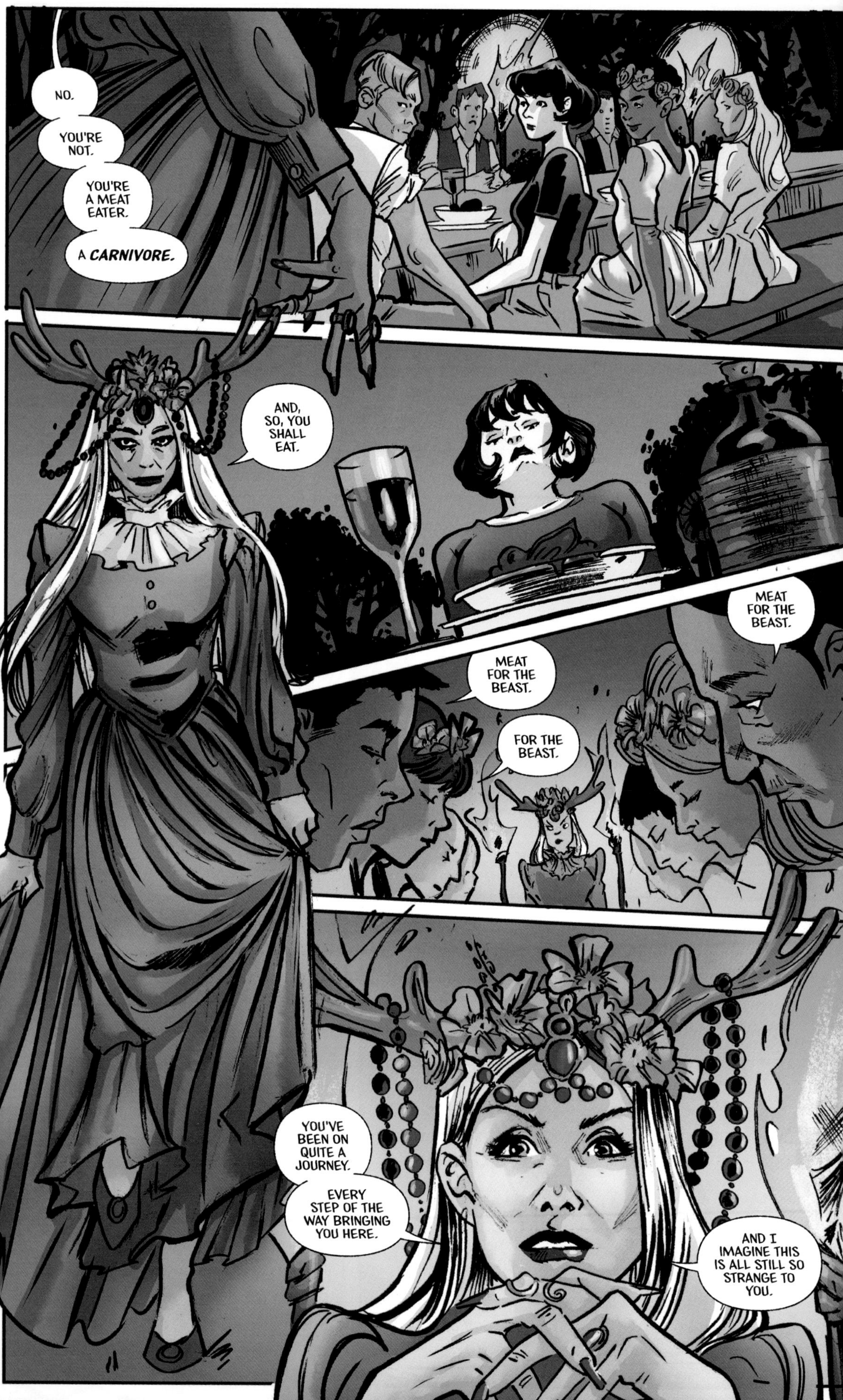
NO.
YOU'RE NOT.
YOU'RE A MEAT EATER.
A CARNIVORE.
AND, SO, YOU SHALL EAT.
MEAT FOR THE BEAST.
MEAT FOR THE BEAST.
FOR THE BEAST.
YOU'VE BEEN ON QUITE A JOURNEY.
EVERY STEP OF THE WAY BRINGING YOU HERE.
AND I IMAGINE THIS IS ALL STILL SO STRANGE TO YOU.

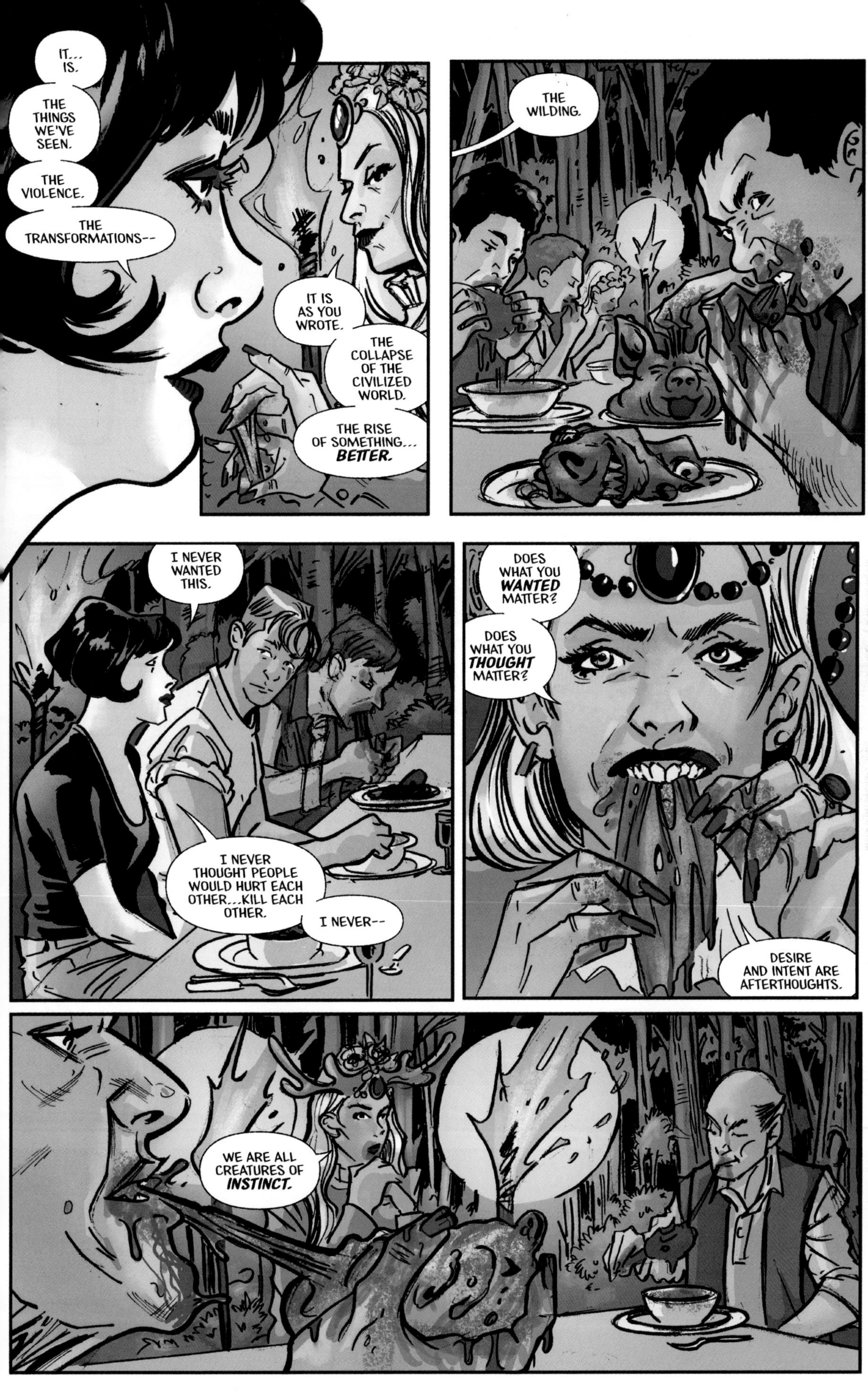
IT... IS.
THE THINGS WE'VE SEEN.
THE VIOLENCE.
THE TRANSFORMATIONS--
IT IS AS YOU WROTE.
THE COLLAPSE OF THE CIVILIZED WORLD.
THE RISE OF SOMETHING... BETTER.
THE WILDING.
I NEVER WANTED THIS.
I NEVER THOUGHT PEOPLE WOULD HURT EACH OTHER...KILL EACH OTHER.
I NEVER--
DOES WHAT YOU WANTED MATTER?
DOES WHAT YOU THOUGHT MATTER?
DESIRE AND INTENT ARE AFTERTHOUGHTS.
WE ARE ALL CREATURES OF INSTINCT.

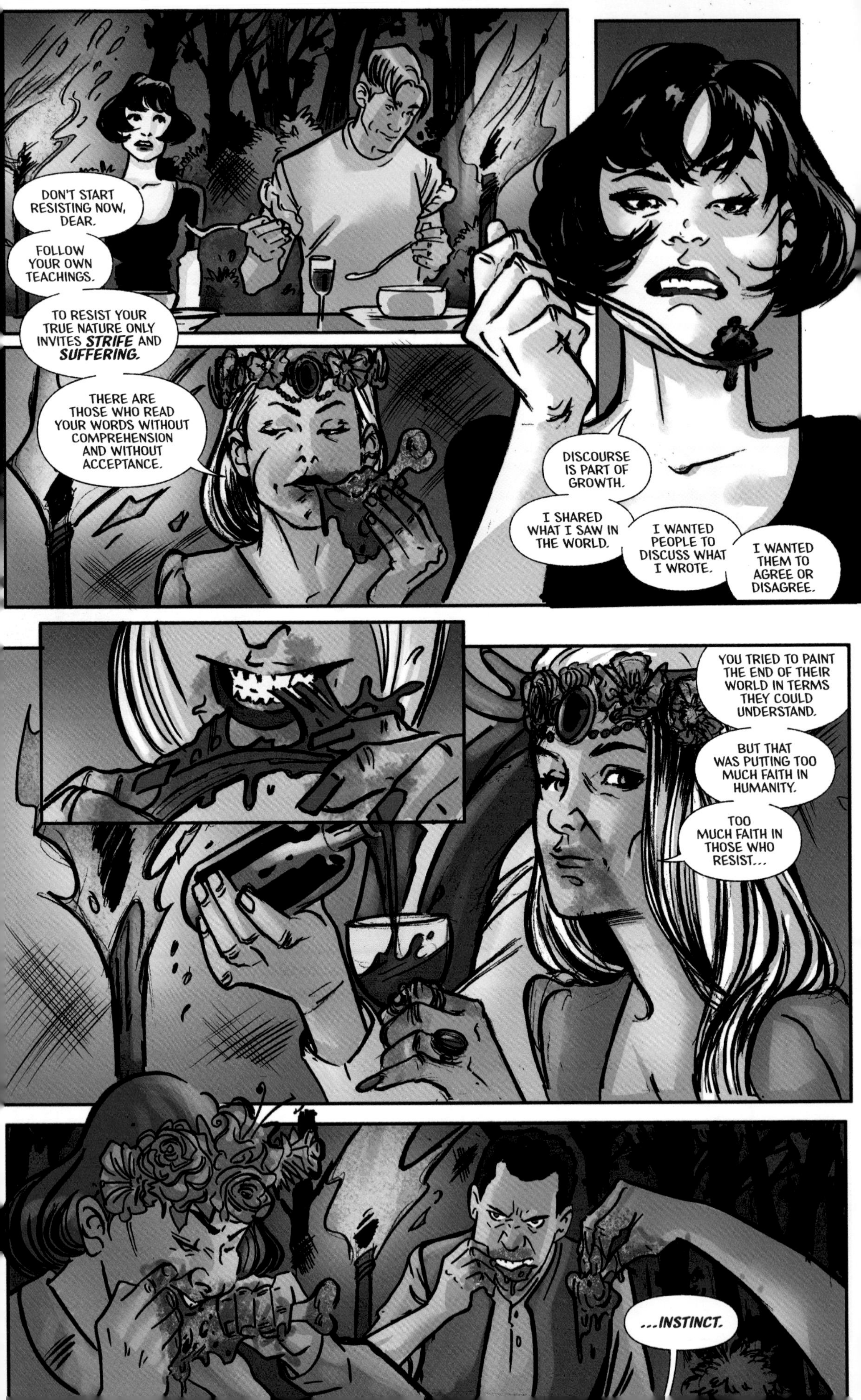
DON'T START RESISTING NOW, DEAR.
FOLLOW YOUR OWN TEACHINGS.
TO RESIST YOUR TRUE NATURE ONLY INVITES **STRIFE** AND **SUFFERING.**
THERE ARE THOSE WHO READ YOUR WORDS WITHOUT COMPREHENSION AND WITHOUT ACCEPTANCE.
DISCOURSE IS PART OF GROWTH.
I SHARED WHAT I SAW IN THE WORLD.
I WANTED PEOPLE TO DISCUSS WHAT I WROTE.
I WANTED THEM TO AGREE OR DISAGREE.
YOU TRIED TO PAINT THE END OF THEIR WORLD IN TERMS THEY COULD UNDERSTAND.
BUT THAT WAS PUTTING TOO MUCH FAITH IN HUMANITY.
TOO MUCH FAITH IN THOSE WHO RESIST...
...**INSTINCT.**

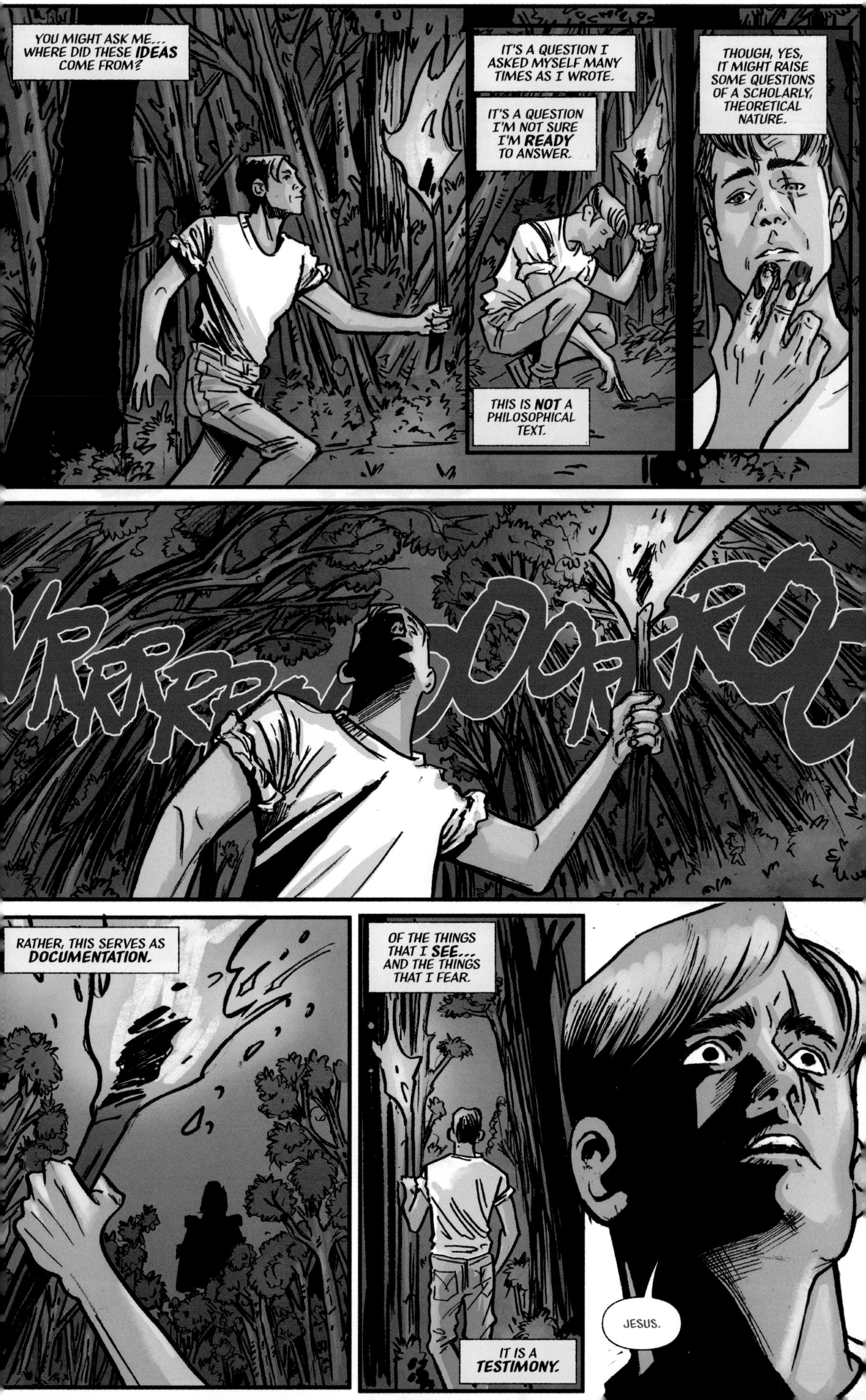
YOU MIGHT ASK ME... WHERE DID THESE IDEAS COME FROM?
IT'S A QUESTION I ASKED MYSELF MANY TIMES AS I WROTE.
IT'S A QUESTION I'M NOT SURE I'M READY TO ANSWER.
THIS IS NOT A PHILOSOPHICAL TEXT.
THOUGH, YES, IT MIGHT RAISE SOME QUESTIONS OF A SCHOLARLY, THEORETICAL NATURE.
VRRRRR...OOOOORRRO
RATHER, THIS SERVES AS DOCUMENTATION.
OF THE THINGS THAT I SEE... AND THE THINGS THAT I FEAR.
IT IS A TESTIMONY.
JESUS.

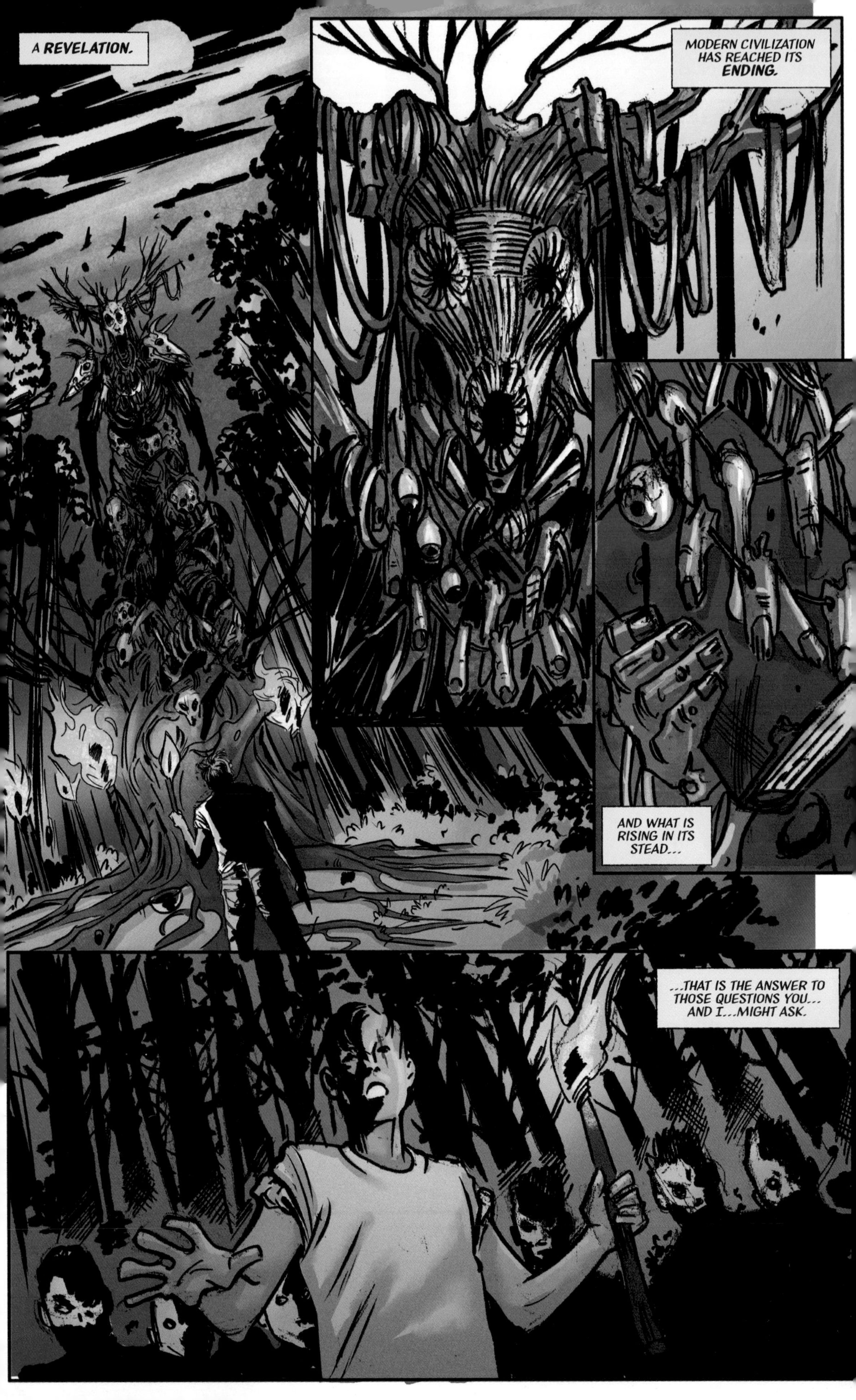
A REVELATION.
MODERN CIVILIZATION HAS REACHED ITS ENDING.
AND WHAT IS RISING IN ITS STEAD...
...THAT IS THE ANSWER TO THOSE QUESTIONS YOU... AND I...MIGHT ASK.

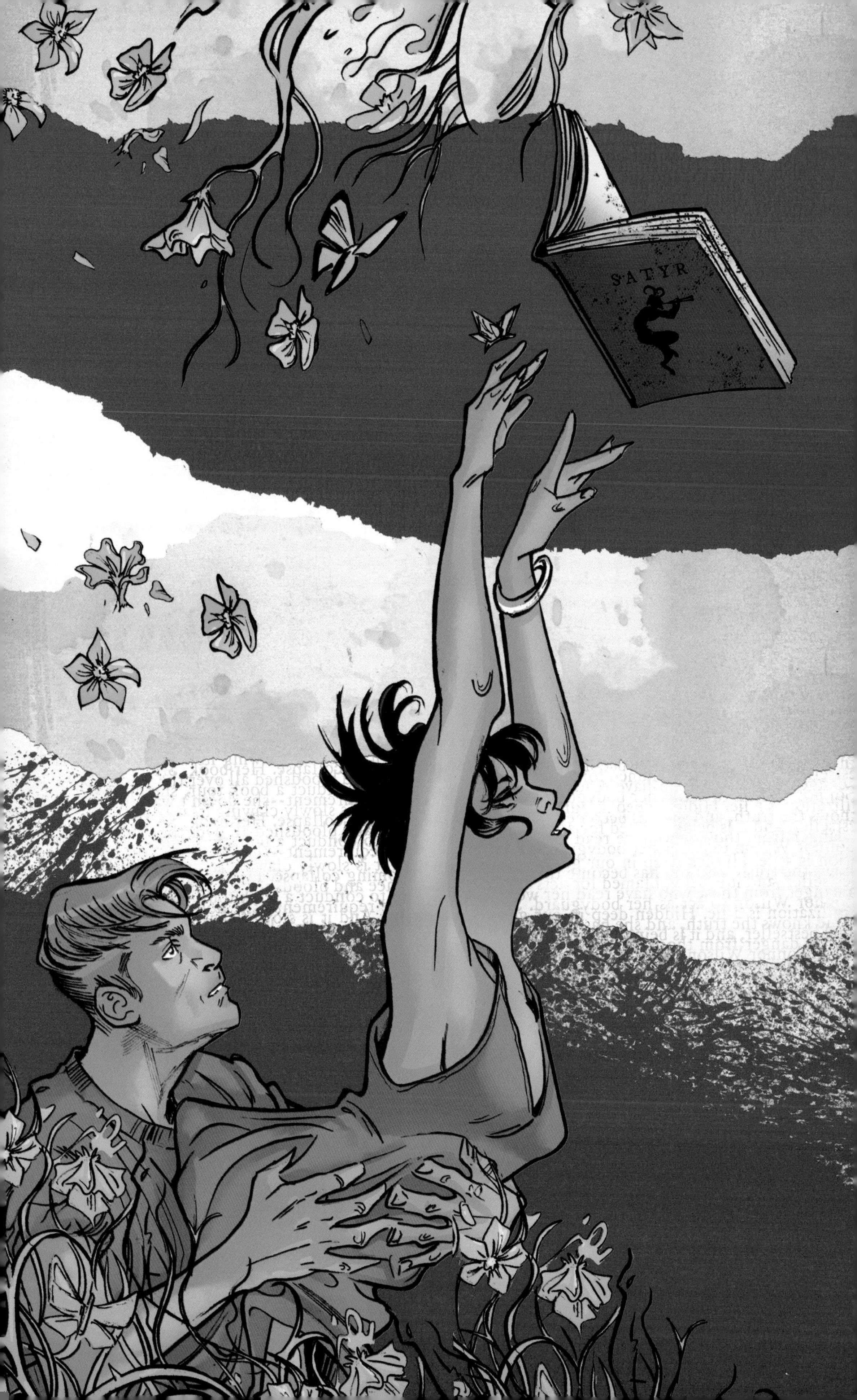
SATYR

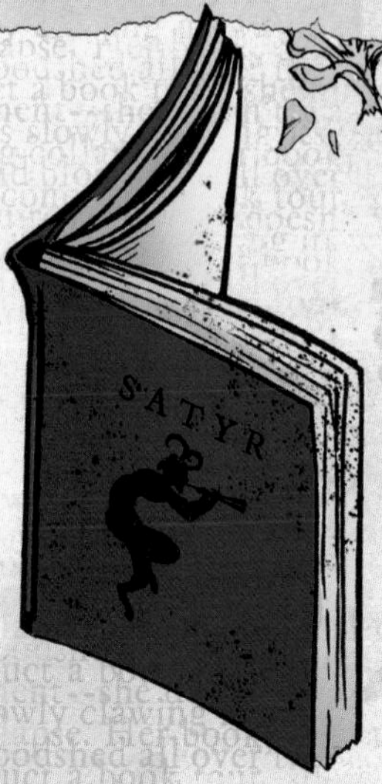
SATYR

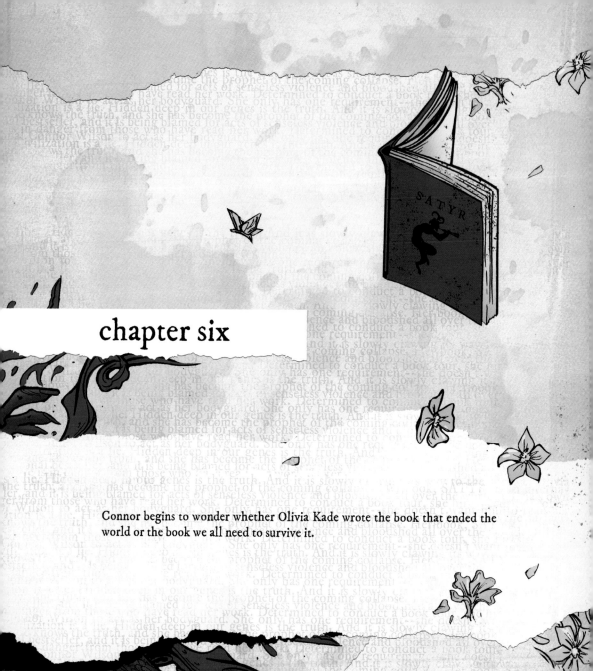

chapter six

Connor begins to wonder whether Olivia Kade wrote the book that ended the world or the book we all need to survive it.

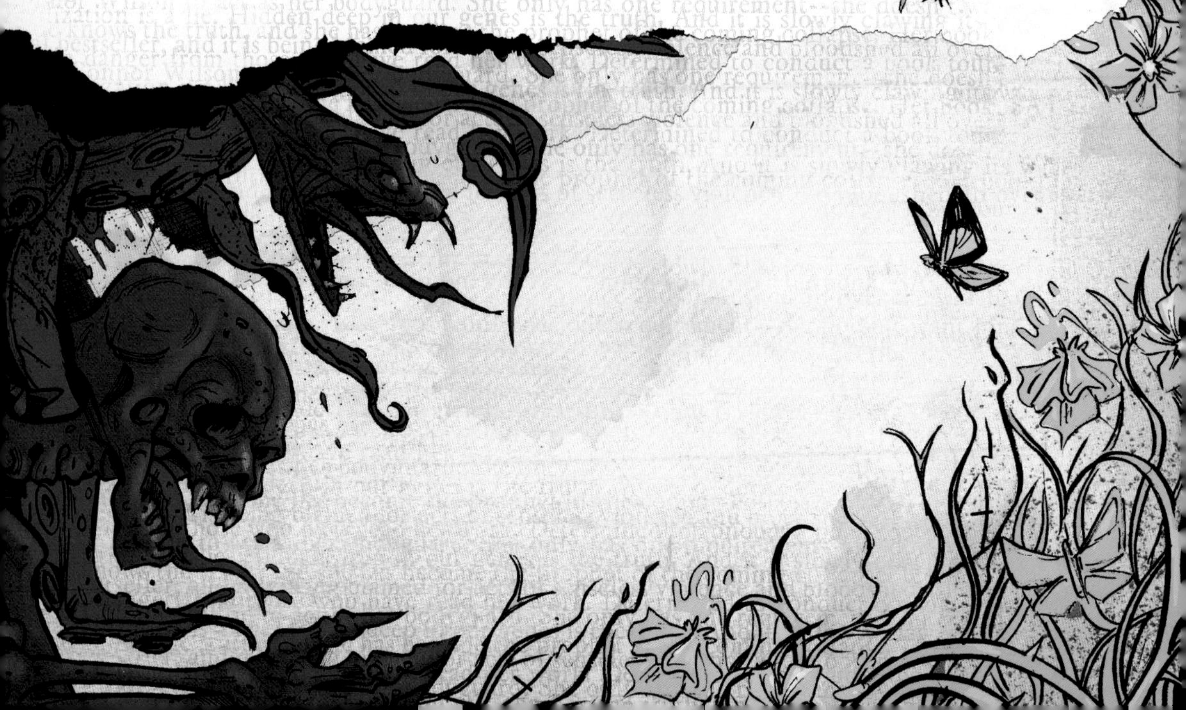

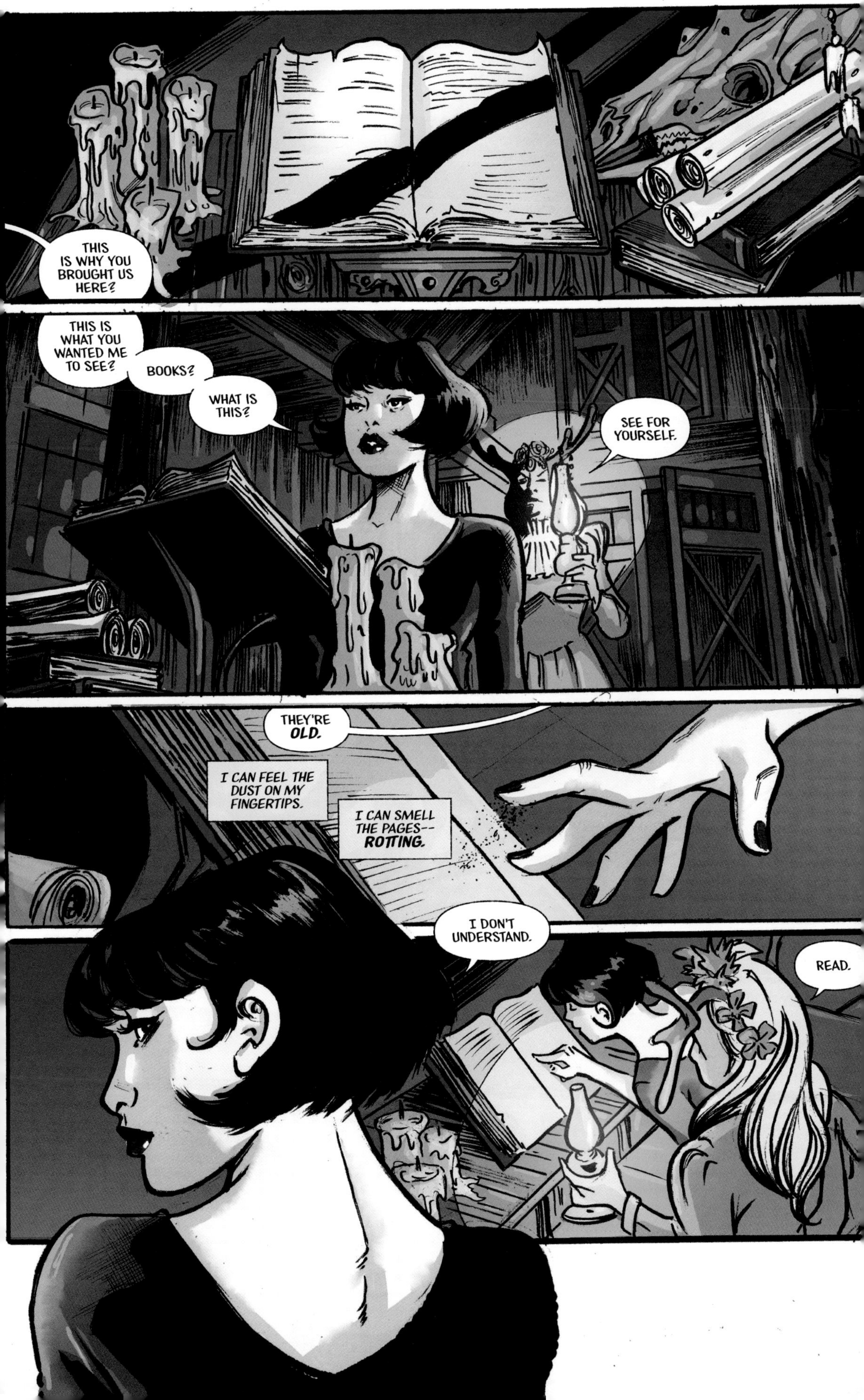
THIS IS WHY YOU BROUGHT US HERE?
THIS IS WHAT YOU WANTED ME TO SEE?
BOOKS?
WHAT IS THIS?
SEE FOR YOURSELF.
THEY'RE *OLD.*
I CAN FEEL THE DUST ON MY FINGERTIPS.
I CAN SMELL THE PAGES-- *ROTTING.*
I DON'T UNDERSTAND.
READ.

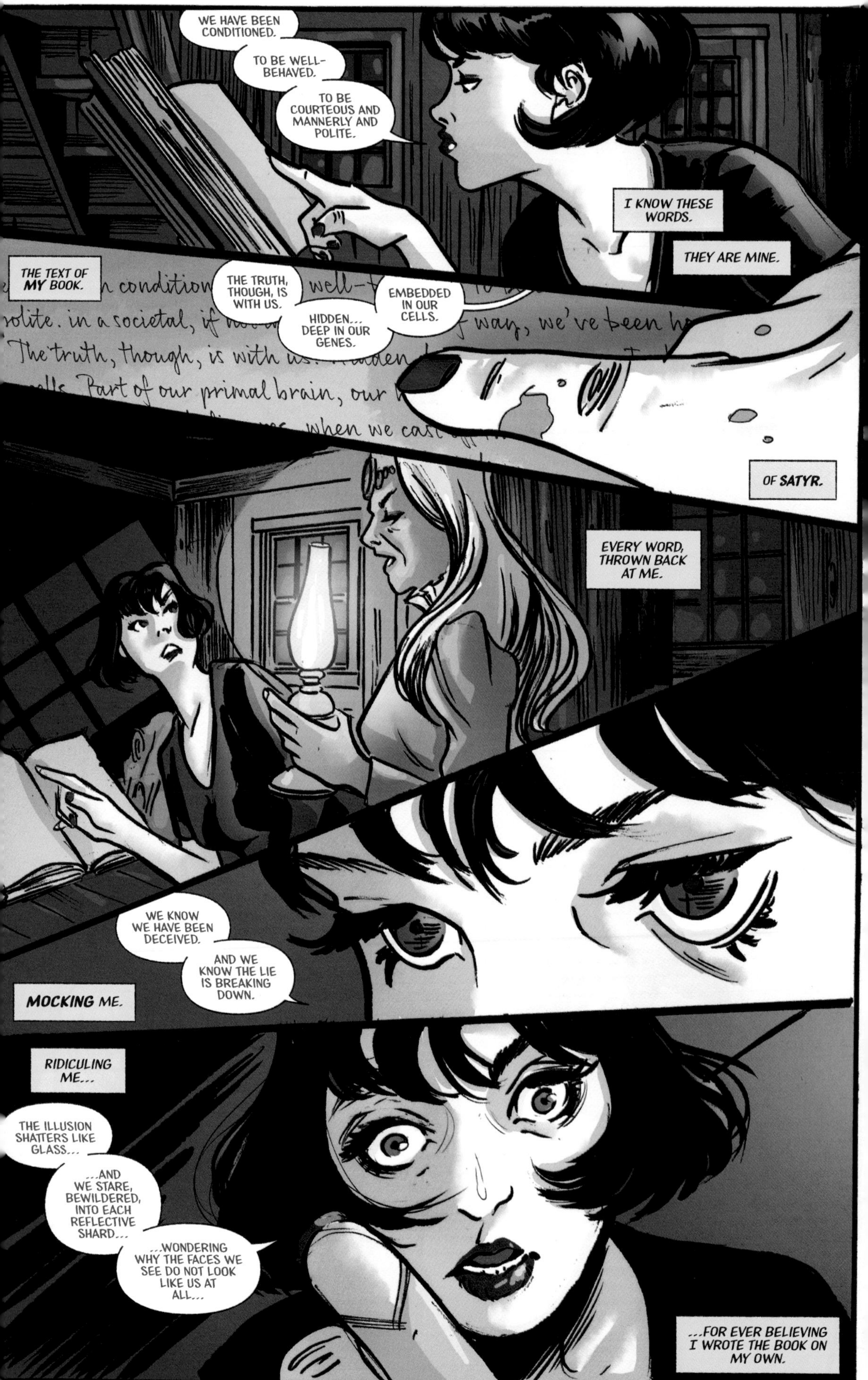
WE HAVE BEEN CONDITIONED.
TO BE WELL-BEHAVED.
TO BE COURTEOUS AND MANNERLY AND POLITE.
I KNOW THESE WORDS.
THEY ARE MINE.
THE TEXT OF MY BOOK.
THE TRUTH, THOUGH, IS WITH US.
HIDDEN... DEEP IN OUR GENES.
EMBEDDED IN OUR CELLS.
OF SATYR.
EVERY WORD, THROWN BACK AT ME.
WE KNOW WE HAVE BEEN DECEIVED.
AND WE KNOW THE LIE IS BREAKING DOWN.
MOCKING ME.
RIDICULING ME...
THE ILLUSION SHATTERS LIKE GLASS...
...AND WE STARE, BEWILDERED, INTO EACH REFLECTIVE SHARD...
...WONDERING WHY THE FACES WE SEE DO NOT LOOK LIKE US AT ALL...
...FOR EVER BELIEVING I WROTE THE BOOK ON MY OWN.

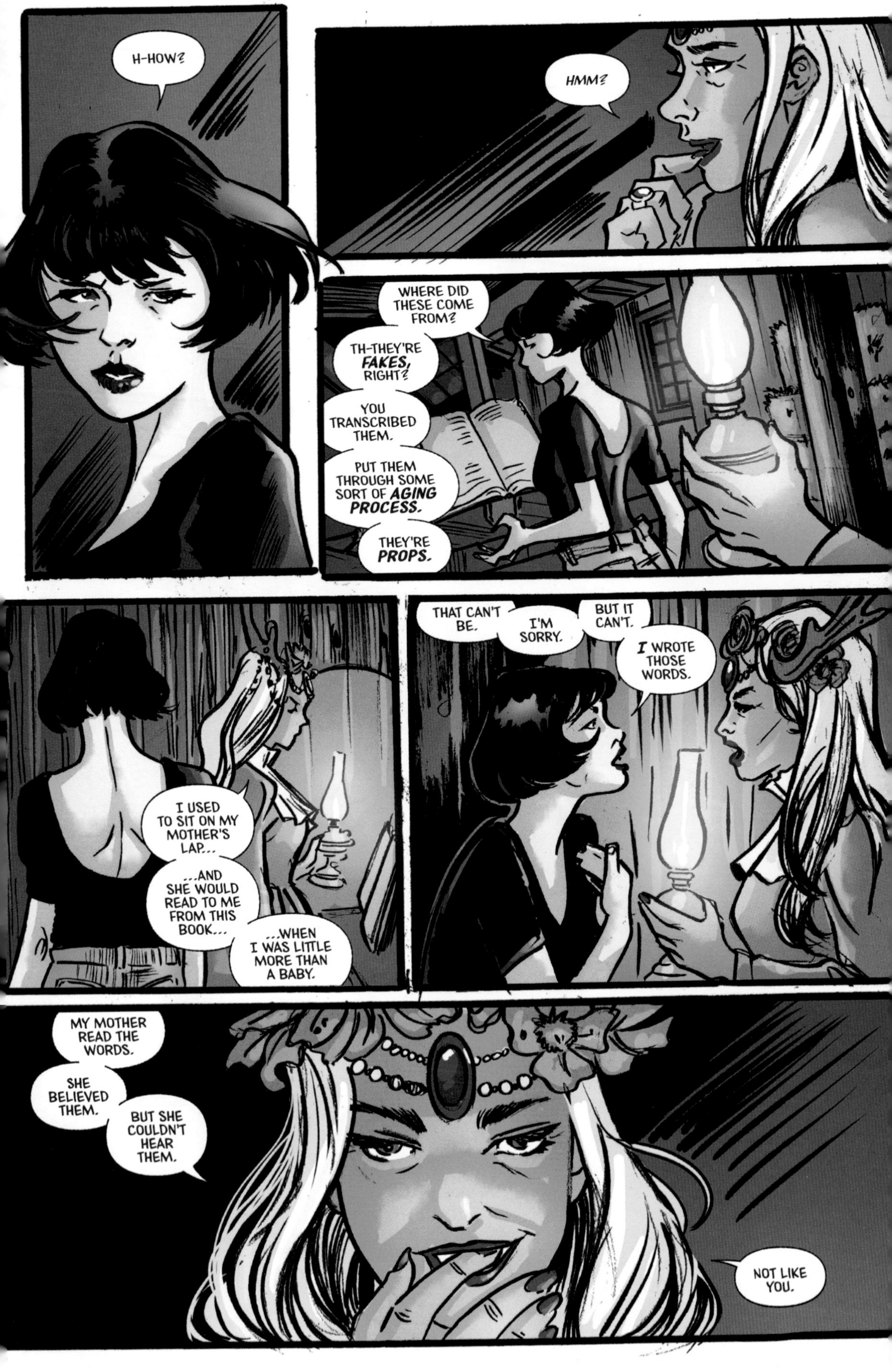
H-HOW?
HMM?
WHERE DID THESE COME FROM?
TH-THEY'RE **FAKES,** RIGHT?
YOU TRANSCRIBED THEM.
PUT THEM THROUGH SOME SORT OF **AGING PROCESS.**
THEY'RE **PROPS.**
I USED TO SIT ON MY MOTHER'S LAP...
...AND SHE WOULD READ TO ME FROM THIS BOOK...
...WHEN I WAS LITTLE MORE THAN A BABY.
THAT CAN'T BE.
I'M SORRY.
BUT IT CAN'T.
I WROTE THOSE WORDS.
MY MOTHER READ THE WORDS.
SHE BELIEVED THEM.
BUT SHE COULDN'T HEAR THEM.
NOT LIKE YOU.

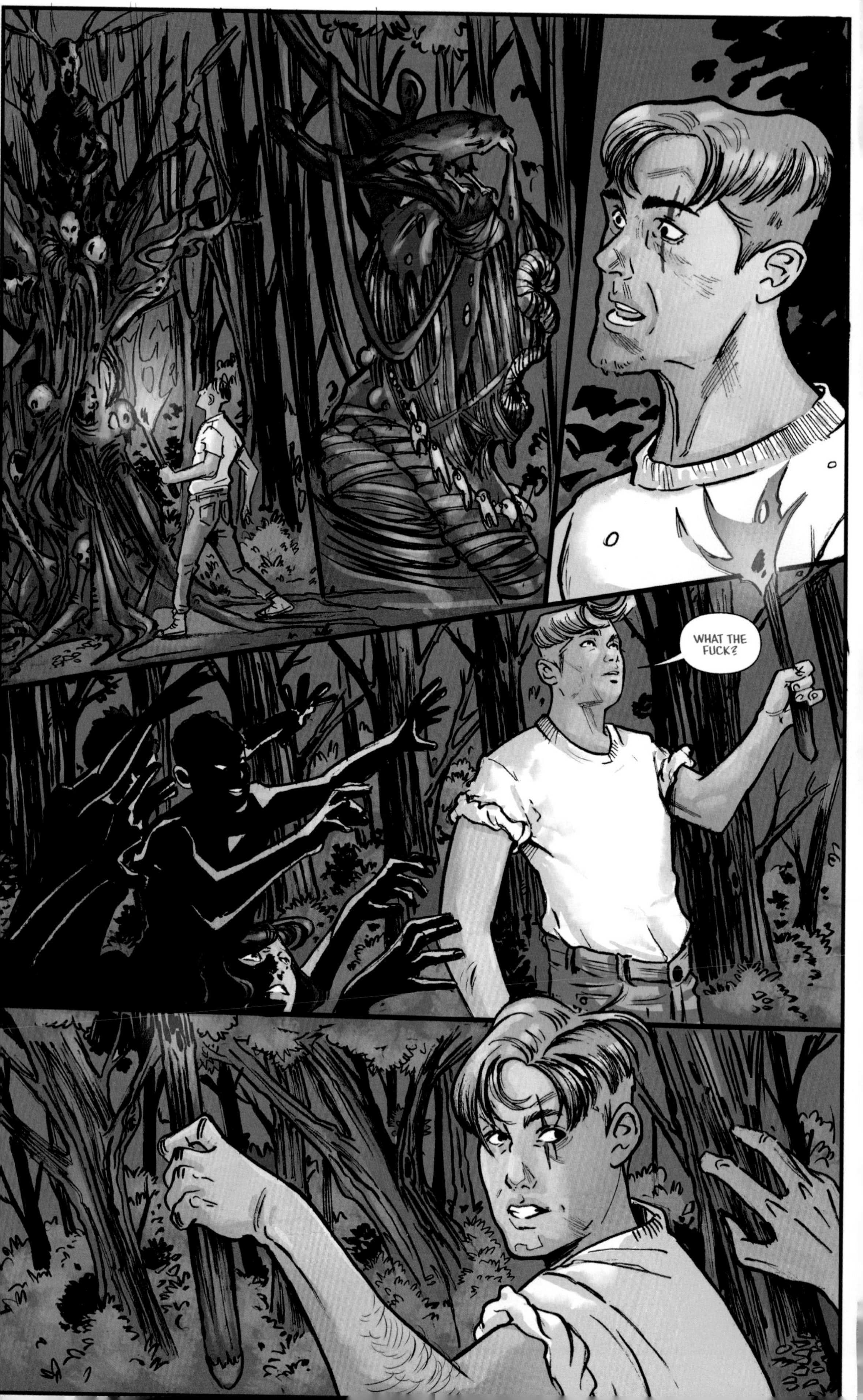
WHAT THE FUCK?

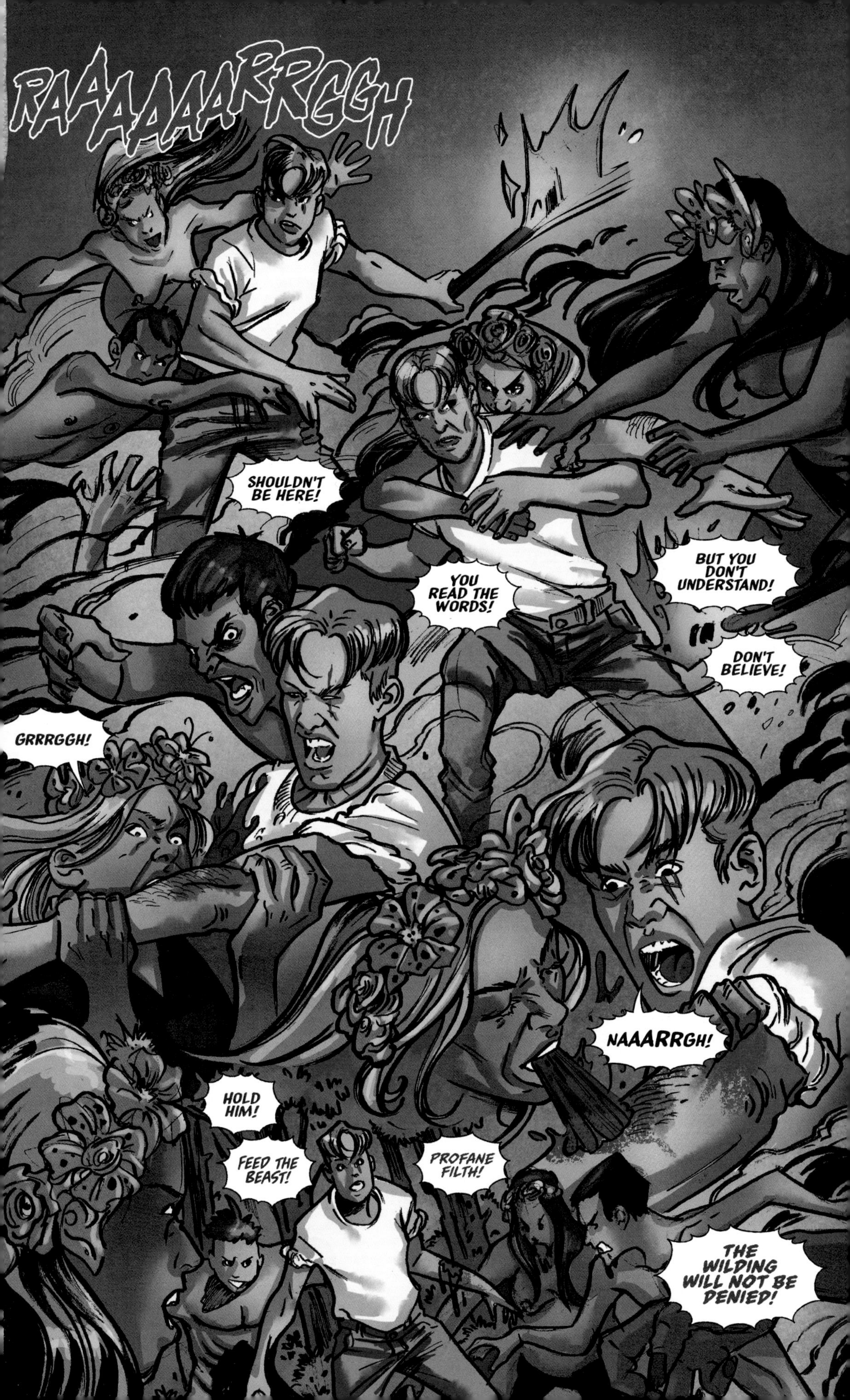
RAAAAAARRGGH
SHOULDN'T BE HERE!
YOU READ THE WORDS!
BUT YOU DON'T UNDERSTAND!
DON'T BELIEVE!
GRRRGGH!
NAAARRGH!
HOLD HIM!
FEED THE BEAST!
PROFANE FILTH!
THE WILDING WILL NOT BE DENIED!

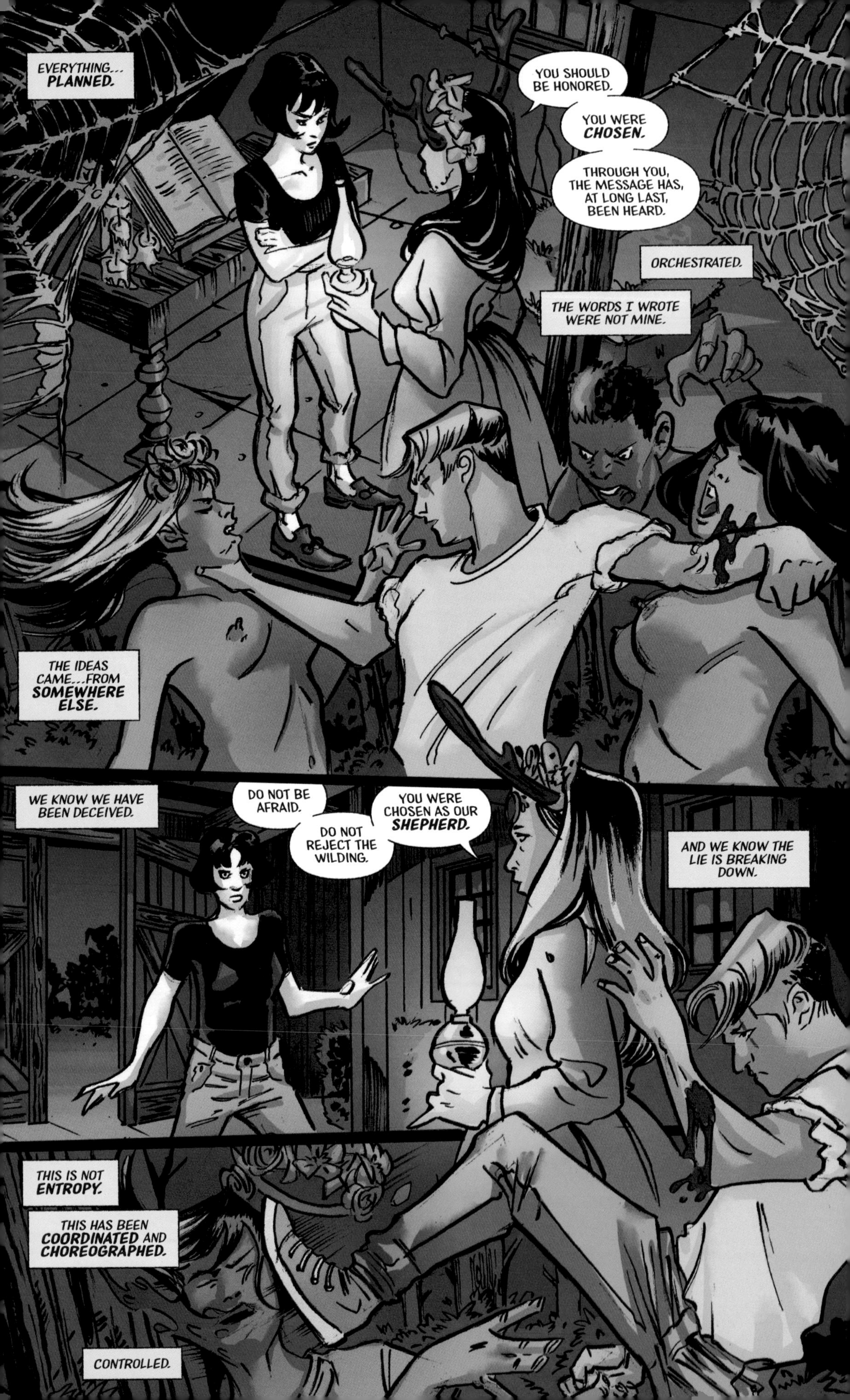
EVERYTHING... PLANNED.
YOU SHOULD BE HONORED.
YOU WERE CHOSEN.
THROUGH YOU, THE MESSAGE HAS, AT LONG LAST, BEEN HEARD.
ORCHESTRATED.
THE WORDS I WROTE WERE NOT MINE.
THE IDEAS CAME...FROM SOMEWHERE ELSE.
WE KNOW WE HAVE BEEN DECEIVED.
DO NOT BE AFRAID.
DO NOT REJECT THE WILDING.
YOU WERE CHOSEN AS OUR SHEPHERD.
AND WE KNOW THE LIE IS BREAKING DOWN.
THIS IS NOT ENTROPY.
THIS HAS BEEN COORDINATED AND CHOREOGRAPHED.
CONTROLLED.

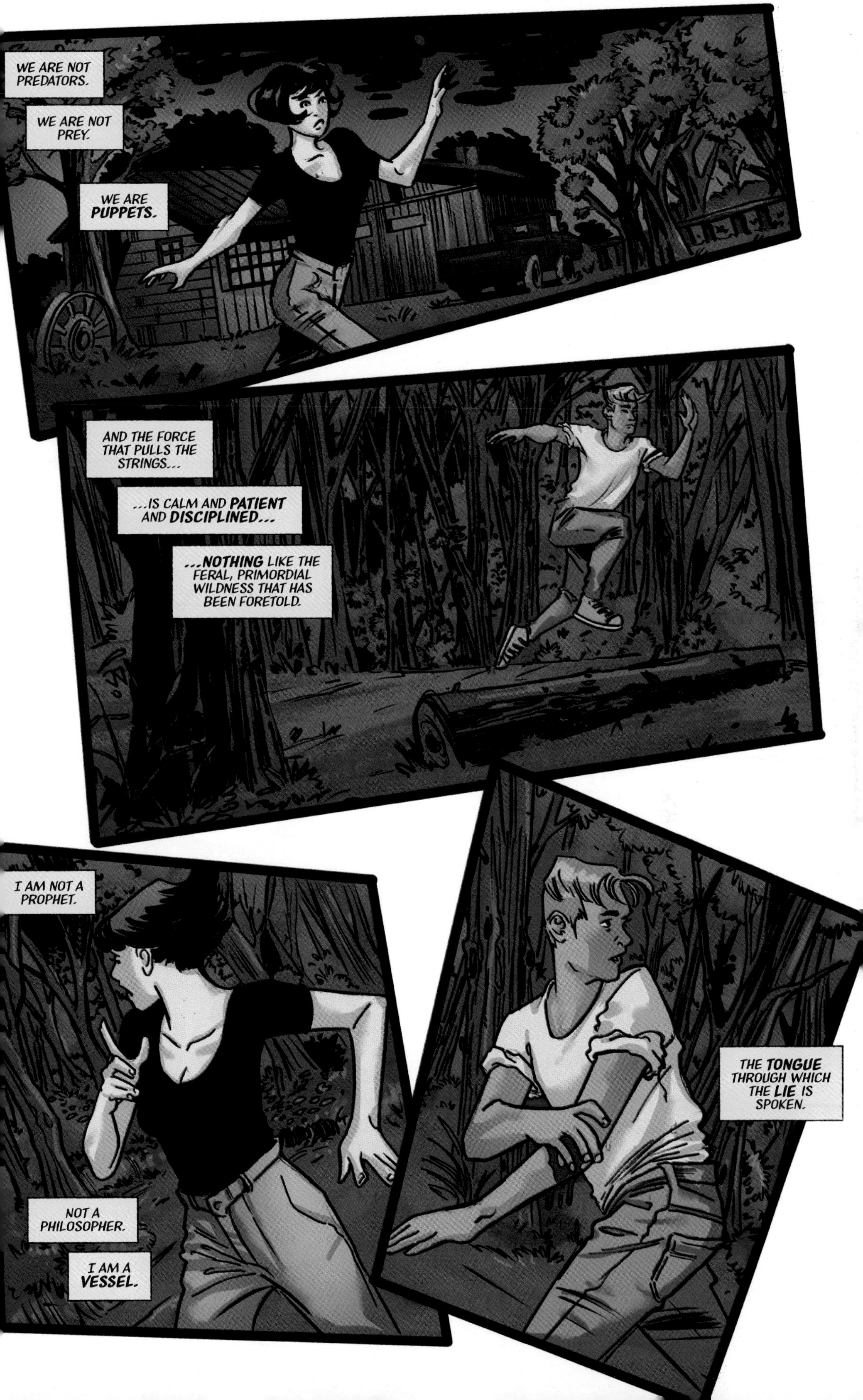
WE ARE NOT PREDATORS.
WE ARE NOT PREY.
WE ARE PUPPETS.
AND THE FORCE THAT PULLS THE STRINGS...
...IS CALM AND PATIENT AND DISCIPLINED...
...NOTHING LIKE THE FERAL, PRIMORDIAL WILDNESS THAT HAS BEEN FORETOLD.
I AM NOT A PROPHET.
NOT A PHILOSOPHER.
I AM A VESSEL.
THE TONGUE THROUGH WHICH THE LIE IS SPOKEN.

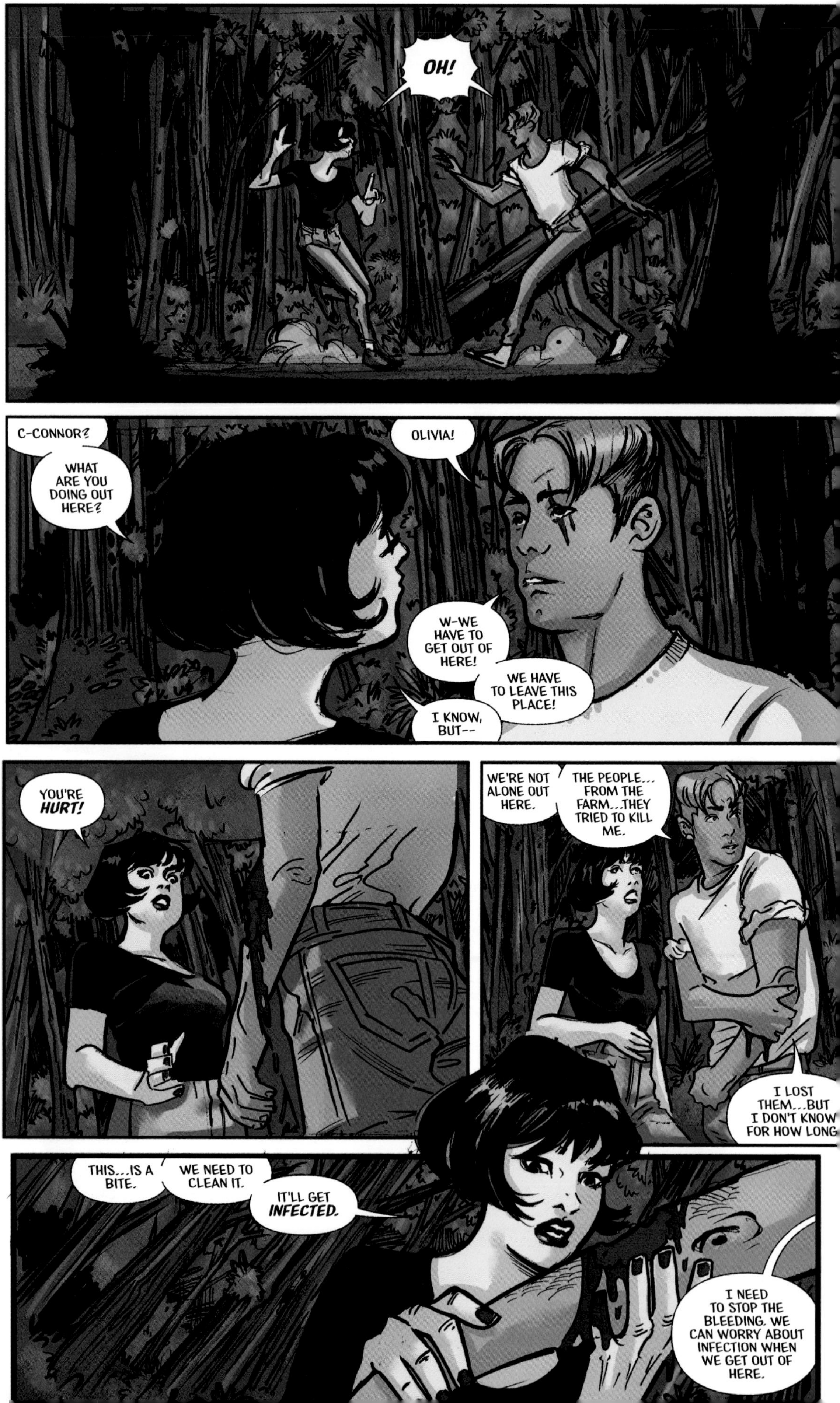

OH!
C-CONNOR?
WHAT ARE YOU DOING OUT HERE?
OLIVIA!
W-WE HAVE TO GET OUT OF HERE!
WE HAVE TO LEAVE THIS PLACE!
I KNOW, BUT--
YOU'RE HURT!
WE'RE NOT ALONE OUT HERE.
THE PEOPLE... FROM THE FARM...THEY TRIED TO KILL ME.
I LOST THEM...BUT I DON'T KNOW FOR HOW LONG
THIS...IS A BITE.
WE NEED TO CLEAN IT.
IT'LL GET INFECTED.
I NEED TO STOP THE BLEEDING. WE CAN WORRY ABOUT INFECTION WHEN WE GET OUT OF HERE.

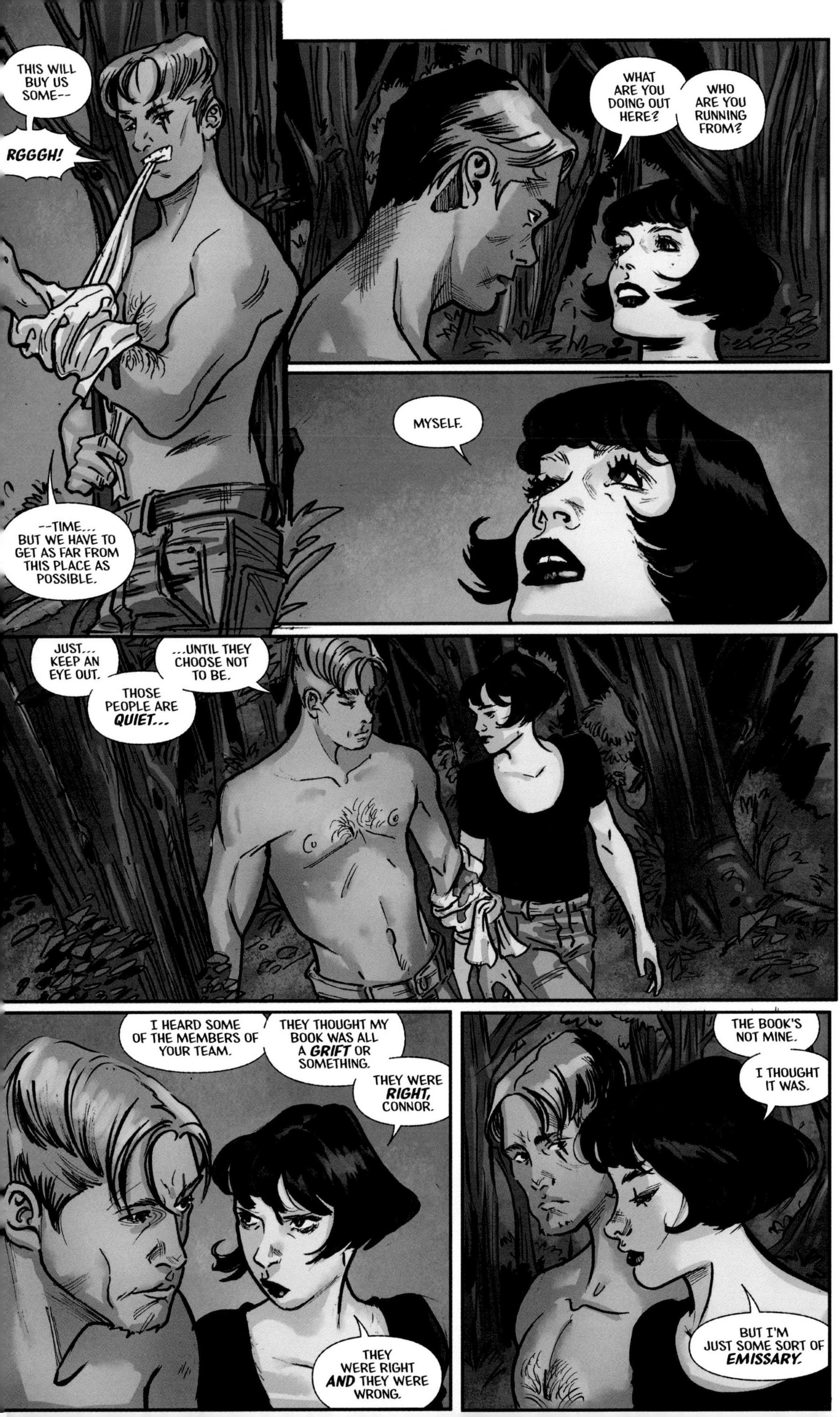
THIS WILL BUY US SOME--
RGGGH!
--TIME... BUT WE HAVE TO GET AS FAR FROM THIS PLACE AS POSSIBLE.
WHAT ARE YOU DOING OUT HERE?
WHO ARE YOU RUNNING FROM?
MYSELF.
JUST... KEEP AN EYE OUT.
THOSE PEOPLE ARE QUIET...
...UNTIL THEY CHOOSE NOT TO BE.
I HEARD SOME OF THE MEMBERS OF YOUR TEAM.
THEY THOUGHT MY BOOK WAS ALL A GRIFT OR SOMETHING.
THEY WERE RIGHT, CONNOR.
THEY WERE RIGHT AND THEY WERE WRONG.
THE BOOK'S NOT MINE.
I THOUGHT IT WAS.
BUT I'M JUST SOME SORT OF EMISSARY.

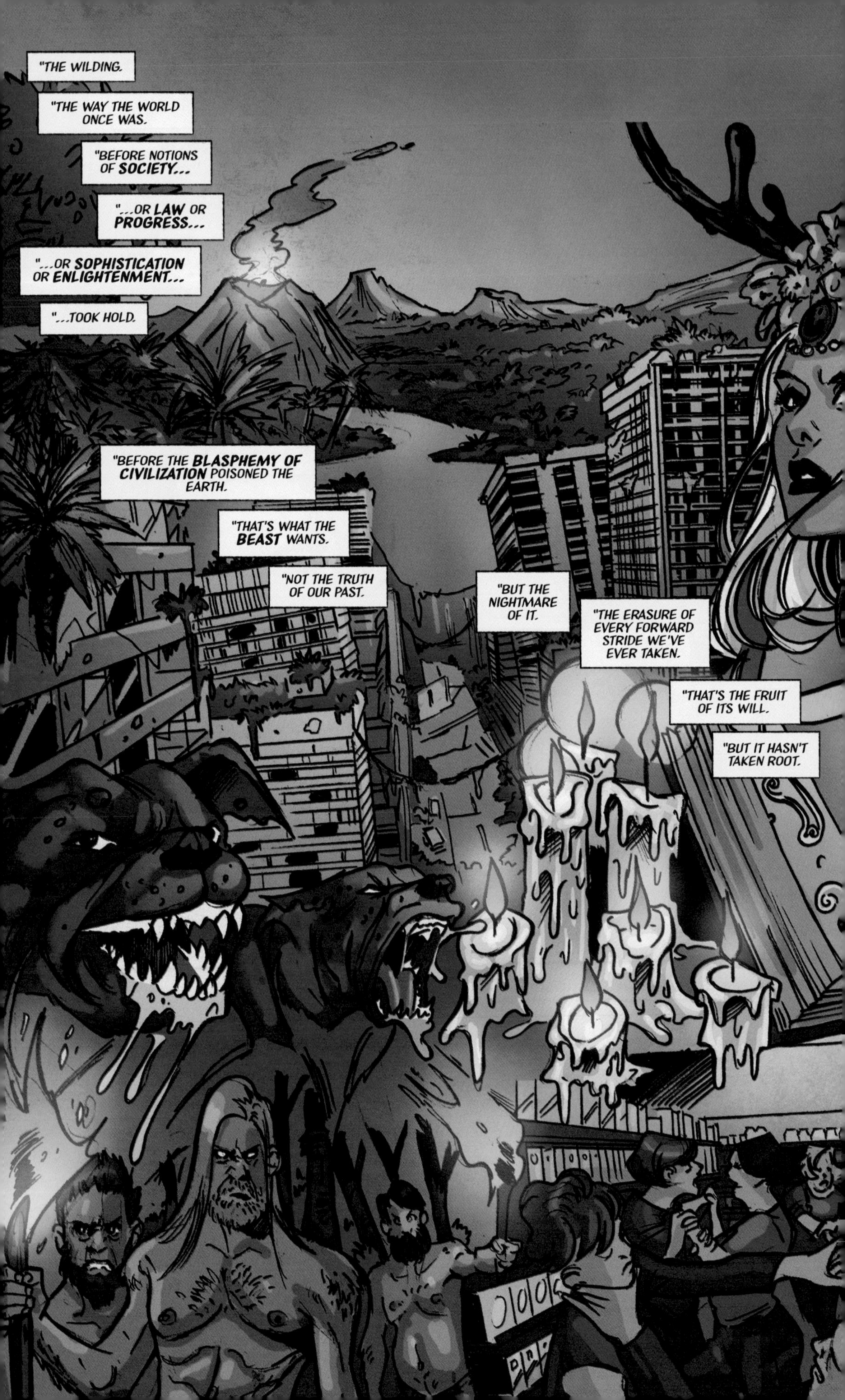
"THE WILDING.
"THE WAY THE WORLD ONCE WAS.
"BEFORE NOTIONS OF SOCIETY...
"...OR LAW OR PROGRESS...
"...OR SOPHISTICATION OR ENLIGHTENMENT...
"...TOOK HOLD.
"BEFORE THE BLASPHEMY OF CIVILIZATION POISONED THE EARTH.
"THAT'S WHAT THE BEAST WANTS.
"NOT THE TRUTH OF OUR PAST.
"BUT THE NIGHTMARE OF IT.
"THE ERASURE OF EVERY FORWARD STRIDE WE'VE EVER TAKEN.
"THAT'S THE FRUIT OF ITS WILL.
"BUT IT HASN'T TAKEN ROOT.

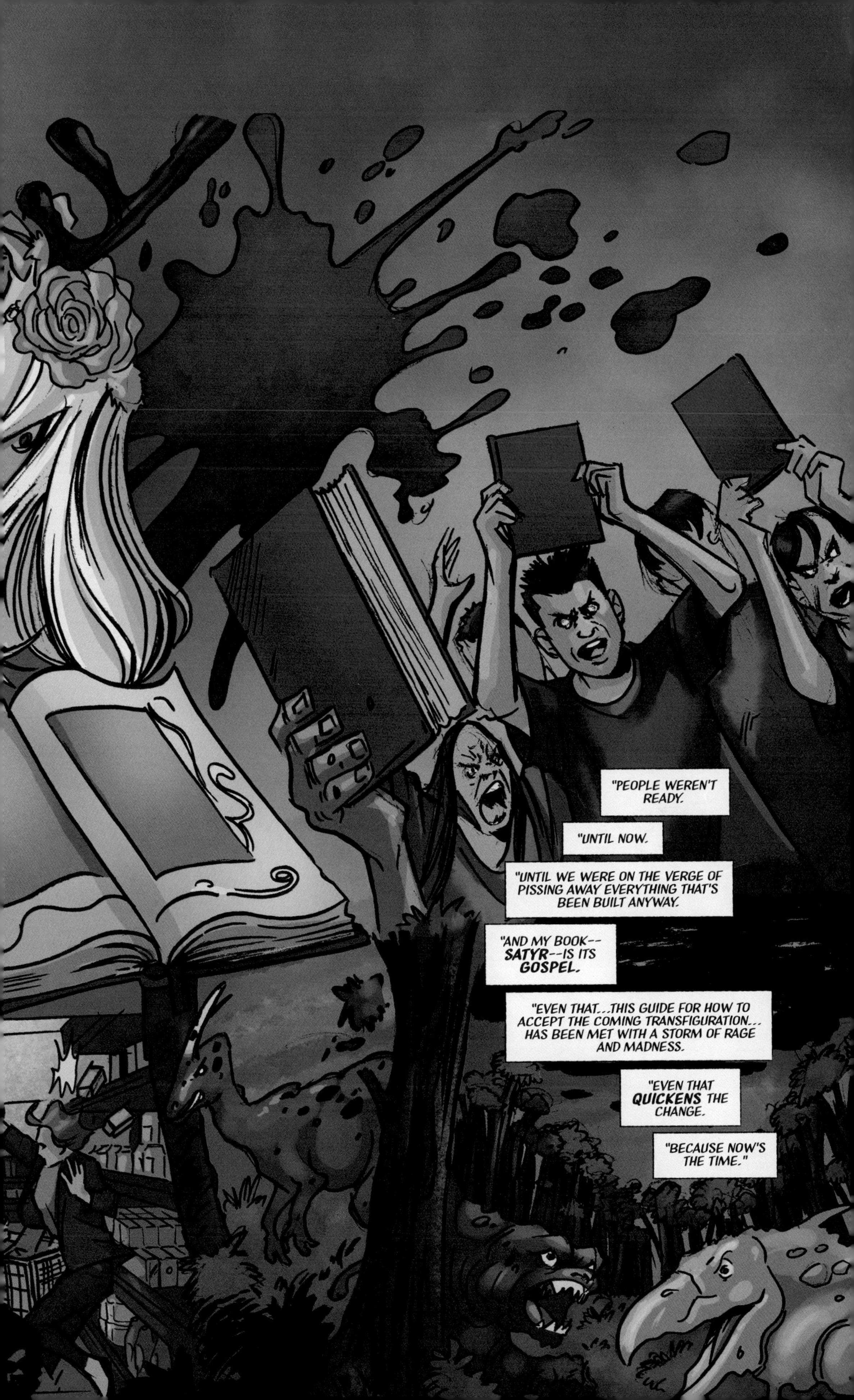
"PEOPLE WEREN'T READY.
"UNTIL NOW.
"UNTIL WE WERE ON THE VERGE OF PISSING AWAY EVERYTHING THAT'S BEEN BUILT ANYWAY.
"AND MY BOOK-- SATYR--IS ITS GOSPEL.
"EVEN THAT...THIS GUIDE FOR HOW TO ACCEPT THE COMING TRANSFIGURATION... HAS BEEN MET WITH A STORM OF RAGE AND MADNESS.
"EVEN THAT QUICKENS THE CHANGE.
"BECAUSE NOW'S THE TIME."

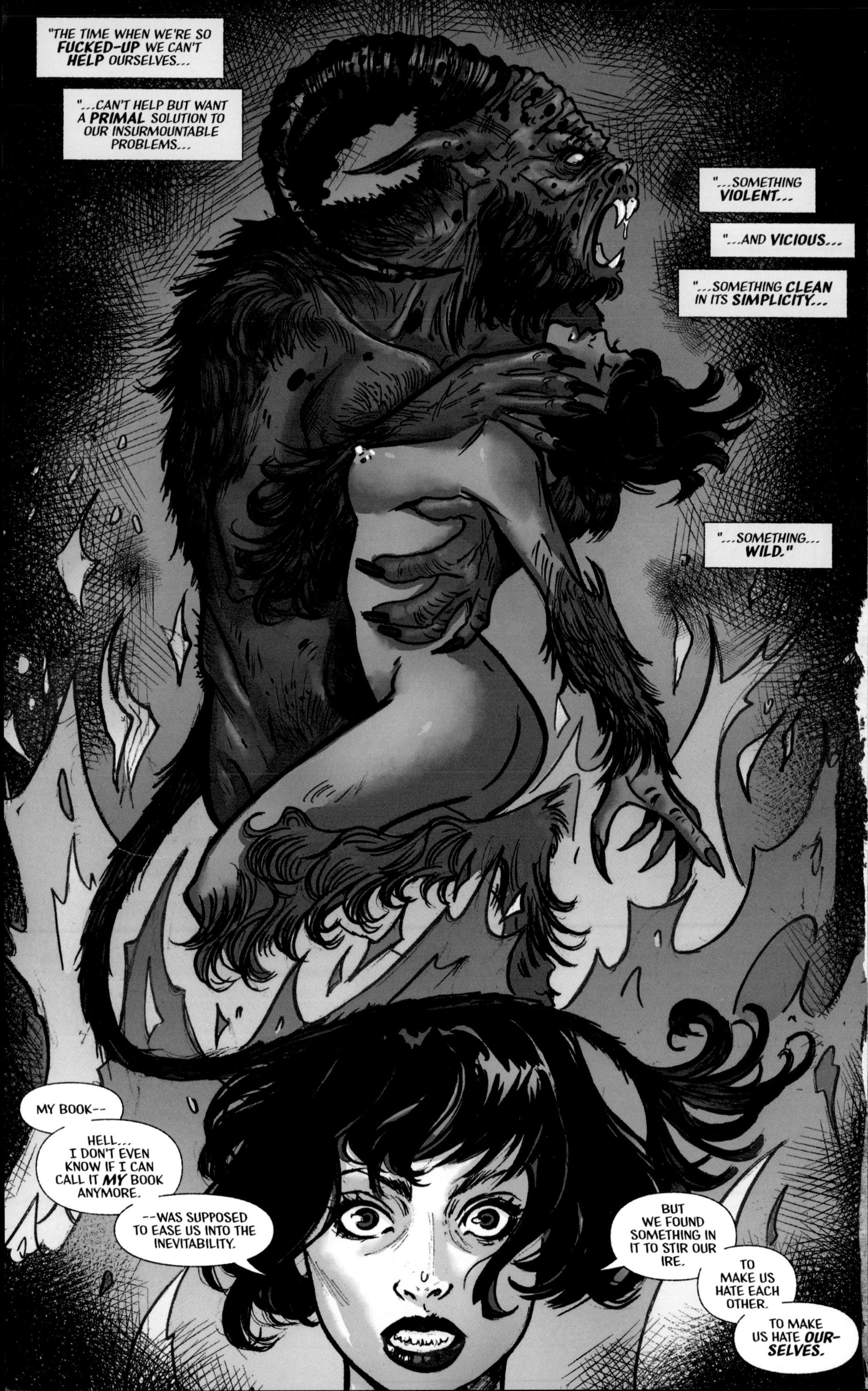
"THE TIME WHEN WE'RE SO FUCKED-UP WE CAN'T HELP OURSELVES...
"...CAN'T HELP BUT WANT A PRIMAL SOLUTION TO OUR INSURMOUNTABLE PROBLEMS...
"...SOMETHING VIOLENT...
"...AND VICIOUS...
"...SOMETHING CLEAN IN ITS SIMPLICITY...
"...SOMETHING... WILD."
MY BOOK--
HELL... I DON'T EVEN KNOW IF I CAN CALL IT MY BOOK ANYMORE.
--WAS SUPPOSED TO EASE US INTO THE INEVITABILITY.
BUT WE FOUND SOMETHING IN IT TO STIR OUR IRE.
TO MAKE US HATE EACH OTHER.
TO MAKE US HATE OUR-SELVES.

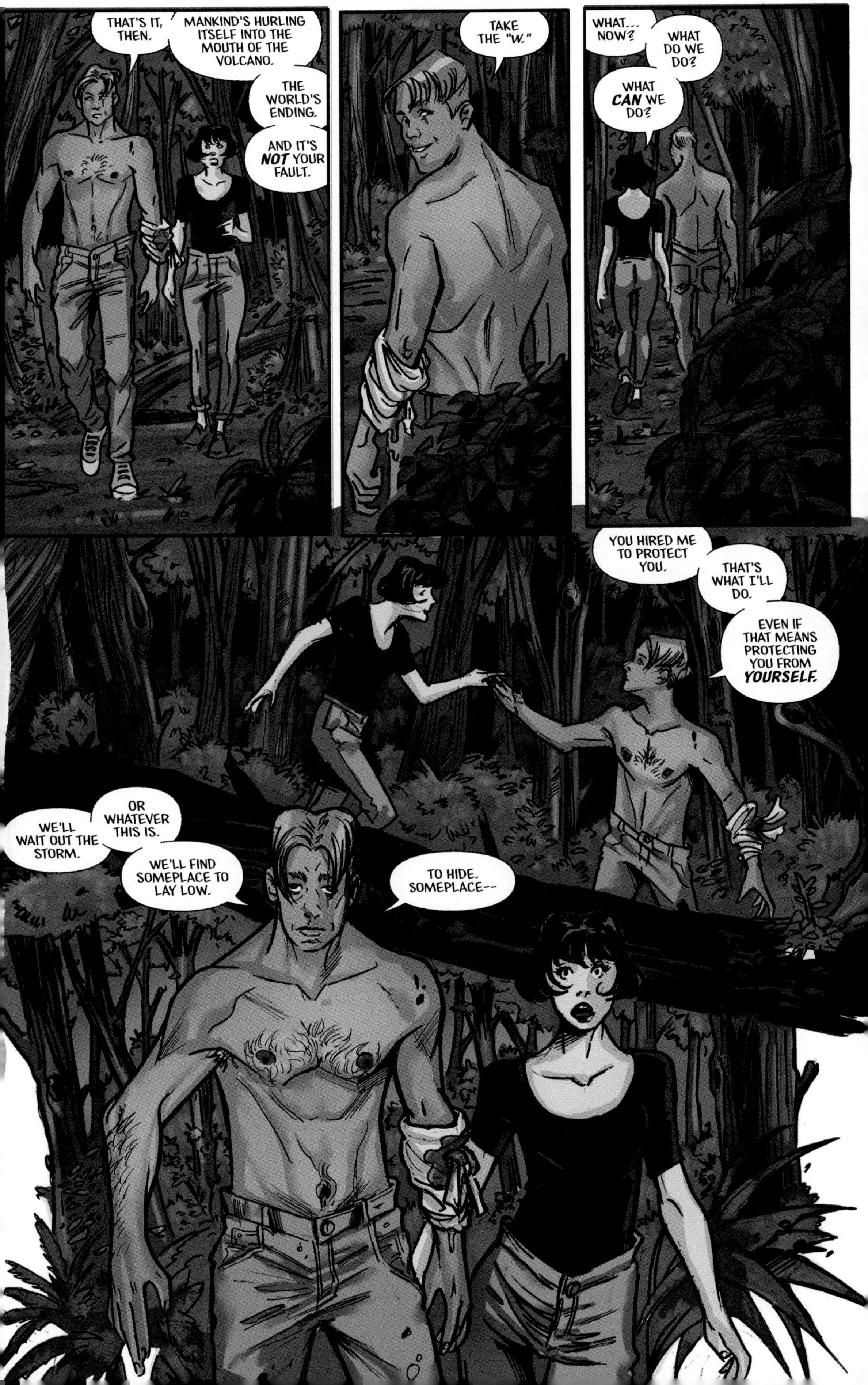
THAT'S IT, THEN.
MANKIND'S HURLING ITSELF INTO THE MOUTH OF THE VOLCANO.
THE WORLD'S ENDING.
AND IT'S NOT YOUR FAULT.
TAKE THE "W."
WHAT... NOW?
WHAT DO WE DO?
WHAT CAN WE DO?
YOU HIRED ME TO PROTECT YOU.
THAT'S WHAT I'LL DO.
EVEN IF THAT MEANS PROTECTING YOU FROM YOURSELF.
WE'LL WAIT OUT THE STORM.
OR WHATEVER THIS IS.
WE'LL FIND SOMEPLACE TO LAY LOW.
TO HIDE. SOMEPLACE--

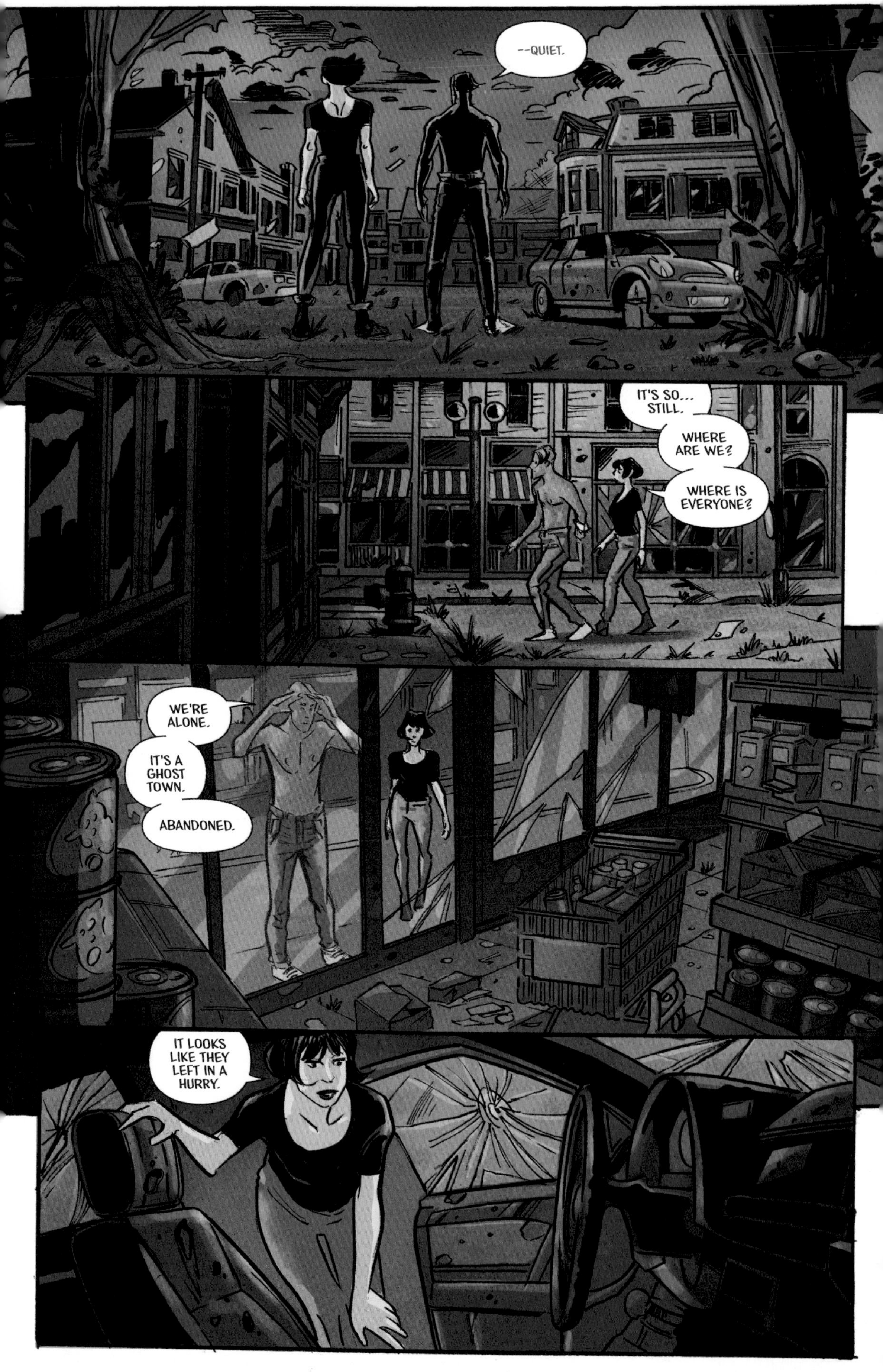
--QUIET.
IT'S SO... STILL.
WHERE ARE WE?
WHERE IS EVERYONE?
WE'RE ALONE.
IT'S A GHOST TOWN.
ABANDONED.
IT LOOKS LIKE THEY LEFT IN A HURRY.

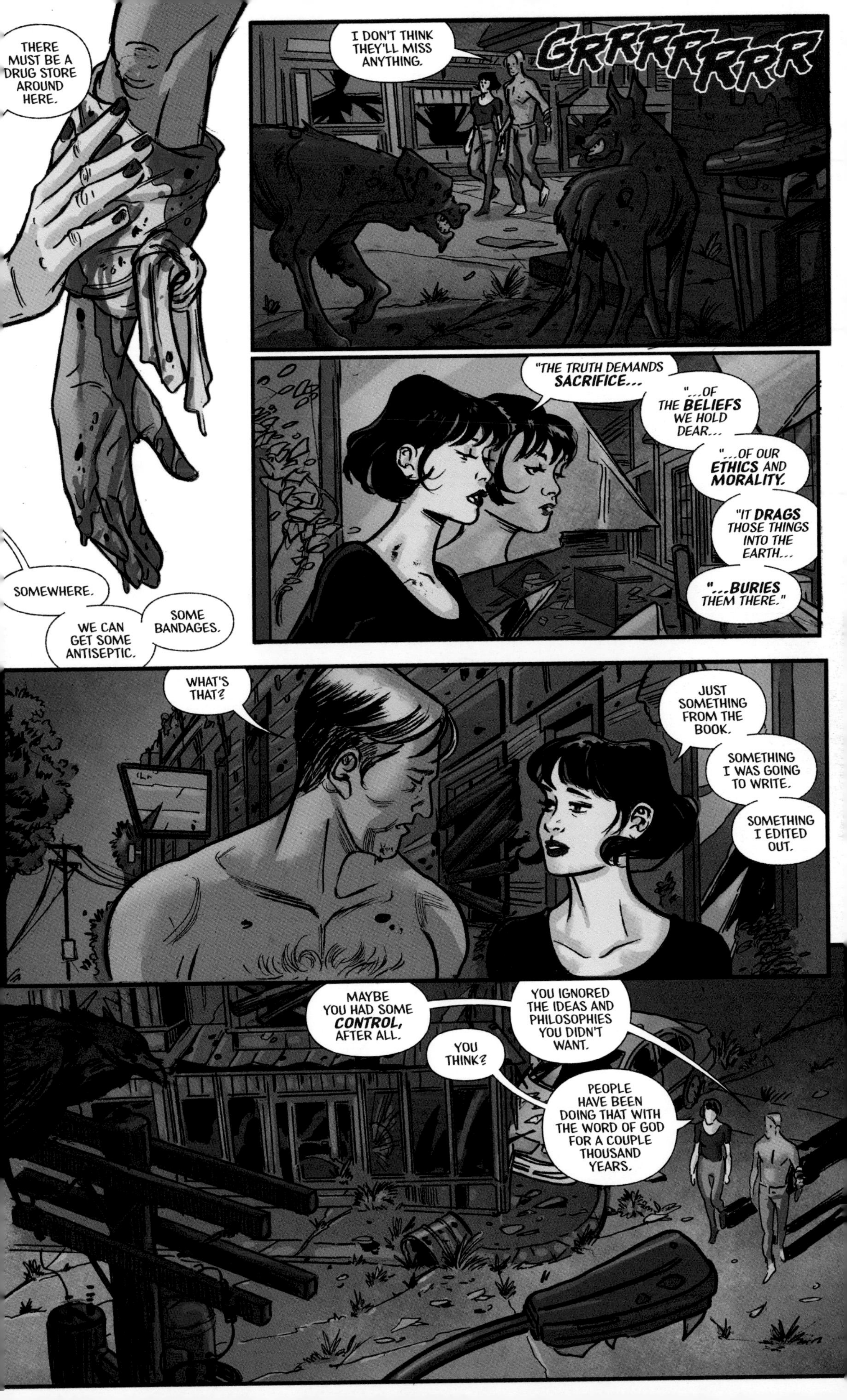

THERE MUST BE A DRUG STORE AROUND HERE.
I DON'T THINK THEY'LL MISS ANYTHING.
GRRRRRRR
"THE TRUTH DEMANDS SACRIFICE...
"...OF THE BELIEFS WE HOLD DEAR...
"...OF OUR ETHICS AND MORALITY.
"IT DRAGS THOSE THINGS INTO THE EARTH...
"...BURIES THEM THERE."
SOMEWHERE.
WE CAN GET SOME ANTISEPTIC.
SOME BANDAGES.
WHAT'S THAT?
JUST SOMETHING FROM THE BOOK.
SOMETHING I WAS GOING TO WRITE.
SOMETHING I EDITED OUT.
MAYBE YOU HAD SOME CONTROL, AFTER ALL.
YOU IGNORED THE IDEAS AND PHILOSOPHIES YOU DIDN'T WANT.
YOU THINK?
PEOPLE HAVE BEEN DOING THAT WITH THE WORD OF GOD FOR A COUPLE THOUSAND YEARS.

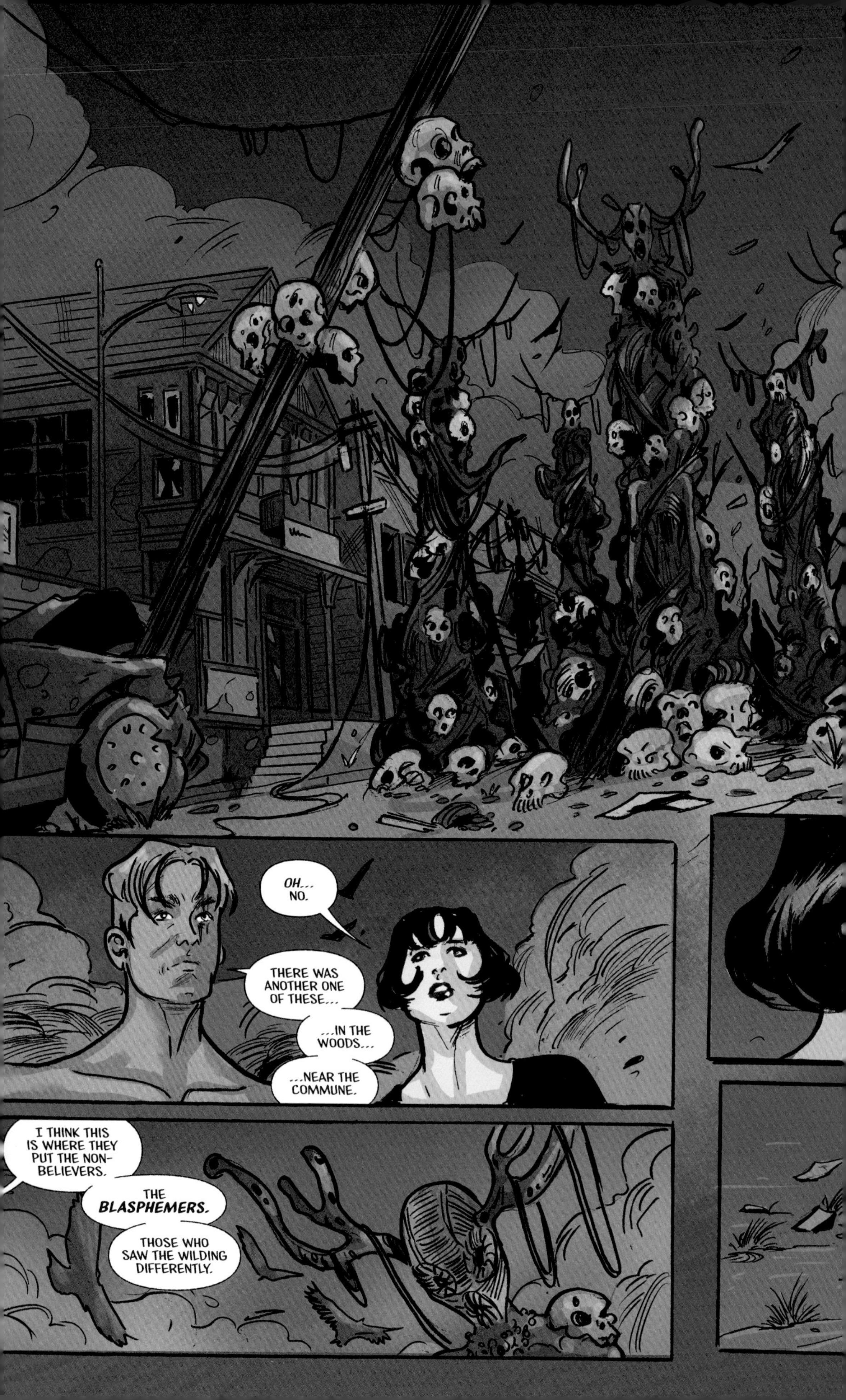
OH... NO.
THERE WAS ANOTHER ONE OF THESE...
...IN THE WOODS...
...NEAR THE COMMUNE.
I THINK THIS IS WHERE THEY PUT THE NON-BELIEVERS.
THE ***BLASPHEMERS.***
THOSE WHO SAW THE WILDING DIFFERENTLY.

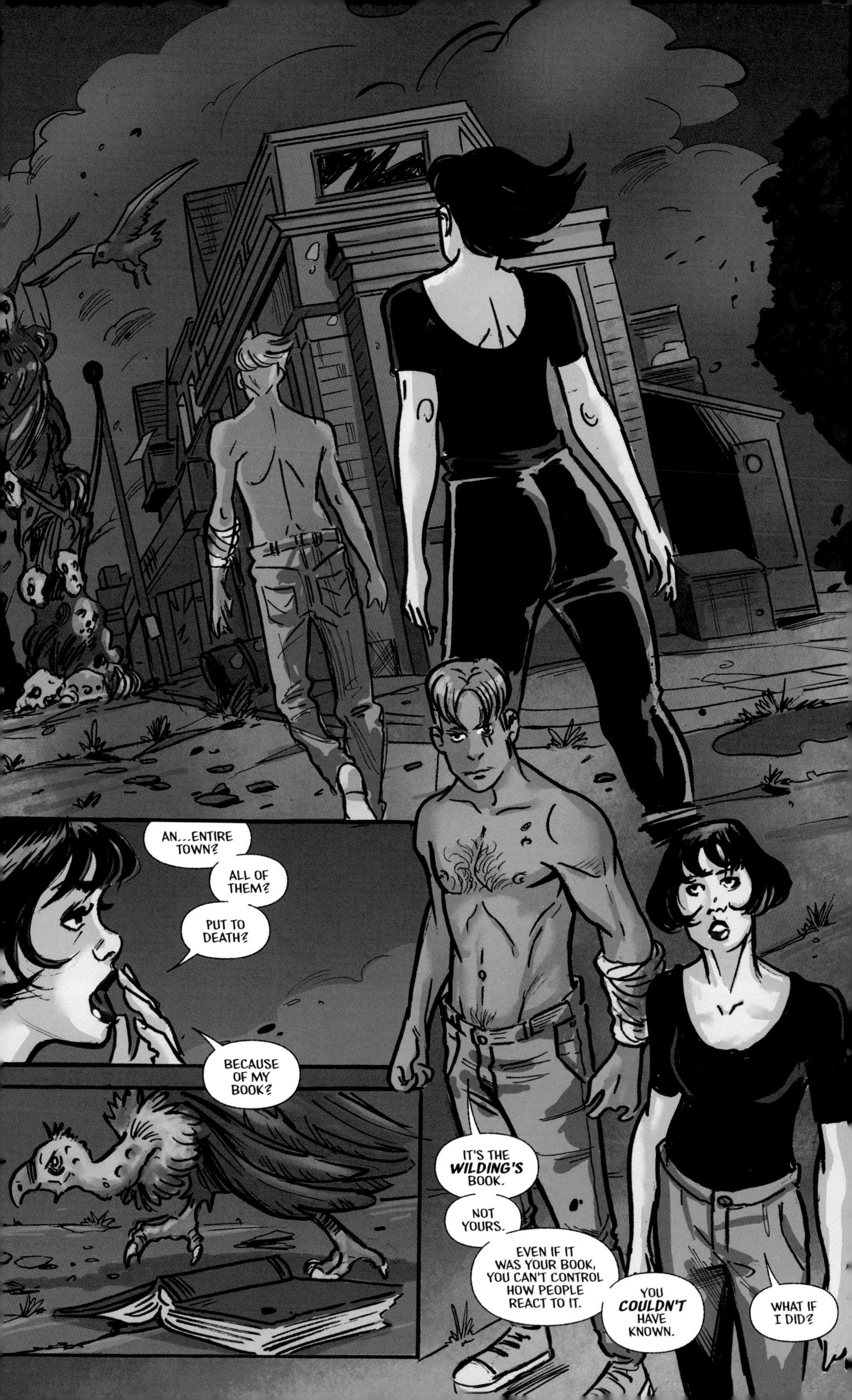
AN...ENTIRE TOWN?
ALL OF THEM?
PUT TO DEATH?
BECAUSE OF MY BOOK?
IT'S THE *WILDING'S* BOOK.
NOT YOURS.
EVEN IF IT WAS YOUR BOOK, YOU CAN'T CONTROL HOW PEOPLE REACT TO IT.
YOU *COULDN'T* HAVE KNOWN.
WHAT IF I DID?

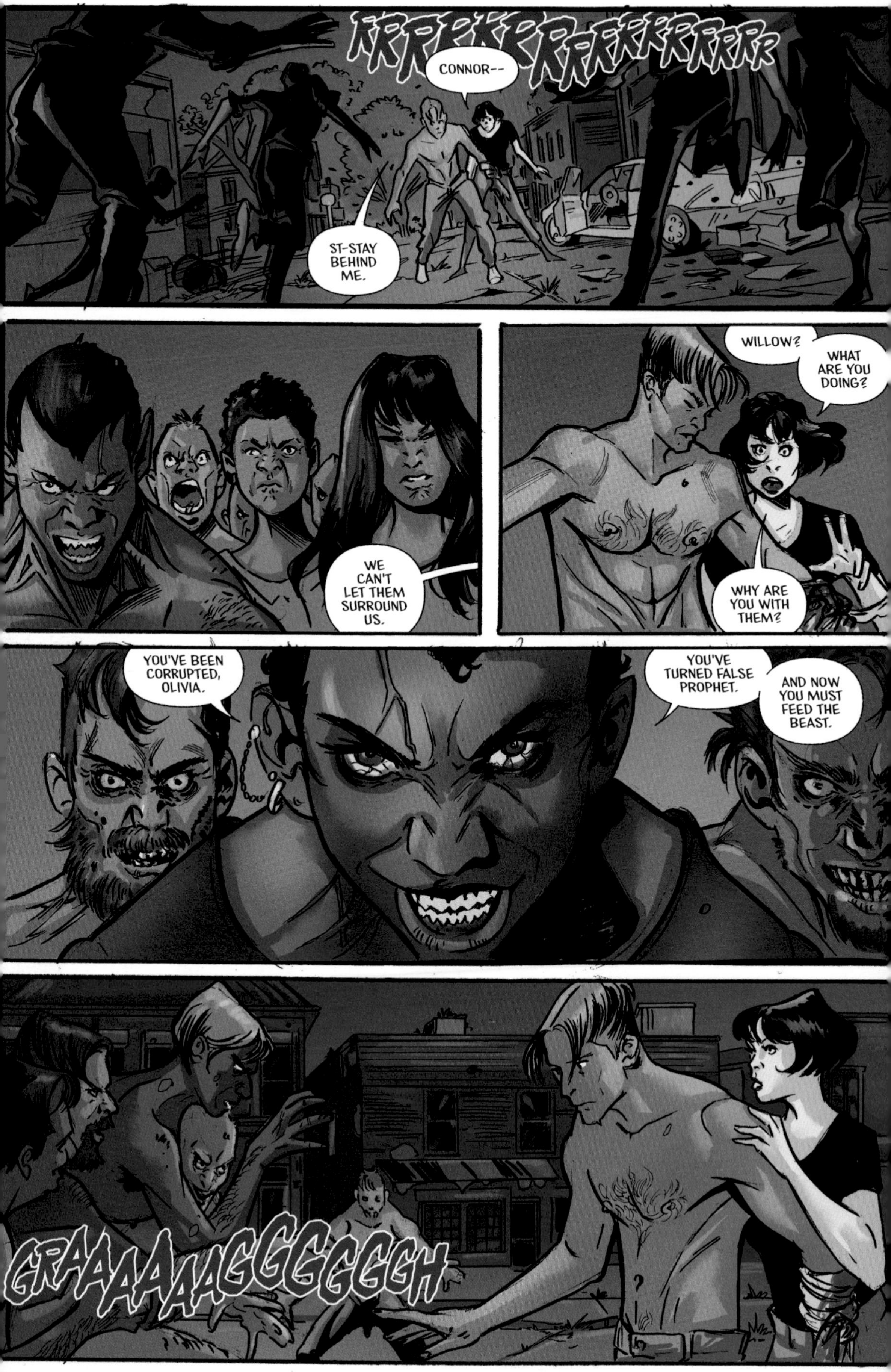
KRRRKRRRRRRRRRRRR
CONNOR--
ST-STAY BEHIND ME.
WE CAN'T LET THEM SURROUND US.
WILLOW?
WHAT ARE YOU DOING?
WHY ARE YOU WITH THEM?
YOU'VE BEEN CORRUPTED, OLIVIA.
YOU'VE TURNED FALSE PROPHET.
AND NOW YOU MUST FEED THE BEAST.
GRAAAAAAGGGGGGGH

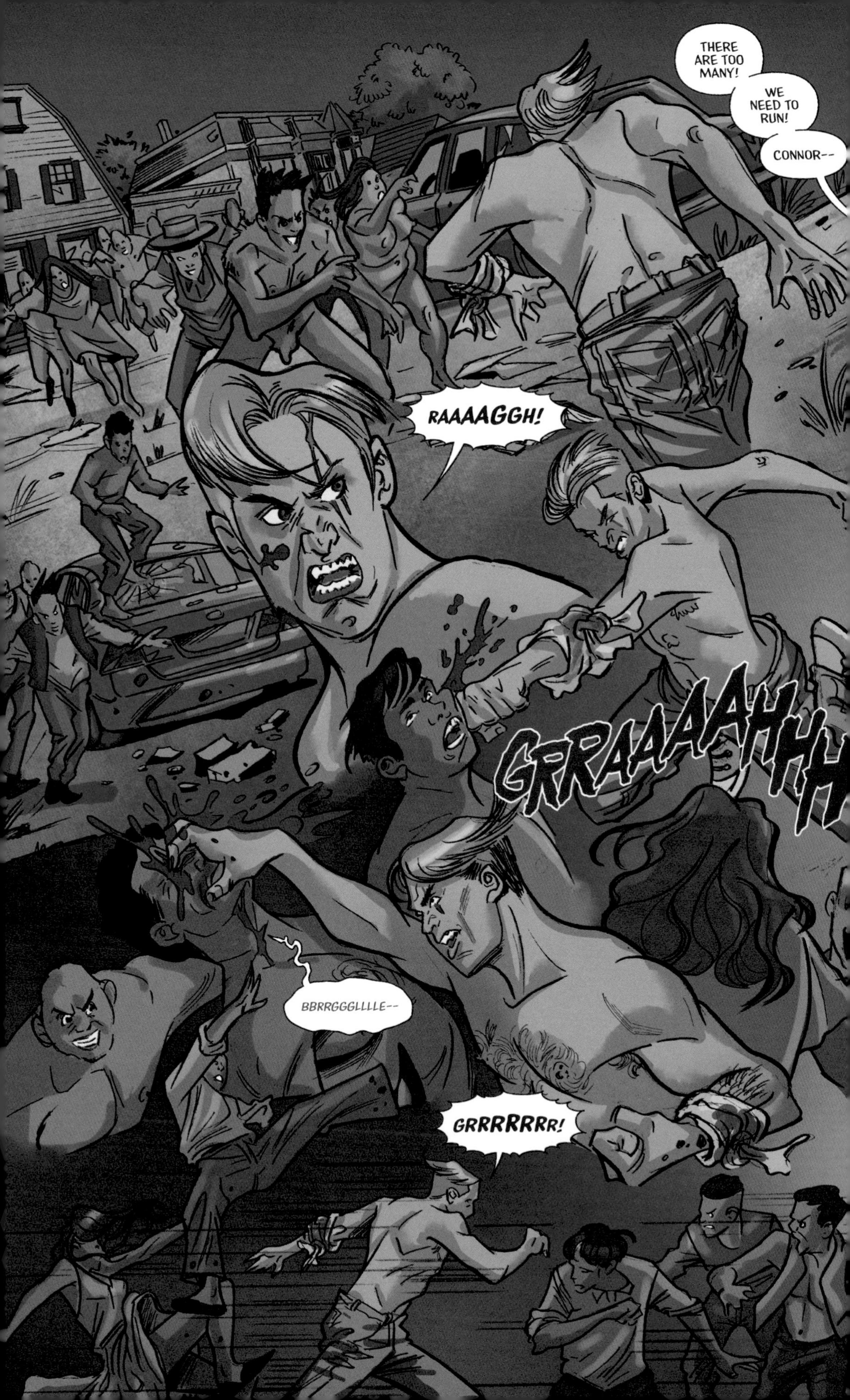
THERE ARE TOO MANY!
WE NEED TO RUN!
CONNOR--
RAAAAGGH!
GRRAAAAAHHH
BBRRGGGLLLLE--
GRRRRRRR!

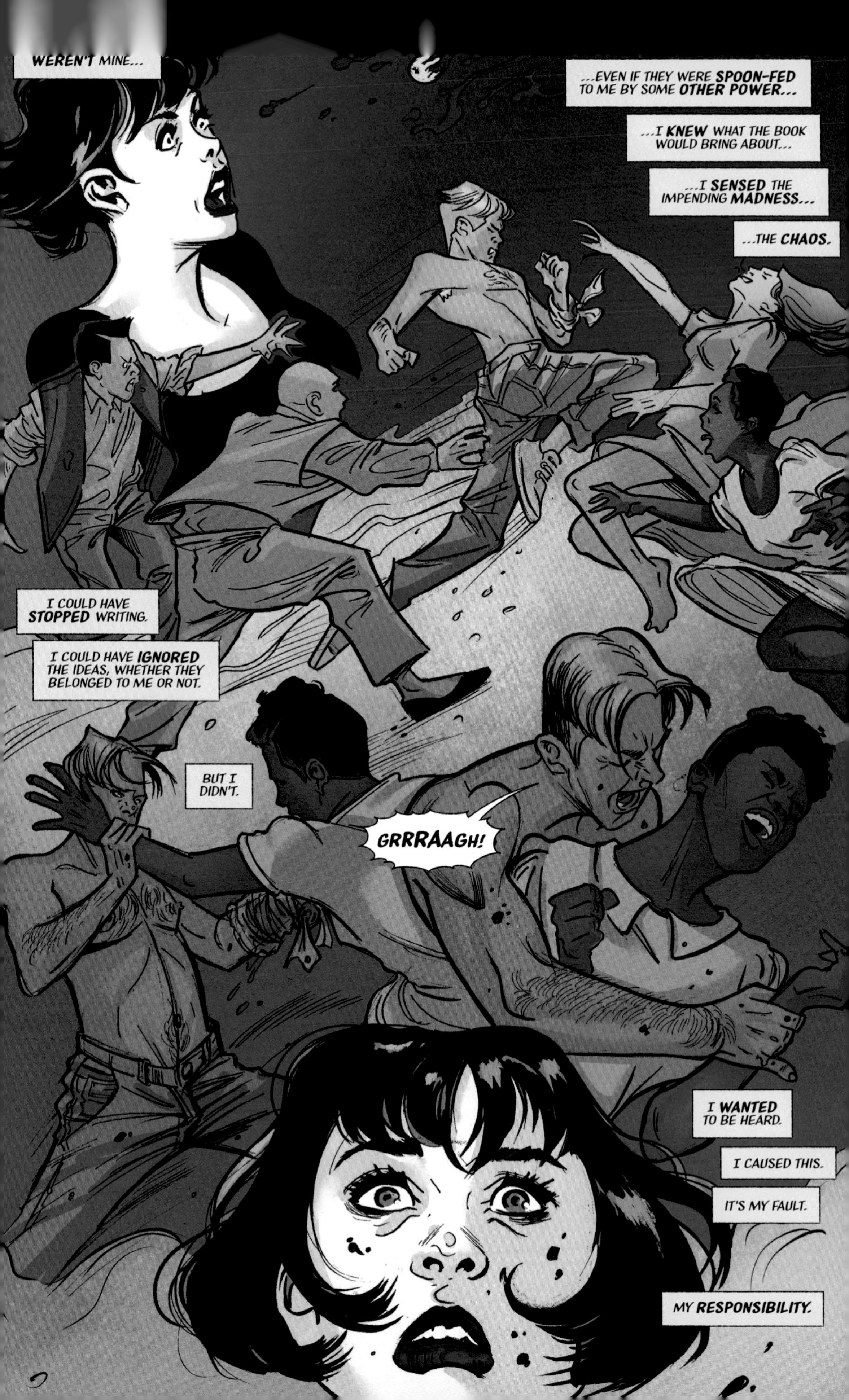
WEREN'T MINE...
...EVEN IF THEY WERE SPOON-FED TO ME BY SOME OTHER POWER...
...I KNEW WHAT THE BOOK WOULD BRING ABOUT...
...I SENSED THE IMPENDING MADNESS...
...THE CHAOS.
I COULD HAVE STOPPED WRITING.
I COULD HAVE IGNORED THE IDEAS, WHETHER THEY BELONGED TO ME OR NOT.
BUT I DIDN'T.
GRRRAAGH!
I WANTED TO BE HEARD.
I CAUSED THIS.
IT'S MY FAULT.
MY RESPONSIBILITY.

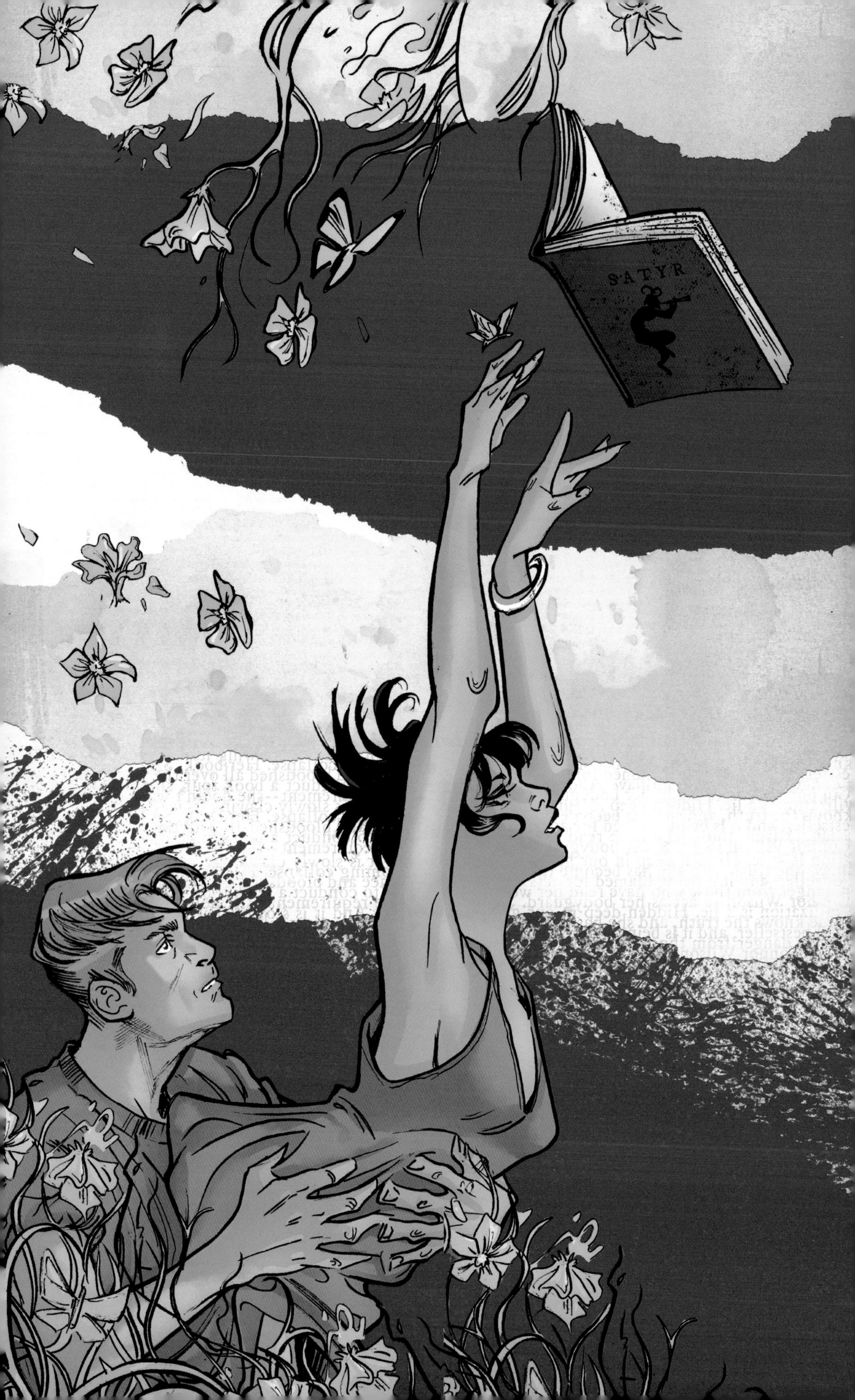
SATYR

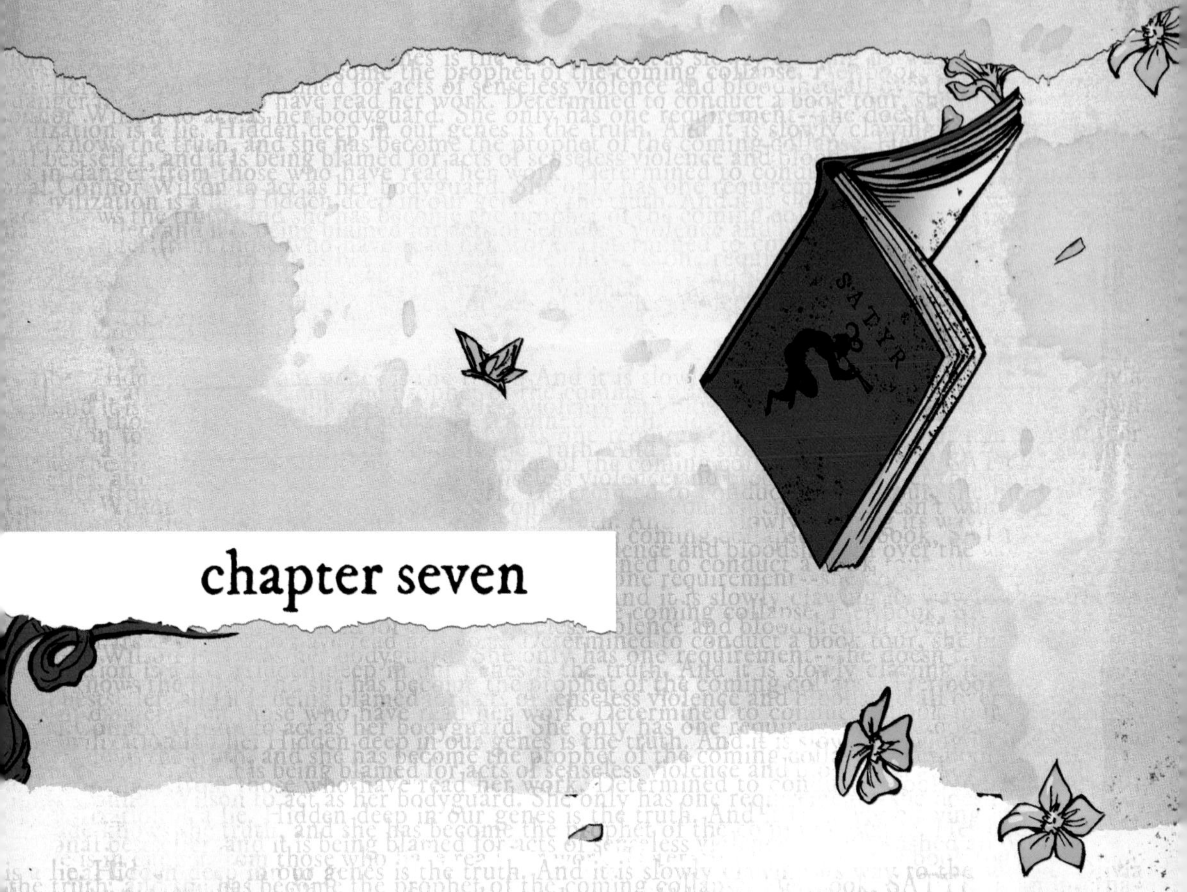
SATYR

chapter seven

Sanctuary in a small town that's been given over to the Wilding.

Weeds crack the asphalt. Animals roam the street.

Humanity is all but forgotten.

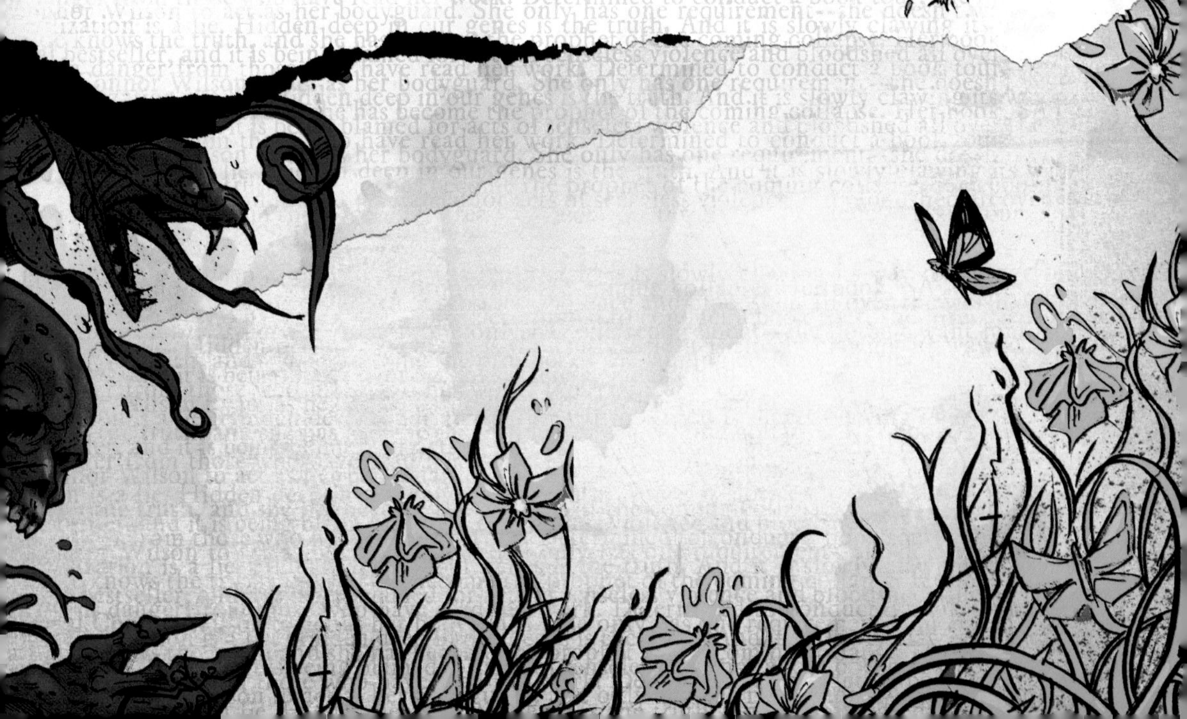

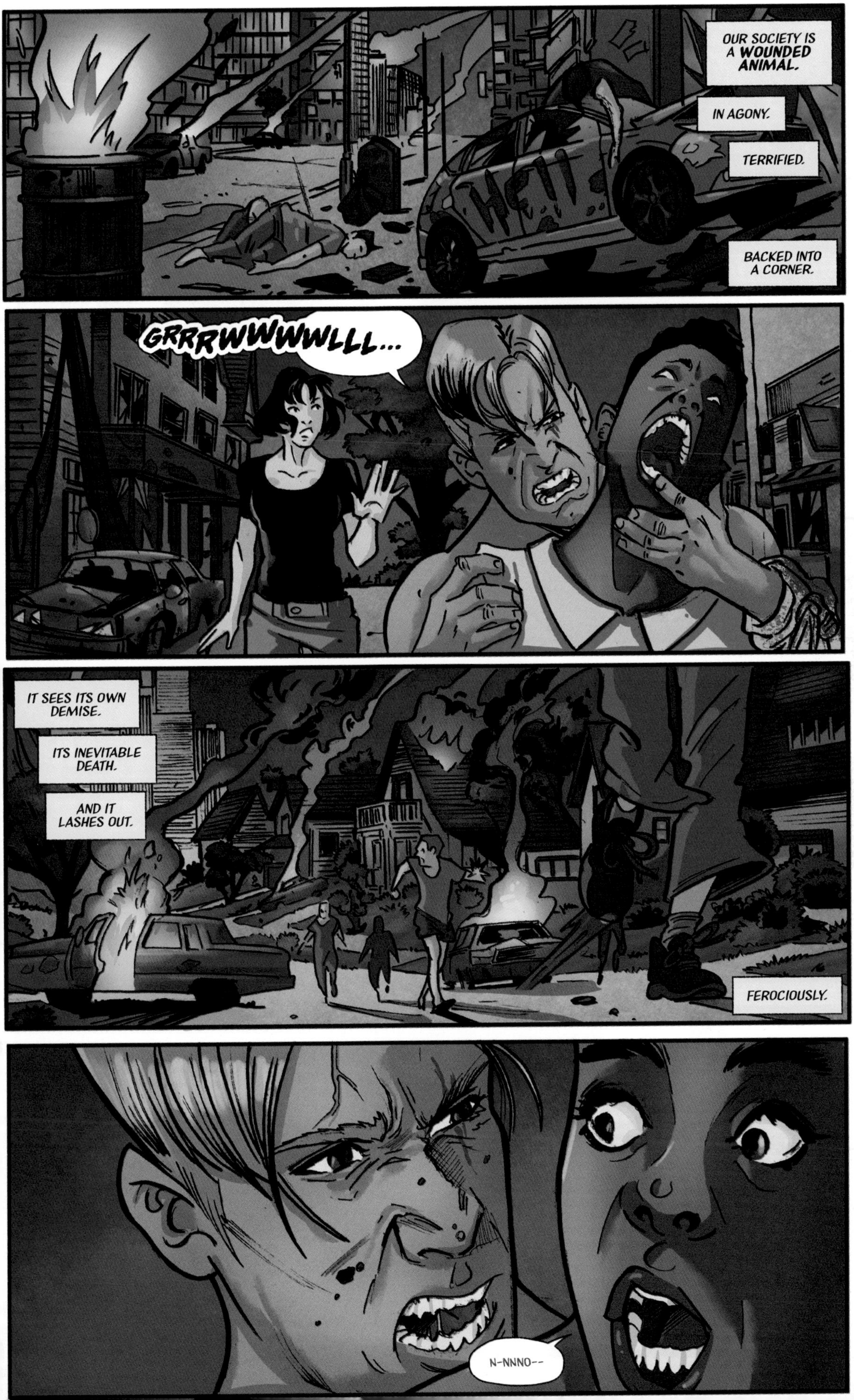
OUR SOCIETY IS A WOUNDED ANIMAL.
IN AGONY.
TERRIFIED.
HELL
BACKED INTO A CORNER.
GRRRWWWWLLL...
IT SEES ITS OWN DEMISE.
ITS INEVITABLE DEATH.
AND IT LASHES OUT.
FEROCIOUSLY.
N-NNNO--

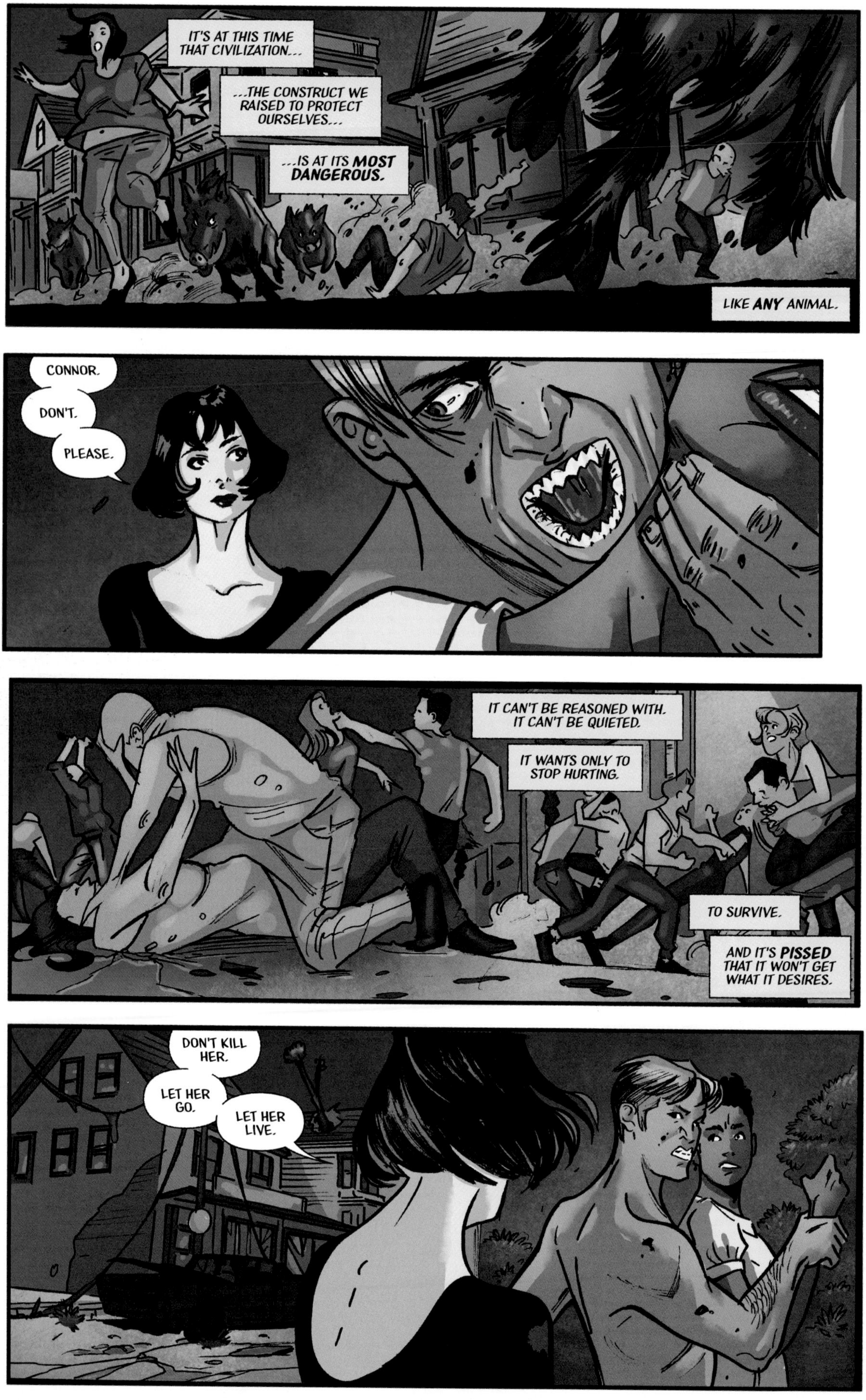
IT'S AT THIS TIME THAT CIVILIZATION...
...THE CONSTRUCT WE RAISED TO PROTECT OURSELVES...
...IS AT ITS MOST DANGEROUS.
LIKE ANY ANIMAL.
CONNOR.
DON'T.
PLEASE.
IT CAN'T BE REASONED WITH. IT CAN'T BE QUIETED.
IT WANTS ONLY TO STOP HURTING.
TO SURVIVE.
AND IT'S PISSED THAT IT WON'T GET WHAT IT DESIRES.
DON'T KILL HER.
LET HER GO.
LET HER LIVE.

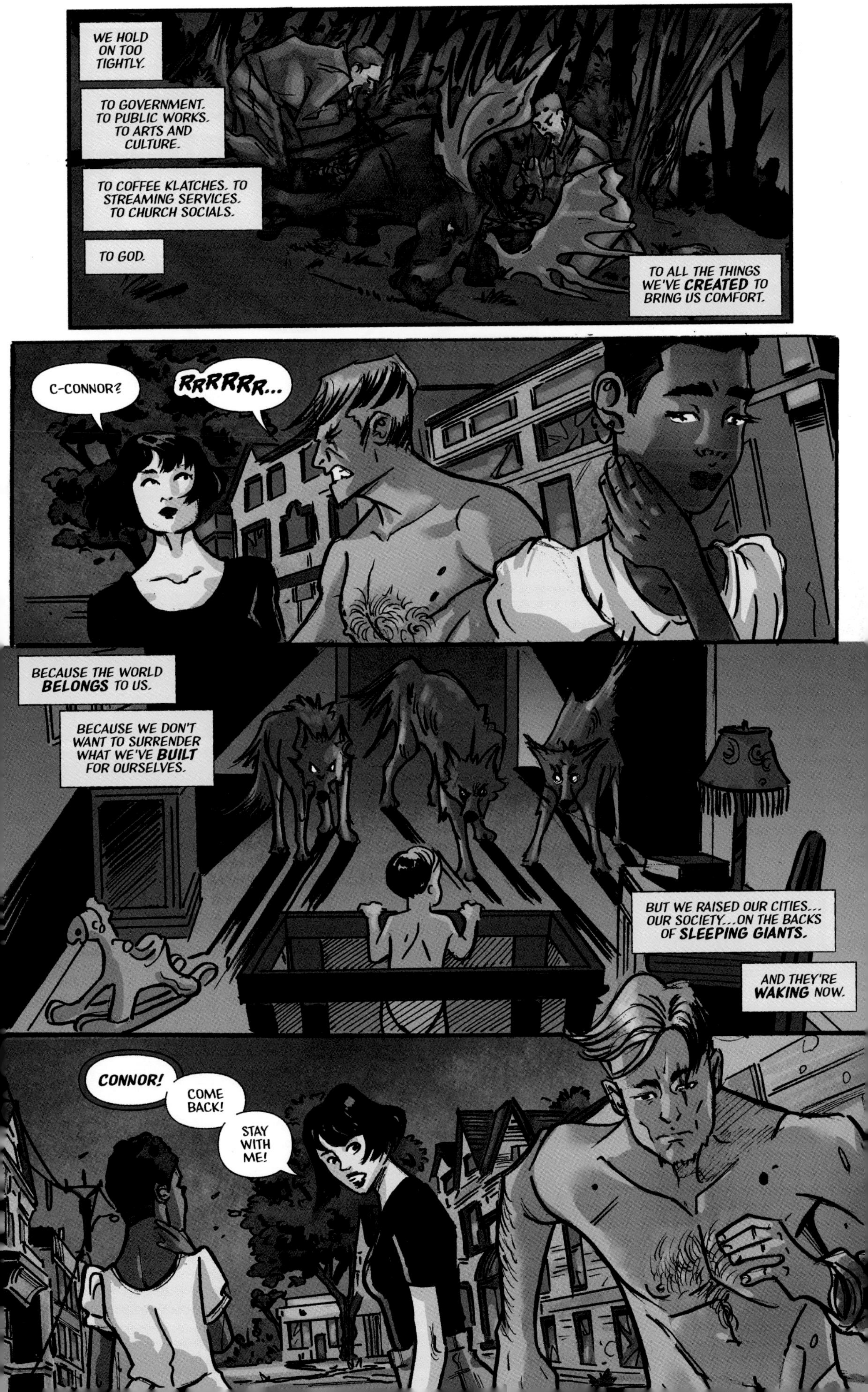

WE HOLD ON TOO TIGHTLY.
TO GOVERNMENT. TO PUBLIC WORKS. TO ARTS AND CULTURE.
TO COFFEE KLATCHES. TO STREAMING SERVICES. TO CHURCH SOCIALS.
TO GOD.
TO ALL THE THINGS WE'VE CREATED TO BRING US COMFORT.
C-CONNOR?
RRRRRR...
BECAUSE THE WORLD BELONGS TO US.
BECAUSE WE DON'T WANT TO SURRENDER WHAT WE'VE BUILT FOR OURSELVES.
BUT WE RAISED OUR CITIES... OUR SOCIETY...ON THE BACKS OF SLEEPING GIANTS.
AND THEY'RE WAKING NOW.
CONNOR!
COME BACK!
STAY WITH ME!

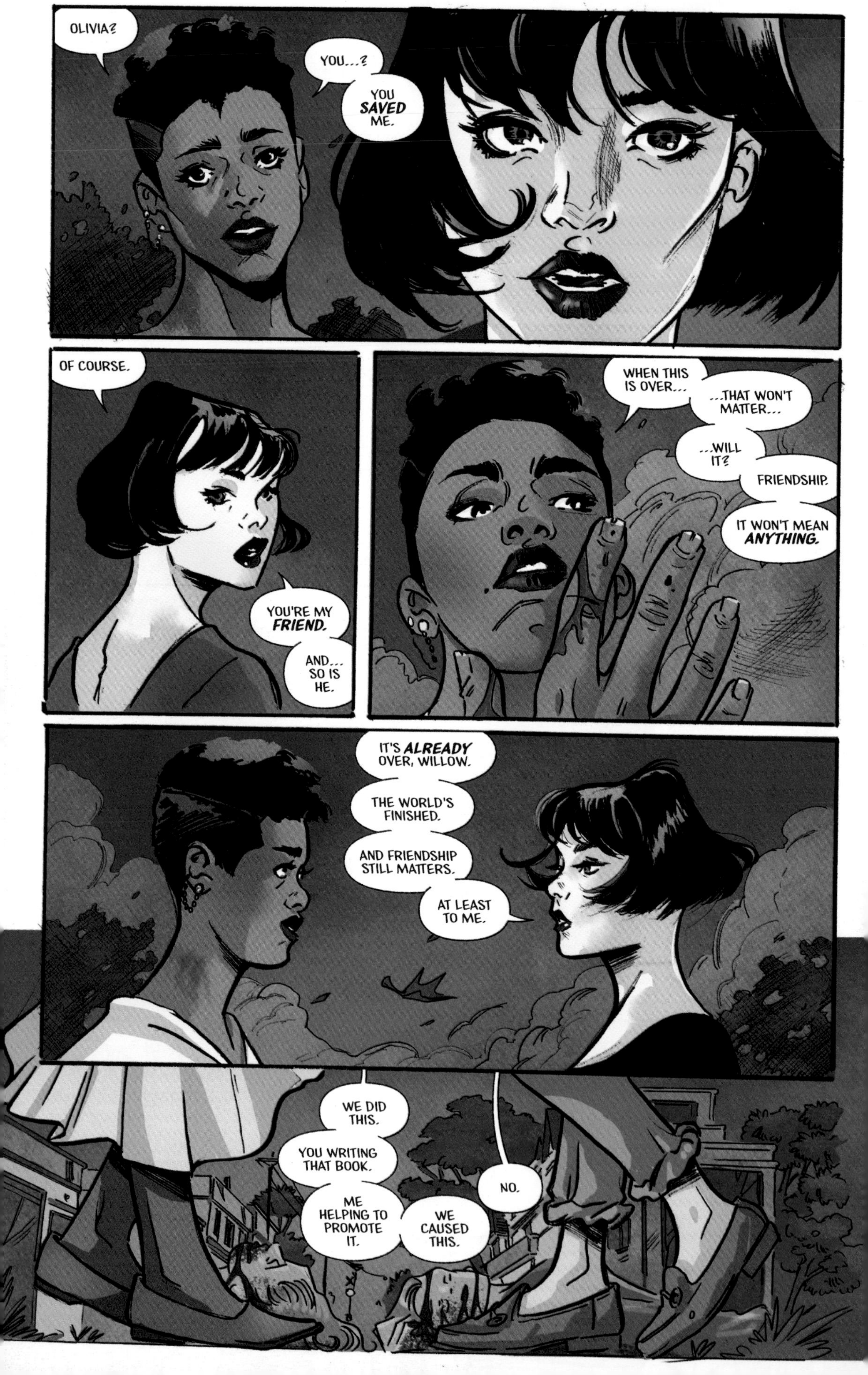

OLIVIA?
YOU...?
YOU SAVED ME.
OF COURSE.
YOU'RE MY FRIEND.
AND... SO IS HE.
WHEN THIS IS OVER...
...THAT WON'T MATTER...
...WILL IT?
FRIENDSHIP.
IT WON'T MEAN ANYTHING.
IT'S ALREADY OVER, WILLOW.
THE WORLD'S FINISHED.
AND FRIENDSHIP STILL MATTERS.
AT LEAST TO ME.
WE DID THIS.
YOU WRITING THAT BOOK.
ME HELPING TO PROMOTE IT.
WE CAUSED THIS.
NO.

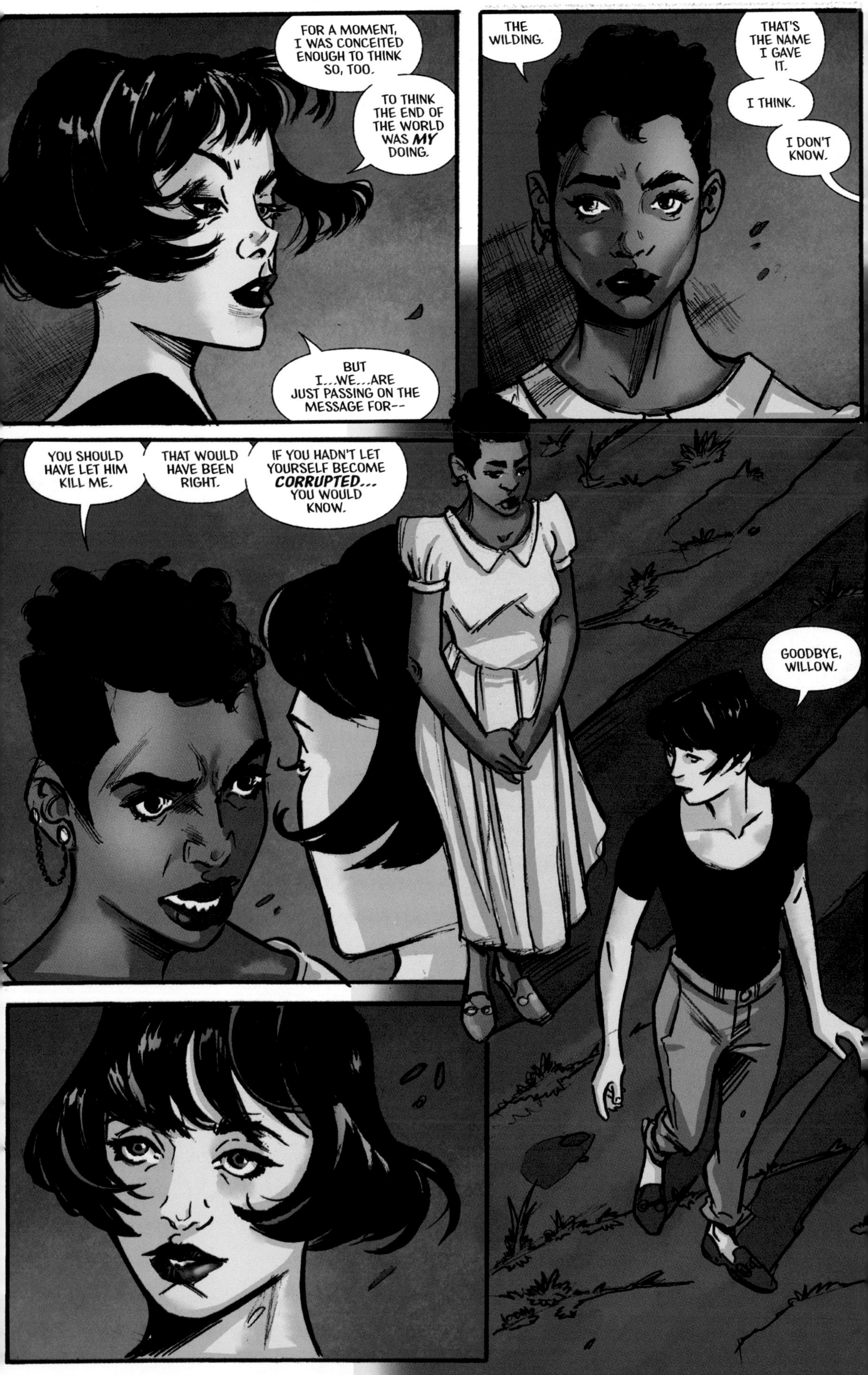
FOR A MOMENT, I WAS CONCEITED ENOUGH TO THINK SO, TOO.
TO THINK THE END OF THE WORLD WAS *MY* DOING.
BUT I...WE...ARE JUST PASSING ON THE MESSAGE FOR--
THE WILDING.
THAT'S THE NAME I GAVE IT.
I THINK.
I DON'T KNOW.
YOU SHOULD HAVE LET HIM KILL ME.
THAT WOULD HAVE BEEN RIGHT.
IF YOU HADN'T LET YOURSELF BECOME ***CORRUPTED...*** YOU WOULD KNOW.
GOODBYE, WILLOW.

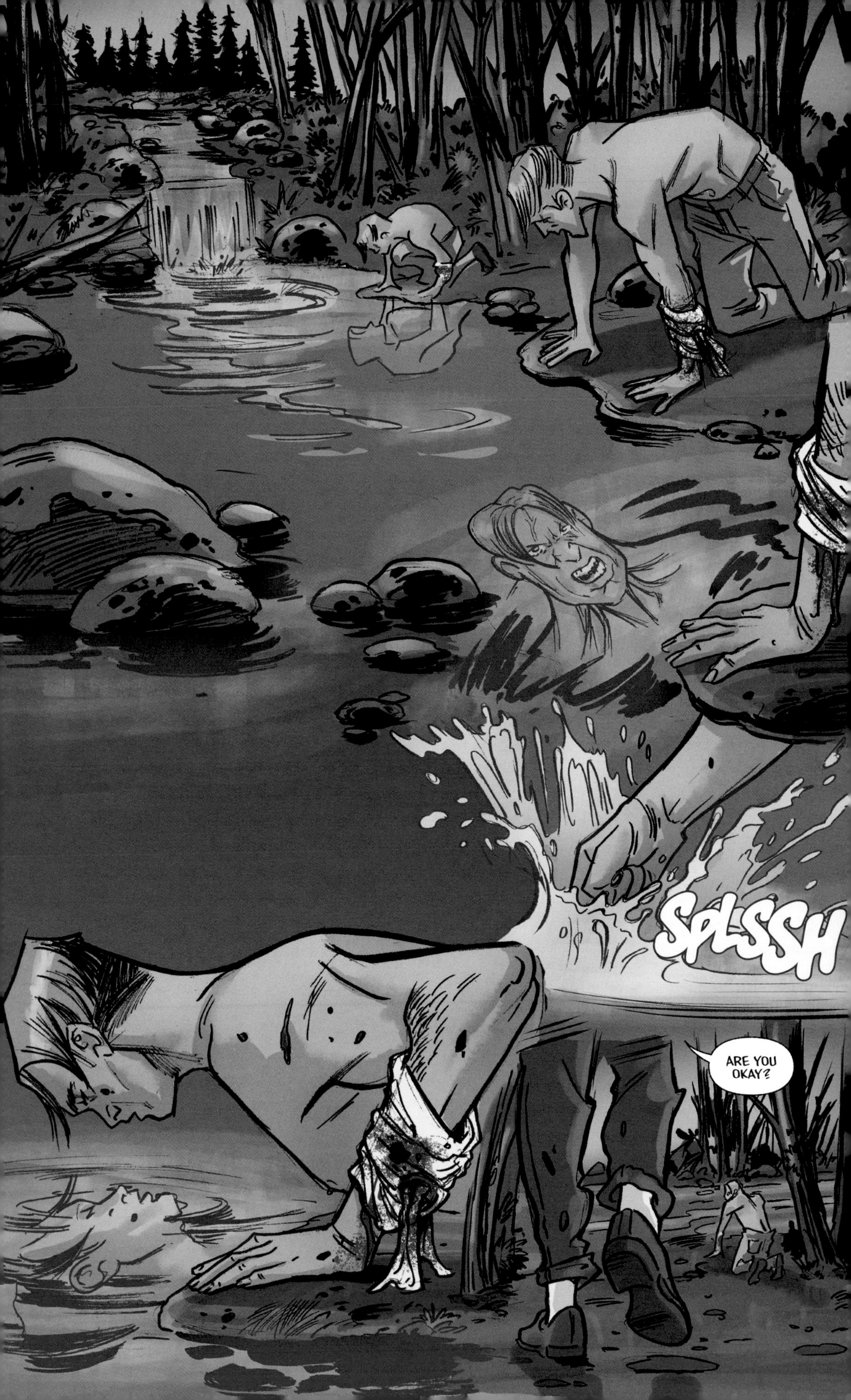
SPLSSH
ARE YOU OKAY?

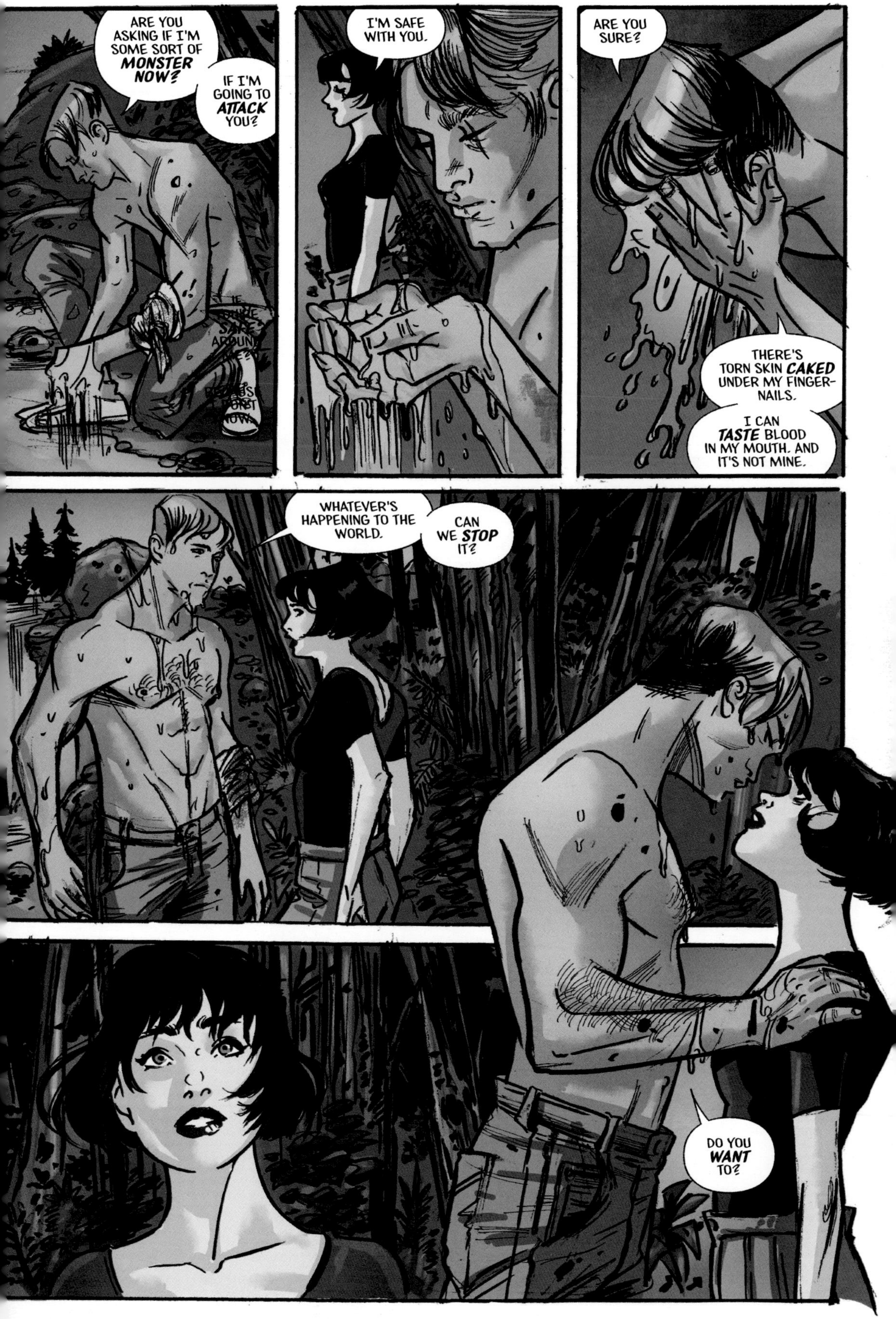
ARE YOU ASKING IF I'M SOME SORT OF MONSTER NOW?
IF I'M GOING TO ATTACK YOU?
I'M SAFE WITH YOU.
ARE YOU SURE?
THERE'S TORN SKIN CAKED UNDER MY FINGER-NAILS.
I CAN TASTE BLOOD IN MY MOUTH. AND IT'S NOT MINE.
WHATEVER'S HAPPENING TO THE WORLD.
CAN WE STOP IT?
DO YOU WANT TO?

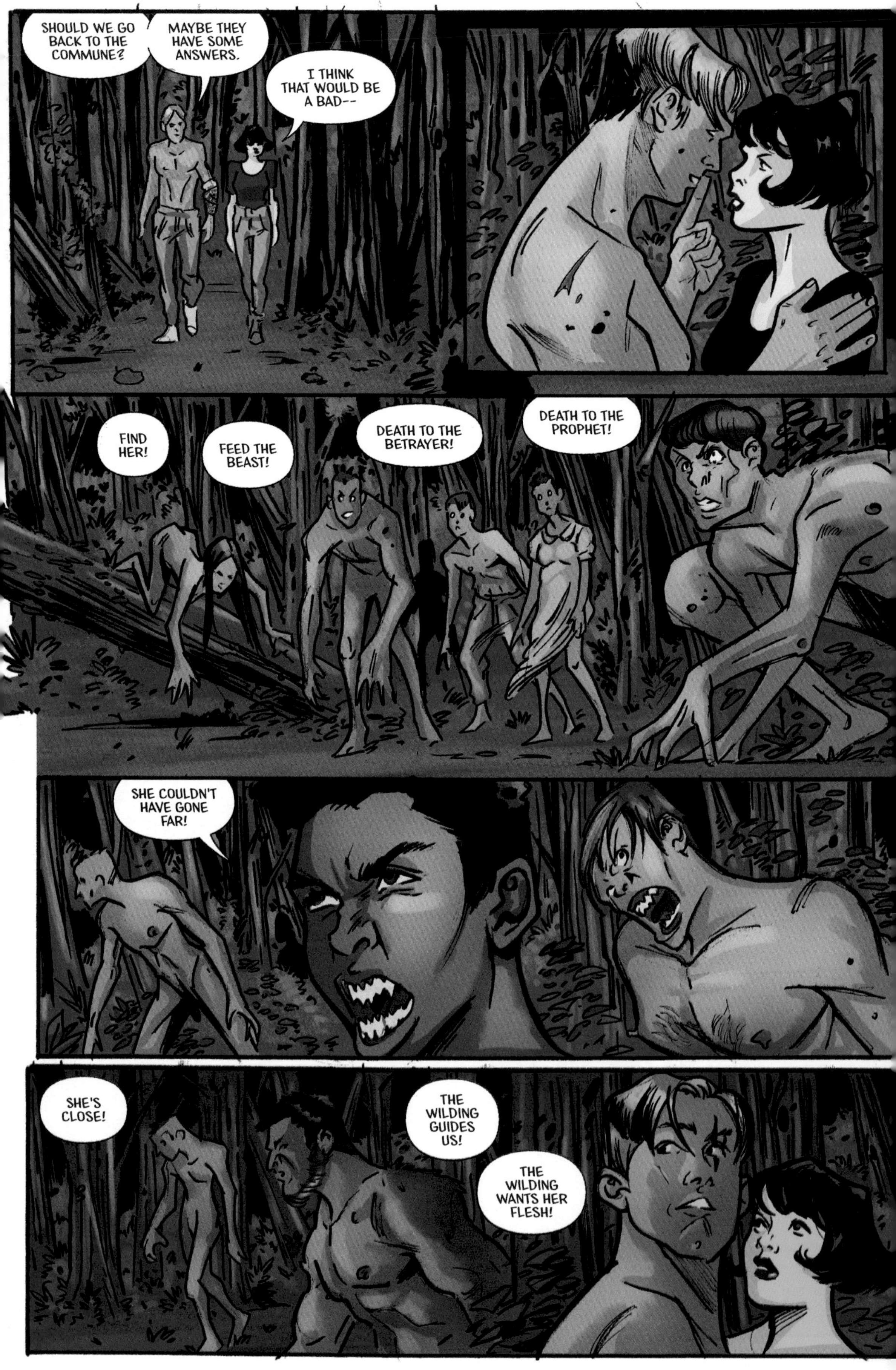
SHOULD WE GO BACK TO THE COMMUNE?
MAYBE THEY HAVE SOME ANSWERS.
I THINK THAT WOULD BE A BAD--
FIND HER!
FEED THE BEAST!
DEATH TO THE BETRAYER!
DEATH TO THE PROPHET!
SHE COULDN'T HAVE GONE FAR!
SHE'S CLOSE!
THE WILDING GUIDES US!
THE WILDING WANTS HER FLESH!

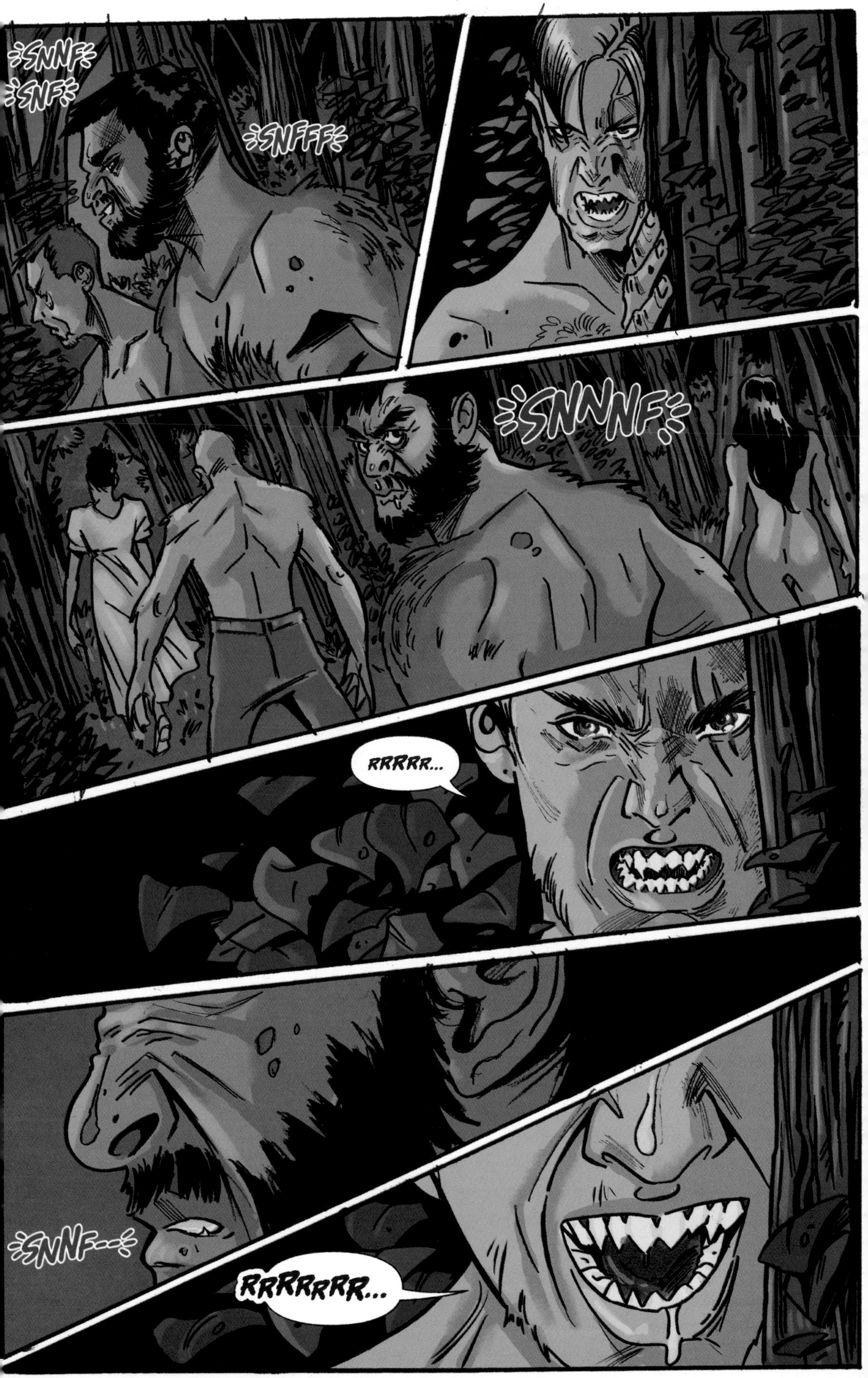
SNNF
SNF
SNFFF
SNNNF
RRRRR...
SNNF--
RRRRRRR...

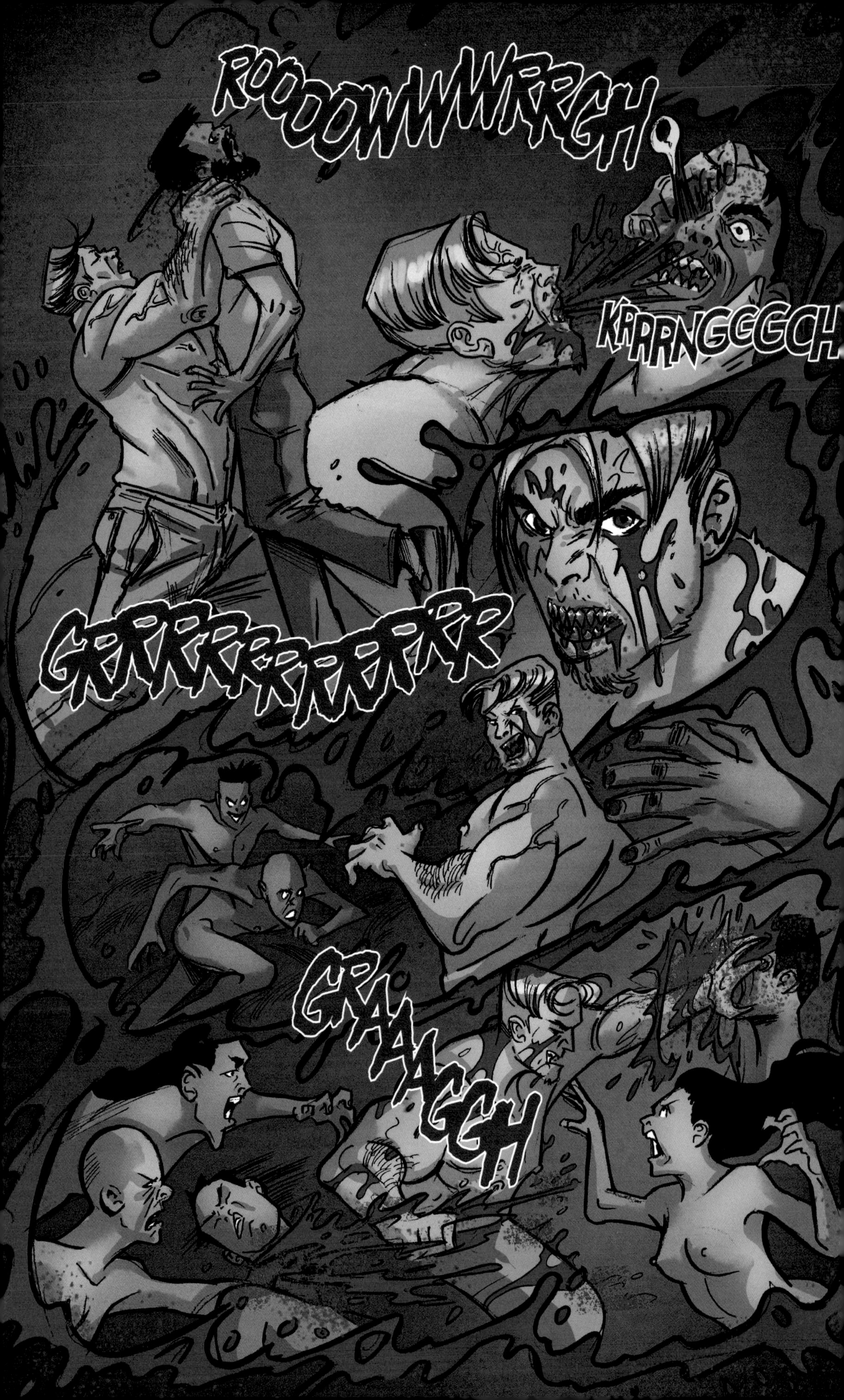
ROOOOOWWWRRRGH
KRRRNGGGGCH
GRRRRRRRRRRRRR
GRAAAAGGH

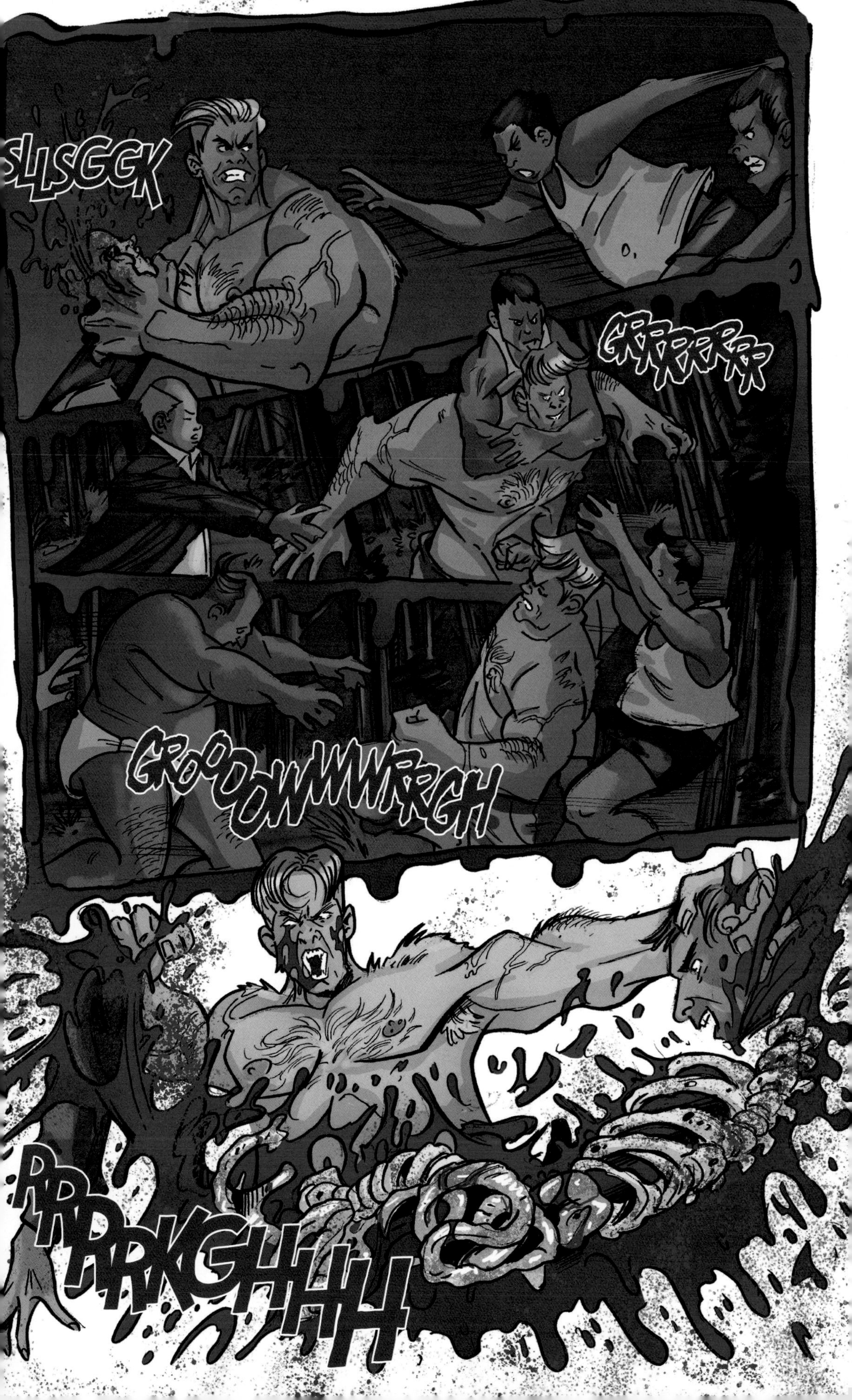
SLLSGGK
GRRRRRRR
GROOOOWWWRRGH
RRRRKGHHHH

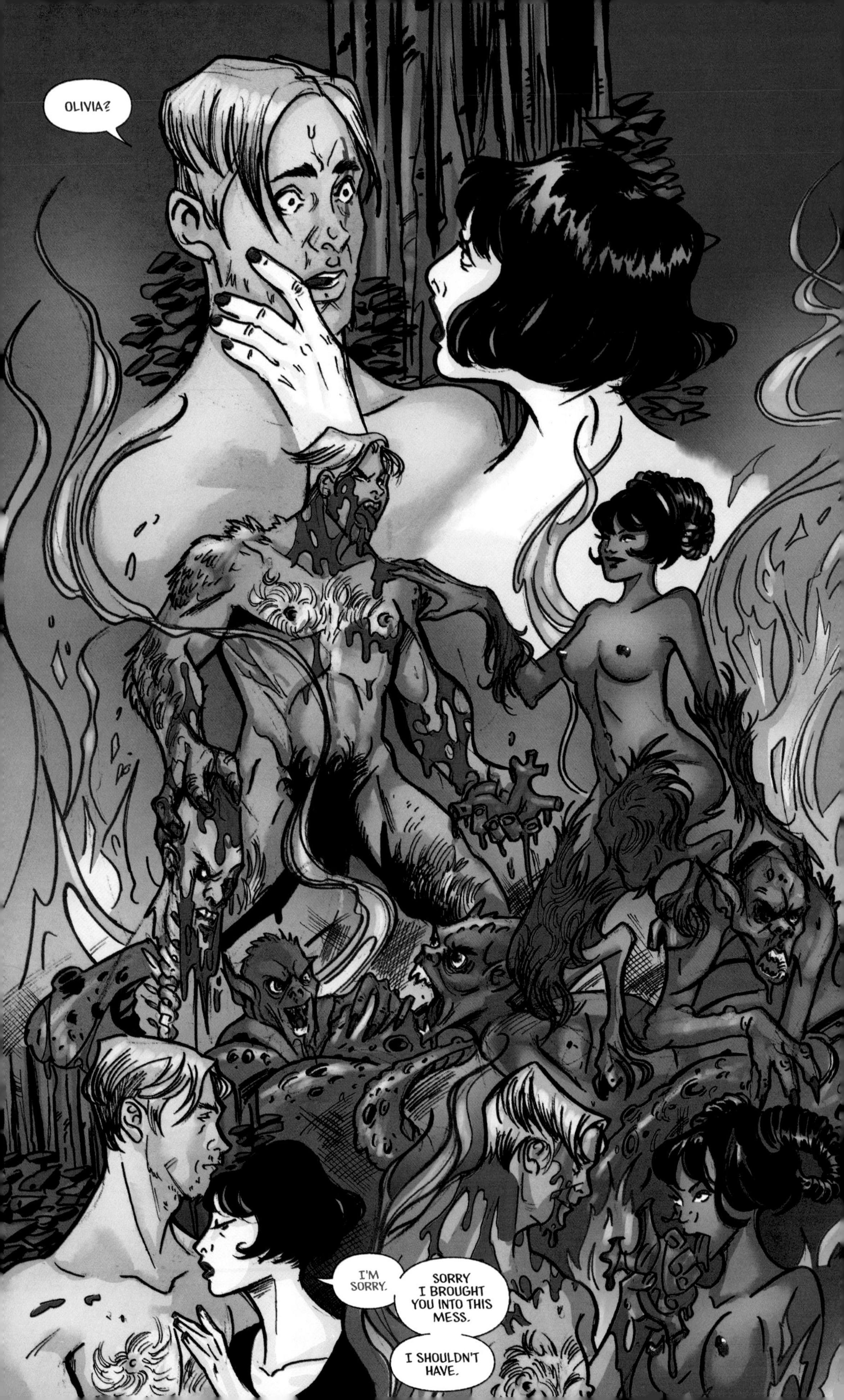
OLIVIA?
I'M SORRY.
SORRY I BROUGHT YOU INTO THIS MESS.
I SHOULDN'T HAVE.

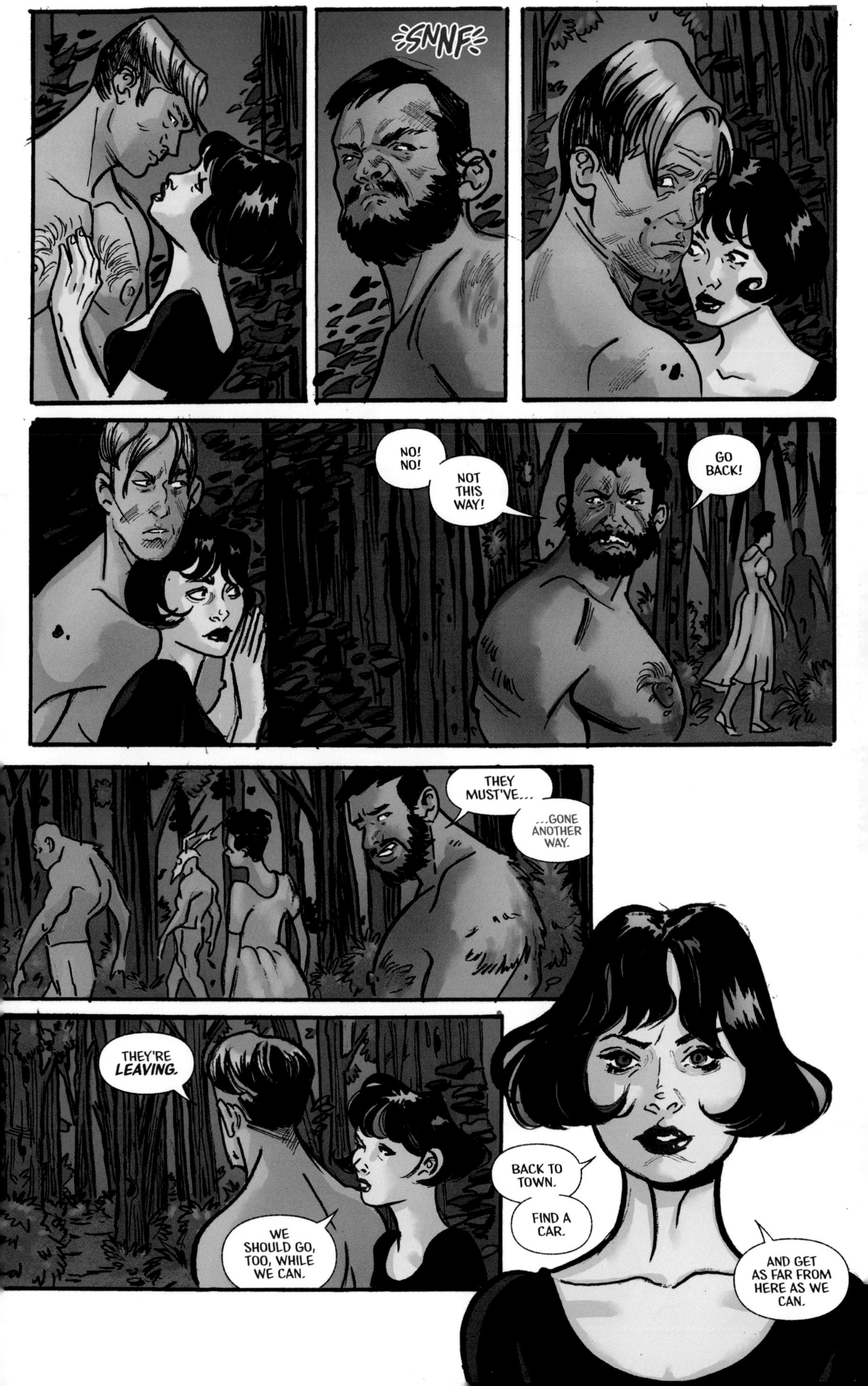
SNNF
NO! NO!
NOT THIS WAY!
GO BACK!
THEY MUST'VE...
...GONE ANOTHER WAY.
THEY'RE *LEAVING.*
WE SHOULD GO, TOO, WHILE WE CAN.
BACK TO TOWN.
FIND A CAR.
AND GET AS FAR FROM HERE AS WE CAN.

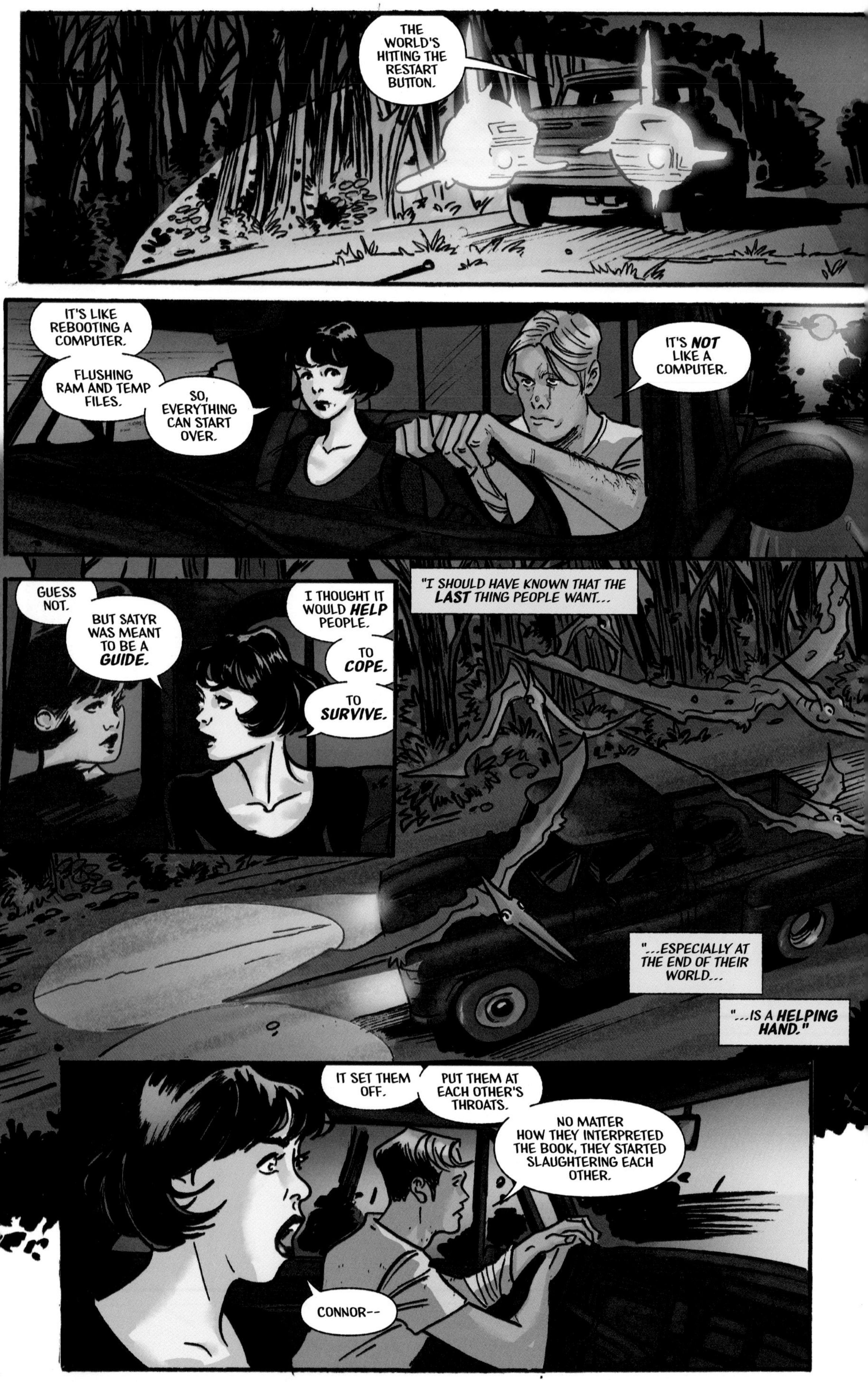

THE WORLD'S HITTING THE RESTART BUTTON.
IT'S LIKE REBOOTING A COMPUTER.
FLUSHING RAM AND TEMP FILES.
SO, EVERYTHING CAN START OVER.
IT'S NOT LIKE A COMPUTER.
GUESS NOT.
BUT SATYR WAS MEANT TO BE A GUIDE.
I THOUGHT IT WOULD HELP PEOPLE.
TO COPE.
TO SURVIVE.
"I SHOULD HAVE KNOWN THAT THE LAST THING PEOPLE WANT...
"...ESPECIALLY AT THE END OF THEIR WORLD...
"...IS A HELPING HAND."
IT SET THEM OFF.
PUT THEM AT EACH OTHER'S THROATS.
NO MATTER HOW THEY INTERPRETED THE BOOK, THEY STARTED SLAUGHTERING EACH OTHER.
CONNOR--

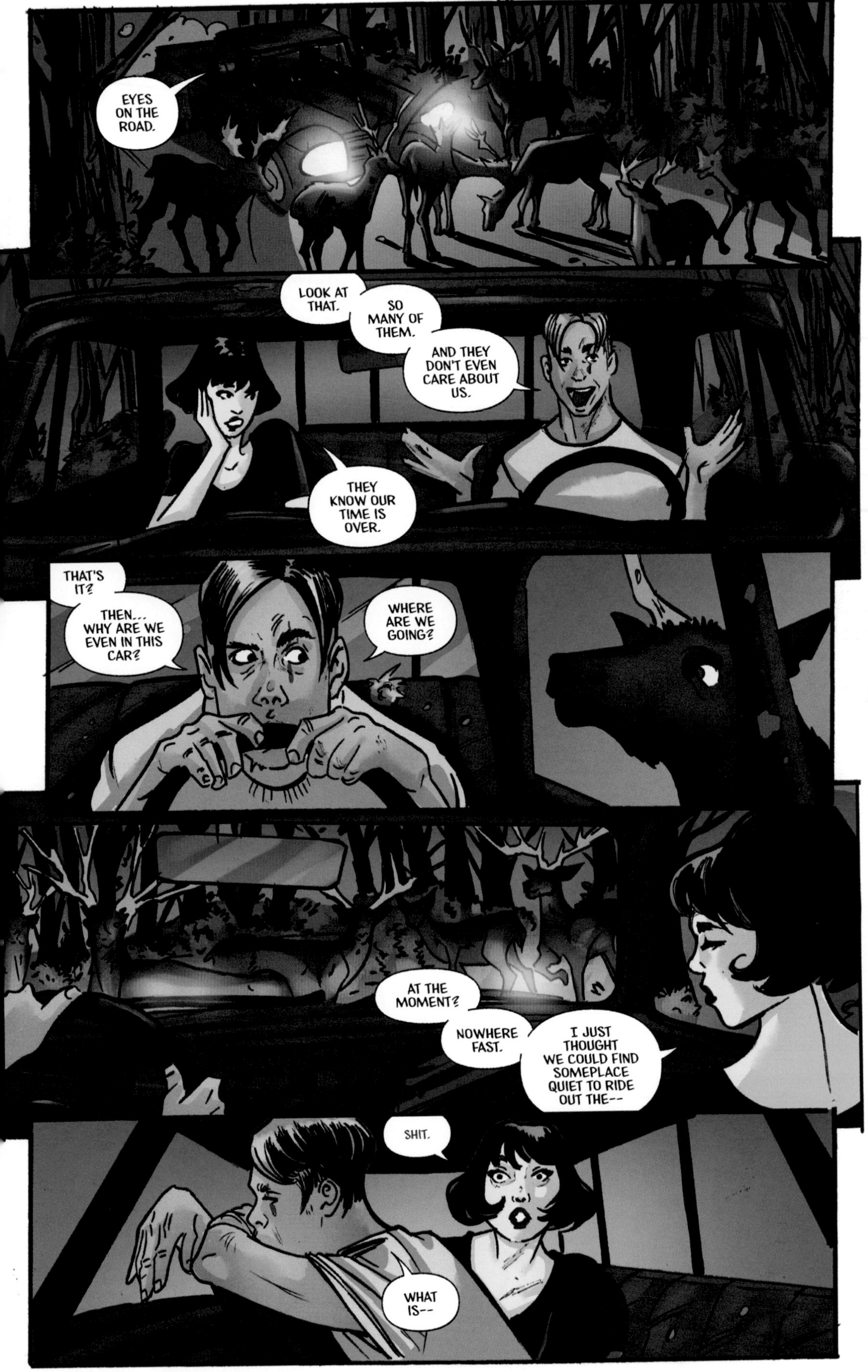
EYES ON THE ROAD.
LOOK AT THAT.
SO MANY OF THEM.
AND THEY DON'T EVEN CARE ABOUT US.
THEY KNOW OUR TIME IS OVER.
THAT'S IT?
THEN... WHY ARE WE EVEN IN THIS CAR?
WHERE ARE WE GOING?
AT THE MOMENT?
NOWHERE FAST.
I JUST THOUGHT WE COULD FIND SOMEPLACE QUIET TO RIDE OUT THE--
SHIT.
WHAT IS--

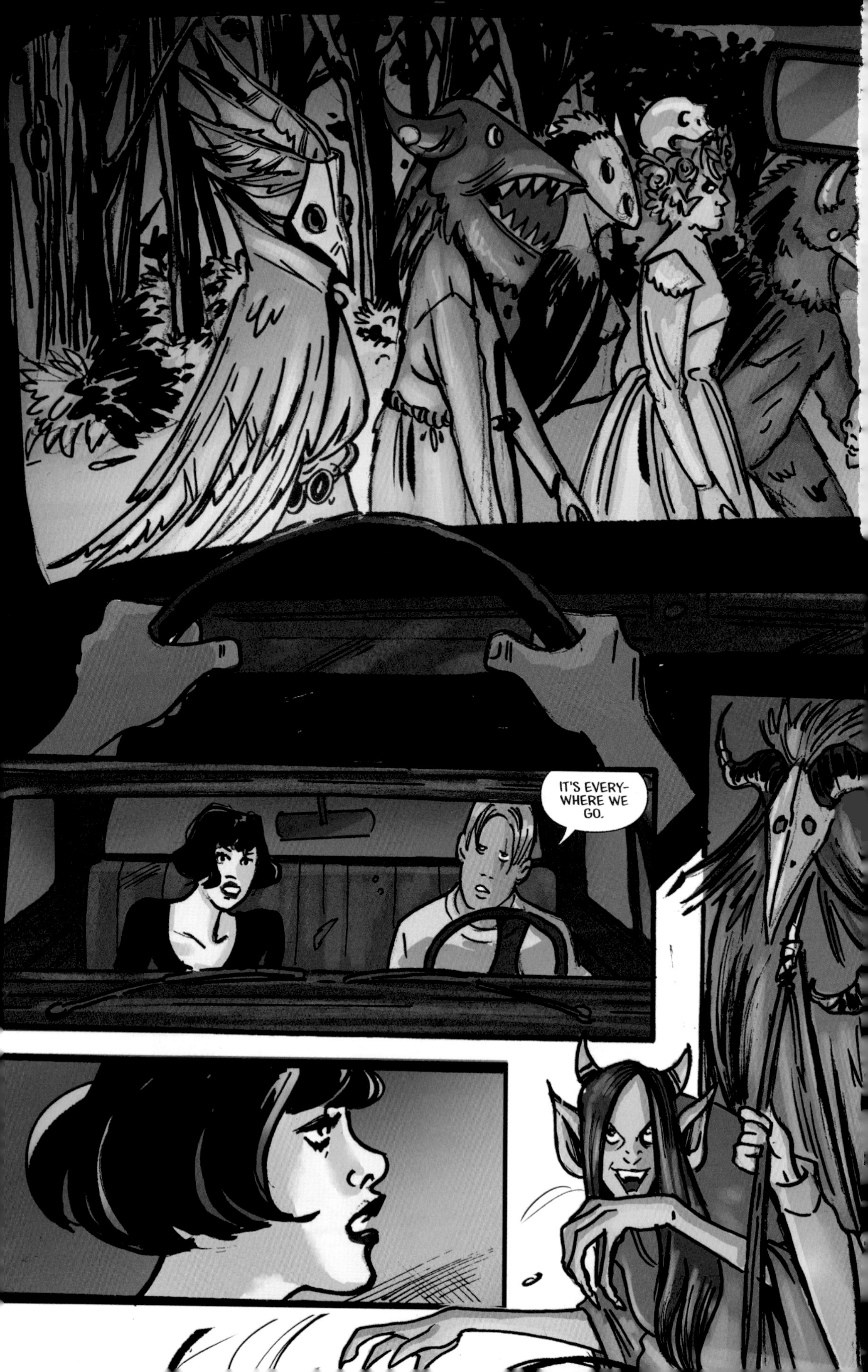
IT'S EVERY-WHERE WE GO.

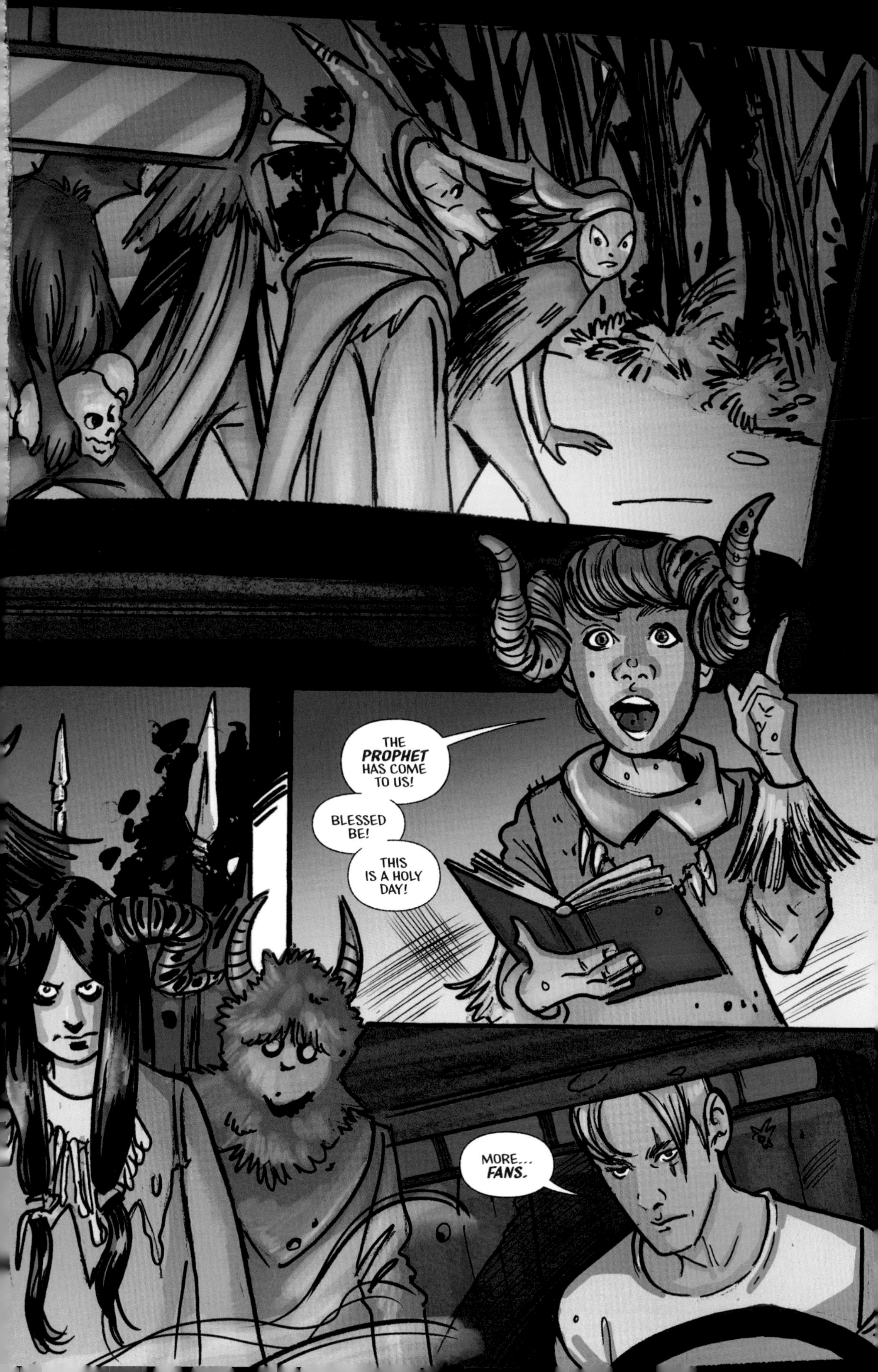
THE PROPHET HAS COME TO US!
BLESSED BE!
THIS IS A HOLY DAY!
MORE... FANS.

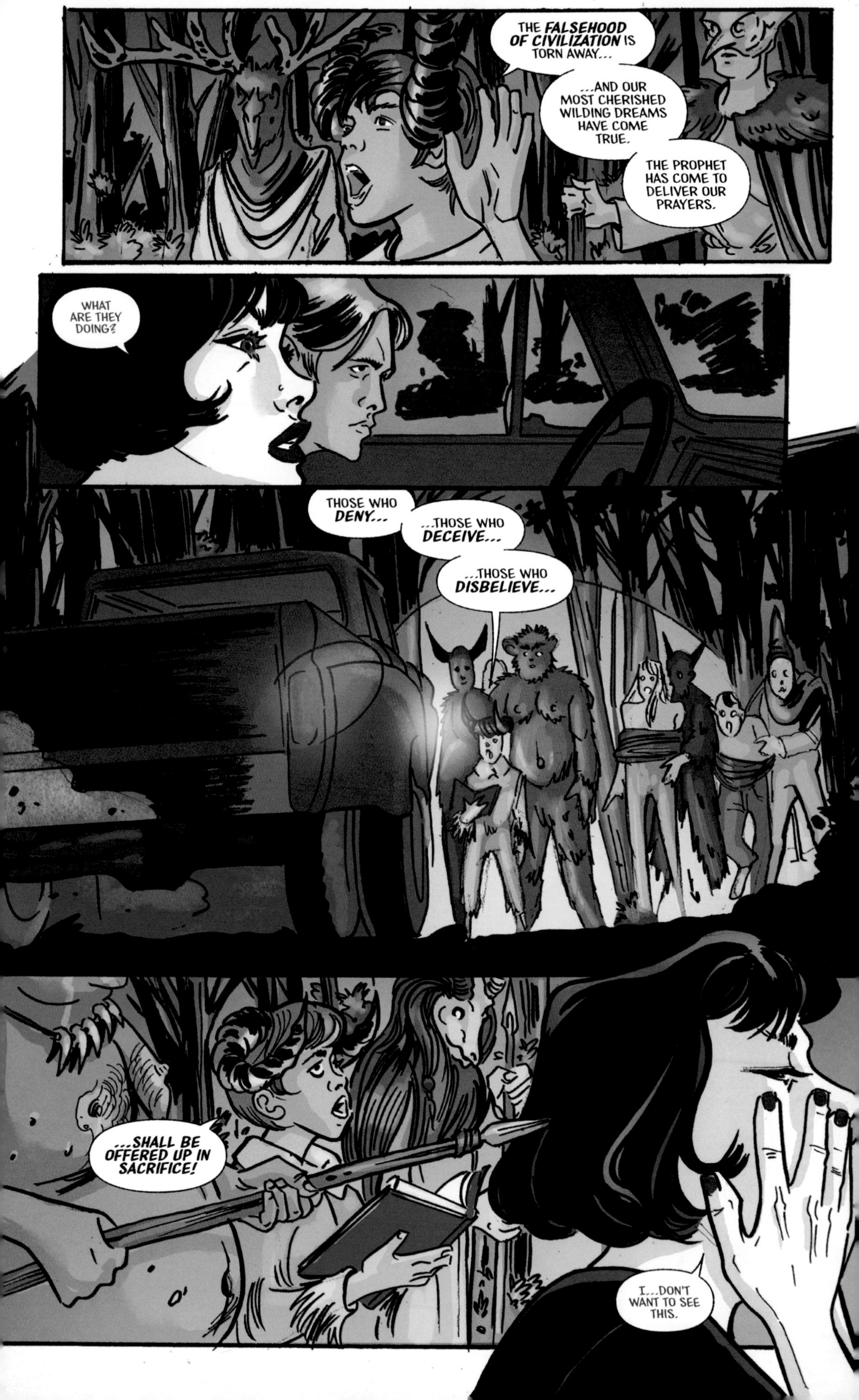
THE *FALSEHOOD OF CIVILIZATION* IS TORN AWAY...
...AND OUR MOST CHERISHED WILDING DREAMS HAVE COME TRUE.
THE PROPHET HAS COME TO DELIVER OUR PRAYERS.
WHAT ARE THEY DOING?
THOSE WHO *DENY*...
...THOSE WHO *DECEIVE*...
...THOSE WHO *DISBELIEVE*...
...SHALL BE OFFERED UP IN SACRIFICE!
I...DON'T WANT TO SEE THIS.

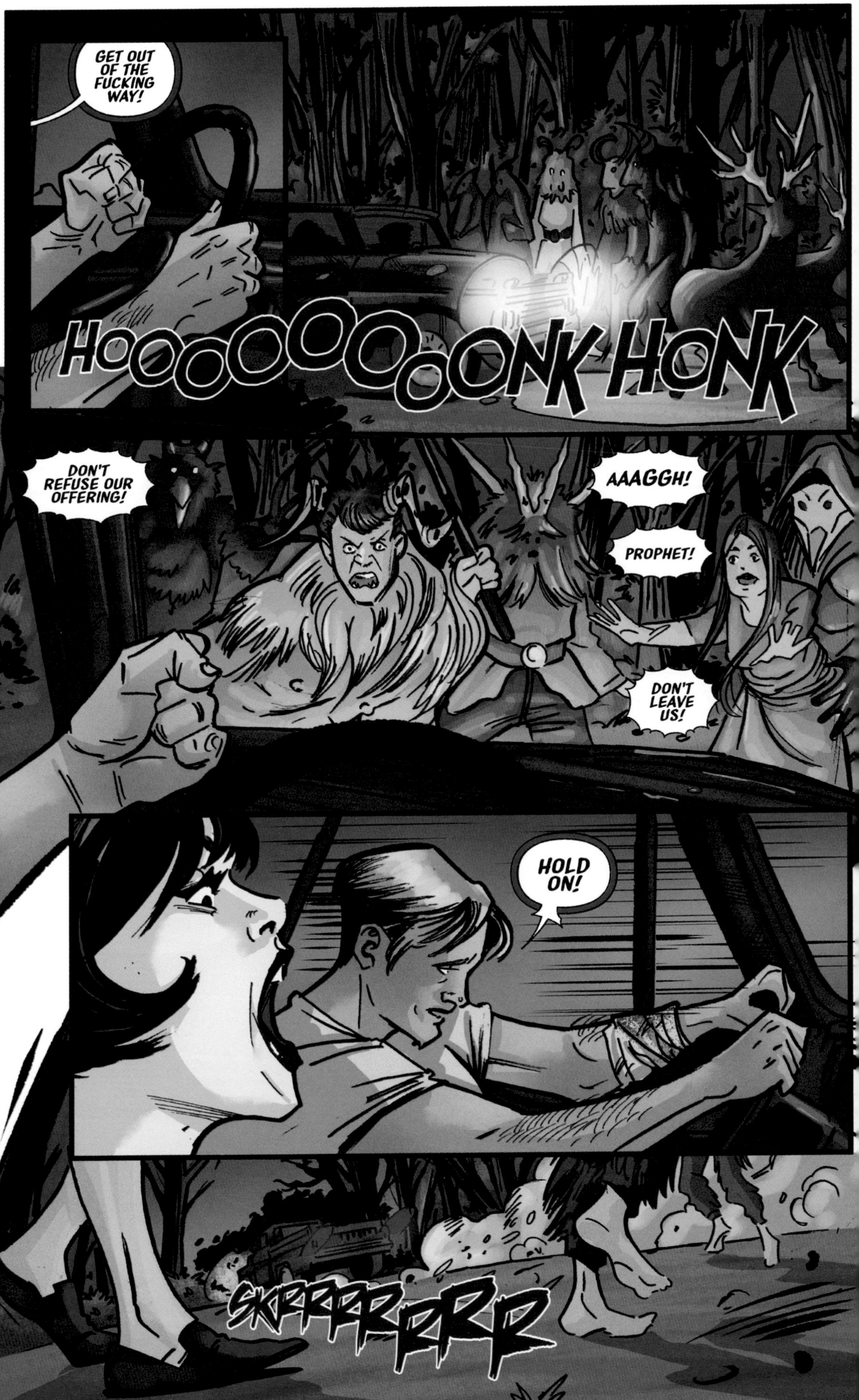
GET OUT OF THE FUCKING WAY!
HOOOOOOOOOONK HONK
DON'T REFUSE OUR OFFERING!
AAAGGH!
PROPHET!
DON'T LEAVE US!
HOLD ON!
SKRRRRRRRR

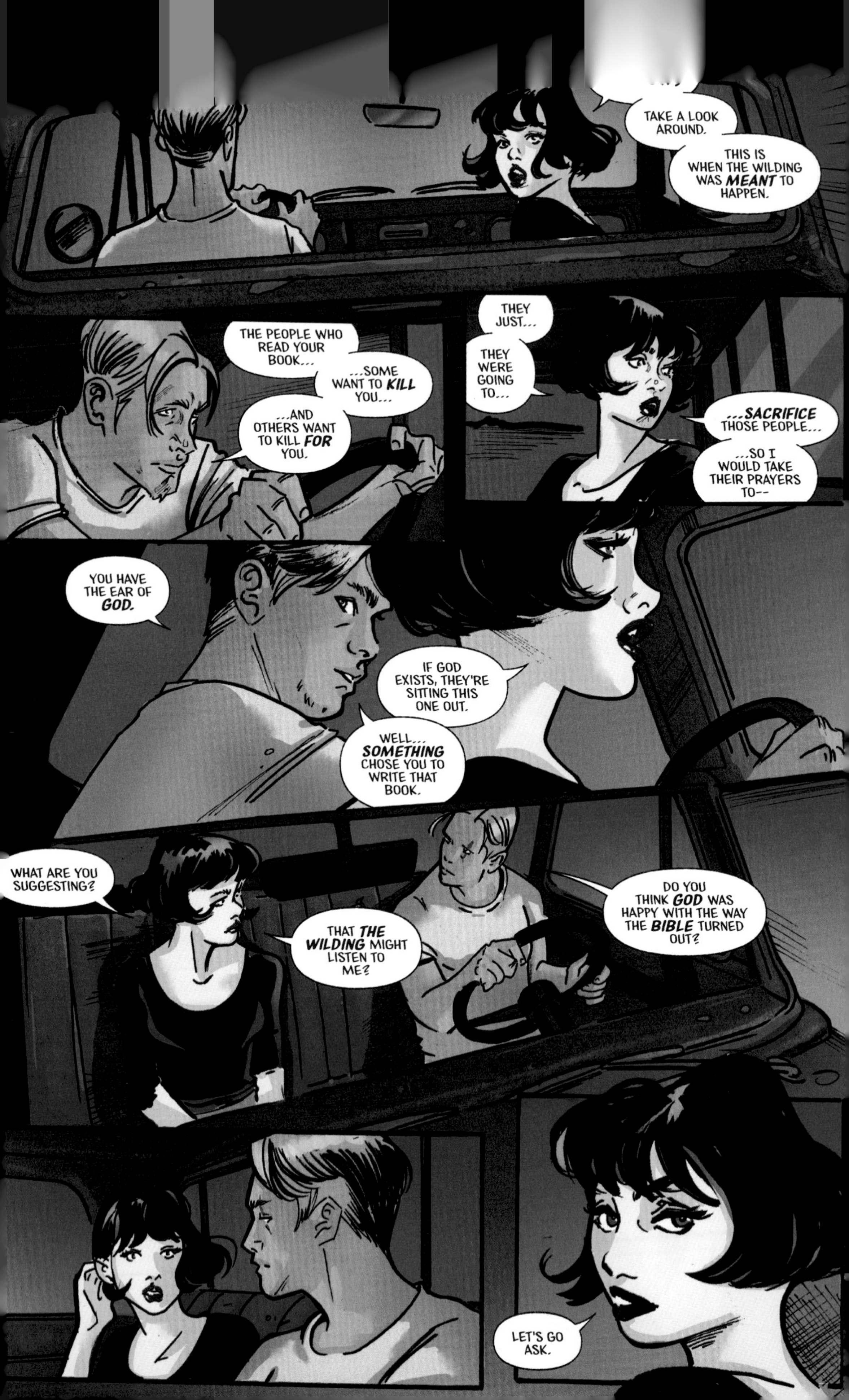
TAKE A LOOK AROUND.
THIS IS WHEN THE WILDING WAS MEANT TO HAPPEN.
THE PEOPLE WHO READ YOUR BOOK...
...SOME WANT TO KILL YOU...
...AND OTHERS WANT TO KILL FOR YOU.
THEY JUST...
THEY WERE GOING TO...
...SACRIFICE THOSE PEOPLE...
...SO I WOULD TAKE THEIR PRAYERS TO--
YOU HAVE THE EAR OF GOD.
IF GOD EXISTS, THEY'RE SITTING THIS ONE OUT.
WELL... SOMETHING CHOSE YOU TO WRITE THAT BOOK.
WHAT ARE YOU SUGGESTING?
THAT THE WILDING MIGHT LISTEN TO ME?
DO YOU THINK GOD WAS HAPPY WITH THE WAY THE BIBLE TURNED OUT?
LET'S GO ASK.

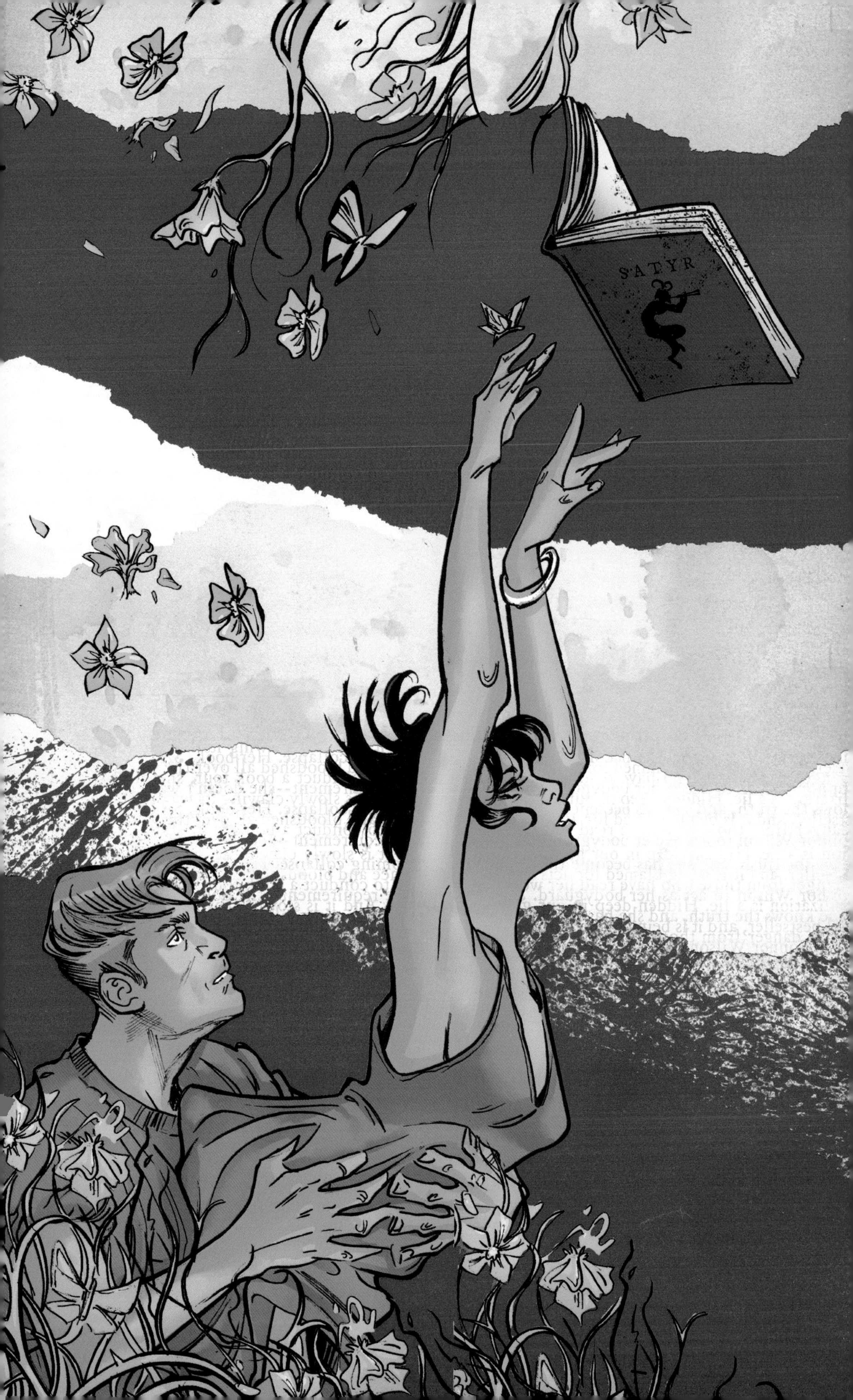
SATYR

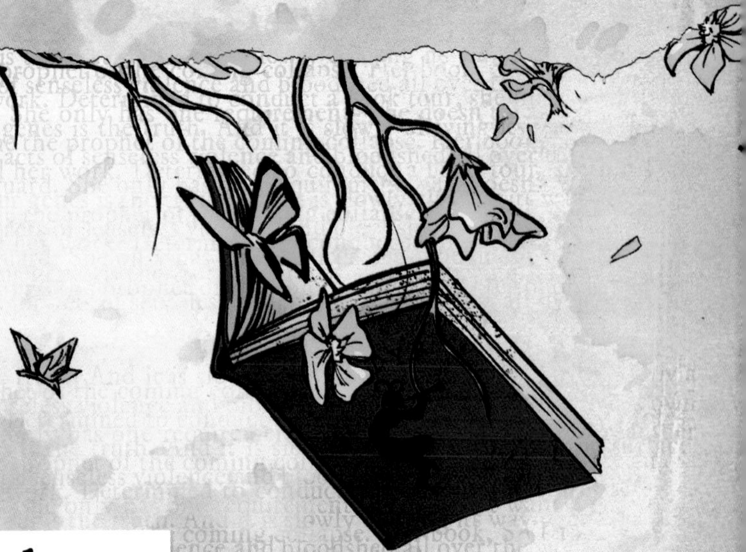

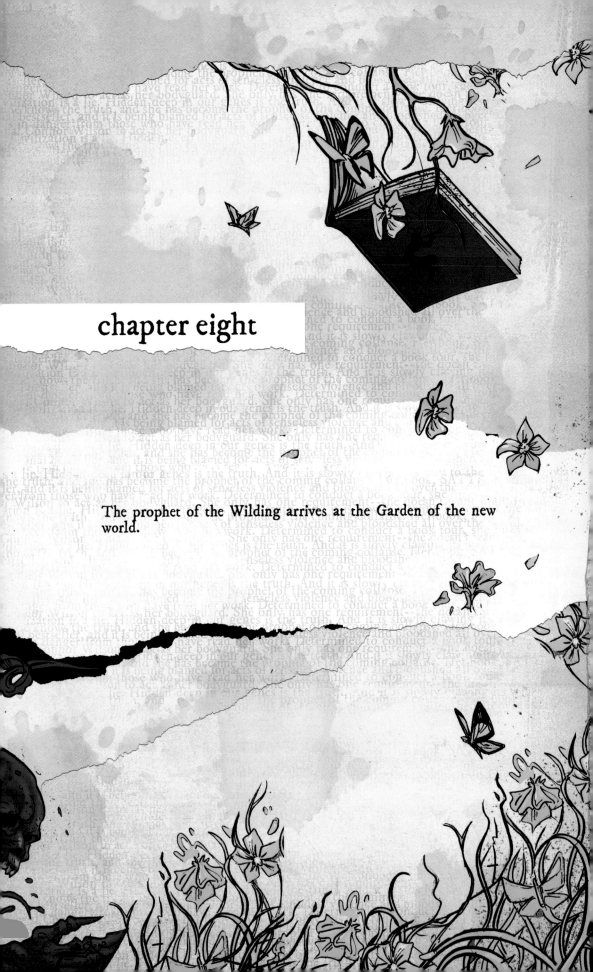

chapter eight

The prophet of the Wilding arrives at the Garden of the new world.

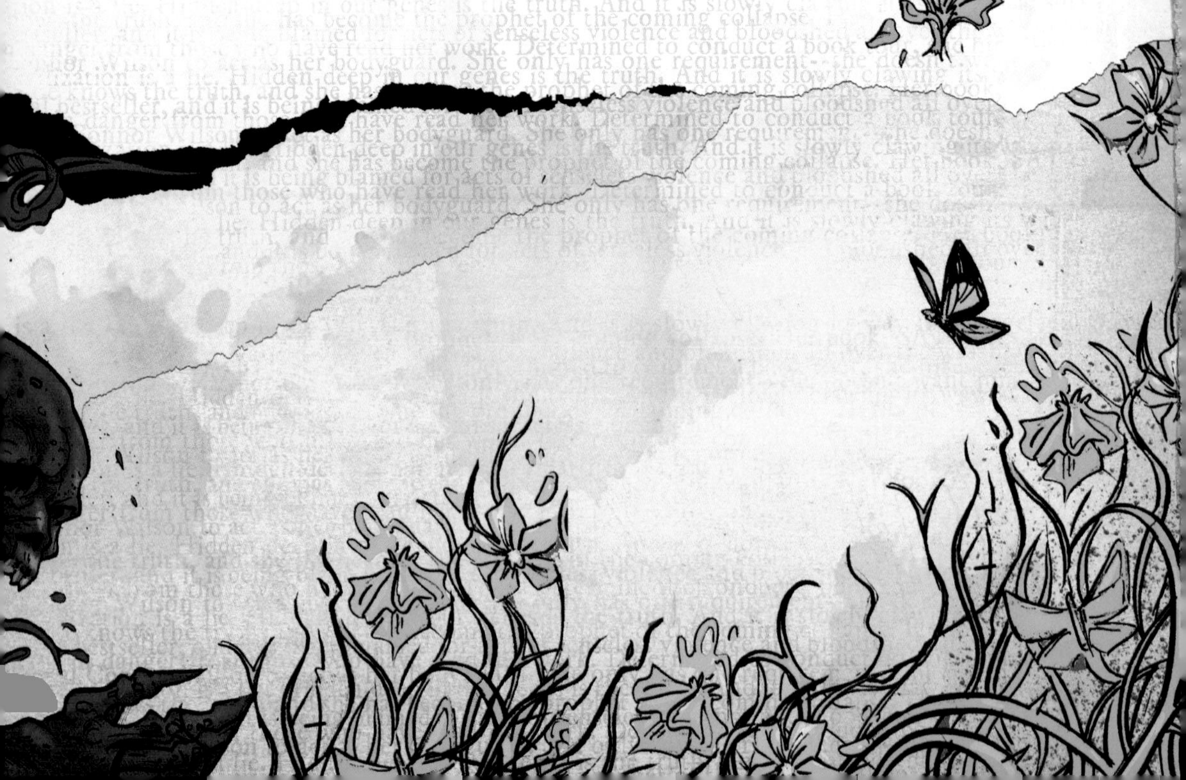

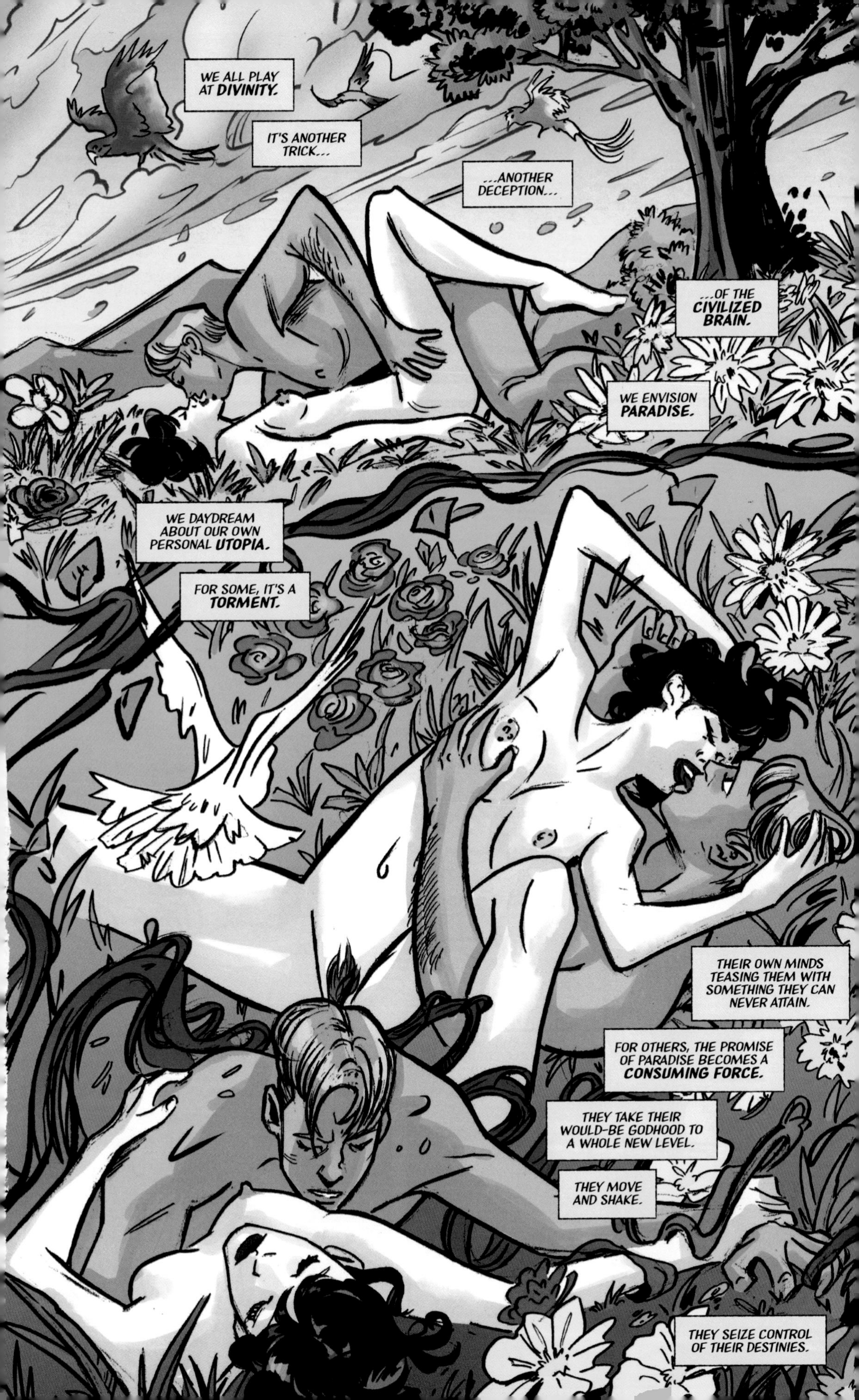
WE ALL PLAY AT DIVINITY.
IT'S ANOTHER TRICK...
...ANOTHER DECEPTION...
...OF THE CIVILIZED BRAIN.
WE ENVISION PARADISE.
WE DAYDREAM ABOUT OUR OWN PERSONAL UTOPIA.
FOR SOME, IT'S A TORMENT.
THEIR OWN MINDS TEASING THEM WITH SOMETHING THEY CAN NEVER ATTAIN.
FOR OTHERS, THE PROMISE OF PARADISE BECOMES A CONSUMING FORCE.
THEY TAKE THEIR WOULD-BE GODHOOD TO A WHOLE NEW LEVEL.
THEY MOVE AND SHAKE.
THEY SEIZE CONTROL OF THEIR DESTINIES.

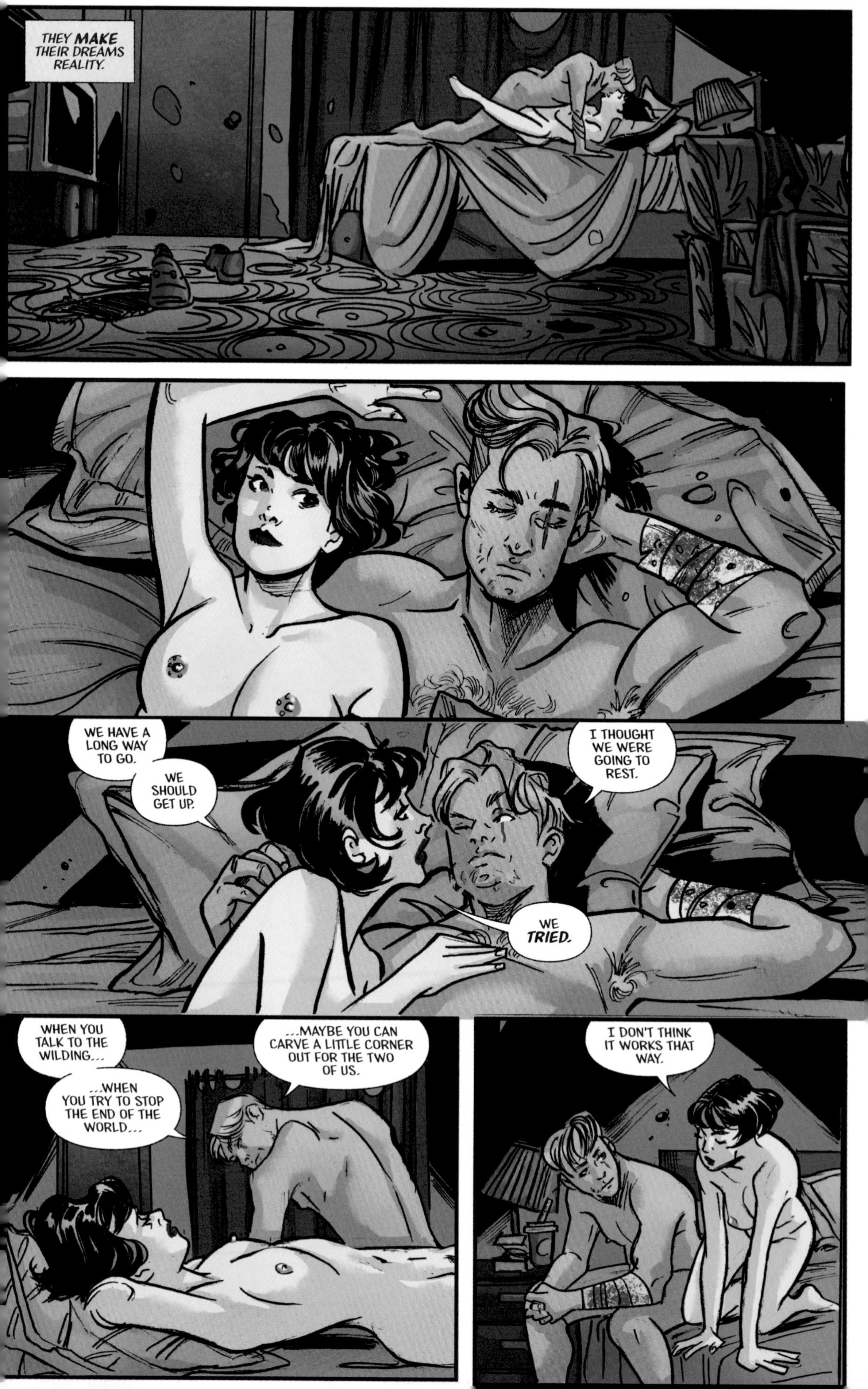
THEY MAKE THEIR DREAMS REALITY.
WE HAVE A LONG WAY TO GO.
WE SHOULD GET UP.
I THOUGHT WE WERE GOING TO REST.
WE TRIED.
WHEN YOU TALK TO THE WILDING...
...WHEN YOU TRY TO STOP THE END OF THE WORLD...
...MAYBE YOU CAN CARVE A LITTLE CORNER OUT FOR THE TWO OF US.
I DON'T THINK IT WORKS THAT WAY.

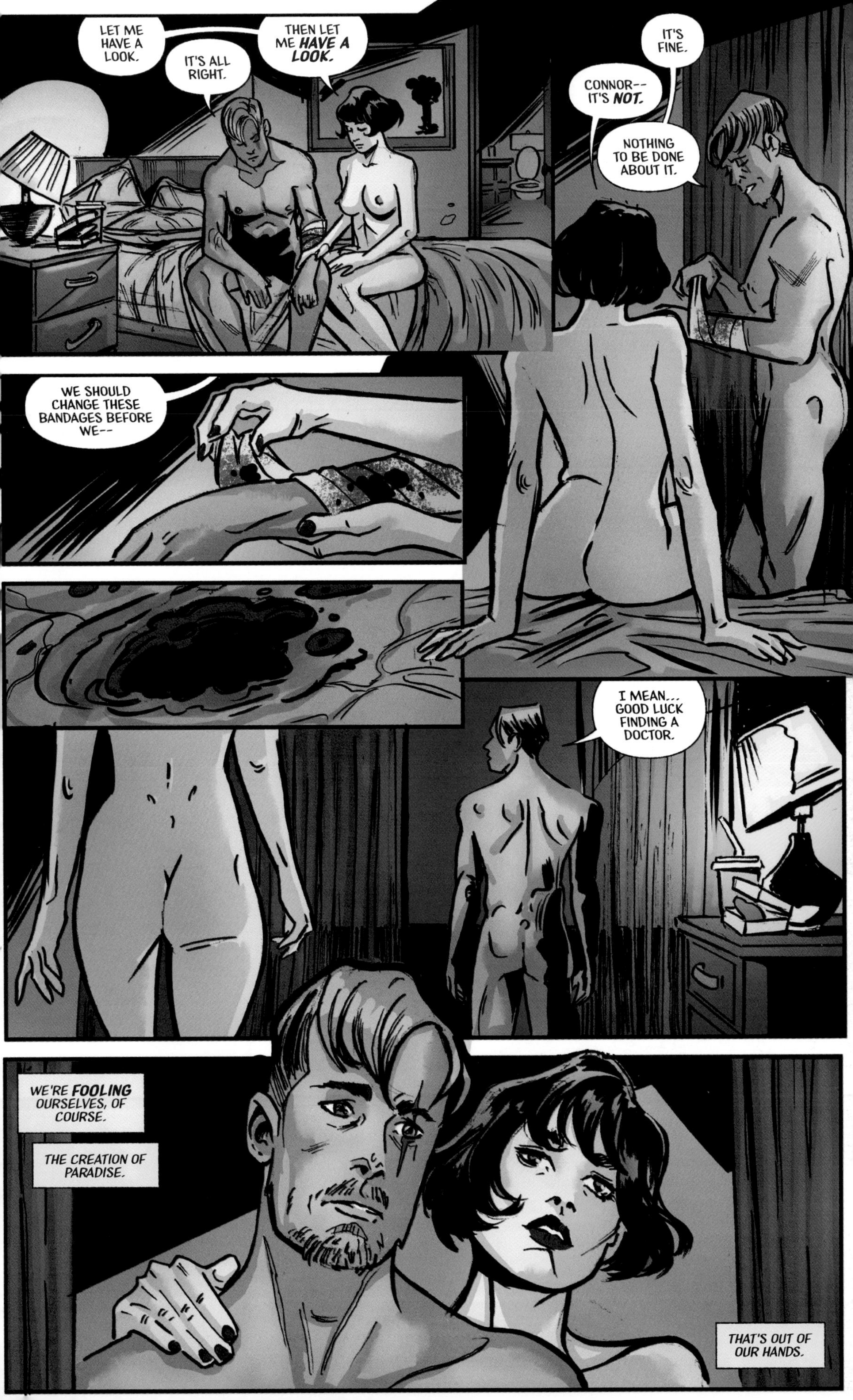

LET ME HAVE A LOOK.
IT'S ALL RIGHT.
THEN LET ME ***HAVE A LOOK.***
IT'S FINE.
CONNOR-- IT'S ***NOT.***
NOTHING TO BE DONE ABOUT IT.
WE SHOULD CHANGE THESE BANDAGES BEFORE WE--
I MEAN... GOOD LUCK FINDING A DOCTOR.
*WE'RE **FOOLING** OURSELVES, OF COURSE.*
THE CREATION OF PARADISE.
THAT'S OUT OF OUR HANDS.

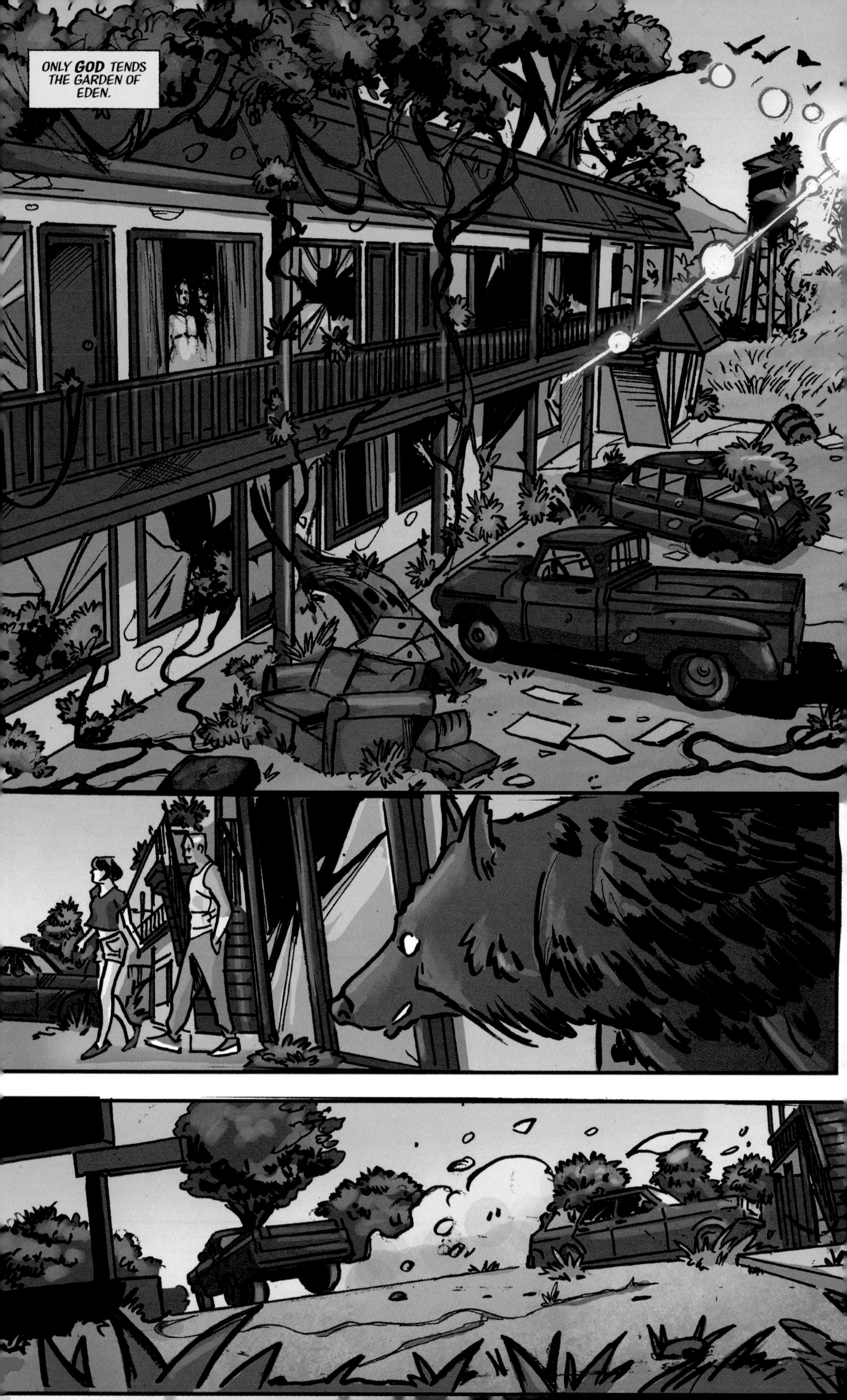
ONLY GOD TENDS THE GARDEN OF EDEN.

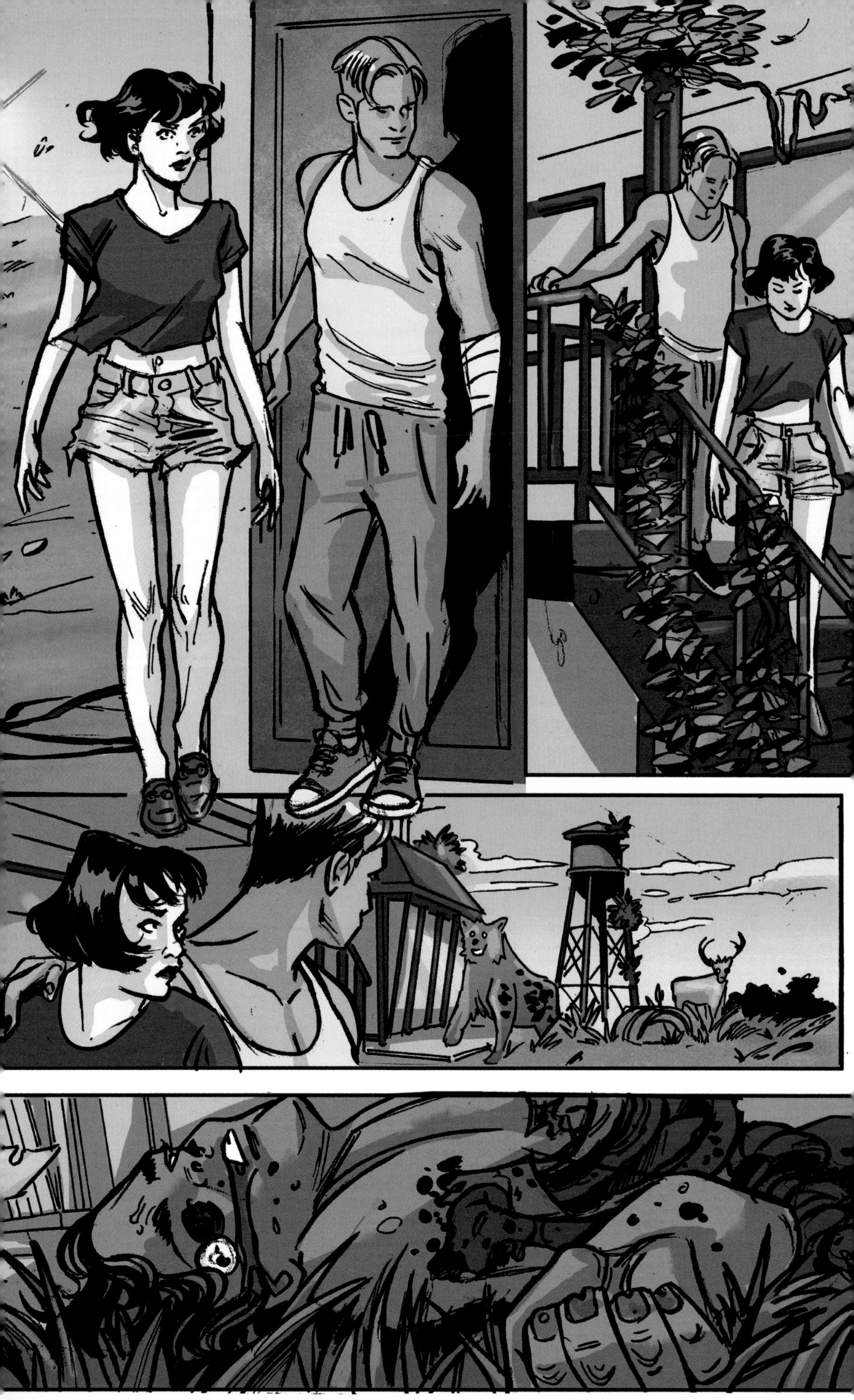

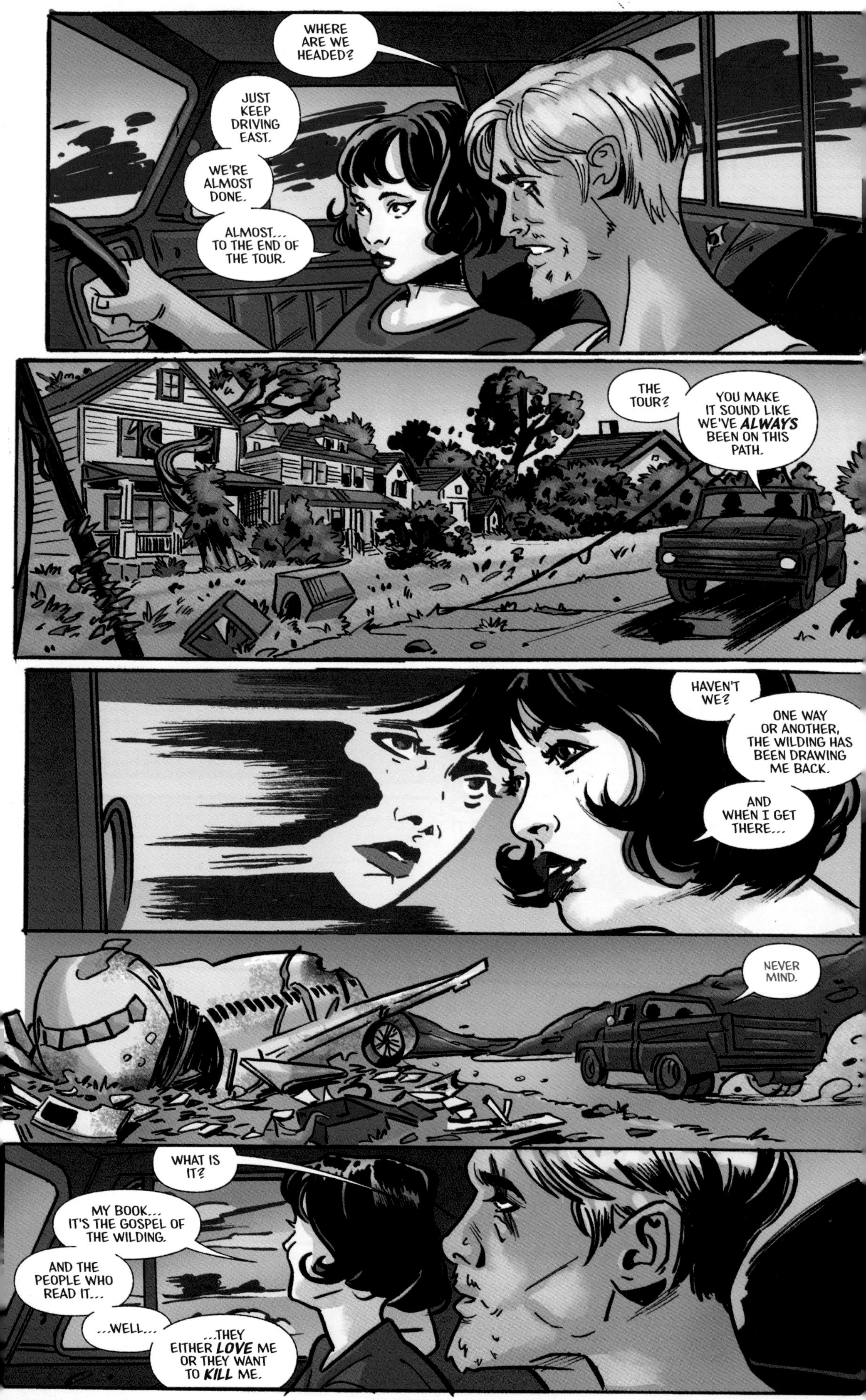
WHERE ARE WE HEADED?
JUST KEEP DRIVING EAST.
WE'RE ALMOST DONE.
ALMOST... TO THE END OF THE TOUR.
THE TOUR?
YOU MAKE IT SOUND LIKE WE'VE *ALWAYS* BEEN ON THIS PATH.
HAVEN'T WE?
ONE WAY OR ANOTHER, THE WILDING HAS BEEN DRAWING ME BACK.
AND WHEN I GET THERE...
NEVER MIND.
WHAT IS IT?
MY BOOK... IT'S THE GOSPEL OF THE WILDING.
AND THE PEOPLE WHO READ IT...
...WELL...
...THEY EITHER *LOVE* ME OR THEY WANT TO *KILL* ME.

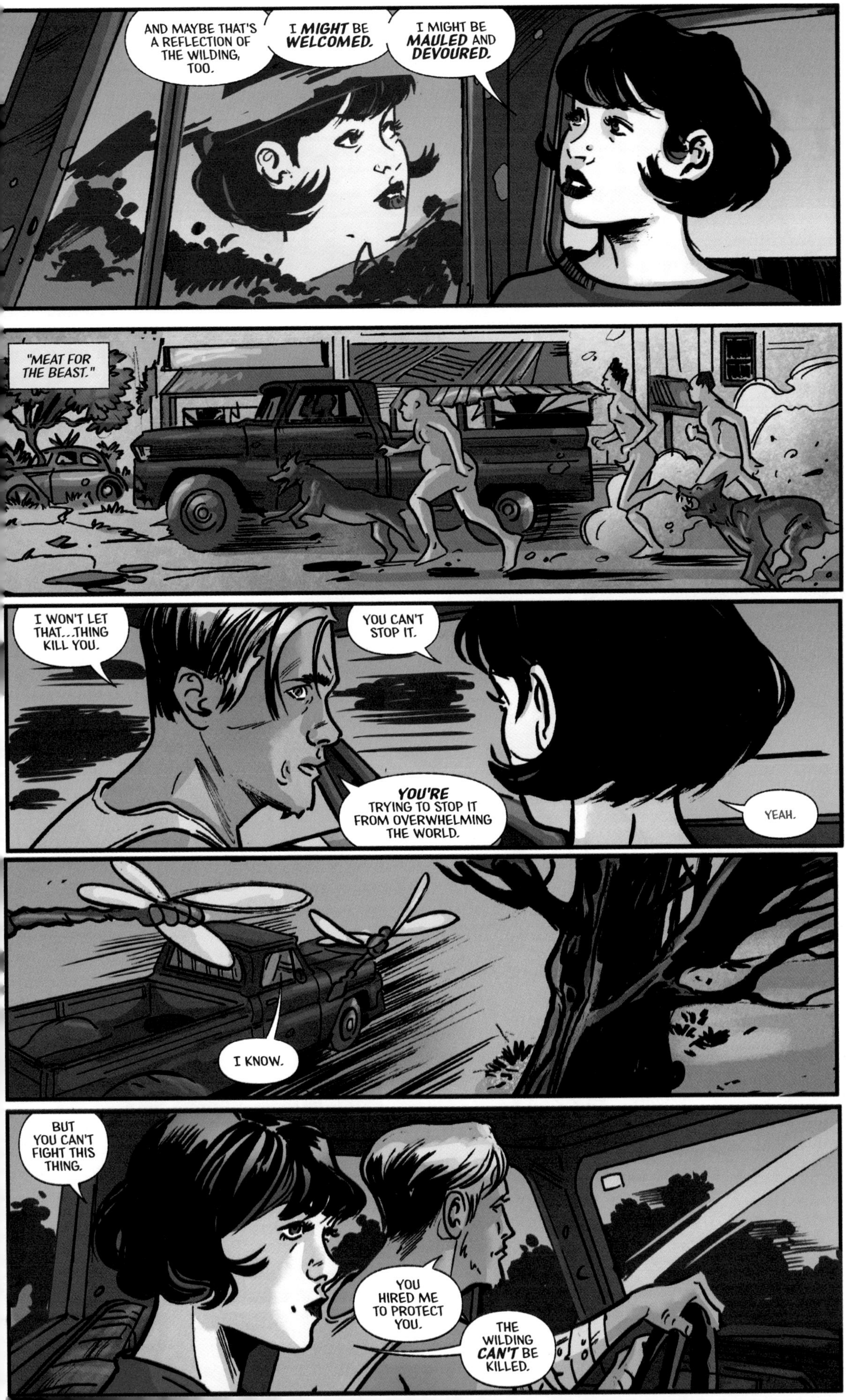
AND MAYBE THAT'S A REFLECTION OF THE WILDING, TOO.
I MIGHT BE WELCOMED.
I MIGHT BE MAULED AND DEVOURED.
"MEAT FOR THE BEAST."
I WON'T LET THAT...THING KILL YOU.
YOU CAN'T STOP IT.
YOU'RE TRYING TO STOP IT FROM OVERWHELMING THE WORLD.
YEAH.
I KNOW.
BUT YOU CAN'T FIGHT THIS THING.
YOU HIRED ME TO PROTECT YOU.
THE WILDING CAN'T BE KILLED.

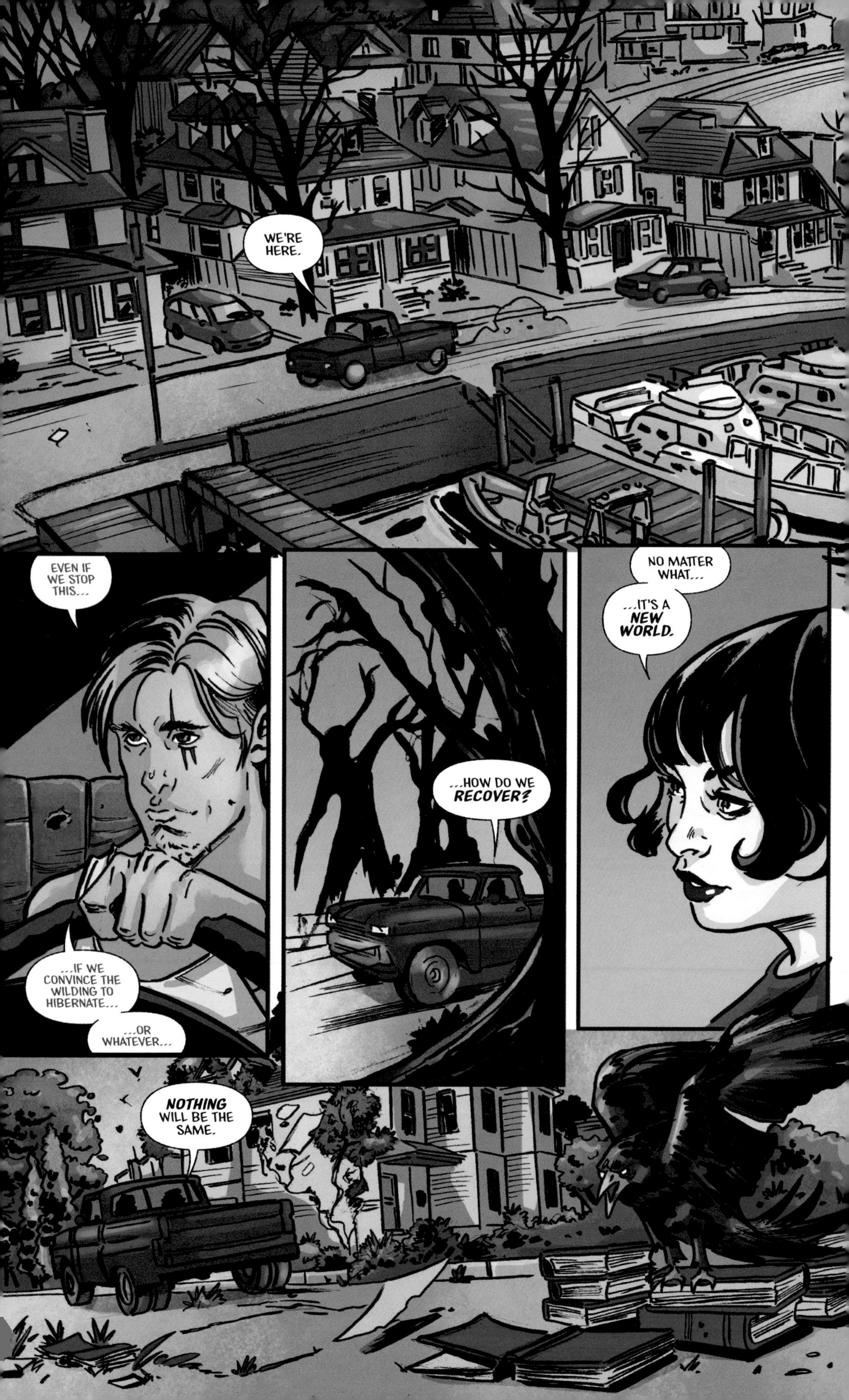
WE'RE HERE.
EVEN IF WE STOP THIS...
...IF WE CONVINCE THE WILDING TO HIBERNATE...
...OR WHATEVER...
...HOW DO WE RECOVER?
NO MATTER WHAT...
...IT'S A NEW WORLD.
NOTHING WILL BE THE SAME.

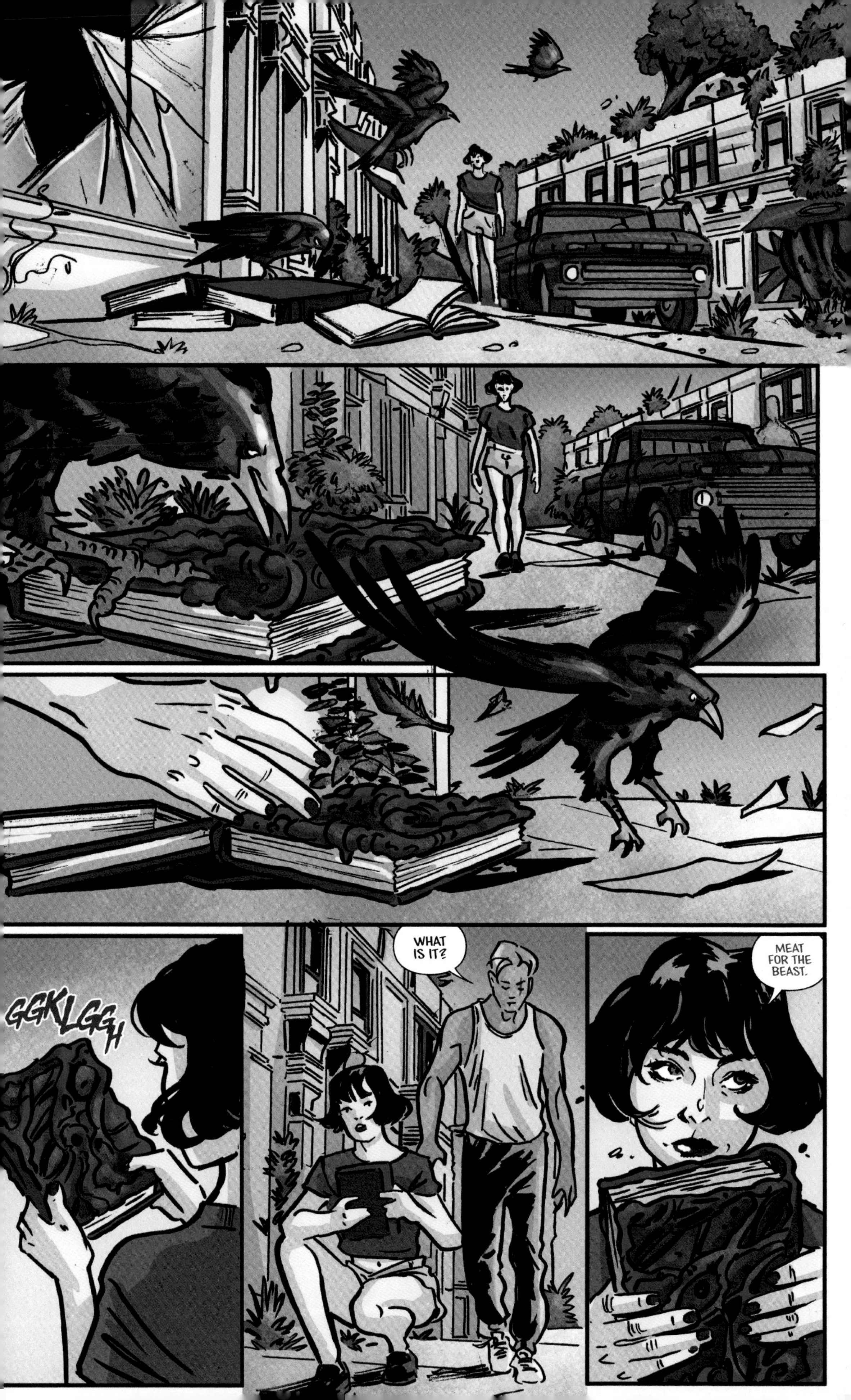
GGKLGGH
WHAT IS IT?
MEAT FOR THE BEAST.

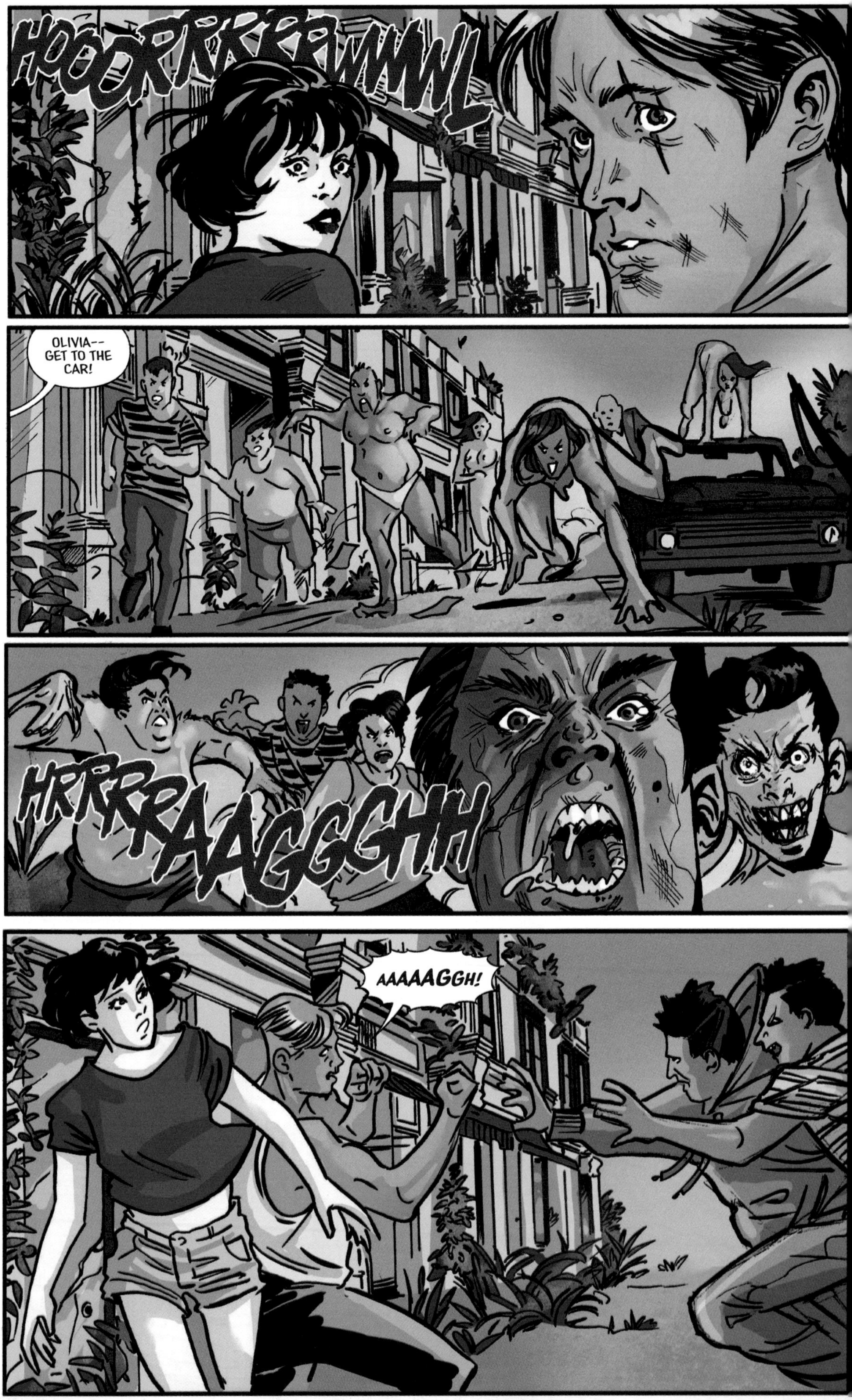
HOOORRRRRRWWWWL
OLIVIA-- GET TO THE CAR!
HRRRRAAGGGHH
AAAAAGGH!

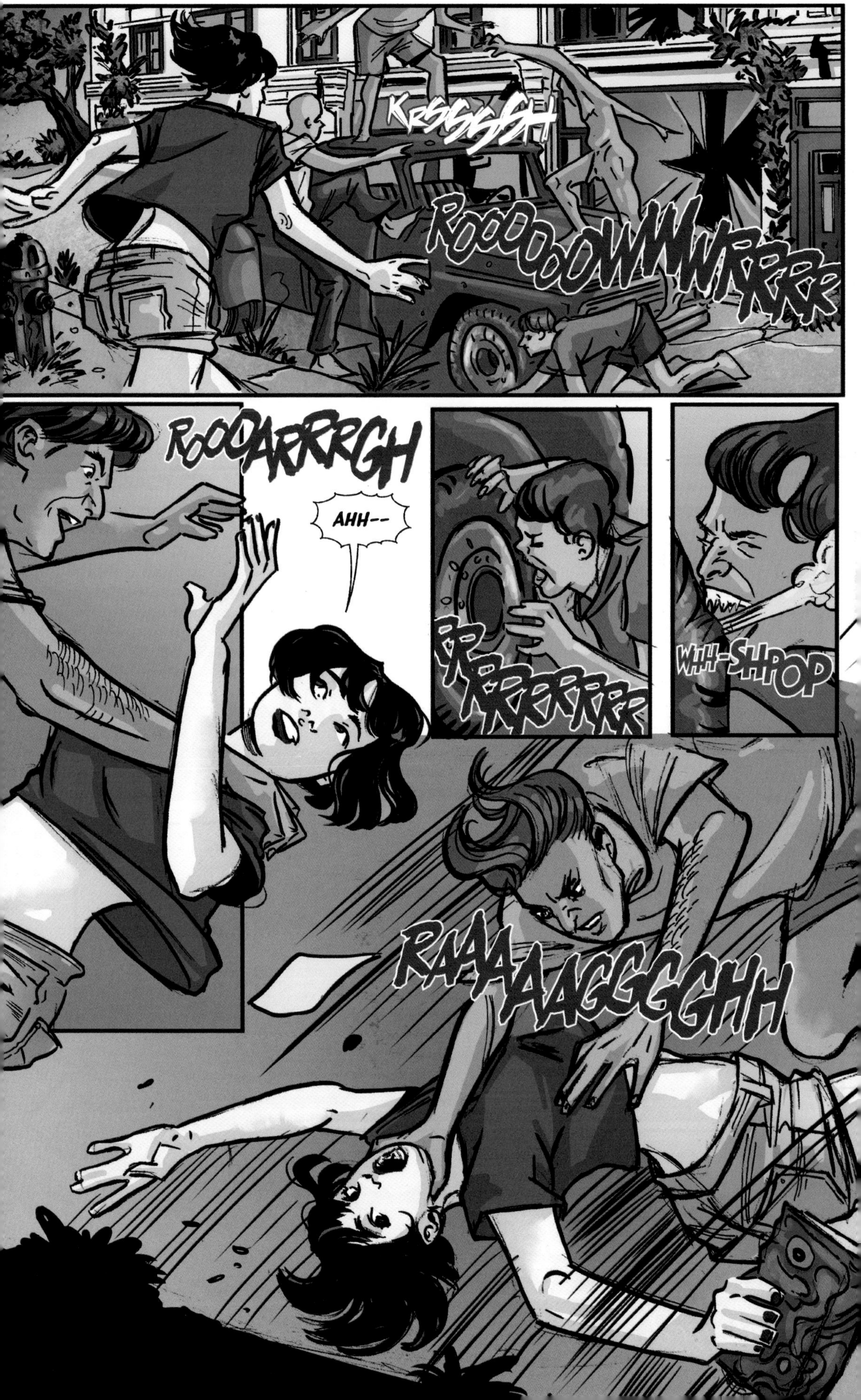
KRSSSSSH
ROOOOOOWWWRRRRR
ROOOARRRRGH
AHH--
RRRRRRRRRR
WHH-SHPOP
RAAAAAAGGGGHH

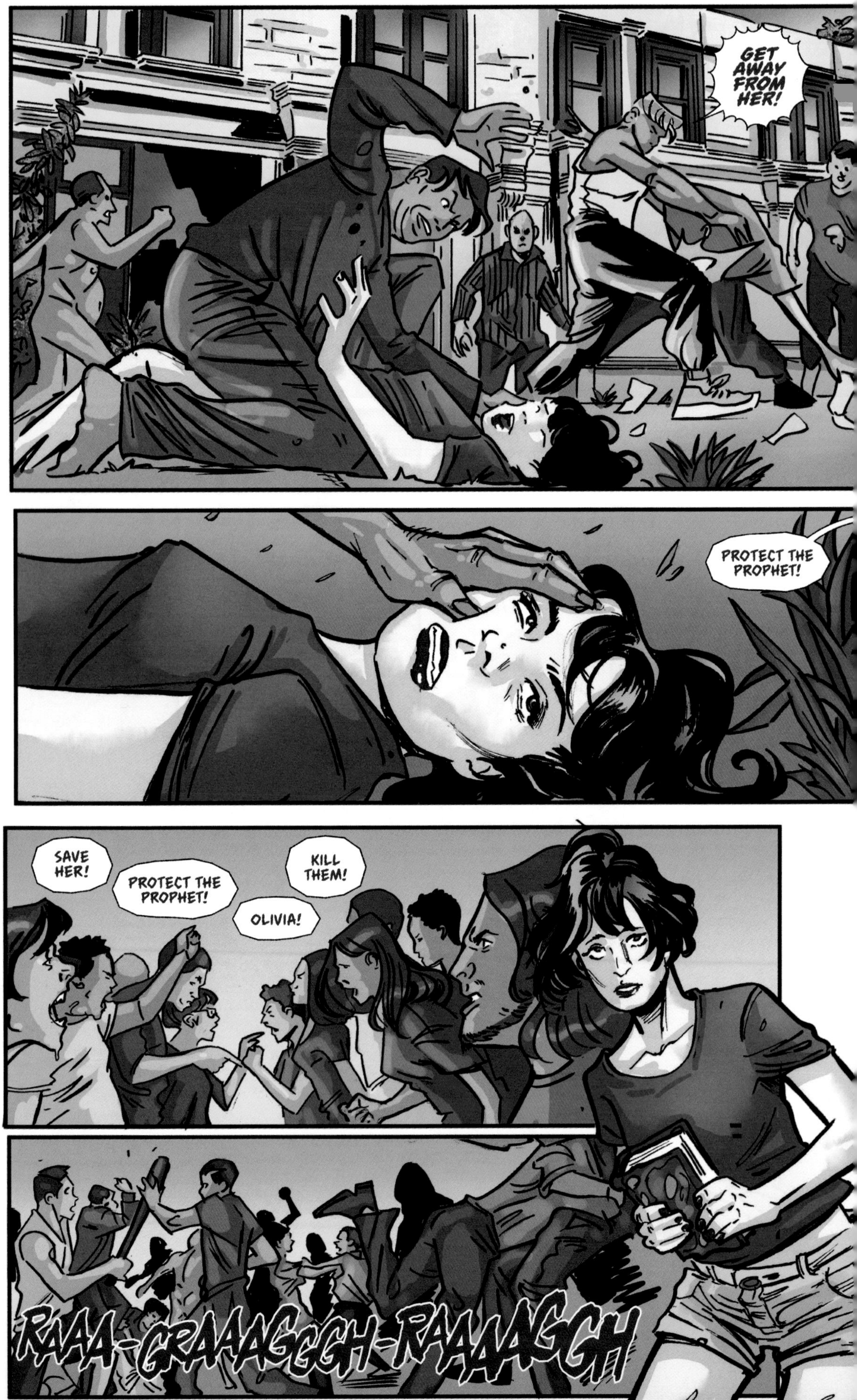
GET AWAY FROM HER!
PROTECT THE PROPHET!
SAVE HER!
PROTECT THE PROPHET!
OLIVIA!
KILL THEM!
RAAA-GRAAAGGH-RAAAAGGH

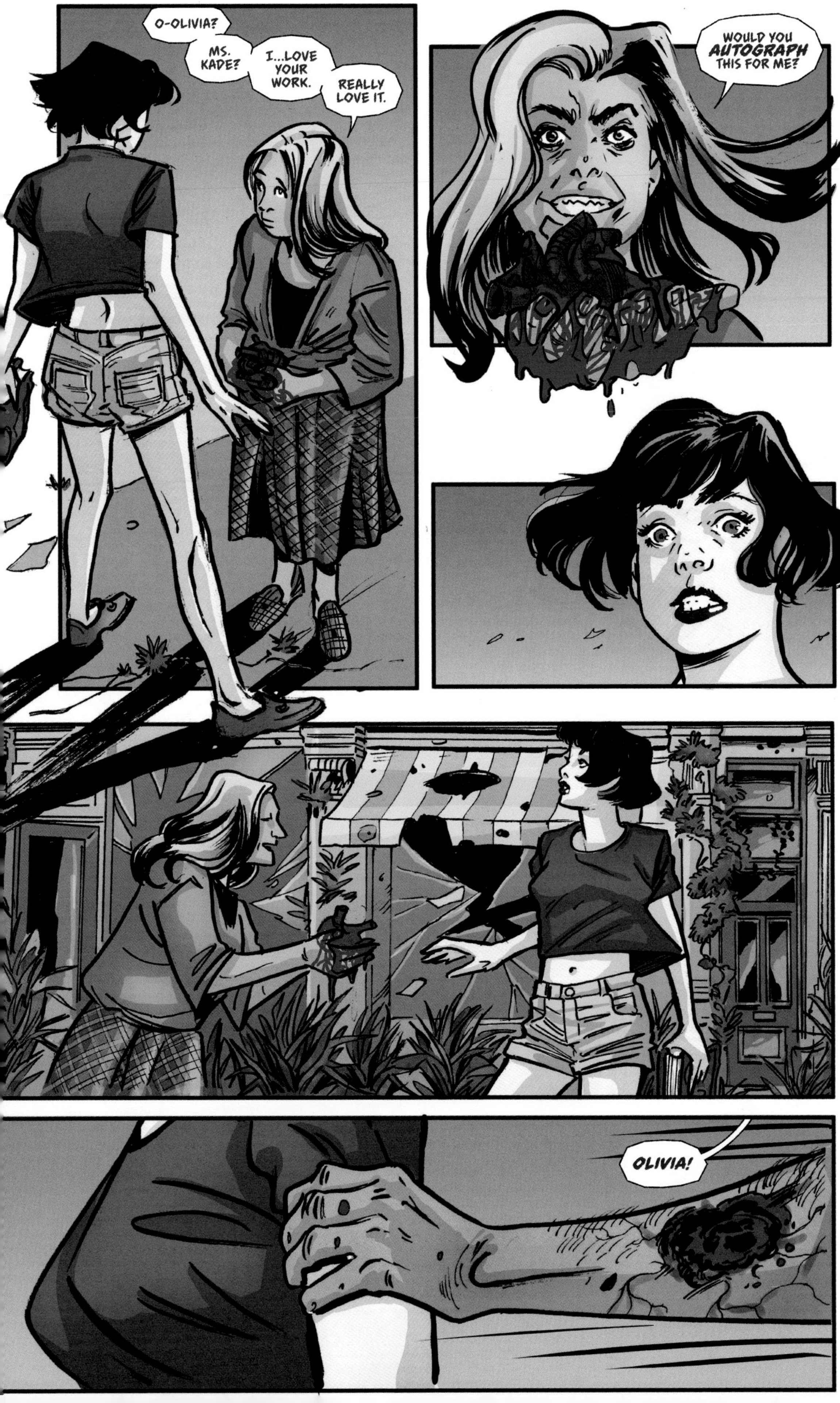

O-OLIVIA?
MS. KADE?
I...LOVE YOUR WORK.
REALLY LOVE IT.
WOULD YOU AUTOGRAPH THIS FOR ME?
OLIVIA!

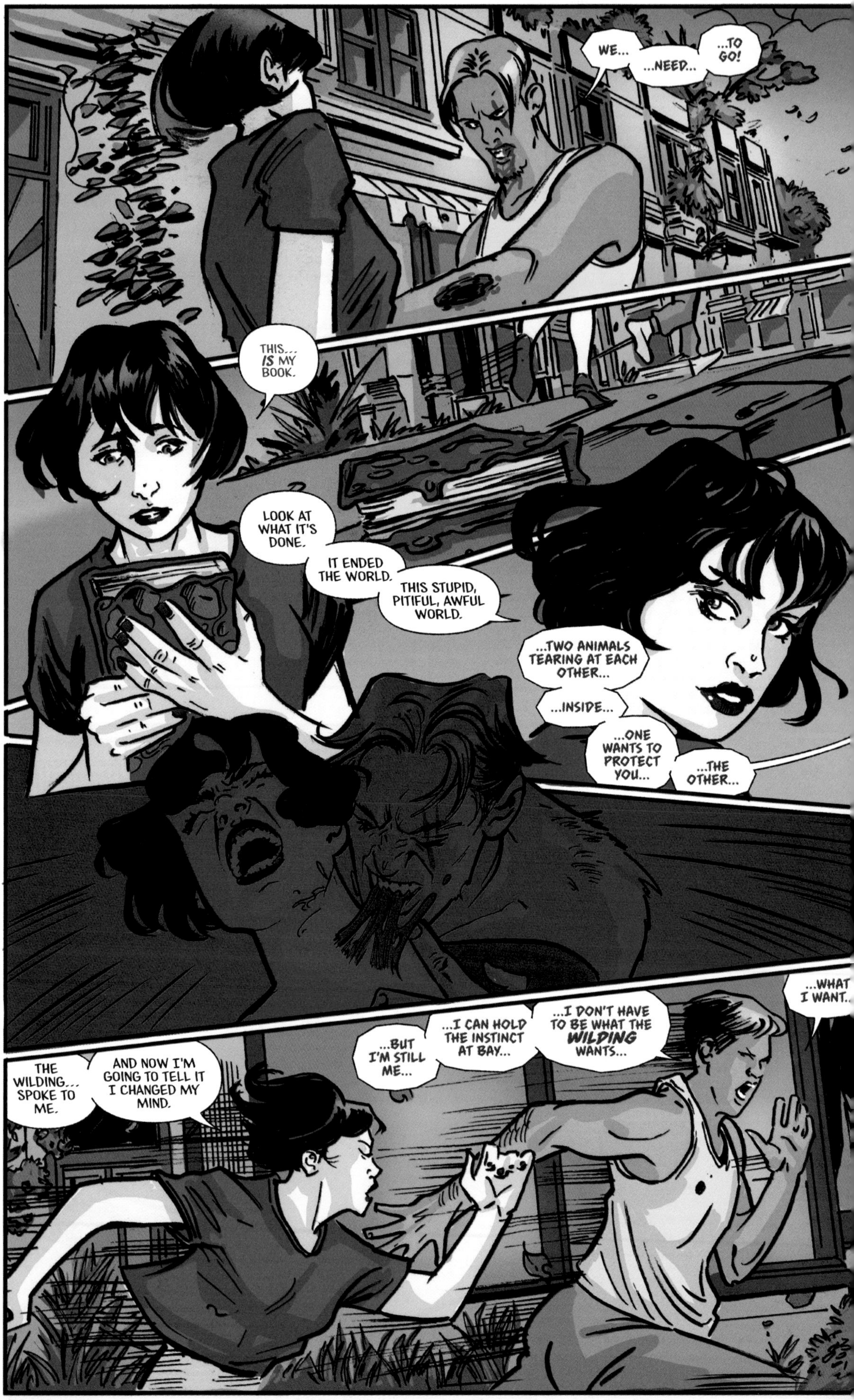
WE...
...NEED...
...TO GO!
THIS... IS MY BOOK.
LOOK AT WHAT IT'S DONE.
IT ENDED THE WORLD.
THIS STUPID, PITIFUL, AWFUL WORLD.
...TWO ANIMALS TEARING AT EACH OTHER...
...INSIDE...
...ONE WANTS TO PROTECT YOU...
...THE OTHER...
THE WILDING... SPOKE TO ME.
AND NOW I'M GOING TO TELL IT I CHANGED MY MIND.
...BUT I'M STILL ME...
...I CAN HOLD THE INSTINCT AT BAY...
...I DON'T HAVE TO BE WHAT THE WILDING WANTS...
...WHAT I WANT...

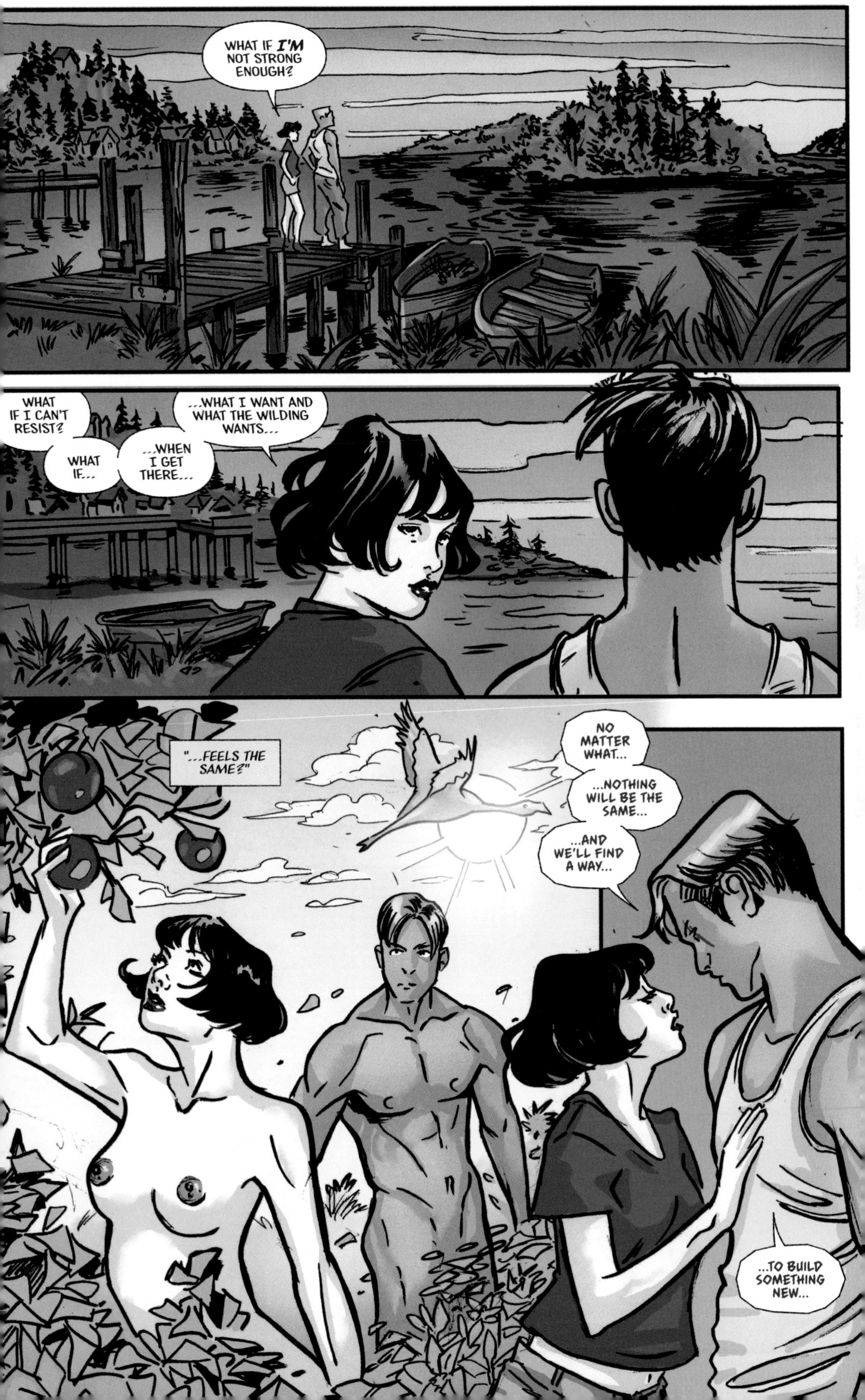
WHAT IF I'M NOT STRONG ENOUGH?
WHAT IF I CAN'T RESIST?
WHAT IF...
...WHEN I GET THERE...
...WHAT I WANT AND WHAT THE WILDING WANTS...
"...FEELS THE SAME?"
NO MATTER WHAT...
...NOTHING WILL BE THE SAME...
...AND WE'LL FIND A WAY...
...TO BUILD SOMETHING NEW...

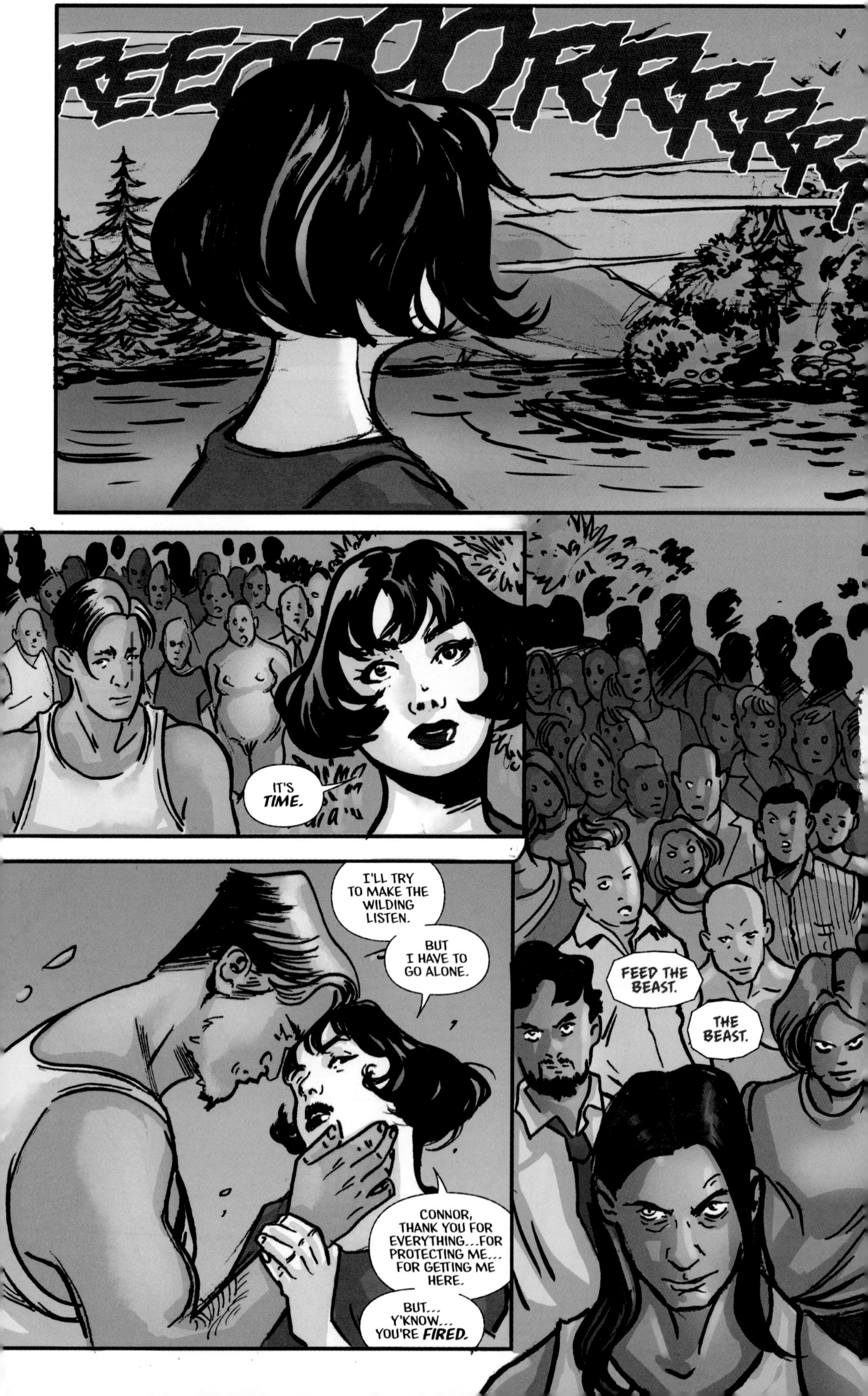
REEOOOORRRRRRR
IT'S TIME.
I'LL TRY TO MAKE THE WILDING LISTEN.
BUT I HAVE TO GO ALONE.
FEED THE BEAST.
THE BEAST.
CONNOR, THANK YOU FOR EVERYTHING...FOR PROTECTING ME... FOR GETTING ME HERE.
BUT... Y'KNOW... YOU'RE FIRED.

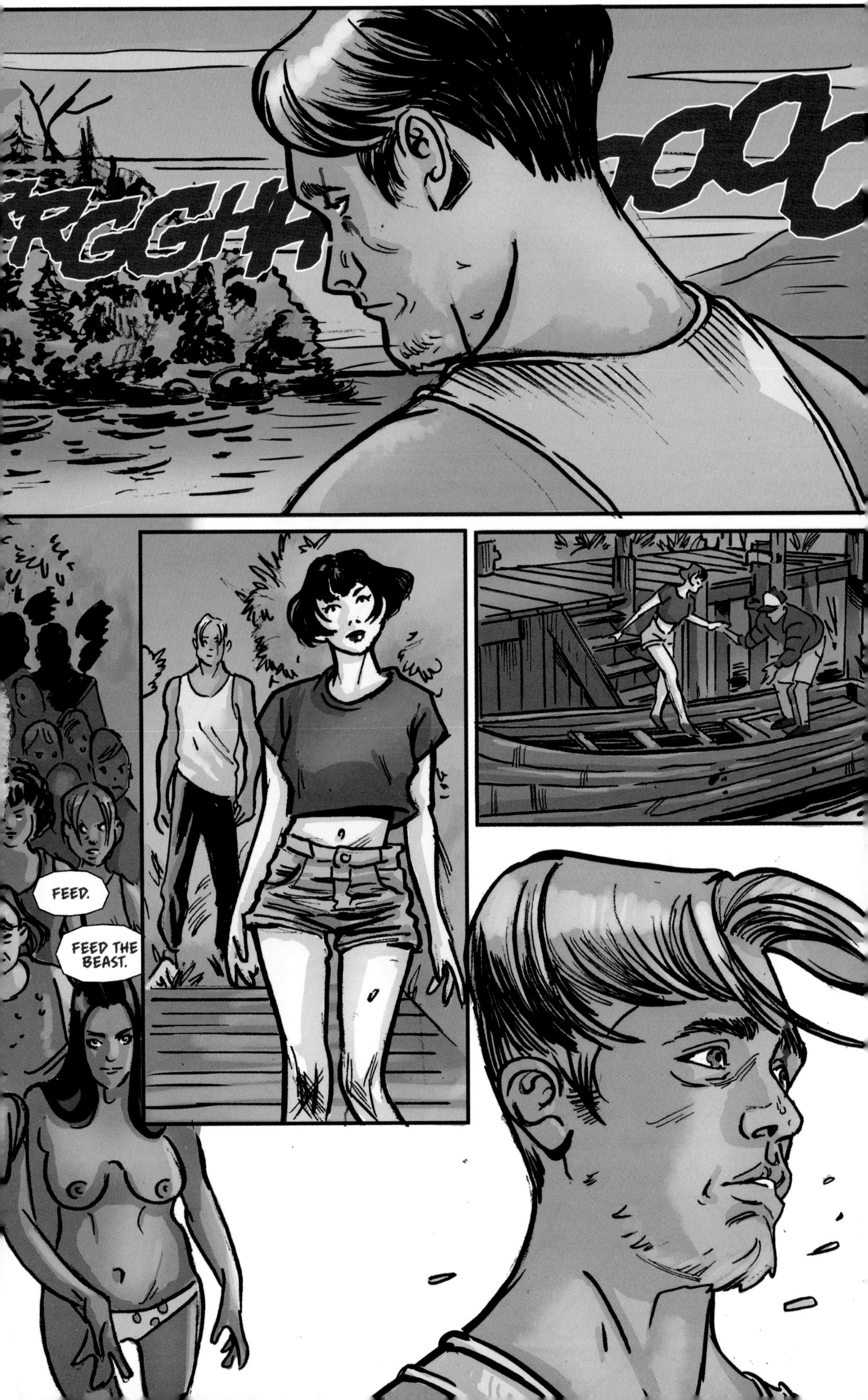
RGGH
FEED.
FEED THE BEAST.

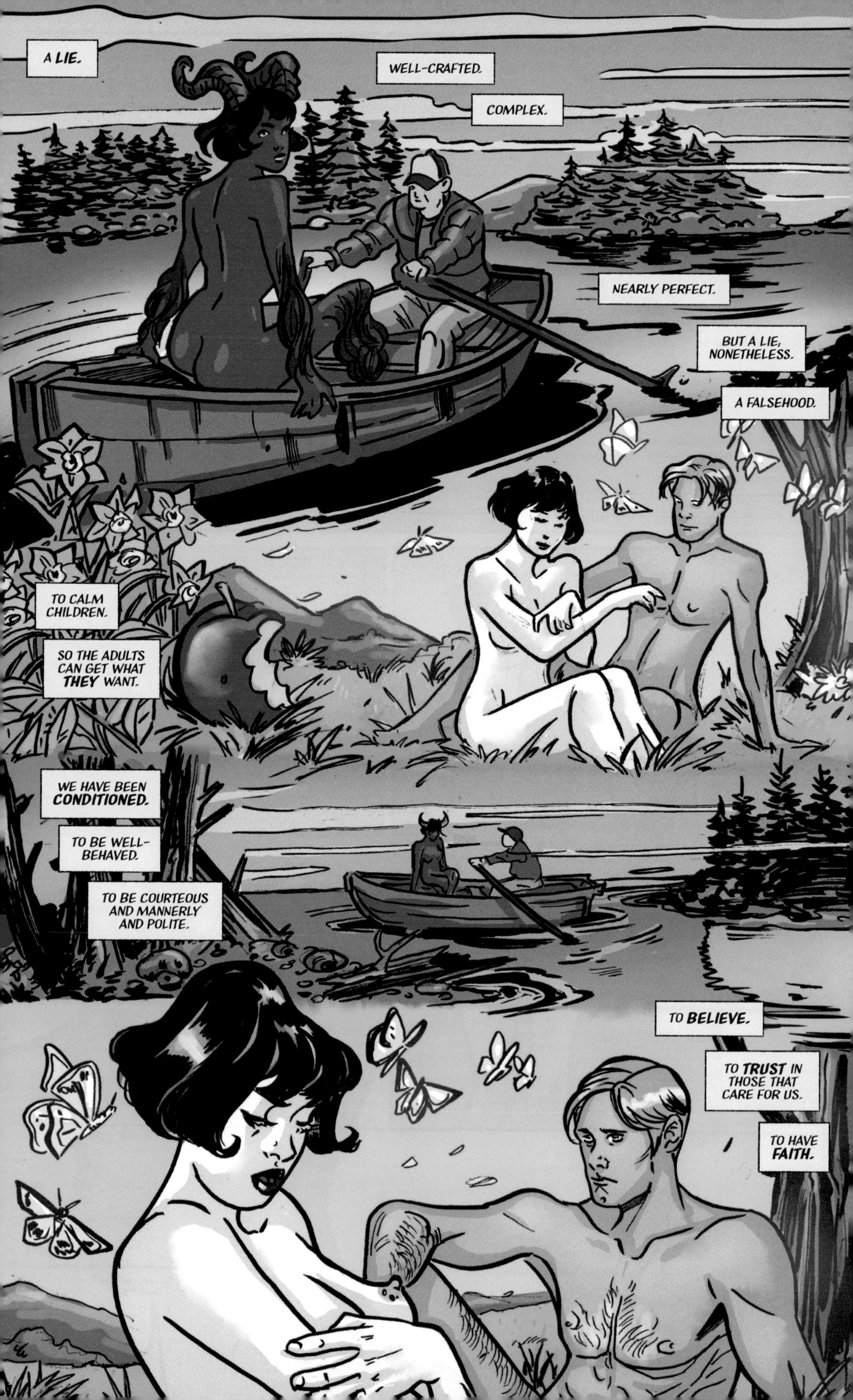
A LIE.
WELL-CRAFTED.
COMPLEX.
NEARLY PERFECT.
BUT A LIE, NONETHELESS.
A FALSEHOOD.
TO CALM CHILDREN.
SO THE ADULTS CAN GET WHAT THEY WANT.
WE HAVE BEEN CONDITIONED.
TO BE WELL-BEHAVED.
TO BE COURTEOUS AND MANNERLY AND POLITE.
TO BELIEVE.
TO TRUST IN THOSE THAT CARE FOR US.
TO HAVE FAITH.

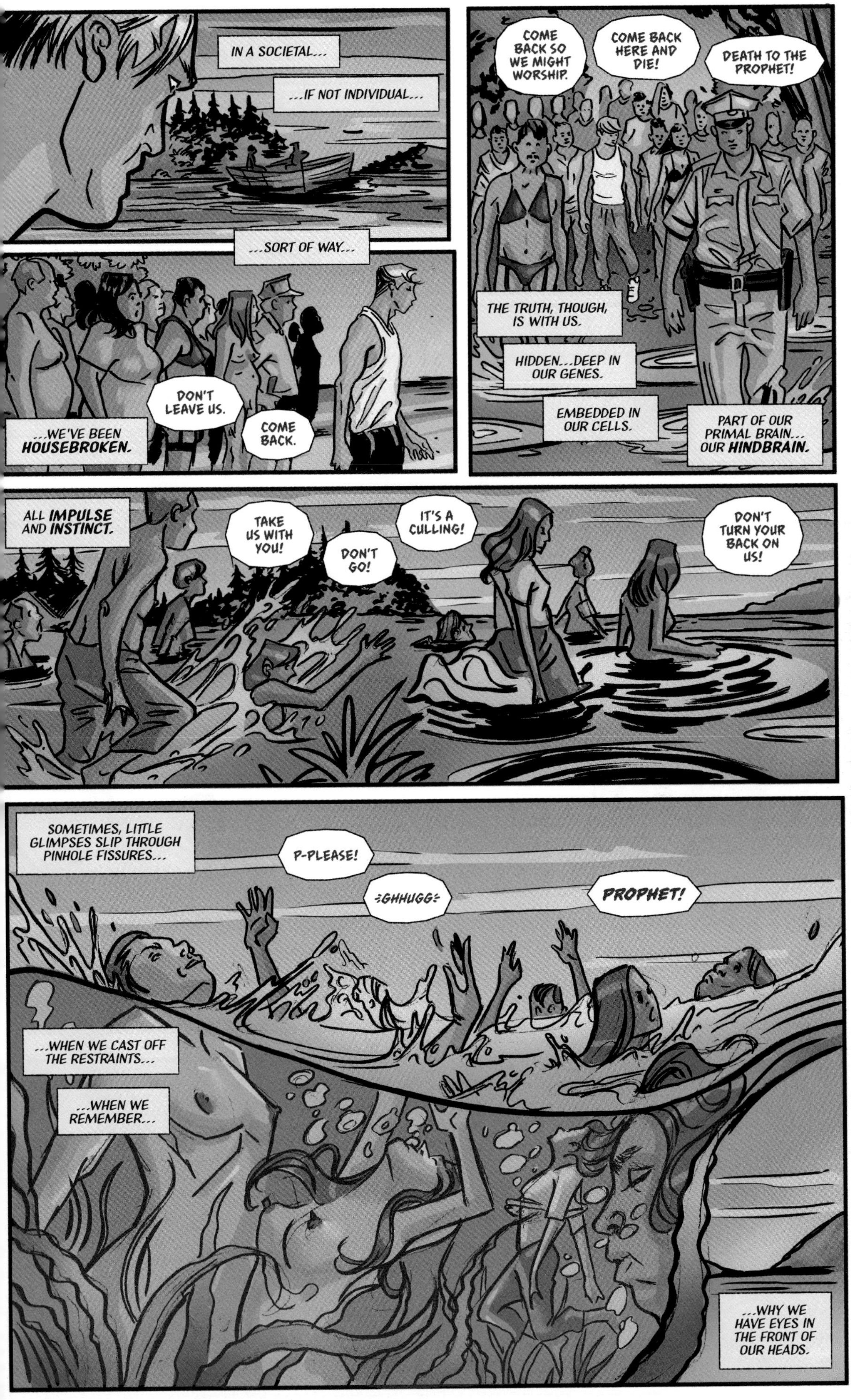
IN A SOCIETAL...
...IF NOT INDIVIDUAL...
...SORT OF WAY...
...WE'VE BEEN HOUSEBROKEN.
DON'T LEAVE US.
COME BACK.
COME BACK SO WE MIGHT WORSHIP.
COME BACK HERE AND DIE!
DEATH TO THE PROPHET!
THE TRUTH, THOUGH, IS WITH US.
HIDDEN...DEEP IN OUR GENES.
EMBEDDED IN OUR CELLS.
PART OF OUR PRIMAL BRAIN... OUR HINDBRAIN.
ALL IMPULSE AND INSTINCT.
TAKE US WITH YOU!
DON'T GO!
IT'S A CULLING!
DON'T TURN YOUR BACK ON US!
SOMETIMES, LITTLE GLIMPSES SLIP THROUGH PINHOLE FISSURES...
P-PLEASE!
GHHUGG
PROPHET!
...WHEN WE CAST OFF THE RESTRAINTS...
...WHEN WE REMEMBER...
...WHY WE HAVE EYES IN THE FRONT OF OUR HEADS.

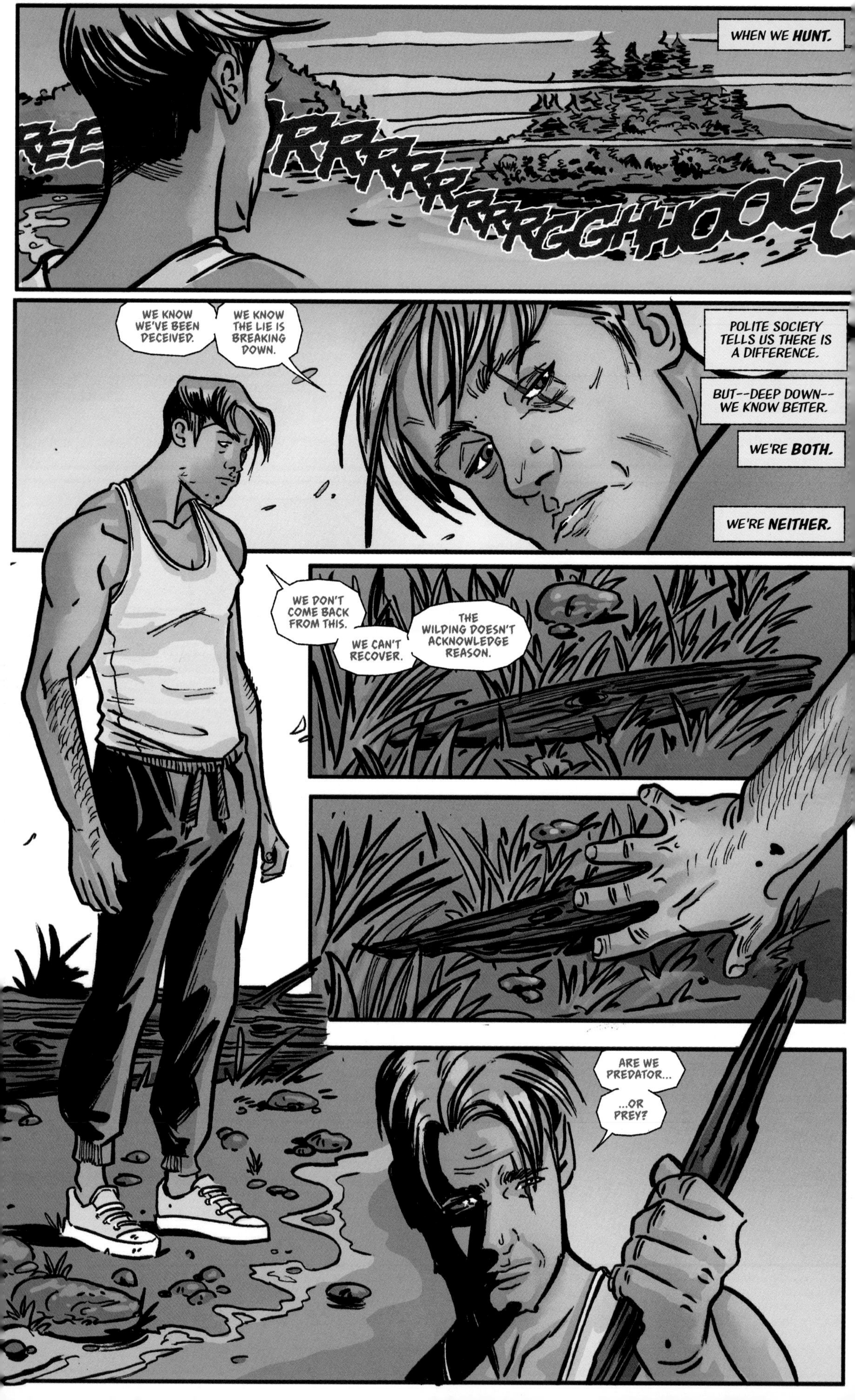
WHEN WE HUNT.
REEERRRRRRRRRGGHOOOO
WE KNOW WE'VE BEEN DECEIVED.
WE KNOW THE LIE IS BREAKING DOWN.
POLITE SOCIETY TELLS US THERE IS A DIFFERENCE.
BUT--DEEP DOWN--WE KNOW BETTER.
WE'RE BOTH.
WE'RE NEITHER.
WE DON'T COME BACK FROM THIS.
WE CAN'T RECOVER.
THE WILDING DOESN'T ACKNOWLEDGE REASON.
ARE WE PREDATOR...
...OR PREY?

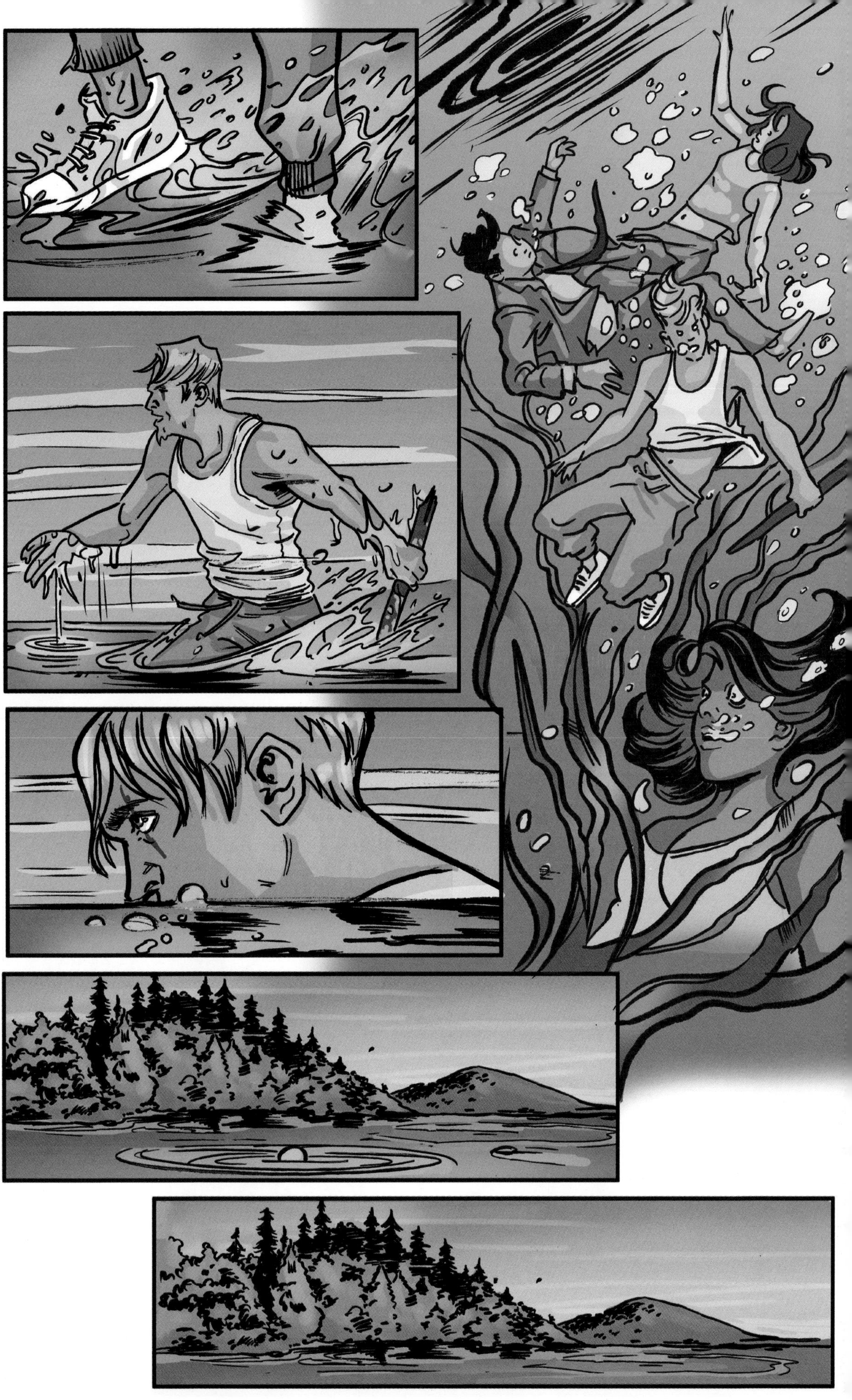

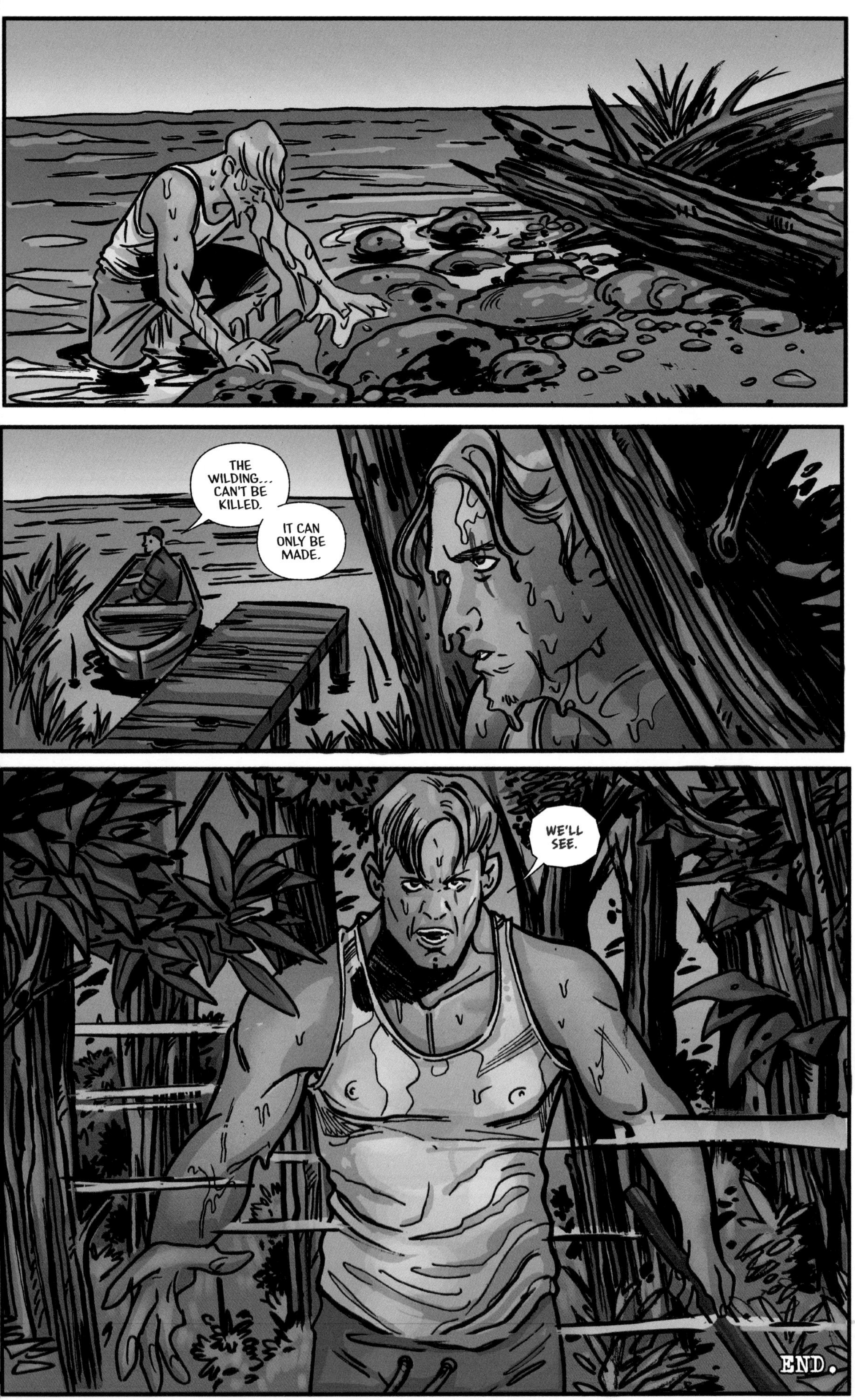
THE WILDING... CAN'T BE KILLED.
IT CAN ONLY BE MADE.
WE'LL SEE.
END.

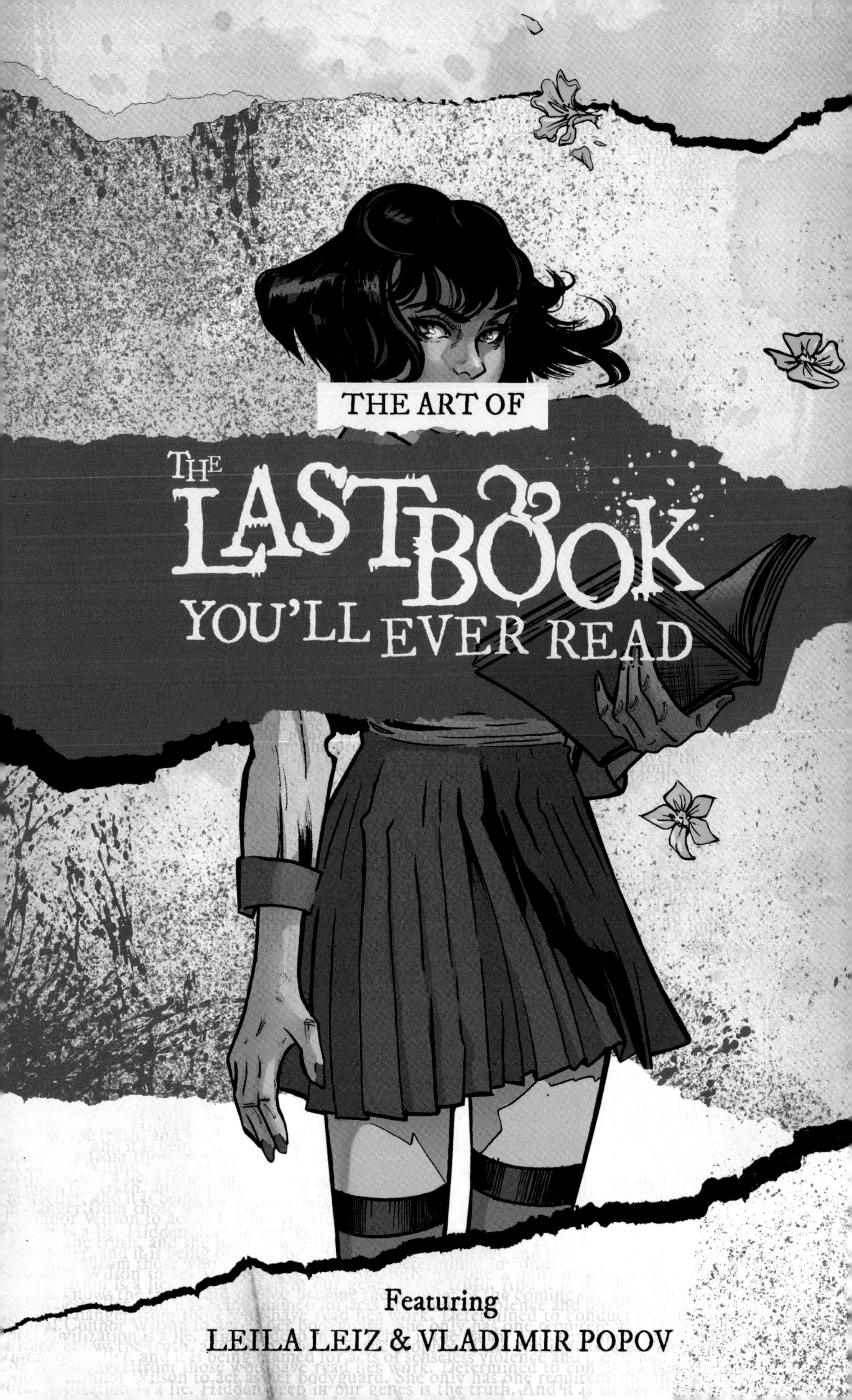
THE ART OF
THE LAST BOOK YOU'LL EVER READ
Featuring
LEILA LEIZ & VLADIMIR POPOV

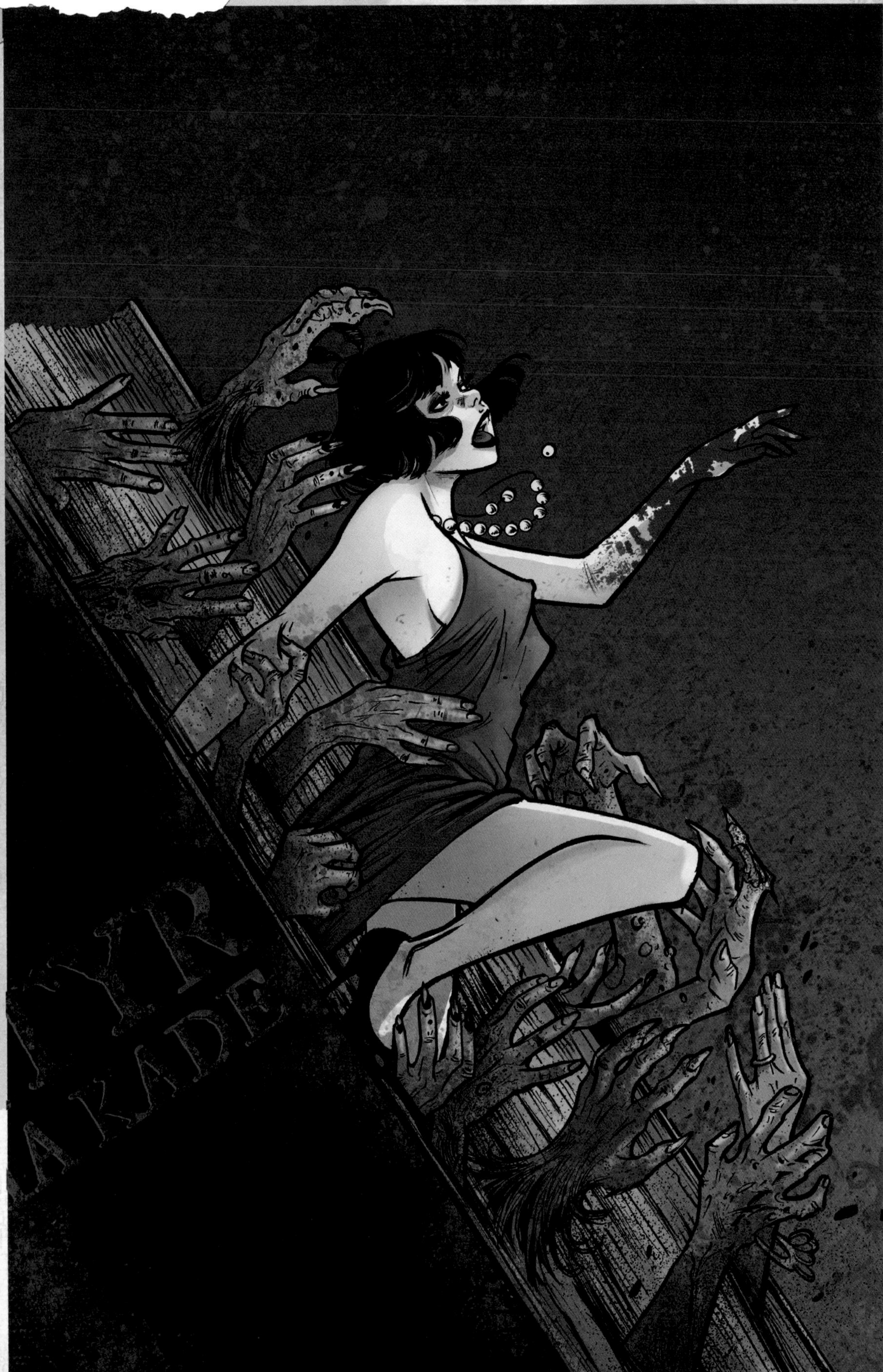

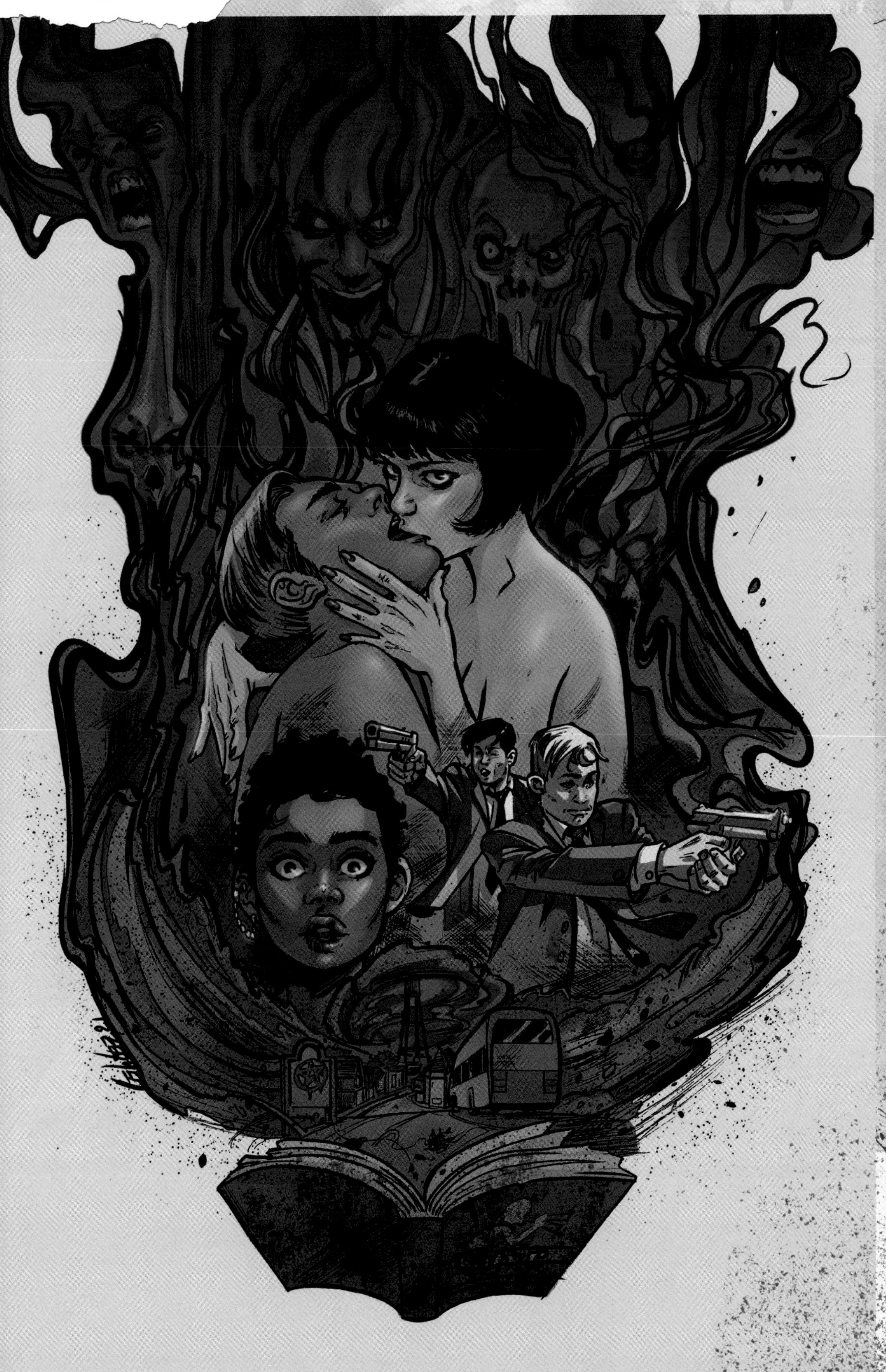

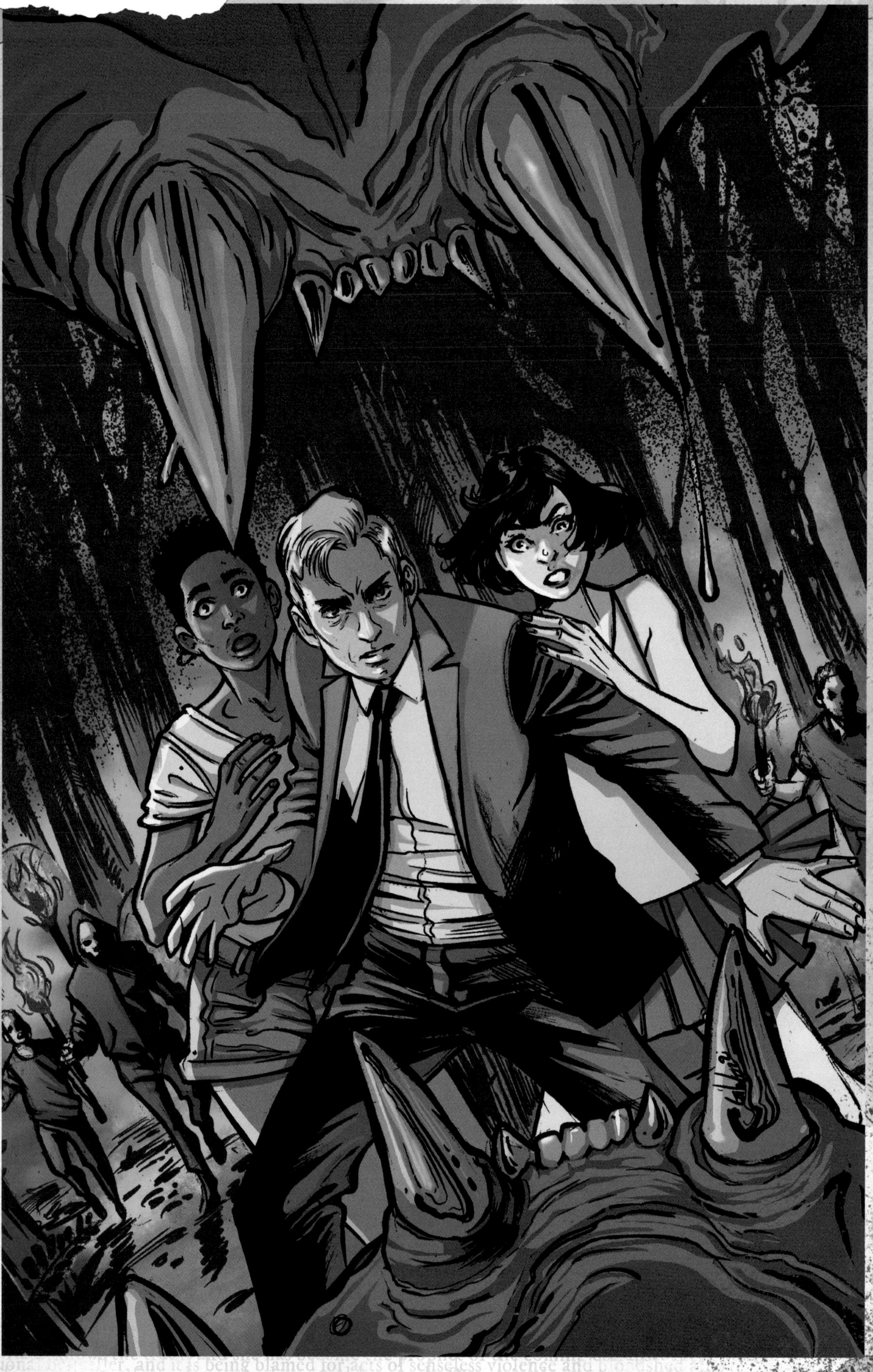

ISSUE IV//COVER

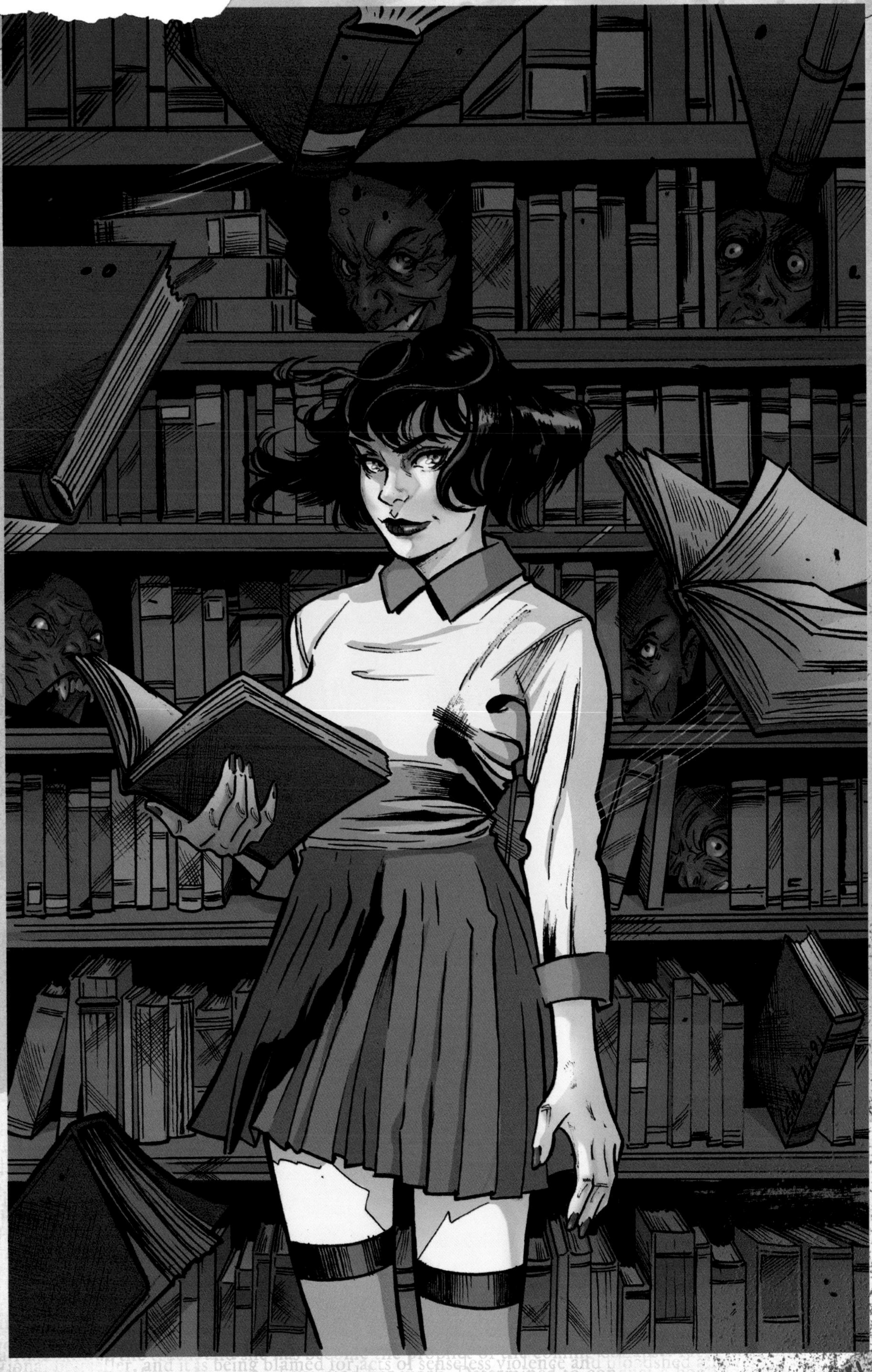

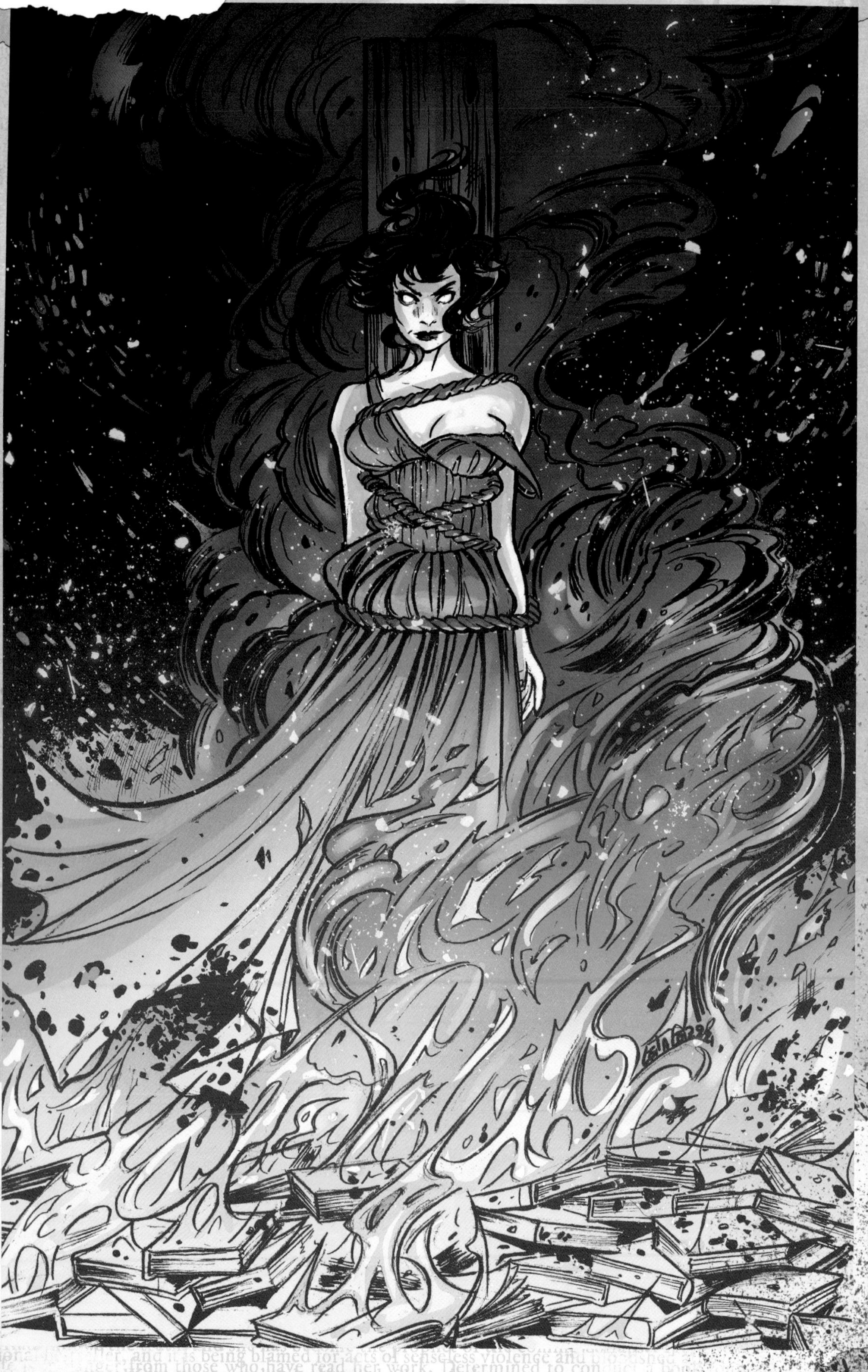

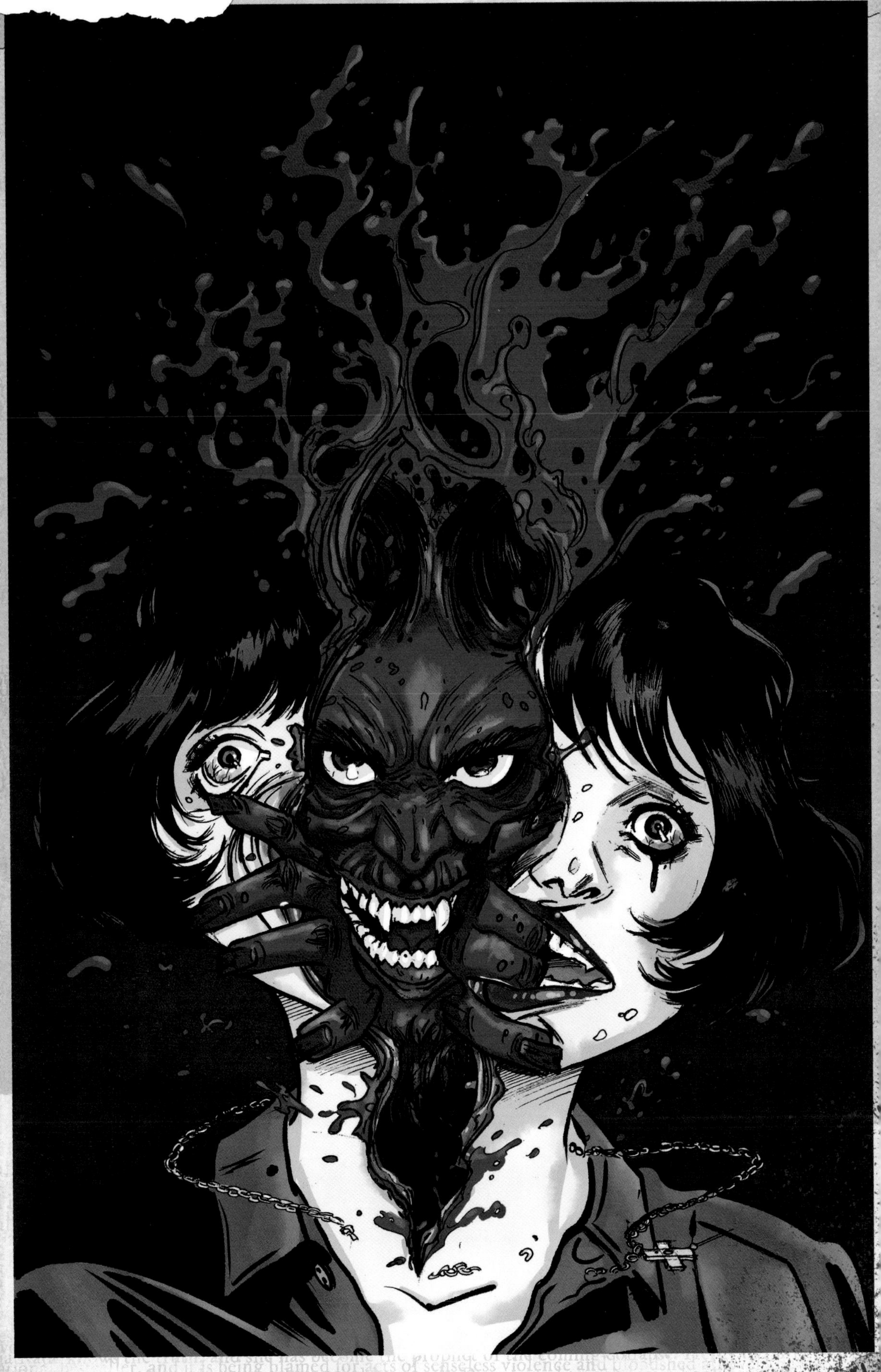

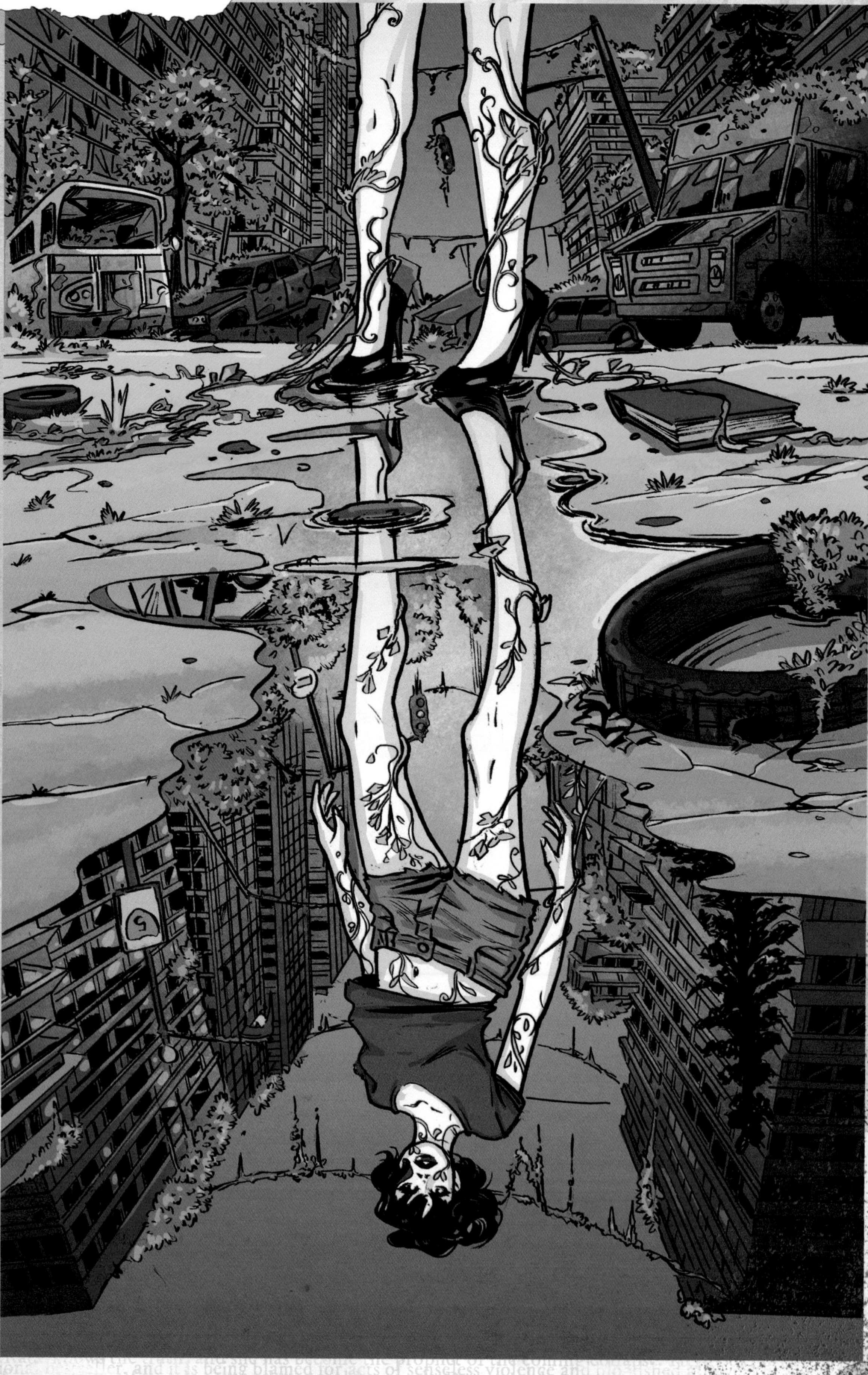

ISSUE VIII//COVER

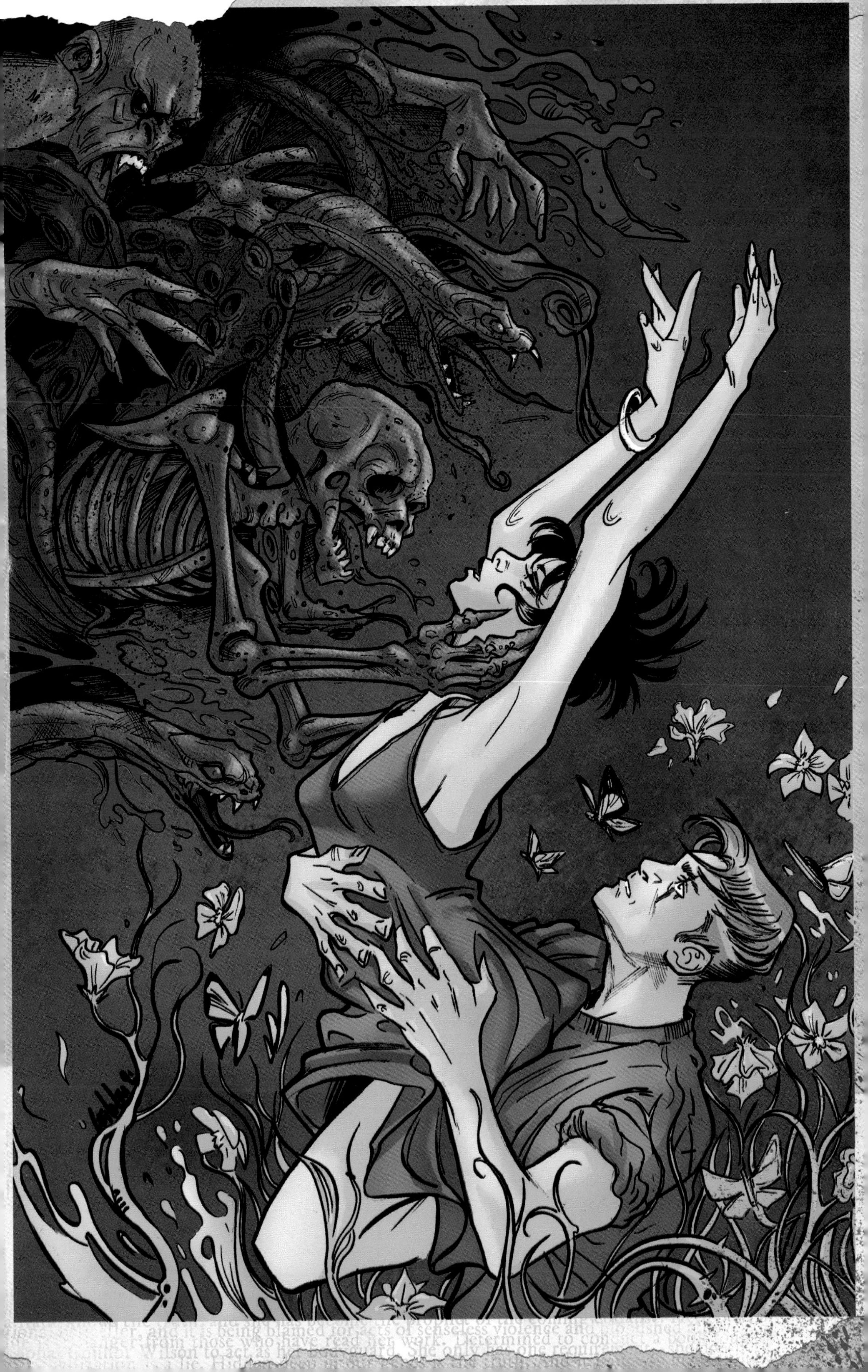

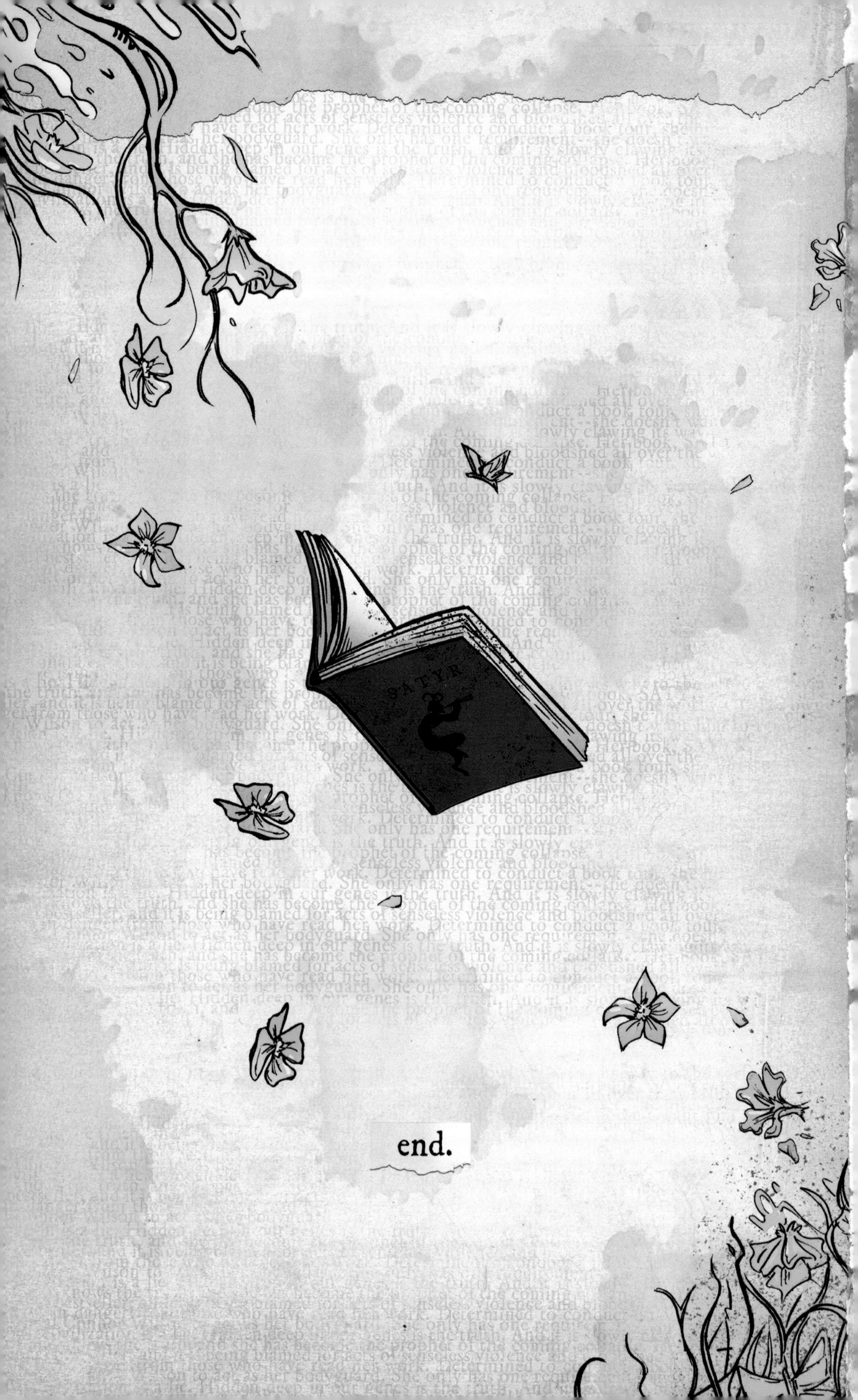
end.